Do political institutions significantly influence policy outcomes? If so, how and why do they make a difference? These essays explain why the differences between governments and national voting systems with a premier and those with a president shape the fundamentals of politics and policy choices in the United States and Japan. The authors explain outcomes ranging from national budgetary priorities through nuclear-power regulations and military-security commitments. They show that the political leadership in both countries is in control of policy, but that political institutions explain why the bureaucracies of the two countries receive different missions and operating procedures. This volume is a powerful contribution to the fields of comparative politics, comparative political economy, comparative foreign policy, and rational choice.

STRUCTURE AND POLICY
IN JAPAN AND THE UNITED STATES

POLITiCAL ECONOMY OF INSTITUTIONS AND DECISIONS

Editors
James E. Alt, Harvard University
Douglass C. North, Washington University of St. Louis

Other books in the series

STRUCTURE AND POLICY IN JAPAN AND THE UNITED STATES

Editors

PETER F. COWHEY
University of California, San Diego

MATHEW D. McCUBBINS
University of California, San Diego

Published by the Press Syndicate of the University of Cambridge
The Pitt Building, Trumpington Street, Cambridge CB2 1RP
40 West 20th Street, New York, NY 10011-4211, USA
10 Stamford Road, Oakleigh, Melbourne 3166, Australia

First published 1995

Printed in the United States of America

Library of Congress Cataloging-in-Publication Data
Structure and policy in Japan and the United States / editors, Peter
F. Cowhey, Mathew D. McCubbins.
p.   cm. – (Political economy of institutions and decisions)
Includes bibliographical references and index.
ISBN 0-521-46151-0. – ISBN 0-521-46710-1 (pbk.)
1. Japan – Politics and government – 1945–   2. United States –
Politics and government.   3. Political planning – Japan.
4. Political planning – United States.   I. Cowhey, Peter F., 1948–   .
II. McCubbins, Mathew D. (Mathew Daniel), 1956–   .   III. Series.
JQ1624.S78   1995
320'.6'0952 – dc20   94-45191
                                                    CIP

A catalog record for this book is available from the British Library.

ISBN 0-521-46151-0 Hardback
ISBN 0-521-46710-1 Paperback

Contents

Contents

Series editors' preface

The Cambridge series on the Political Economy of Institutions and Decisions is built around attempts to answer two central questions: How do institutions evolve in response to individual incentives, strategies, and choices, and how do institutions affect the performance of political and economic systems? The scope of the series is comparative and historical rather than international or specifically American, and the focus is positive rather than normative.

This pioneering book brings intellectual products of the "new institutionalism" to a new context, the comparative study of the political economy of public policy in Japan and the United States. There is a feast for scholars here, whether in its provision of a mass of new empirical data for Japan or in the host of novel perspectives and propositions the Japanese case contributes to the comparative study of legislator-voter and legislator-bureaucrat relationships in democratic polities. The book brings both the unusual American separation of powers and the unusual Japanese electoral system, often seen as the sources of the "exceptionalism" of each of these countries, within the ambit of comparative generalizations. In this way it takes us a big step down the road toward more systematic comparisons between parliamentary and presidential systems of government and their impact on public policy. But the book goes beyond comparing governmental structures: the team of authors that Cowhey and McCubbins have assembled in this volume offer new and distinctive views about a variety of policy areas of great contemporary interest, including technology, nuclear power, budget management, and foreign policy. Even so, the chapters display an underlying unity of purpose, which is ultimately to show how institutions affect political and economic outcomes.

Preface

The purpose of this book is to provide a common framework from which to study politics in two very different countries, Japan and the United States. That framework relies heavily on understanding the implications for political behavior and policy outputs of differences in the institutions and processes that govern policy making. As such, we see the approach as a quite general one, applicable to any number of policy areas in most stable democracies.

The chapters in this book were written in 1992 and 1993, and the Introduction was written in the fall and winter of 1993. Of course, a great deal has changed in Japan since the book was basically completed. After thirty-eight years of uninterrupted rule, the Liberal Democratic Party (LDP) finally lost its majority in the Lower House of the Diet and was replaced first by a seven-party coalition in the summer of 1993, then for two months by a five-party minority government. And now, the LDP is back in power, in coalition with their long-standing opponents, the Japan Socialist Party.

As of this writing (August 1994) the Japanese government has just passed a sweeping reform of the electoral system, eliminating the single nontransferable vote in favor of a mix of plurality and proportional representation elections, and restricting the financing of electoral campaigns. A redistricting plan has been proposed to the Cabinet, but has not yet been submitted to the Diet. As the reader will soon become aware, the electoral system plays a very important role in our authors' explanations of both party organization and policy outputs, so a change in the electoral rules should affect almost everything discussed in the chapters that follow.

Hence, in one sense, this book should be read as a discussion of Japanese politics and policy during the four decades of LDP rule. However, from a theoretical standpoint, the theme of this book remains unaffected by the recent changes in Japanese institutions. The authors argue that the structure and process of policy making matter a great deal for policy outputs, and a change in one of the explanatory variables should perhaps more properly be considered as a test of this thesis. In the Conclusion, we discuss the recent changes in Japan and reflect upon their implications for the conclusions of the substantive chapters of the book, but we chose to leave the chapters themselves untouched. In the meantime, we look forward to discovering how political decision making will progress in postreform Japan.

Acknowledgments

The editors of this volume and the authors of the chapters herein owe a debt of gratitude to the generous foundations and institutes that supported the research reported on here. Collectively, we thank the Ford Foundation for its support of the research reported on in this volume. The editors also thank the University of California's Institute of Global Conflict and Cooperation; U.C. San Diego's Project on International and Security Affairs, Law and the Behavioral Sciences; and the American Political Institutions Project for their support of this volume. McCubbins, Rosenbluth, and Noll thank Soka University for support administered through the Pacific Basic Research Project at Harvard University. McCubbins and Noble also thank the support of the University of California Pacific Rim Program for support of their data collection. McCubbins also thanks the U.C. San Diego's Committee on Research for support of Japanese budgetary data collection and the Center for Institutional Reform and the Informal Sector at the University of Maryland for partial support of the research on Japanese nuclear energy regulation.

The editors and authors also owe a tremendous debt of gratitude to the research assistants who worked tirelessly (although not always happily) on the editing, revision, and production of this volume, as well as assisting in the research reported on here. We thank Andrea Campbell, William Heller, Jonathan Katz, Chieko Numata, Brian Sala, Atsuko Suzuki, and Michael Thies. Our debt to them is great. We hope to repay it eventually in a different currency (God forbid we should have to repay it in kind).

We also thank referees and commentors whose advice and criticism helped to make the papers included herein far better than they would otherwise have been. For their service we thank: Vince Crawford, John McMillan, Ken Shepsle, Mark Ramseyer, Thomas Schwartz, Rod Kiewiet, Rodney Fort, Jack Montgomery and his students at the John F. Kennedy School of Government, Skip Lupia, Kaare Strom, and John Campbell. Words aren't enough, of course; we hope to repay them in kind.

Acknowledgments

The intellectual heritage of this book derives from the scholarship of the leading lights of the new institutionalist approach to political science and economics. The work of Jim Alt, Gary Becker, Kenneth Boulding, James Coleman, John Ferejohn, Mo Fiorina, Paul Joskow, Mick Laver, Doug North, William Riker, Ken Shepsle, Barry Weingast, and Oliver Williamson broke new ground in the explanation of the importance of institutional and organizational structures for social, economic, and political outcomes. In putting this volume together, we sought to extend the research program of eminent students of comparative politics including Joel Aberbach, Bob Bates, Maurice Duverger, Bernie Grofman, Arend Lijphart, Gerry Loewenberg, Pat Patterson, Bing Powell, Bob Putnam, Doug Rae, and Bert Rockman. We owe each of these scholars a great deal for showing us the path.

PFC and MDM
La Jolla, California, August 1994

Contributors

LINDA COHEN is a professor of economics at the University of California, Irvine. Professor Cohen has written extensively on subjects ranging from the economics of nuclear power regulation to technology development, and on law and economics. She is co-author of *The Technology Pork Barrel* and has published articles in a number of journals, including the *American Economic Review,* the *Georgetown Law Journal,* and *Law and Contemporary Problems.*

PETER F. COWHEY is a professor of political science at the University of California, San Diego. He has written extensively on international political economy and on the domestic political roots of trade policy. He has published numerous articles in scholarly journals, most recently *International Organization.* His most recent book is *Managing the World Economy: The Consequences of Corporate Alliances.*

GARY W. COX is a professor of political science at the University of California, San Diego. His recent research has focused on the political effects of electoral rules. Professor Cox is author of *The Efficient Secret* (a study of the development of political parties in Victorian England) and co-author of *Legislative Leviathan* (a study of party government in the U.S. House of Representatives), and he has written numerous articles for journals such as *Legislative Studies Quarterly,* the *American Journal of Political Science,* and the *American Political Science Review.*

HARUHIRO FUKUI, formerly a professor of political science at the University of California, Santa Barbara, now teaches at the University of Tsukuba (Japan). He is an expert on Japanese politics and is the author of *Party in Power: The Japanese Liberal-Democrats and Policy-Making,* a co-author of *The Textile Wrangle: Conflict in Japanese-American Relations, 1969–71,* and editor of *Political Parties of Asia and the Pacific,* as well as a number of articles in such publications as the *Journal of Japanese Studies* and the Japanese political science journal *Leviathan.*

MATHEW D. MCCUBBINS is a professor of political science at the University of California, San Diego. An expert on the U.S. Congress, Professor McCubbins is co-author of two books on U.S. national politics. The first, *The Logic of Delegation,* looks at the appropriations process in Congress; the second, *Legislative Leviathan,* examines the structure of congressional policy making. He also has published numerous articles in political science, economics, and law journals, most recently in the *Journal of Law, Economics, and Organization* on congressional oversight of the bureaucracy.

GREGORY W. NOBLE is an assistant professor of political science at the University of California, Berkeley. Professor Noble has written extensively on political economy in East Asia. He is author of a forthcoming book, *Regimes and Industrial Policy: The Politics of Collective Action in Japan and Taiwan,* on the politics of industrial policy in Japan and Taiwan.

ROGER G. NOLL is the Morris Doyle Professor of Economics at Stanford University. Professor Noll's expertise extends from regulatory and antitrust policy to administrative law to the economics of sports. He has published more than 100 articles in books and scholarly journals. His most recent book, *The Technology Pork Barrel,* examines the politics of government development and contracting of high-tech projects. Among his recent publications is an article in *Scientific American* on science and technology policy.

FRANCES MCCALL ROSENBLUTH is a professor of political science at Yale University. An expert on Japanese politics, Professor Rosenbluth is author of *Financial Politics in Contemporary Japan* and co- author of *Japan's Political Marketplace* and *The Politics of Oligarchy: Institutional Choice in Imperial Japan.* She has published articles in a number of scholarly journals, including the *American Political Science Review, Electoral Politics,* and the *British Journal of Political Science.*

M. STEPHEN WEATHERFORD is a professor of political science at the University of California, Santa Barbara. A specialist on American politics and economic policy making, Professor Weatherford has written on the interplay between international economic trends and national economic policy making, and on macroeconomic policy coordination between Japan and the United States. His articles have been published in *The American Political Science Review, International Organization, The British Journal of Political Science,* the *American Journal of Political Science,* and others.

1

Introduction

PETER F. COWHEY AND MATHEW D. MCCUBBINS

Academics and nonacademics alike agree that Japan and the United States are interesting and exceptional political entities. These two countries stand out in the world for, among other things, their economic prowess and democratic political stability. As such, they attract attention and invite comparison. Japan, while possessing a parliamentary form of government, practices electoral politics that are quite distinct from those of most other parliamentary systems. Diet members spend lavishly on their reelection efforts, and Liberal Democratic Party (LDP) members participate in the policy-making process – through membership on Policy Affairs Research Council (PARC) committees – much more than do backbenchers in most European parliaments. At the same time, the Japanese bureaucracy often is said to be very powerful and the cabinet very weak, relative to bureaucrats and cabinets in other parliamentary systems. Bureaucrats in Japan make high-level policy decisions with an authority only dreamed of by bureaucrats in other parliamentary states, while the cabinet at times seems almost headless as various faction leaders and ministers vie for public attention.

The United States also has long been the subject of "exceptionalism" studies. As the most prominent and longest-lived example of presidentialism, it often is cast as an anomaly in comparative political studies. The U.S. experience with "divided government" virtually sets it apart as a system in which the divided sovereignty inherent in the constitutional system of separated powers makes the very idea of identifying the "government" problematic.[1]

Our purpose is to demonstrate that politics in the United States and Japan are not exceptional, at least not in ways that render general comparative analysis problematic. All of the essays in this volume share a

---

[1] However, some recent work on parliamentary systems has reopened the "exceptionalism" question from the perspective of challenging the conventional interpretation equating parliamentarism with majoritarian government. See, e.g., Strom (1990).

1

common theme. They approach the study of political behavior from the standpoint that the structure of decision-making matters – that who gets to make what political decisions when, and with what informational resources, materially affects the choices that people make. By "structure" we mean the formal (legal, constitutional, or party) rules that bind political actors and that shape their motivations, including the rules that define a party's internal organization. The "new institutionalism" literature, of which this volume is a part, concerns itself largely with the motivational effects of formal institutions, such as national constitutions, statutes, and formal administrative regulations. The electoral rules that govern the selection of governments and the constitutional structures that define how policy is to be made provide the starting points for the comparative analyses presented by the authors in this volume.[2] Thus, while this volume focuses its case studies rather narrowly on Japan and the United States, its mission is more ambitious. We seek a new synthesis between the theoretical impetus of a whole tradition of political thought – the rational choice, or new institutionalism school – with the driving questions of comparative politics. By identifying how long-standing political institutions shaped policy choices, this volume will help analysts assess the likely consequences of political reform in both countries.

The study of institutions in the United States has a long, respected history, stretching back to the debates of the American Revolution and Constitutional Convention and earlier. The political debates surrounding the framing of the Constitution involved quite explicit and sophisticated arguments about the effects of different institutional designs on the responsiveness of political officials to popular interests, and on the nature of policy choices that would result.

The essays by Hamilton, Jay, and Madison that form the *Federalist Papers* are classic statements of the role that institutions play in shaping the behavior of political agents. The people cannot be sure to choose virtuous and omniscient leaders. Hence, argued the *Federalist* authors, the people must structure government to encourage less-than-perfect leaders to act in the interests of the governed.

Modern institutionalist theorists have continued to study the ways in which institutional design affects the motivations of politicians, voters, interest groups, and bureaucrats. The essayists here explore the consequences of two important differences between American and Japanese political institutions. The first is the choice of parliamentary as opposed to presidential government. On the one hand, the dependence of the parlia-

---

[2] Admittedly, representative democracies are relatively easy cases, in that the motivations of elected officials are fairly simple to trace. But as recent work on political behavior in China (e.g., Shirk 1993; Zhao 1989) and the Former Soviet Union (e.g., Roeder 1993) suggests, the institutionalist approach is not limited to the realm of democratic politics.

mentary executive on legislative confidence may weaken it relative to a president with constitutionally guaranteed powers. On the other hand, this very interdependence gives parliamentary parties the incentive to hold together more tightly than might parties in legislatures that do not fear the fall of the government if they experience defections from the party line on an important vote. This is especially true given the possibility of divided government in presidential systems.

The second important explanatory variable in these essays is the structure of the electoral system. If we accept that the (at least instrumental) goal of legislators everywhere is to be reelected, then the rules by which elections take place are important determinants of their incentive structures. On this dimension, the Japanese system is unique among modern democracies. The Japanese Lower House system of multimember districts wherein voters may cast a single nontransferable vote creates contradictory incentives for candidates who wish to be reelected, *and* to be part of the majority coalition (to see as many of their copartisans elected as possible). Any party seeking a majority in such a system must win more than one seat per electoral district, and therefore will find its candidates competing against each other within their electoral districts. At the same time the party must guard against intraparty policy disputes that might undermine the program of and support for the government.

Ultimately, we are interested in political institutions not for their own sake, but for the ways in which they shape the policy outputs of governments. This volume covers policy areas from budgets, to energy and telecommunications, to defense and foreign economic policy, in order to demonstrate that the same simple institutional variables go a long way in explaining differences between Japan and the United States in any number of issue areas. Thus, we demonstrate that the institutional approach to the study of political decision making is no more bound by issue area than it is by national borders.

1. STRUCTURES OF REPRESENTATIVE DEMOCRACY IN JAPAN AND THE UNITED STATES

Modern democracies come in two fundamental types, parliamentary and presidential. Scholars have long observed some general behavioral differences between political actors in the two types of systems. For example, in parliamentary systems, parties generally are more disciplined than legislative parties in presidential systems. Whereas votes in parliaments typically follow strict party lines and are noteworthy when they do not, legislators in presidential systems deviate from their party's line quite regularly, although the majority party nonetheless wins on most issues (Linz 1990). Similarly, regarding the composition of legislation, we see a good deal more amending activity on the floor and within legislative committees (and hence, in the public eye) in the United States than we see in most parliamentary systems, including Japan. Whereas the legislative programs of parliamentary governments seem to spring fully formed from the foreheads of cabinet members, the U.S. Congress rarely considers and almost never passes a presidential proposal without significantly altering it.[3]

Cox (1987; see also Epstein 1967) argues that one successful electoral strategy employed by British parliamentary parties has been to present a united front in parliamentary debate. This strategy is enforced and advertised by centralizing party policy-making authority into the hands of party leaders and cabinets or shadow cabinets, which often debate policy and make decisions behind closed doors. As a result, party members' electoral fates tend to be tied very closely to the fate of the party.[4] Many continental parliamentary systems have gone one step further, by using various proportional representation electoral rules, which directly tie party candidates' fates to one another by limiting voters' ability to reward or punish separately individual candidates on a party slate.[5]

In presidential systems, the multicameral policy-making structure clouds the issue of who speaks for "the party." Some scholars have gone so far as to suggest that there are multiple, overlapping "parties" in the United States bearing the same names – different "Democratic" parties in

---

[3] It is noteworthy that one of the common criticisms of the U.S. Congress made by American scholars is that legislators defer *too much* to the executive branch. Yet, in comparative perspective, the U.S. president's influence over the form and language of legislation appears to be almost nil relative to the influence most scholars see wielded by prime ministers.

[4] Whether the "efficient secret" of centralized responsibility over policy making and candidate recruitment is a consequence or a cause of voters' relative emphasis on the party-label aspect of electoral competition is a matter of some debate. Cox (1987) comes down on the supply side, emphasizing the key role played by party elites in the mid to late nineteenth century in creating collective responsibility. But once the system was in place, regardless of origins, it proved to be self-sustaining. Even though scholars have recently found evidence that personal vote activities do play a role in British elections, the collective reputation continues to far outweigh anything that most candidates can do on their own to win votes (Cain, Ferejohn, and Fiorina 1987). In our view, this stability speaks volumes for the role that extralegislative party rules and structures play in stabilizing intralegislative partisan activities. For an in-depth discussion of these issues with an application to U.S. congressional parties, see Cox and McCubbins (1993).

[5] It is important to note, however, that in many parliamentary cases, electoral rules (even if they are part of the written constitution) can be changed by simple majority votes of Parliament. Hence, we hesitate to lay too much emphasis on the stability-enforcing consequences of electoral rules per se. Rather, such rules reflect more general, equilibrium behaviors bound up in party rules and the structure of government coalitions. In countries where single-party majorities rule, the electoral rules must reflect underlying agreements that hold the majority party together. In countries most often ruled by multiparty coalition governments, electoral rules will tend to reflect a "lowest common denominator" of interests between coalition partners, since changes to the rules can be vetoed by pivotal members of the coalition.

the House, Senate, and presidency, for example. As a result, U.S. voters are less sure about what a candidate's party label means and, therefore, more attentive to other signals that candidates send when trying to win votes. In this case, individual legislators have a greater incentive to cultivate a "personal vote" (Cain, Ferejohn, and Fiorina 1987; Cox and McCubbins 1993; Cox and Rosenbluth, Chapter 2 herein). One method by which to do this is to claim credit publicly for changes to legislation.[6]

In a parliamentary government such as Japan's, the constitutional authority to make law is concentrated in the national legislature, and the executors of law are, formally, that legislature's appointed agents.[7] Likewise, the overseer of bureaucratic enforcement of legislative intent, the judiciary, is an appointed agent of the legislature and lacks the means – frequently by constitutional design – to act as a check on the legislative power. Parliament is sovereign – it alone determines what laws are constitutional and what judicial interpretations of its intent will stand. There is no check on the government other than the self-imposed one arising from the threat of rejection by voters in the next election. Hence, we focus first on the nature of political competition at the polls arising from national electoral laws.

In presidential government, by contrast, the authority to make law is shared by the legislature and a separately chosen executive, who also holds the authority to implement most or all legislation.[8] In the United States, the president has no constitutional role in proposing legislation, but holds a veto over all legislative proposals drafted by Congress.[9] If the ruling legislative coalition and the president have different interests, arising from

---

[6] Another response scholars have seen to this credibility problem has been for voters to demand, and candidates to offer, different kinds of services for different offices. Jacobson (1992) argues that voters expect different policy emphases from presidents than from legislators. As a result, he argues, "presidential" parties and "congressional" parties have specialized somewhat, reestablishing the reliability of informational cues sent by party candidates, but also changing the relative probabilities of success for party candidates from the respective parties, all else equal. He sees Republicans as advantaged in presidential elections but Democrats advantaged in legislative elections by this specialization in party labels and incumbent behavior.

[7] Parliaments typically delegate broad authority over policy making and governance to an appointive executive committee, the cabinet.

[8] As recent work by Shugart and Carey (1992) highlights, the degree to which the lawmaking authority is shared between president and legislature varies widely across countries. The implementation function, as well, varies across countries; it also varies within countries, across different policies. For example, while the U.S. Constitution vests the "executive power" in the office of the presidency, Congress frequently has by law vested authority to direct policy implementation in other officers, some of whom the president alone cannot remove from office during their legally prescribed terms (e.g., the comptroller general, who heads the General Accounting Office, and members of the Federal Reserve Board, who manage monetary policy).

[9] The U.S. president also has several other constitutional roles, shared with the Senate, such as appointment of top executive officials and judges and the negotiation of treaties.

their different electoral constituencies, this additional constitutional step will likely rule out many policy changes that a parliamentary majority could otherwise enact. Shared law-making authority broadens the nature of the coalition necessary to change policy.

Further, the constitutional assignment of the executive power to the president affects the kinds of delegations of authority that legislatures are willing to make. In order to determine what alternatives they would prefer to existing policy, legislators must forecast how the executive will implement policies. This is because any attempts by Congress to overturn executive actions legislatively require the acquiescence of the executive himself (or an extraordinary majority, as defined in the Constitution). By contrast, parliamentary majorities face neither the constitutional impediment to reversing policies that they dislike (the veto), nor the concern that they are delegating authority to an executive that they cannot control. Thus, the second part of this volume focuses on the structure of policy making. Together, studies of electoral motivations and organizational imperatives for policy choice allow us to build a broad understanding of political behavior in Japan and the United States, despite the many obvious cultural differences that distinguish the two societies.

In order to provide a general background for the chapters in this volume, we will briefly describe here the electoral systems and policy-making structures in Japan and the United States. The interested reader should bear these specific institutional details in mind while reading the essays in this book, in order to maintain focus on our central question: What limitations or opportunities do these details imply for the choices various political actors make in Japan and the United States?

In Japan, Parliament (the Diet) is divided into two chambers: the House of Councillors, or Upper House, and the more powerful House of Representatives, or Lower House. From 1948 to 1993, the members of the House of Representatives were elected for terms lasting up to four years, from districts with two to six members each.[10] The electoral districts are drawn by the Diet, and elections were conducted under a single-nontransferable-vote (SNTV) electoral rule. Under this rule, each voter casts one vote for one candidate, although the district as a whole will elect more than one representative. Candidates win office in an M-member district by ranking in the top M candidates in votes received.[11] For the Upper House's 252 members, 152 are elected similarly from large districts

---

[10] In the 1993 election, there were 511 members elected from 129 districts. Both the size of the legislature and the number of electoral districts has varied over the postwar period, although the general trend has been upward for both figures. For several elections, there was one district, the Amami Islands, that sends only one member to the Lower House, but it was reabsorbed into a larger district for the 1993 poll.

[11] In other words, SNTV is a "first M past the post" system. Votes "wasted" on clear winners or losers are not redistributed to other candidates.

by SNTV; the remaining 100 members are elected separately in a nation-wide, closed-party-list election.[12] Terms for the Upper House are six years, with half of the membership (of each group) standing for reelection every three years.[13]

In the United States, the legislature is divided into two chambers with equal legislative authorities under the Constitution. As is largely true in Japan, the members of each chamber design and enforce their own rules of procedure, subject only to a few broad constitutional stipulations. The 435 members of the House of Representatives are elected by plurality rule from single-member districts every two years. Districts within each state are drawn by their respective state governments, with each state's allocation of seats (greater than one) determined, under the Constitution, by its share of the national population.[14] Senators, two for each of the fifty states, serve six-year terms, with one-third standing for reelection every two years. In addition, a national executive – the president – is elected by an electoral college once every four years. The electoral college is essentially a weighted voting rule whereby each state has as many votes as it has members of Congress.[15] The president, under the Constitution, also has a role in creating legislation, by virtue of a limited veto over any measure passed by both houses of Congress.

The American policy-making structure sets up multiple obstacles to policy change. The House, the Senate, and the president share policy-making authority, and overlapping checks ensure that no one branch will monopolize power. All legislation originates in either the House or the Senate and upon passage in that chamber must then be passed in identical form in the other.[16] Upon the agreement of both houses, the president

---

[12] The allocation rule for the list candidates is proportional representation with d'Hondt divisors (see Taagepera and Shugart 1989).

[13] These rules obtained through the Lower House election in July 1993. However, the LDP lost its majority for the first time in that election, and the new anti-LDP coalition government has made electoral reform the centerpiece of its platform. The most likely reform, as well as its implications for the policy areas covered in this book, will be discussed in the Conclusion to the book.

[14] This is not strictly true, of course. State-by-state seat allocations are determined by law. The Constitution requires Congress to allocate seats according to state population as determined by decennial census, but does not stipulate how this is to be done. Hence, Congress must choose a mechanism, both for conducting the census and then for translating census counts into allocations of seats. Both of these processes can and have raised serious political conflicts in Congress. Furthermore, state districting is itself subject to federal legislation – which requires, among other things, single-member districts – and to oversight by the federal courts, which have imposed various limitations on how districts can be drawn.

[15] In 1961, the twenty-third amendment to the Constitution gave the District of Columbia, which has no voting representation in Congress, a minimum of three electoral votes (and a maximum roughly determined by its proportion of the national population).

[16] All bills may be initiated in either chamber, except for revenue bills, which must originate in the House. The Senate can amend revenue bills as it pleases (as with any bill), however.

may either agree to the bill as is, or send it back to Congress for reconsideration. If the president vetoes the bill, it becomes law, without his approval, only if both houses repass it by two-thirds majorities.

The U.S. system is further complicated by constitutional provisions for two other sets of institutional actors: state governments and the courts. The Constitution reserves certain specific policy matters (and all residual powers generally thought to adhere to governments) to the states. The courts in the United States are most often thought of as a third branch of government. While many judges in the United States do not have popular constituencies per se (since they receive lifetime appointments), their role in policy making is subject to both constitutional prescriptions and statutorily defined structures and procedures.

The Framers saw to it that the various institutions that must agree on legislation would have incumbents with contradictory incentive structures. As discussed, the electoral constituencies and terms of office of the three national branches (House, Senate, and presidency) and the state offices are different, so that office holders are responsible to disparate groups. "Ambition [is] made to counteract ambition"; this was Madison's solution to the threat of tyranny (*Federalist* 51).

The Japanese policy-making structure is streamlined in comparison to the American system. The Diet holds complete sovereignty, so the party or coalition that governs the Diet enjoys sole authority over the political affairs of the nation. The only real veto gate in the Japanese government – that is, the only real point in the decision process where a proposal may be rejected – as in any parliamentary system, is the majority coalition.

Most legislation is introduced by the Cabinet to the House of Representatives.[17] For "ordinary" legislation, upon approval by a majority of representatives, the House of Representatives then sends bills to the House of Councillors, which may approve the bill in the same form, change it, vote it down, or simply do nothing. In the first scenario, the bill becomes law. In any of the other scenarios, the House of Representatives (if it can muster a two-thirds majority) may legislate over the heads of the Upper House. Alternatively, it may agree to whatever changes the Upper House has proposed. However, in the case of budgets, treaties, or the choice of the prime minister, the House of Representatives is sovereign. Article 60 of the Japanese Constitution reads, "When the House of Councillors makes a decision different from that of the House of Representatives, and when no agreement can be reached . . . the decision of the House of Representatives becomes the decision of the Diet."

---

[17] Article 73 of the Constitution of Japan stipulates that budget bills must originate in the Cabinet.

2. INSTITUTIONAL INCENTIVES AND
INDIVIDUAL BEHAVIOR

This book is about the implications of institutional differences for individual political behavior in the United States and Japan. Any analysis of the effects of institutions is of course founded upon a more basic assumption about individual behavior. We wish to make the weakest reasonable assumption applicable to everyone everywhere. Some scholars speak of people as being "hard-wired" by their sociological or cultural environments to behave in certain identifiable ways (see for example, Sen 1970). The historical record, however, points out numerous instances of broad-based protest movements or deviant behavior specifically challenging cultural norms (see, e.g., Esherick 1987; Upham 1987). And even within the Western "Protestant ethic," for example, there are a wide variety of competing approaches to political and social organization. This causes us to look beyond overarching societal ethics for an understanding of what motivates individual behavior.

We do not argue with the statement that people in a particular culture have a great deal in common. However, we think it more useful to conceive of culture as one of many constraints on political behavior – what North (1990) calls "informal institutions." We still need a basic assumption for how individual actors respond to various incentives and constraints created by culture and by the institutions of politics.

We begin with a fundamental assumption of individual rationality: that, given a complete "preference ordering" of possible states of the world (i.e., a listing of outcomes to which individual actions can be mapped, ranked according to the individual's subjective determination of how desirable each outcome is), individual actors are efficient in pursuing their own objectives. In other words, individuals choose actions that lead to the highest-ranking outcome that they can achieve (all else constant) and, when more than one action by an individual maps to the same desired outcome, the individual follows the rule of choosing the action that "costs" him the least. Note that this assumption itself says nothing at all about what those objectives might be. For example, we can imagine an altruist who wishes to save a baby trapped in a burning building. There is nothing irrational about caring for others, even to the point of risking one's life to save someone else. The only presumption that rationality implies is that the altruist, given his knowledge of the building and the fire, will seek the shortest effective route in and out of the fire.

The efficiency assumption is very general. By overlaying a variety of institutional structures and the incentives they create onto our basic assumption about individual behavior, we open the door to explicitly comparative work. We can then map out the effects of different institutions on observed behavior in order to study a great variety of issues of interest. Such an approach is common in models of economic activity, such as studies of buyers and sellers in competitive markets, where the efficiency assumption implies that the seller, who cannot affect market price, maximizes his profits by minimizing his costs, whereas the buyer makes purchasing decisions about identical goods largely on the basis of price.

Political institutions create incentives for individual behavior by raising the costs of some actions (the most obvious example is the criminal-justice system) and facilitating or rewarding individuals for choosing other actions (e.g., merit pay for teachers). It is widely recognized that the requirement in constitutional democracies that many responsible government officials secure frequent reelection, motivates them to promote what they see as their constituents' interests (Mayhew 1974a; Fenno 1973).

Although bureaucrats do not run for reelection, these unelected policy makers nonetheless are subject to performance reviews. A bureaucrat's promotions, pay raises, and professional growth, as well as the fate of his agency, depend in no small part on performance reviews – but by elected government officials rather than by the public at large.

Furthermore, institutions affect incentives by constraining choices. In the United States, for example, the behavior of House members must be based on their expectations of future actions by the Senate, the president, the courts, and the bureaucracy, each of which has the ability to affect the policies that House members seek. In Japan, the ruling party's leadership is limited in its range of policy options by party backbenchers. A recent and explosive illustration of this check on leadership was backbencher recalcitrance within the then-ruling LDP with respect to leaders' efforts to reform the electoral system.

Institutions often are designed to protect certain groups (Lijphart 1977) or to advantage certain political parties. As the studies in this book demonstrate, the design of bureaucratic institutions reflects the fundamentals of electoral competition and the division of power in government. Many other incentive effects may have been unintended, though perhaps not unforeseen. Regardless, it is these institutional details that prescribe behavior for political actors and, accordingly, these institutional details are the focus of this book.

3. THE OUTLINE OF THE BOOK

Inevitably, in any project with broadly comparative scope, some nuances of the individual national landscapes will be given short shrift. That is the nature of theoretically driven comparative political studies. We are trying to stake out, as clearly as possible, one particular perspective in the ongoing debate over how, why, and by whom policy choices are made in various national governments. We are seeking a certain clarity of vision that allows us to understand key aspects of the policy making process in different national settings and to explain various policy choices. To do so, this volume unabashedly assumes a rational choice, or new institutionalist, approach to comparative-political studies.

The new institutionalism approach to comparative politics highlights two particular structural issues: regime type (presidential vs. parliamentary) and electoral system. While each of these issues can be found in the comparative literature, the new institutionalism brings a new way of understanding the implications of different structural choices in these areas. This volume is organized into two parts, each reflecting our attention to questions about regime type, electoral systems, and how each relates to the design and implementation of governance institutions. Part I addresses the two main arguments: that a nation's choice of electoral system shapes the incentives that legislators face in trying to manage bureaucratic activity, and that a nation's choice of regime type (presidential or parliamentary) affects the scope, nature, and appearance of the delegations that legislators make to bureaucrats as well as the structure and process legislators employ to manage policy administration. The second part of the book focuses more narrowly on the structures used by the Japanese and U.S. legislatures to manage domestic and foreign policy.

3.1. Part I: Structure and Politics

The United States and Japan seem to converge in their electoral politics, despite clear differences in regime type, because Japan's SNTV system instills intraparty competitive electoral incentives that any majority-seeking party must find ways to control. The first two chapters in Part I explore the institutional incentives within the electoral systems in the two countries. Cox and Rosenbluth introduce and measure the concept of "electoral cohesiveness" – that is, the degree to which candidates of the same party share a common fate in elections. They compare Japan and the United States, measured against Great Britain as a base, and then explain the differences across cases as resulting from incentives and constraints inherent in the structure of government and the electoral system in each country. In Chapter 3, McCubbins and Rosenbluth argue that the incentives built into the Japanese SNTV system provide the key to understanding the internal organization of the ruling party; they conclude that the party has institutionalized the provision of particularistic goods. The next two chapters in Part I, both by McCubbins and Noble, explore the governance institutions in Japan, in light of what institutionalists have learned about comparable institutions the United States. McCubbins and Noble first argue that delegations by the U.S. Congress and the Japanese Diet to their respective bureaucracies have not become an abdication of power by those legislatures to the executive. The bureaucratic predominance in policy-making activity observed by many scholars and commentators in both countries is more apparent than real. They argue that there is ample reason, both empirical and theoretical, to show that the legislatures in both countries can and do shape bureaucratic behavior to respond to legislator interests. In Chapter 5, McCubbins and Noble examine several commonly accepted theories of how Japanese governmental institutions work. Budgeting is at the core of politics and governing. If reigning theories about Japanese institutions are correct, budgets and the budget process should show it. McCubbins and Noble therefore test the implications of those theories against a data set of Japanese budgetary allocations over most of the postwar period and, based on the results of these tests, reject much of the conventional wisdom on Japanese budgeting. They suggest that a new approach to Japanese budgets is needed in order to account for the opportunity and motivations that members of the Diet have to affect expenditure programs.

3.2. Part II: Politics and Policy

Where Part I of this volume is more concerned with developing a general view of the linkages between voters, legislators, and bureaucrats, the chapters in Part II concentrate on how governance and electoral institutions have shaped policy in different ways in the United States and Japan. Both countries have experienced sharp demographic, economic, and cultural changes in recent decades.[18] Their different responses to these changes provide a base for comparing the effects of differing institutional structures in the two countries – a method of theory testing known as *comparative statics*. What do external shocks such as changes in constituency bases or party cohesion mean for policy in the two countries? The authors in this section highlight specific aspects of policy-making structure in order to show how similar economic, demographic, or cultural changes in each nation result in very different effects on policy outcomes.

The chapter by Noll and Rosenbluth on telephone regulation and the chapter by Cohen, McCubbins, and Rosenbluth on nuclear power regula-

---

[18] In the case of Japan, it is widely argued that politicians have become increasingly interested in policy making – that many Diet members are no longer content to leave policy decisions to the bureaucrats. Diet members have become perhaps more interested in developing policy reputations and demonstrating independence from party leaders. In the United States, by contrast, the dominant Democratic party appears to have reemerged in the 1980s as a cohesive, effective organization, as southern electoral districts became more urbanized and as black voting power was restored for the first time since Reconstruction. The behavior of southern Democrats, long seen as a party within a party, has converged with that of Democrats elsewhere in the country, expanding the scope of policy issues on which the Democrats are willing to take cohesive action (Rohde 1991).

tion both seek the key to understanding the shape of policy adaptation to external shocks. First, Noll and Rosenbluth argue that increased international telecommunications competition and the emergence of new technologies changed the form but not the substance of Japanese regulation. Both the United States and Japan introduced competition in the provision of telephone services; unlike in the United States, however, regulatory change in Japan did not affect the identities of winners and losers in the telecommunications market. In Japan, telephone regulation is national and is designed to subsidize equipment manufacturers at the burden of consumers. In the United States, the regulatory burden is split between state authorities and the national government. The U.S. response to technological change was to deregulate long distance phone services and introduce competition in equipment supply and cellular communication. By separating local services, for which competition is difficult to maintain (especially in sparsely populated areas) from long distance services, the United States dramatically lowered the costs of long distance services and exotic computer/telephone services, and thus benefited consumers at the expense of equipment suppliers.

Cohen, McCubbins, and Rosenbluth tell a similar story for electric utility regulation. In Japan, national regulation serves to subsidize electric utilities and electrical-equipment manufacturers in Japan. In the United States, with decentralized regulation, utilities face much greater impediments to making large capital investments, such as building new generating capacity. The push for nuclear power in Japan is a result of policies to reward capital investment by utilities and to increase industrial demand for electricity. The U.S. nuclear power plant construction industry died because of overlapping vetoes – including some controlled by localities that opposed the construction of expensive new capacity – and key changes at the national level in the structure of nuclear power policy making, which led to sharp cuts in effective federal subsidies for new nuclear power capacity.

In both the telecommunications and nuclear power cases, structures of governance and electoral institutions shaped the outcomes. Telephone deregulation and the end of nuclear power plant construction in the United States both follow as a result of checks and balances, in terms of state–federal relations and of the multiplicity of veto gates that policy must negotiate strictly at the national level. Each veto point provides prospective opponents of a policy change an arena in which to make their case. And, because of the different modes of election to the various veto offices, the probability of consensus among veto players is quite low. By contrast, monopolistic telephone and utility regulation in Japan and subsidies from consumers to utilities and equipment manufacturers result from electoral incentives inherent in SNTV that lead the LDP to provide distributive favors to various well-organized interests, and from the LDP's ability to control all of a smaller number of veto gates in their parliamentary system.

Scholars often argue that foreign policy is unique because diplomacy requires greater executive discretion and insulation from routine domestic politics. As such, foreign policy should be a hard test for our claims about the consequences of domestic political institutions. Two chapters in Part II show that though international bargaining matters, diplomacy does not fall outside our analytic framework.

Peter Cowhey's chapter examines the nature of security commitments and the linkages between military procurement and regional economic policies in the two countries. He finds that the variables of electoral incentives, division of powers, and the structure of delegation to the bureaucracy explain how the countries reacted to the choices posed by diplomacy. The United States' preeminent strategic position after 1945 required new strategic commitments, but Cowhey argues that domestic political factors explain much of their scope and credibility. The U.S. electoral system provided incentives for undertaking major commitments, and divided powers then made it politically difficult to retreat from them. Cowhey further demonstrates that the powers of the new national security bureaucracy (and the requirements for transparency in the policy process) fit the pattern of tightly controlled delegations of powers that we would expect in a country with divided powers. At the same time, divided powers and numerous veto points made it difficult to turn military procurement programs into long-term commitments for specialized, regional industrial complexes in the United States.

Cowhey shows that in Japan, by contrast, political institutions impeded security commitments but favored linkages between military and regional development programs. The same incentives in the Japanese electoral system that worked against consumer interests also discouraged politicians from expanding security commitments. Yet a parliamentary government under a single party can undertake new security arrangements far more easily than a country with divided powers. This meant that a prime minister could have initiated security policies that were politically unrewarding from the viewpoint of the LDP Diet members. Because the primary veto gate in the Japanese government is the majority coalition, would-be prime ministers discovered that the road to power required prominent political pledges to the LDP to follow a low military profile. By preemptively binding their hands politically at home, prime ministers could then argue to Japan's allies that to expand Japan's security commitments would be to risk a major political crisis. At the same time, just as the LDP liked to aid telecommunications and nuclear power equipment suppliers, it wanted to foster the fortunes of military suppliers interested in spin-off civilian products, especially in aerospace. LDP control over the decision process allowed it to reengineer the defense bureaucracy and devise extraordinary budgetary procedures to create credible, long-term support for companies and their regional production centers.

Finally, Fukui and Weatherford use the different institutional features in Japan and the United States to explain national approaches to exchange rate policies and the outcome of the major 1985 agreement on the exchange rate between the yen and the dollar (the Plaza Accord). They argue that both learning from necessity (Japan was more reliant on international trade than the United States for many years) and a parliamentary system dominated by a single party have permitted the Japanese financial bureaucracy to operate with considerable discretion in maintaining a consistent policy. This usually helps Japan in diplomacy over exchange rate policy. In contrast, the United States's system of divided powers with different constituencies for Congress and the president made exchange rate policy more politically volatile. During the 1985 crisis over exchange rates and trade deficits between the United States and Japan, however, divided powers made it possible for the president to promise the carrot of no trade sanctions if Japan compromised on exchange rates, and to argue that he could not shield Japan from the stick of congressional trade sanctions in the absence of such a compromise. The president, in turn, knew that the Japanese government could deliver a new exchange rate despite the skepticism of its financial bureaucrats. Under a parliamentary system, when the LDP leadership can obtain a consensus on a policy it wants changed, the ministries have no means with which to resist. Thus, the divisions of power in the two countries altered the credibility of their bargaining positions and the outcomes of the negotiations.

3.3. Reforming the political process?

Our studies could not come at a better time. In the conclusion to the book, we look at the electoral reforms on the front burner in both the United States and Japan. The most prominent U.S. reforms are piecemeal, as various states have recently adopted term limits that restrict the number of terms that their representatives may serve. What consequences will such changes – if they are not nullified by the courts – have for American-style federalism as it has been described here? If reelection is no longer a goal of some significant subset of legislators, what effect can we expect to see on party organization and, ultimately, on policy outputs? The concluding chapter of the volume will discuss this question, as well as the policy implications of term limitations in the context of U.S. policy making.

In Japan, on the other hand, reform is likely to be much more comprehensive. The LDP fell from power after a party split and the subsequent Lower House election. The new coalition government, which included all parliamentary parties except for the LDP and the Communists,[19] then passed a set of bills drastically changing the electoral rules for the Lower House, imposing new districts, new allocation rules, and new campaign finance restrictions. The SNTV system was abandoned in favor of a system that combines 300 single-member constituencies with 200 seats elected by proportional representation from eleven large districts. Since, as most of the chapters in this volume discuss, the peculiarities of SNTV are key to a great deal of Japanese policy making, this change is likely to have widespread repercussions. These questions, too, will be taken up in the final chapter.[20]

Together, the essays in this volume constitute an important extension of the methods and emphases of the new institutionalist approach to political institutions and behavior outside of the United States. By explicitly comparing aspects of American and Japanese electoral and policy-making institutions, we can show the power and generality of the institutionalist approach, and continue to build toward a truly general science of politics.

[19] Thus, the Socialists, who have been the leading opposition party for four decades, find themselves in coalition not only with the traditional centrist parties, but also with three conservative parties, two of which broke off from the LDP in June 1993.

[20] The coalition that passed the electoral reform broke up and was replaced first by a minority government containing the same group of parties minus the Socialists and the small Sakigake party, and then by a coalition comprising these two parties and the LDP. At the time of this writing, the map for the 300 new single-member districts has just been submitted to the Socialist prime minister, and it remains to be seen in what way (if any) this redistricting will be altered by the new political coalition.

PART I

Structure and politics

2

The structural determinants of electoral cohesiveness: England, Japan, and the United States

GARY W. COX AND FRANCES MCCALL ROSENBLUTH[1]

Political scientists interested in assessing the electoral importance of parties have devised a wide range of quantitative measures. Survey researchers in the United States, for example, have used a seven-point scale to measure levels of "party identification" in the American electorate since the 1950s (Campbell et al., 1960). At any given time, these scales allow an assessment of the electoral importance of parties both in terms of the percentage of voters who identify with one of the two major parties and in terms of how well self-declared partisanship predicts reported voting choices. American scholars using aggregate electoral returns have tapped into somewhat different aspects of the electoral impact of parties by estimating such statistics as the split voting rate (e.g., Burnham 1965), the frequency of split returns (e.g., Wattenberg 1986), and the "nationalization" of electoral forces (e.g., Stokes 1965).

In this chapter, we measure the electoral importance of parties in terms of their *electoral cohesiveness* – by which we mean *the extent to which the electoral fates of incumbent candidates of the same party are tied together.* Electoral cohesiveness is high when what happens to the party's incumbents as a whole is a good predictor of what will happen to any one of them; it is low when collective and individual fates are dissociated. To put it in a way that clarifies our connection to the literature on the nationalization of electoral forces, electoral cohesiveness is high when politics is nationalized and partisan, consisting of a series of statistically related referenda on the government's decisions. Conversely, electoral cohesiveness is low when politics is localized and personal, consisting of a series of statistically independent trials of strength over unrelated issues.

[1] Cox's and Rosenbluth's work was supported by the National Science Foundation under grant numbers SES-9208753 and SES-9113738, respectively. We thank the participants of the conference on comparative institutions held in February 1992 at the University of California, Irvine, for their helpful comments.

Our interest in electoral cohesiveness stems from several sources. First, the extent to which incumbents of the same party are subject to similar electoral forces is of interest in itself and provides one way of measuring the importance of nationwide partisan forces. Second, electoral cohesiveness has been tied theoretically to the strength and cohesiveness of legislative parties in the United States by a number of scholars (Brady, Cooper, and Hurley 1979; Cox and McCubbins 1993; Rohde 1991). In the future, cross-national measurements of electoral cohesiveness may allow an assessment of the importance of electoral cohesiveness in producing "strong" legislative parties in comparison to such structural factors as parliamentarism or presidentialism. Third, we think the notion of electoral cohesiveness is less difficult to measure operationally than is the closely allied notion of nationalization (as we explain later in this chapter).

The outline of our investigation of electoral cohesiveness is as follows. In Section 1, we review the nationalization literature, noting that extant measures of nationalization do not adequately capture localities' differential responses to national forces. We prefer the notion of electoral cohesiveness because it preserves some of the intuition behind the metaphor of partisan "tides" while avoiding the problem of differential response that besets the nationalization studies. Section 2 presents a statistical methodology for measuring electoral cohesiveness. Sections 3 and 4 present our results – estimates of the electoral cohesiveness of England, Japan, and the United States – and discuss the factors underlying the cross-national differences we uncover. Section 5 concludes.

1. THE NATIONALIZATION OF ELECTORAL FORCES

Donald Stokes's (1965) application of analysis of variance techniques to U.S. congressional elections spawned a sizable – though still largely Anglo-American – literature on the "nationalization" of electoral forces. In Stokes's conceptualization, elections were nationalized when voters' choices were shaped predominantly by national rather than local or regional influences: "We have . . . three distinct classes of forces which may influence the voter: those which favor one party or the other across a whole nation, those which favor one party or the other across a whole state, and those which favor one candidate or the other within the individual congressional district" (1965: 63).[2]

---

[2] Stokes's actual question was, "Where are the political actors whose performance is salient to the voter?" But we know from his subsequent discussion that he was less interested in actors per se than in the range of forces at the national, state, and constituency levels of electoral aggregation. His rationale for including the state level, for example, features the

Stokes proposed to measure the magnitude of national effects by comparing the variance of party votes within and among several levels of electoral aggregation. After partitioning the variance of the Republican Party's share of the two-party vote into national, state, and district components, Stokes concluded that district-level forces seemed to predominate in the United States, overshadowing the effects of national- and state-level forces by a wide margin. He contrasted this result with that obtaining in Britain, where the national component was much larger.[3]

In a subsequent article, Stokes (1967) noted that nationalization as measured in his first work would be maximized when the Democratic percentage of the vote was the same in all districts, even if the Democratic swings were quite different. In order to get at the nationwide uniformity of electoral change, Stokes used swing as the dependent variable in a subsequent analysis (1967).

Stokes's work has been widely cited and has generated a series of attacks, refinements, and sequels. Most scholars agree that the relevant concept to capture is electoral response to national forces, rather than convergence in partisan configurations across districts and regions.[4] But as Katz (1973) and Flanigan and Zingale (1974) point out, analysis of variance identifies only a lower bound on the size of the electoral response to national forces. This is because national forces do not necessarily have uniform effects throughout the polity. As with John Kennedy's Catholicism (the example Stokes used in 1965), national issues often split the electorate in a variety of ways. It is quite possible to imagine an election driven entirely by national issues that nonetheless exhibits nothing close to a uniform nationwide swing.

Katz suggested an alternative model that would attribute electoral changes across districts and states to national forces as long as the timing of the changes was correlated, even if the magnitude and direction of change were different. The obvious problem with this proposed solution, however, is the danger it runs of affirming the consequent. Short of exhaustive research on the impact of national issues in each district and

variety of ballots across states, some of which have a party line or party designations and some of which do not.

[3] In his 1967 article, Stokes drew the U.S.–U.K. comparison more explicitly. The average total variance of Labour and Conservative strength was less than half the total variance in Republican and Democratic strength from 1950–66. But districts are more competitive in the United Kingdom – there is more massing of constituencies within a competitive range there (Stokes 1967: 199). In the 1955 parliamentary election, 53 percent of seats were won with less than 60 percent of the vote; in the 1954 U.S. election, only 42 percent of the congressional districts were won with less than 60 percent of the vote (Stokes 1967: 201). Even with the greater amplitude in vote swings in the United States, members of Congress are in no more danger of losing their seats than are British MPs.

[4] See Claggett, Flanigan, and Zingale (1984) for a fuller discussion of these alternative definitions of nationalization.

state, it would be impossible to rule out coincidence rather than differential responses as the cause of simultaneous electoral change across districts. Furthermore, Katz provided no statistical model for how even an omniscient observer would differentiate between coincidence and national responses.[5] As we explain in Section 2, we prefer a mode of analysis that avoids the choice altogether.[6]

Beyond the problem of measuring only the net effect of national forces, three other problems beset the use of analysis of variance in comparative research. First, the typical measurement offered of the size of the "national component" in swing – the normalized variance component (Stokes 1965) – is essentially just a partition of the adjusted R^2. Comparing these normalized variance components across different samples (countries) is an endeavor very similar to comparing the R^2's of different samples, and is fraught with potential pitfalls (Achen 1982; King 1986).

Second, although it may be reasonable to compare electoral swings in the United States to those in the Britain, since both have single-member electoral districts, comparisons with multimember district systems should factor in the greater consequences for incumbent politicians of electoral swings of a given size.[7] To make this point clearer, consider Japan and England. The average candidate's vote percentage is quite a bit larger in England than in Japan for the simple reason that England has one-seat districts while Japan has mostly three-, four-, and five-seat districts, so that the number of candidates running (and splitting the vote) is smaller in England than in Japan. Larger vote percentages in England, however, translate into larger vote swings and larger standard deviations of vote

---

[5] The nationalization literature is also beleaguered by other problems that need not concern us here. There is, for example, the issue of how to interpret a decline in the local variance component when not accompanied by a rise in the national component. Claggett, Flanigan, and Zingale (1984) contend that Stokes (1967) made intemperate claims when he wrote, on the basis of this pattern, that "the primary conclusion to be drawn from the turnout and partisan components in the U.S. over most of a century is the substantial decline of a constituency as a distinct arena of conflict in congressional elections" (p. 196).

[6] Stokes (1965, 1973) claims that the covariance terms in his model, designed to pick up differential effects, were statistically insignificant. In Stokes's words, "The test made me aware of how important it is to distinguish real from chance effects. Katz's failure to do so almost certainly leads him to overestimate the importance of national forces" (1973: 831). Flanigan and Zingale (1974) picked up only modestly larger differential effects with a two-way variance design. In their model, "all variation not explained by the election factor or the sub-unit factor is 'explained' by the combination of the two, i.e., the idiosyncratic effects of that election on that sub-unit . . . From the standpoint of developing interpretations of patterns of electoral change, it is reassuring to note the relatively small amounts of change which are idiosyncratic" (p. 67).

[7] We also question the usefulness of comparing electoral swings in U.S. states with regional or other local swings in nonfederal countries. Indeed, as with Katz's "differential response" problem, the utility of any intermediate-level comparison rests on the value of the information about the intermediate levels and their comparability as units of analysis.

swings.[8] Thus, if we take the standard deviation of the swings to individual candidates as a measure of the electoral cohesiveness of parties (as analysis of variance does), we end up concluding that Japanese parties, with much smaller standard deviations, are much more electorally cohesive.[9]

Third, the only political information included in standard analyses of variance is the vote swing. But it is possible that candidates from the same party face similar vote swings without being at the same risk of losing their seats. And it is the latter – the possibility of losing one's seat – that we presume motivates candidates.[10]

2. MEASURING ELECTORAL COHESIVENESS

In this section, we consider how best to measure the extent to which the electoral fates of incumbents of the same party are tied together.[11] Our approach is to measure what we call the *typical impact* of partisan electoral tides in each polity under study. The typical impact, defined briefly (perhaps too briefly for clarity), is the *expected probability decrement suffered by a randomly sampled incumbent candidate when the swing against his or her party changes from nil to average.*

This quantity is measured in the context of a probit equation in which the unit of analysis is an incumbent candidate (of one of the two largest

---

[8] Why should we expect larger swings in England than Japan? Because larger swings are needed in England to change electoral outcomes, and changing electoral outcomes is what competing politicians aim at. English-sized swings in Japan would suggest an inefficient use of votes from some party's point of view. Larger swings lead in turn to larger standard deviations of swings because in both polities there will be districts in equilibrium (producing small swings) and districts in disequilibrium (with strong challenges producing large swings), but in England the large swings will be much larger than in Japan.

[9] Recognition of a similar problem in the context of a U.S.–U.K. comparison led Stokes (1967) to use two-party percentages rather than simple percentages. But this will not work for Japan, where more than two candidates are elected from most districts. It might also be noted that things are not helped by working with aggregate district swings rather than individual candidate swings.

[10] A couple of other possible measures of the electoral importance of parties are problematic for cross-national comparative purposes. Simply asking voters whether "party" was important in determining their vote, as is sometimes done, ignores the structural differences between Japan, on the one hand, and England and America, on the other. As Rochon (1981) has pointed out, since Japanese voters routinely face a choice among several candidates of the same party, they can hardly be expected to identify "party" as the sole or perhaps even chief criterion of guiding their choice. Using split voting rates (often seen in the "party decline" literature in the United States) would ignore the differences in number and structure of offices between federal America, on the one hand, and unitary England and Japan, on the other.

[11] For this purpose, if some national issue splits the party, then so be it. Such differences mean that the party's members do not face identical electoral circumstances because their electorates do not respond identically to national issues. The fact of the difference is what matters, not the source of the difference.

parties in the polity) and the dependent variable, WIN, equals one for incumbents who win reelection, and zero for those who do not. The analysis includes two independent variables: (1) LASTMARGIN, equal to the percentage margin of victory enjoyed by the incumbent in the immediately preceding election; and (2) PARTYSWING, equal to the average swing to all other incumbents of the same party in the same year.

The coefficient on the PARTYSWING variable is the key to measuring the typical impact. However, as with all probit coefficients, it is a bit difficult to interpret in its raw form. The coefficient reveals how much a decrement in PARTYSWING decreases the probability of an incumbent's reelection, but the answer it gives depends on two other bits of information: first, the incumbent's initial or baseline probability of reelection;[12] second, the size of the decrement in PARTYSWING.[13]

The typical impact is constructed so as to be comparable between polities. One might think that this entails comparing incumbents with the same initial probabilities of reelection facing the same decrements in PARTYSWING, but this is not really a suitable procedure. A probability of reelection of .95 is routine for U.S. representatives but well above average for Japanese representatives; thus, holding constant the initial probability compares "average" U.S. incumbents to "exceptional" Japanese ones. Similarly, as noted above, a 1 percent swing is about average for Japan, but well below average for both the United States and England; so holding constant the swing (at 1 percentage point) compares the impact of average Japanese swings to that of anemic American and English swings.

To take account of these problems, the typical impact is defined as follows: For each polity, the initial probability is set equal to the actual reelection rate for incumbents in that polity; this is typical (in the sense that averages convey typicality) for that polity. The question then becomes, what is a "typical" decrement in the PARTYSWING variable? Here, we define a "typical" decrement as a fall from a nil swing, in the initial state, to an average-sized negative swing.

By adopting the definition just noted, we contrive a comparison between typical incumbents in Japan facing decrements in PARTYSWING of a size typically encountered there and typical incumbents in America or England facing decrements in PARTYSWING of a size typical for those polities. The analysis in the next section provides some results of applying this measurement technique to Japan, England, and America.

[12] For example, an incumbent with a .9999 initial probability of reelection will be less affected by 1-percentage-point decline in the swing to his party than will one with a .5 initial probability of reelection.

[13] The exact formula showing how the probability decline depends on initial probability, coefficient, and size of decrement is: probability decline $= i - F(F^{-1}[i] - c^*s)$, where i is the initial probability of reelection, c is the probit coefficient of PARTYSWING, s is the size of the decrement in PARTYSWING, and F is the cumulative normal distribution function.

3. RESULTS: PART 1

The results in this section pertain to Japanese elections held between 1960 and 1990 (inclusive), to U.S. elections held in the same period, and to English elections held between 1955 and 1979 (inclusive). In all three polities, only incumbents of the two largest parties competing in general elections were included in the analysis.[14]

As can be seen in Table 2.1, which presents estimations of the probit equation specified in the previous section, results for each of the three polities are broadly similar. The coefficient on LASTMARGIN is positive for all three countries (the bigger an incumbent's margin of victory in the immediately preceding general election, the better his or her chances of reelection), ranging only from .04 (for the United States) to .08 (for Japan) to .10 (for England). The coefficient on PARTYSWING is also positive in all three countries (the bigger the swing to the incumbent's party, the better his or her chances of reelection) and ranges from .15 for the United States to .19 for England to .22 for Japan.

On the face of it, these results suggest that electoral cohesiveness is largest in Japan and smallest in the United States. For example, the coefficients imply that an incumbent with an initial .85 probability of reelection who faces an exogenous 1-percentage-point decline in the swing to his party will suffer a decrement in his initial probability of reelection of .06 in Japan, .05 in England, and .04 in the United States. As we have noted, however, such a comparison is misleading in that it compares average Japanese incumbents facing average swings to rather weak English and U.S. incumbents facing anemic swings. If we want to get at the typical impact for each polity, a different comparison is needed.

This comparison is presented in panel C of Table 2.1 (panel B having given the means of the variables involved in panel A). As one can see, the typical impact of partisan swings is estimated to be .119 in England, .089 in the U.S., and .065 in Japan.

These numbers in principle allow cardinal comparisons between the three countries, representing as they do probability decrements suffered by typical incumbents facing average-sized negative swings rather than nil swings. Thus, for example, it is meaningful to say that the electoral cohesiveness of parties in England looks to be nearly twice as high as it is in Japan, with the United States closer to Japan than England, but near the midway point between them.

These findings jibe to a certain extent with conventional wisdom: Most

---

[14] We have not explored cross-sectional differences between or among parties. We plan in future work to divide the cohesiveness measure by party, to get a more nuanced view of the partisanship-versus-stability components of our measure.

Table 2.1. *Probit estimation of incumbent reelection chances*

PANEL A
Dependent variable: WIN = 1 if major party incumbent is reelected, 0 otherwise

Independent Variables	Japan, 1960–90 Coeff.	(t)	U.S., 1960–90 Coeff.	(t)	England, 1959–79 Coeff.	(t)
Constant	.77	(18.3)	.82	(13.2)	.51	(7.5)
Lastmargin	.08	(11.7)	.04	(13.1)	.10	(16.5)
Partyswing	.22	(9.9)	.15	(13.3)	.19	(12.4)
N =	3,886		3,575		2,986	
pseudo-R^2 =	.42		.74		.72	

PANEL B
Means of variable

Variable	Country Japan	U.S.	England
Win	.841	.935	.909
Lastmargin	5.91	28.87	18.78
Partyswing[a]	1.09	3.31	2.78

[a]The absolute mean of Partyswing is presented in this table.

PANEL C
Typical impacts, by country

Country	Typical incumbent's initial probability of victory	Impact on typical incumbent's chances of an average swing against party
Japan	.841	-.065
U.S.	.935	-.089
England	.909	-.119

observers believe party to be more important in English than American elections; and the weakness of party as an electoral cue in Japan is widely reported in the Japanese literature. Rather than go through all the previous arguments that might be pertinent to explaining our results, we simplify radically in order to focus on two fundamental features of a polity that predispose it to high or low levels of electoral cohesiveness.

The first of these fundamental features is governmental structure, by which we mean (1) whether executive and legislative powers are fused or separated, and (2) whether legislatures are dissoluble at any time or only at fixed intervals. These two aspects of governmental structure are in principle independently variable, but in practice parliamentary systems (with fused powers and fully dissoluble legislatures) contrast with presidential systems (with separated powers and fixed terms).[15]

The second broad feature affecting electoral cohesiveness is electoral structure. If our study included a more diverse set of countries, we might need to describe electoral structure in terms of many characteristics. But the present study includes only Japan, England, and the United States, all of which use the single nontransferable vote (SNTV). That is, in all three countries, voters have a single vote that they can give to one and only one candidate, without any provision for that vote being transferred to another candidate. All three countries also use the plurality rule to translate voting outcomes into an allocation of seats: in each, the top M vote-getting candidates win seats, where M is the district magnitude.[16] The only major structural difference between Japanese elections, on the one hand, and U.S. and English elections, on the other, is that M equals 1 in the United States and England, while M ranges from 1 to 6 in Japan. Thus, in this study, the only aspect of electoral structure that we shall recognize is the dichotomy between systems employing single-member districts (SNTV-SMD systems) and systems employing multimember districts (SNTV-MMD systems).

Putting the two contrasts just discussed together – that between parliamentary and presidential governmental systems and between SMD and MMD electoral systems – we have a two-by-two matrix of possible structures (Figure 2.1). England occupies the parliamentary/SMD cell, Japan the parliamentary/MMD cell, and America the presidential/SMD cell. Obviously, we leave much out of our analysis, even of a structural nature. But much of what we do not consider is influenced by the two structural variables we identify. For example, the degree of party control over electoral endorsements, while potentially an important factor in determining electoral cohesiveness, is strongly affected by governmental structure.

In any event, the question is not whether everything follows from governmental structure and electoral rules, but whether something important about electoral cohesiveness does. We think so. By our reading, the extant literature suggests two abstract propositions about electoral cohesiveness, both of which go somewhat beyond the specific countries in our sample:

Proposition 1: Parliamentary governmental systems with SNTV-SMD electoral systems will have greater electoral cohesiveness than otherwise similar presidential systems with SNTV-SMD electoral systems.

Proposition 2: Parliamentary systems with SNTV-SMD electoral systems will have greater electoral cohesiveness than otherwise similar parliamentary systems with SNTV-MMD electoral systems.

[15] Norway, with fused powers and fixed legislative terms, is an exception.
[16] For a more extended defense of the way we use the terms SNTV and electoral formula, see Cox (1990, 1991).

27

Figure 2.1. *A typology of politics – single nontransferable vote and:*

	Single-member districts	Multimember districts
Parliamentary	U.K.	Japan
Presidential	U.S.	–

Both of these propositions deal with macropolitical characteristics, and as such are difficult to prove. Nonetheless, there are arguments in the literature pertinent to both.

As regards proposition 1, the difference between dissoluble and fixed-term legislatures is the key. Legislative majorities organizing in a dissoluble legislature will tend to be more internally cohesive than otherwise similar groups organizing under a presidential system, because the costs of internal dissension are much higher – including, as they do, the downfall of the government and the holding of new elections.[17] Thus, voters in parliamentary systems will be presented with more cohesive parties and will, other things equal, be more party-oriented. This in turn should tie the electoral fates of incumbents of the same party more tightly together.

As regards proposition 2, the key is whether members of the same party are put into direct competition with one another at general elections. In SNTV-SMD systems, there is no direct electoral competition among members of the same party. It is thus feasible for candidates to run primarily on the party platform, if they so choose.[18] In systems with SNTV and multimember districts, in contrast, direct electoral competition among members of the same party is guaranteed, at least if there are any parties that seek majority status in the legislature. This competition among co-partisans makes it impossible for them to run simply on the party platform, since that does not provide voters with a reason to vote for one of them in particular. The incentives to create a personal campaign organiza-

[17] The governmental structure of parliamentary systems essentially places governing parties or coalitions in the same position that the Nazis put Polish villagers in during World War II, when they promised collective punishment for any violence against the occupying forces. The difference, of course, is that members of parliamentary parties choose to constrain themselves with strong party leadership to avert, in game-theoretic terms, the mutual defection of cabinet collapse and poorly timed elections.

[18] Indeed, the parliamentary system with SNTV and single-member districts is essentially the same as a parliamentary system with closed-list proportional representation electoral rules, if the parties control nominations; for then the only difference is the district magnitude.

tion and to cultivate a personal vote in one's constituency (both of which serve to insulate the incumbent from nationwide tides for or against their party) are thus large.

Although the structural features we have identified generate rather clear predictions of higher electoral cohesiveness in England than in the United States (parliamentary versus presidential rule) and Japan (single-member versus multimember districts), there does not seem to be a straightforward argument, merely from looking at governmental or electoral rules, telling us what to expect between the United States and Japan. The difficulty is that the United States has one factor decreasing electoral cohesiveness (a presidential structure) while Japan has another (an SNTV-MMD electoral system), and we do not know which of these ought in principle to produce the larger effect. We do know, however, that at least over the 1960–90 period, the level of electoral cohesiveness was higher in the United States than in Japan.

4. RESULTS: PART 2

The previous section looked at the typical impact of partisan tides only as an average over a fairly lengthy period of time. In this section, we address the question of how much variation in electoral cohesiveness is hidden in these overtime averages.

If our structural variables – type of governmental and type of electoral system – were the whole story, then presumably there would be little variation over time within a given polity. But of course describing the governmental and electoral structure of a polity in our spare vocabulary leaves many other variables unmentioned, and these unmentioned variables may well have differential impact over time.

As an example, consider the question of how stable, or close to equilibrium, a polity is. On one end of a continuum, imagine a polity in which all electoral allegiances are apolitical artifacts of political socialization, in the sense that every voter is socialized to support one or another party and never questions that socialization later in life. In such a polity (absent fluctuations in turnout that benefited one party or another, and absent net partisan gains due to the different socializations of those entering and exiting the electorate), the vote would never change. The swings to incumbents would be zero everywhere, and hence partisan swings would be nil. But this would in turn put the level of electoral cohesiveness at zero, since we measure it in terms of the typical *response* to partisan swings (and if there is nothing to respond to . . .). Thus, even though "party allegiance" proximally determines all of voting behavior in this hypothetical example, our measure of the electoral cohesiveness of parties would nonetheless be zero.

29

On the other end of the continuum, we might imagine a polity in which all voters were "floating," ready to change their votes in response to the short-term political successes and failures of the parties. Here too, we might specify that all voters reacted solely to what the parties did, so that the electoral importance of party is in some sense held constant between this and the previous example. What differs is that in this example the parties "do something" and voters react to what they do, thus producing net partisan swings on occasion. In this case, our measure of electoral cohesiveness would more accurately catch the importance of party, simply because there are changes in party fortune to be assessed.

The general point here is that cycles or fluctuations in the stability of the partisan division of the vote may have important consequences for the observed level of electoral cohesiveness, independent of either the structural variables we have identified or the "actual importance" of parties. Two empirical examples where this point plays out concern two-party realignments in the United States and multiparty realignments in Japan.

A large niche in the literature on American elections is occupied by studies of so-called critical elections and realignments. The basic assumptions underpinning critical elections theory are very simple: First, it is assumed that the primary long-term factor determining outcomes in American elections is the underlying distribution of partisan loyalties or identifications in the electorate (Campbell et al. 1960). Second, it is assumed that if one classifies American elections along a continuum from "no change in the underlying distribution of partisan loyalties" to "important or decisive change," one will find a markedly bimodal distribution, with many "no change" elections, a few "decisive change" elections, and nothing to speak of in between.[19] The key supposition in the critical-elections literature is that there is not a process of continual incremental change in the underlying partisan distribution. Instead, it is argued, incremental demographic shifts and other forces for change are "pent up" until they burst forth in periodic realignments. If this is true, then the United States should exhibit cyclic increases and decreases in electoral cohesiveness, with large typical impacts around realignments, and small or declining typical impacts during the stable periods between realignments.

If the stability of a polity – or how close the underlying distribution of partisan loyalties in that polity is to a long-run equilibrium – is important in explaining observed levels of electoral cohesiveness, then the next question is: Do some polities suffer disequilibrium systematically more often

---

[19] The "no change" elections are called "maintaining" or "deviating," depending on whether short-term forces deflect the outcome from what it would have been based on partisan loyalties alone or not. The "decisive change" elections are called "realigning" or "converting," depending on whether a new majority party emerges or whether the position of the old majority party is reinforced.

or in a different pattern than others? One might conclude that this is so from the American realignment literature. Part of that literature's argument is that the structure of the U.S. system produces periodic crises (see especially Burnham 1970). The implicit comparison is with systems in which government is unitary and elections translate popular wishes more smoothly and continuously into party policy. So perhaps we should expect more variability over time in levels of electoral cohesiveness in the United States than in the United Kingdom.

In Japan, where parliamentary government generates strong party discipline, one would not predict a pattern of electoral realignments on the American model. But electoral politics in Japan does realign: New parties are formed on occasion, and conflict among the factions of the dominant Liberal Democratic Party heats up and cools down.

Consider first the creation of new parties. In the period under scrutiny here, Japan has witnessed the formation of four new parties: the Democratic Socialist Party (1960), the Komeito (1964), the Social Democratic League (1978), and the New Liberal Club (1976). The first three are still in business, having discovered viable electoral niches to occupy; the New Liberal Club was reabsorbed into the LDP in 1986. The creation of each new party ought, to the extent that it represented a nationwide electoral force detrimental to incumbents of *both* major parties, to have increased the level of electoral cohesiveness measured here. Of course, some of the new parties, notably the Democratic Socialist Party, hurt the Japan Socialist Party (JSP) while benefiting the LDP – and so, since we do not disaggregate by party here, the effect is more or less a wash. A larger effect comes with the creation of the centrist Komeito and New Liberal Club, which competed against incumbents of both major parties successfully.

Consider next the level of electoral competition among the factions of the LDP. Cox and Rosenbluth (1993) have shown that the electoral fates of LDP factions were negatively correlated in the 1960–79 period, but positively correlated thereafter. At the same time, the size of interparty swings increased substantially. Thus, intraparty electoral competition seems to have given way to interparty electoral competition in the 1980s. Given that the LDP was about two and a half times the size of the JSP by the 1980s, one expects overall electoral cohesiveness to go up as intra-LDP fighting goes down.

In the United States, incumbents are likely to respond to demographic changes and the postrealignment shrinking of partisan platforms by insulating themselves from party swings with the personal vote (Cain, Ferejohn, and Fiorina 1987). In Japan, the majority party's leadership may wield more potent instruments with which to rein in errant incumbents, but its hands are tied by its own dependence on the personal vote to return

Table 2.2. *Typical impacts of partisan tides over time in the United States, Japan, and England*

Years	Typical Impact
The United States	
1960–64	.164
1966–70	.225
1972–76	.101
1978–82	.065
1984–90	.024
Japan	
1960–67	.034
1969–79	.066
1980–90	.093
England	
1959–66	.102
1970–79	.123

a majority to the legislature. We should therefore expect periodic realignments in Japan as well, though because of Japan's multimember district electoral system, the realignments are likely to entail a reshuffling of constituencies among multiple parties and factions.[20]

We have given reasons that electoral cohesiveness in both the United States and Japan should be more variable than in the United Kingdom, but our mode of analysis does not lead to a prediction as to which of the two is likely to be more variable than the other.

Turning now from expectations to data, one can see from Table 2.2 that the United States shows the largest variability over time in electoral cohesiveness. There is a significant decline in the typical impact of partisan tides in the United States from .164 and .225 in 1960–64 and 1966–70 to .024 in 1984–90. This is largely consistent with the conventional view in the literature that partisan ties in the American electorate went into secular decline in the 1960s.[21]

---

[20] We interpret the LDP's current consideration of electoral overhaul as the party's reevaluation of its long-term electoral viability under the existing rules. Should the Japanese legislature adopt some variant of the proposals combining single-member district and proportional representation rules, we would expect indicators of electoral cohesiveness in Japan to come to resemble those in the United Kingdom more closely.

[21] That the U.S. coefficients for the two earliest periods are so high, even higher than the corresponding British figures, reflects two things. First, uncontested races, most of which occurred in the South, are discarded from the U.S. analysis. The remaining incumbent

Japan also shows variation, with a steady increase in the typical impact. From historical accounts of those years, it seems plausible that this rise in electoral cohesiveness reflects the declining electoral success of both the LDP and the Japan Socialist Party in the face of successful competition from the entrepreneurial, largely urban, Komeito and Democratic Socialist Party.[22] Electoral cohesiveness in the United States has been decreasing, while it has been increasing in Japan.

5. CONCLUSION

This chapter has offered a method of measuring electoral cohesiveness, applying this measure to the United States, the United Kingdom, and Japan. We drew initial inspiration from the "nationalization" literature, which has attempted to quantify the extent of national, or partisan, influences on electoral change. Nevertheless, we parted company with that stream of scholarship, choosing to measure electoral cohesiveness (the degree to which members of the same party share a collective electoral fate) instead of nationalization, because we find it both conceptually more intuitive and empirically more tractable.

We hasten to add that our measure is also less than perfect. Electoral cohesiveness is based on change, and will understate the degree to which electoral fates are tied together when partisan configurations in the electorate are in equilibrium. Nonetheless, low electoral cohesiveness for a particular party, when coupled with declining proportions of the vote, suggests difficulty in acting collectively. Conversely, high electoral cohesiveness may indicate, as in the case of Japan for the 1969–79 period, the inability of one or more large parties to respond to new political issues.

In explaining the cross-national patterns we observed, we suggested that the United Kingdom's parliamentary government and single-member district electoral system both contribute to electoral cohesiveness, while in the United States and Japan governmental structure and electoral rules

candidates are thus predominantly nonsouthern, and the electoral fates of this somewhat homogenized group are more closely tied together than would be the fates of all major-party candidates. Uncontested races would also be discarded from the U.K. sample, if there were any. Since there are not, the full diversity of the U.K. sample remains in the data analyzed. Second, the large U.S. coefficient for 1966–70 also reflects the peculiarities of the 1966 election. Forty incumbents lost their seats in 1966, the fifth-highest figure in the postwar era. Since it is the loss of seats by incumbents that drives the party-swing variable's coefficient up, the 1966–70 coefficient is rather large, even though most measures of the "incumbency advantage" go up in this period. See Jacobson 1990: 56.

22 It is important to bear in mind that in Japan the cohesiveness of incumbents reflects anti-incumbent swings within the LDP as well, whereas this is not the case in the United States or the United Kingdom. In other words, the LDP has maintained some degree of responsiveness to the changing electorate by way of LDP challengers who run against LDP incumbents.

influence electoral cohesiveness in cross-cutting directions. Our framework does not predict, and our data are inconclusive about, whether electoral cohesiveness will be stronger in presidential/SNTV-SMD systems or in parliamentary/SNTV-MMD systems. We leave systematic investigation of this question for future research.

3

Party provision for personal politics: dividing the vote in Japan

MATHEW D. MCCUBBINS AND
FRANCES MCCALL ROSENBLUTH

1. INTRODUCTION

Japanese politics is widely perceived to be exceptional. On the one hand, its government structure is British parliamentary: Voters cast ballots for individual candidates who bear party labels; winning candidates are then collectively responsible for directing and managing the activities of the bureaucrats who execute policy. There is no popularly elected executive to whom legislators can allocate either authority or blame for policy outcomes. On the other hand, Japanese government processes seem more American than British. Japanese elections are expensive and candidate-centered, much like U.S. congressional races. Japan's ruling Liberal Democratic Party, moreover, is seen as having a decentralized power structure. The party manages policy in large part through an extensive system of committees, each of which carries responsibility for overseeing its own set of cabinet ministries and bureaucratic agencies, much as the U.S. Congress relies on its own standing committees to oversee the executive branch.

Moreover, despite its parliamentary structure, Japanese politics seems highly particularistic and personalized. The LDP's Policy Affairs Research Council's system of standing committees spreads policy-making authority broadly among party backbenchers, reinforcing American-style individual responsibility for policy outcomes rather than the British model of collective responsibility centered on the prime minister and cabinet. The effects of this individualized policy-making process are seen in how the LDP distributes budgetary resources. The Japanese budget emphasizes spending on highly targetable benefits and programs, such as public works and small-business subsidies. The proportion of all general account spending going to public construction projects (roads, harbors, dams, housing, and so forth), energy production, and the like, is typically around 30 percent in Japan, compared to 15–20 percent of the supply estimates in

35

Britain, or 21 percent. Additionally, Japan typically subsidizes loans for projects and small businesses (outside of the regular budget) to the equivalent of about 40 percent of the total general account budget through the Fiscal Investment and Loan Program (FILP). Britain and Canada have no equivalent loan-subsidy programs.

Particularistic tendencies permeate the whole range of Japanese policies. Tax and regulatory policy decisions steer benefits to certain constituents (Rosenbluth 1989; Sakakibara 1991). The government also guarantees unsecured loans made by local credit associations to small manufacturers (Friedman 1988). Through these and other means, the government creates and protects markets for a panoply of interests (Lincoln 1990; Okimoto 1989; Ramseyer 1983). Thus, a cursory glance at Japanese policy outcomes reveals that the ruling party relies heavily on particularistic policies.

In this chapter, we provide a simple explanation for why British-style parliamentary structures in Japan yield U.S.-style electoral behavior and policy outcomes. Our explanation is institutional and is premised on the structure of incentives arising from Japan's electoral laws. Japan's electoral system, we argue, forces any majority-seeking party to apportion votes for the party in most districts among multiple candidates. In order to divide the votes of party loyalists efficiently, parties must devise an incentive-compatible scheme for grouping party voters with party candidates – a way for candidates to enhance their individual reputations without detracting from the party's overall appeal to voters.

We argue that the LDP's strategy to solve these collective dilemmas has been to distribute to its incumbent candidates effective property rights over aspects of policy making (through cabinet posts and the Policy Affairs Research Council [PARC] committee assignments), thus giving each candidate the opportunity to build his own reputation with voters on policy making. Thus, the party can limit competition between its candidates on policy grounds and at the same time provide voters with incentives to vote for particular party candidates. The LDP has made this strategy effective by devoting a large share of the budget (and off-budget spending, such as FILP) to policies that are amenable to narrow targeting and for which individual LDP members can plausibly claim credit.

The remainder of the chapter elaborates these ideas. In Section 2 we describe in greater detail the single nontransferable vote (SNTV) electoral system used in Japan and the incentives that system creates for candidates and voters. We then introduce the concepts of collective reputation, personal reputation, and personal vote coalitions and show why the LDP has an interest in subsidizing and managing its candidates' personal vote coalition–building activities. In Section 3, we present an explanation for how the party could contribute to these coalitions, and we present some evidence on budgetary policy that supports our interpretation of party involvement in reelection activities. Section 4 describes the structure of the LDP and presents evidence that shows that the party has taken care to differentiate its incumbents in each district on policy grounds. Section 5 concludes.

2. SNTV AND CANDIDATES' INCENTIVES

In experimenting with different electoral rules, the Meiji oligarchs who dominated Japanese politics at the turn of the century chose new, democratic political structures with an eye toward keeping the party movement in check. They sought to divide the political landscape into a number of parties with medium-sized districts rather than single-member or large districts, and to dampen the degree to which the new parties would be unified on questions of policy and strategy. They did this by imposing the limited vote, SNTV electoral system rather than party-list proportional representation or the single transferable vote (Fukui 1988; Soma 1986).

Recent scholarship on the effects of electoral laws on political outcomes confirms the strategic wisdom of the oligarchs' choices (Lijphart, Pintor, and Sone 1987; Taagepera and Shugart 1989). These authors argue that SNTV is particularly good at allowing for representation of minority parties, largely because major parties tend to be too conservative in nominating candidates and not very good at dividing their votes.

Japan had a brief stint with a single-member district system between 1919 and 1925, when Prime Minister Hara apparently convinced oligarch Aritomo Yamagata that single-member districts would be an effective way to minimize Communist/Socialist representation in the Diet. It seems the only prospect that haunted Yamagata more than party democracy was socialism, though he was determined to avert either. But Prime Minister Hara's Seiyukai won an absolute majority in 1920, which changed Yamagata's mind about the wisdom of single-member districts. The medium-sized districts and SNTV introduced in 1925 are the basis for the current electoral system (Soma 1986; Fukui 1988).

After World War II, U.S. occupation officials rejected Japan's prewar electoral structure on the dubious grounds that the electoral rule may have contributed to the rise of militarism. The occupation introduced a large-district, proportional representation electoral system in 1946 as a way to draw in new political forces, but after the 1946 election gave the Diet a strong Socialist contingent (93 out of 464 seats), MacArthur relented to Liberal Party leader Shigeru Yoshida's request to return to the prewar electoral system. The Liberal and Democratic parties, which together commanded a Diet majority, revised the election law to reinstate the 1925 multimember district system. Despite this revision, neither of the conservative parties did as well at the polls in 1947 as was expected, and the Socialists actually took the lead with 143 seats over 131 for the Liberals and 124 for the Democrats.[1] The conservative parties, however, rebounded by the next election (Fukunaga 1986: 445–446).

Yoshida's choice of the SNTV electoral rule was not obvious, since it poses clear problems for a party trying to gain or maintain a majority of legislative seats. Because each district elects two or more legislators, a party must run more than one candidate in each district to attempt to win a majority.[2] This creates two important problems: Party leaders cannot easily control loyal voters' choices among party candidates, and the party cannot control candidates' individual campaign efforts.

In casting their ballots, voters make decisions based on their preferences for individual candidates as well as party reputations and policy platforms. If voters were to cast their ballots purely on partisan grounds – as if they cared only for their party and were indifferent to distinctions between its candidates – then any particular party's voters would face a problem of pure coordination, with the concomitant possibility of an inefficient outcome.

A party's voters all want the same thing – to maximize the number of successful candidates from their party. But in the absence of some mechanism for allocating their votes, they risk spreading their combined votes too thinly among too many candidates and winning fewer seats than their share of the total vote would merit. Alternatively, they might concentrate their votes too tightly, thus electing a small number of candidates even though their combined votes could have elected more candidates had they been better allocated. In practice, the problem is worse still. Each candidate has personal characteristics that make him or her attractive to voters. In the case of a particularly charismatic candidate, these personal characteristics can draw too many voters, so that the charismatic candidate wins a glorious victory with surplus votes, to the detriment of the party.

On its face, the vote-division problem may seem a simple one to solve. Why could not each party instruct its loyal voters how to vote more efficiently? In other words, why couldn't the parties instruct their voters for whom they should vote, devising a means – by telephone number or address, for example – to divide votes among the party's candidates?

---

[1] Newspapers predicted that the Liberals would capture a plurality with 160 to 170 seats, that the Democrats would run a close second with 150 seats, and that the Socialists would come in third with 125 seats. Part of the conservative parties' problem seems to have been the purge of local conservative politicians who formed the core of their personal support systems.

[2] At present, the 512 members of the Lower House are elected from 130 districts. Thus, to garner a simple majority of 257 seats, a party would have to win an average of just under two seats per district.

Political parties in prewar Japan's SNTV system were reportedly somewhat successful in dividing the votes among candidates within each district through outright vote buying, brokered by local notables.[3]

If it were technically feasible for voters to carry out the voting instructions handed down by the party, the plan would work only if voters cared more about the party's electoral fortunes than they favored any particular candidate. The personal vote would have to be very weak (Cain, Ferejohn, and Fiorina 1987). However, the secret ballot makes it exceedingly difficult for any party to enforce such informal contracts or even to identify with certainty its core constituents, to whom instructions would be given (Cox 1987).[4] Voters' incentives would not be aligned with those of the party; rather, voters would have an incentive to deviate from instructions. Even if we assume that the personal vote is weak in Japanese elections, and that voters have preferences only over public goods, a party would be unable to assure itself of a majority (indeed, a party would be unable to assure itself of a likelihood much beyond zero of winning a majority) on its ideological appeal alone. While ideological information might be sufficient for a voter to hold preferences for one party, it is clearly insufficient for choosing individual candidates within that party.

Moreover, from the standpoint of the candidates, members of the same party must end up competing with each other for the same votes. By contrast, the single transferable vote (STV) rule, which transfers votes to the party's next candidate as soon as the first choice wins the minimum number of votes for a seat, gives candidates of the same party little incentive to compete against each other. Another name for the SNTV system might be the "first M past the post" system, where M is the number of members to be elected from the district (the "district magnitude"). Every candidate is in competition with every other candidate to get past the post (the threshold for election) regardless of party label.

Intraparty competition could cause the party to lose seats. Consider the example of a three-member district in which two candidates run from

---

[3] The closest thing to a centralized electoral machine in postwar Japan was the Komeito's electoral organization, used to divide its voters among its candidates in the nationwide district in Upper House elections. (Note that the Komeito and other small parties do not need an electoral machine for the Lower House elections since they typically do not have enough voters to elect more than one representative in most districts, and so can run on the basis of a party label.) The Komeito's primary base of electoral support is the fervent Soka gakkai sect of Nichiren Buddhism, which is extremely well organized into local blocs, allowing the party to allocate votes geographically to maximize its electoral clout. The LDP finally changed the rules in 1981 to a party-list system when its own Upper House electoral performance began slipping. This nullified the Komeito's organizational advantage and mitigated the LDP's problem in dividing the vote in the nationwide district, which is too large for personal support networks to operate effectively.

[4] See Cox (1987) for a discussion of the changes in British party organization resulting from the introduction of the secret ballot in the nineteenth century.

each of two parties, Party A and Party B. Party A's first candidate is popular in the district and is able to garner 66 percent of the votes cast in the election. Both of Party B's candidates are able to capture only 12 percent of the votes, while Party A's second candidate is assured of only 10 percent of the vote. In this case Party A, though winning 76 percent of the votes, captures only one of three seats. If Party A could find a way to divide votes more equitably between its two candidates, it could win two seats easily. Indeed, if the party were exceptionally good at dividing votes it could field another candidate and win all three seats.[5] Both the Liberal and Democratic parties, in the interim between World War II and their 1955 merger, apparently recognized the importance of efficient vote division. Both made ample use of the personal vote as a way of dividing votes among their own party's candidates in any given district, with some success (Soma 1986).[6]

By contrast, in a closed party-list system, where only the party leadership determines the ordering of party candidates on the ballot, candidates can and will rely exclusively on the party label. Emphasizing individual character or personal abilities should have only a marginal effect on the candidate's electoral chances, and is more costly for both the candidate and the party than relying on the party's collective reputation.[7] But Cain, Ferejohn, and Fiorina (1987) point out that the dynamics are different in a plurality system, in which, absent party control of access to the ballot, the electoral "market" is contestable.[8] That is, just about anyone can run for office and get on the ballot by satisfying some nominal requirements, such as paying a small fee or having a certain number of eligible voters sign a

---

[5] In this counterfactual example we have assumed that the number of candidates does not affect voter turnout. There is evidence, however, that new LDP candidates sometimes mobilize voters who otherwise would have stayed at home (Matsubara and Kabashima 1984).

[6] In a more recent example, the Socialist party today has resorted to distinctions in personal style. When it runs two candidates in a district, one is typically a labor union candidate while the second is often a woman with an environmentalist or feminist platform. Though doubtless better than no vote division at all, this strategy based on personal style has been relatively ineffective.

[7] This depends to some extent on how the ordering of the list is decided. For Japan's Upper House list, LDP leaders rank candidates by their past vote-getting record and future vote-getting promise. Candidates have a strong incentive to bring in registered party supporters, often paying dues on their behalf, to demonstrate their popular appeal.

[8] A perfectly contestable market has perfectly free entry and exit. Thus, the market for bearing the party label is contestable to the degree that entry and exit into competition for use of that label in the general election are free. U.S. House primaries are a good example. Nevertheless, the party as a collectivity clearly decides who, within the House, does and does not get the *ex post* benefits of the party label. Parties can sanction members, for example, by refusing to give them committee assignments. A majority party can effectively deny particularistic benefits to any member's district, and can prevent any member's sponsored legislation from being considered on the floor of the House, thus denying that member of most of his opportunities for Mayhewian credit claiming.

petition. Individual candidates will have a strong incentive to supplement the party label with a personal vote that can serve as a barrier to entry in the face of would-be challengers. Further, the market for the party label itself may be contestable: Others can seek to capture the party label in primary elections or through some other form of party endorsements. Thus, even within a single party, potential candidates have an incentive to build personal vote coalitions.

It follows that majority-seeking parties in an SNTV system cannot rely on either their voters or their candidates to divide the vote efficiently. Any system developed to divide a party's vote must be incentive compatible, both for the voters and for the party's candidates. The alternative, in a country where votes count and parties compete, is to lose the voters' support and the candidates' allegiance. If the system were structured so that party and individual incentives were in conflict, the party would have to invest heavily in a centralized authority structure (party leaders) and a set of tools and sanctions at those leaders' disposal to discourage shirking and slippage (Cox and McCubbins 1993; Kiewiet and McCubbins 1991). Such systems are of course possible, but they are susceptible to what has been called Madison's dilemma: the problem of striking a balance between delegating too little or too much authority to a central agent.

More important, such centralized, "party-controlled" vote divisions are incompatible with the incentives facing individual candidates in district elections. In what we have described as the "first M past the post" system, candidates have an incentive to pursue votes on their own. Since the vote, once cast, is fixed on a specific candidate and cannot be transferred, each candidate has an incentive to give voters reasons to vote for him rather than some other candidate of the same party. Once having obtained office, an incumbent member is in an advantaged position to use the resources of his office to further secure his position.[9]

Instead of fighting the incentives within SNTV for the personal vote, a majority-seeking party would be better off controlling the creation and maintenance of members' personal vote coalitions so as to make the vote division induced by personal vote incentives more efficient. Such a strat-

[9] Thus, the literature on the incumbency advantage in the U.S. Congress, for example, emphasizes the resources at a member's disposal, such as the franking privilege, paid staff, and position as a monopoly supplier of bureaucratic "fix-it" services to the member's district (Fiorina 1977). The fact of being an incumbent also may mean easier access to "free" media, such as being interviewed on television, and it sends a signal to potential campaign contributors that this candidate is a proven vote winner, and thus might be a good investment. Japan's Public Offices Election Law is also biased in favor of incumbents. Prohibitions on door-to-door canvassing, a short election period (forty days in the case of the Lower House), and strict limits on the means and amount of advertising make it extremely difficult for challengers to make a strong impression during the campaign period (Baerwald 1986; Curtis 1988; Hrebenar 1986; Jichi sho senkyobu [ed.] 1991; Tajima 1991).

egy increases the probability that the party may win a majority of seats. Everyone in the party, leaders and backbenchers alike, is better off if the party efficiently uses the total number of votes cast for its candidates to elect the maximum number of legislators, up to the point where the probability of attaining a simple majority of seats is maximized. In this sense, it is a second-best solution, but the best outcome that can be achieved given the circumstances.

Of course, voting and elections are not purely personalistic. To attract voters, parties will create and defend collective reputations about their positions over public goods. These collective reputations, or party labels, serve as information shortcuts for voters sifting through vast amounts of information in making their choices at the polls (Cox and McCubbins 1993; Downs 1957; Popkin 1991). Because the perceived ability to deliver public or private goods rides on reputation, and this reputation is costly to build on one's own, candidates for office have a strong incentive to tap into one of these party labels. Indeed, without attachment to a party, candidates cannot credibly claim to be able to offer anything beyond a very narrow range of private goods, since the probability of any single member being decisive in any legislative vote is effectively zero when all winning coalitions of members are equally likely (see, e.g., Schwartz 1986).

The outcome of this second-best solution – to manage the resources available to candidates for building personal vote coalitions – is a stable division of the electorate. As enforcement is lacking, this division can be established without explicit coordination on the part of voters.[10] Candidates in district systems will identify voters likely to vote for them on the basis of their personal vote, and will cultivate them. In order to do so, a candidate will adopt a "home style" – a public persona to which he/she thinks voters will respond (Fenno 1978). Voters, for their part, will identify with certain candidates. If voters have preferences for particularistic goods provided by the government, and elections are district-based, voters will be inclined to vote for the individual legislators who could plausibly claim credit for the goods they care about most (Fenno 1978; Fiorina 1977; Mayhew 1974). The equilibrium will be that candidates cater to their voting coalition in the district, and that voters will remain loyal to these candidates (Cox and McCubbins 1986). The goal for the party, then, is to help its members build personal vote coalitions that also support the collective reputation of the party.

---

[10] This does not imply that all voters identify with any particular candidate. However, the strength of the personal vote in Japan's Lower House is evidenced by the consistently stronger returns of LDP in the Lower than in the Upper House, where the party label is more important.

3. BUILDING PERSONAL VOTE COALITIONS

How do candidates go about establishing a personal vote? The first means is to court voters with personalized attention. Japanese politicians attempt to draw constituents into personal support organizations (*koenkai*).[11] Politicians coddle citizens with small favors in exchange for votes. Journalistic reporting as well as scholarly analyses of Japanese elections invariably focus on individual candidates' support networks and the enormous sums of money needed to build and maintain them. LDP politicians are famous for showing up at weddings and funerals, helping voters with job placement, and sending bottles of sake for neighborhood festivals (Hirose 1989). Each LDP candidate is said to have spent the equivalent of $3 million to $12 million for the February 1990 Lower House election.[12] While there is a spurt of spending on general advertising during the formal campaign period in the weeks leading up to the election, the bulk of expenditures goes to year-round activities of each candidate's fifty to eighty personal support organizations. These activities typically include candidate-subsidized new year's parties and group trips to hot springs, as well as policy discussion circles and "study tours" of the Diet for constituents.

From the standpoint of the LDP, the problem with personalized attention is that it offers little advantage to the governing party, since any party can undertake these activities.[13] All Japanese politicians can and do build personal support networks and go out of their way to appear more personable, accessible, and attentive than the competition.

Facilitation services are a second means of creating personal vote coalitions. This method, more than personalized attention, has special advantages for the governing party. The governing party can be expected to use its institutional position to determine when and if bureaucratic decision-making processes are to be changed or specific decisions overturned. We therefore expect that, in equilibrium, bureaucrats will be more responsive

---

[11] For more on how these *koenkai* are organized and operate, see Baerwald (1986); Curtis (1971; 1987); Hrebenar (1986); Kamishima (1985); and Stockwin (1987).

[12] *Economist*, February 3, 1990. This is roughly between $50 and $120 per constituent. In comparison, recent research on U.S. House elections has found that incumbents spend less than $1 per constituent (Gary Jacobson, personal communication).

[13] The majority party, of course, has something of an advantage in raising money for these little favors because it can sell regulation to big contributors. But other parties have other advantages. The Japan Communist Party (JCP) runs a popular and highly profitable publishing business, in most years making the JCP the "wealthiest" party according to publicly revealed campaign finance data. See, for example, Hrebenar (1986). The Komeito, while less flush with funds, has an army of volunteers from the Soka gakkai sect. The Japan Socialist Party and Democratic Socialist Party also each have a loyal core of union supporters who volunteer at election time. The LDP is said to be the only party without free help during the campaign season.

to the complaints and inquiries of ruling party members than of opposition party members. As Fiorina (1977) argues about the American case, bureaucracies can be designed to create opportunities for legislators to intervene personally on the behalf of individuals or groups of constituents, thus allowing legislators a never-ending stream of personalized, credit-claiming activities that can help build personal vote coalitions.

LDP members also use government resources to cultivate supporters. Members of PARC committees make a great show of pushing for their constituents' interests in intraparty discussions, and claim credit for policy decisions that benefit their constituents. Agricultural policy making provides an example. During the annual negotiations when the government decides how much it will pay farmers for rice, members of the PARC's agricultural division are vocal backers of a high price on behalf of their agricultural constituents. Even in recent years, as the party leadership has imposed a lower price than the agricultural division has recommended, the division members still claim credit for pushing as hard as possible in the face of the leadership's countervailing considerations, and for achieving some concessions (Fukui 1987).

The party in control of the government has, of course, a distinct advantage in creating personal vote coalitions for its candidates because it monopolizes policy and budgetary favors. As long as the majority party can pass its legislation through the Parliament and can direct bureaucrats effectively, it can enact (or have bureaucrats implement) particularistic policies that facilitate the creation and maintenance of personal vote coalitions.

If the majority party pursues a strategy of building personal vote coalitions for its members, it follows, all else constant, that the more such coalitions the party has to maintain (the more members the party has to provide for), the greater will be expenditures out of the part of the budget used for vote coalitions, which we usually label as particularistic spending. The main counter argument is that spending on particularistic programs increases when the party is doing badly – when it has to protect (see, e.g., Calder 1988b). Districts are said to be flooded with particularistic expenditures in such situations, in order to buy votes for the LDP. This is basically a Japanese version of the thesis forwarded in the U.S. context by Tufte (1975). We can, of course, test the implications of our model of how Japanese elections are organized by examining expenditures on particularistic programs.

If we are right that the electoral connection in Japan leads to incentives to create personal vote coalitions, which in turn lead to incentives to use particularistic resources to create and maintain those coalitions, then we should be able to test whether or not expenditures on particularistic programs increase as the size of the LDP coalition within the Diet increases.

Our hypothesis is simple: the larger the LDP coalition within the Diet, the more it needs to spend, all else constant, in order to maintain the personal vote coalitions of its members, and to help divide the district vote. The null hypothesis against which we test our alternative is that changes in the size of the LDP coalition in the Diet have no effect on spending in these programs. Another alternative hypothesis, which we also test, is that decreases in the size of the LDP coalition lead to increases in spending.

We test our hypothesis by looking at budgetary data for forty-nine general account items and seven special accounts for all years between 1952 and 1989. We selected our set of Japanese budget items from the larger data set used by McCubbins and Noble (Chapter 5 of this book), and is summarized in the Appendix. McCubbins and Noble selected data to cover the two major flows of funds in the general budget: expenditures in the general account, which is funded by tax and bond revenues, and subsidies to the various special accounts from the general account. We restrict our data set to items that McCubbins and Noble defined as either semipublic or particularistic.[14]

We test our hypothesis by pooling the expenditure data for all the agencies listed in the Appendix for fiscal years 1952–89 into a single regression. This allows us to test our hypothesis with a single regression coefficient. Our dependent variable in this regression is the percentage change in spending for an agency from one year to the next.[15] The independent variables are listed in Table 3.1. There are four types of variables that we include in our regression. First is the percentage of seats held by the LDP in the House of Representatives (lagged, so that the size of the LDP coalition corresponds to the time at which decisions for the fiscal year under study were made). The coefficient on this variable tests our main hypothesis. Second, we also included dummy variables to represent election years for both the lower chamber and the upper chamber of the Diet. We included these because McCubbins and Noble report that there is good reason to believe that spending increases on many items in election years, including the items in our analysis. Third, we included dummy variables that represent the ministry in which the program resides. This is to capture different spending trends for different broad categories of policy. In the end only those dummy variables that were significant were

---

[14] The authors categorized all budget items as "public," "particularistic," or "semipublic" from the description of the items in government manuals and by examining the legislative charters of the various agencies. Of course, a taxonomy as simple as the one they use draws too fine a line, as nearly every government program contains some aspects of both publicness and particularism. Nonetheless, the labels do provide a rough indication of the general tenor of a particular program. See the appendix to McCubbins and Noble (Chapter 4, this volume) for details.

[15] The actual dependent variable is the partial log of the budget item, where the partial log for a budget item Y_t is $\log(Y_t/Y_{t-1})$.

Table 3.1 *Japanese budget regression*[a]

Independent variable	Estimated coefficient	Standard error	t-statistic
Constant	-0.63695	0.12224	-5.21082
Percentage change in budget remainder	1.24191	0.23015	5.39599
Percent LDP	1.04807	0.23272	4.50362
Lower House election	2.77452e-02	1.98918e-02	1.39480
Upper House election	1.94724e-02	2.27005e-02	0.85780
Ministry of Education	6.96370e-02	2.48803e-02	2.79888
Ministry of Posts & Telecom	-5.60421e-02	1.76490e-02	-3.17536

Note: Number of observations = 1,593
R-squared = 5.69691e-02
[a]Dependent variable: Partial Log of Real Budget for item i in year t.

included in the table.[16] Last, we included a variable to account for overall trends in expenditures,[17] which is the percentage change in the remainder of the general account budget (subtracting from total expenditures the spending for the program in question, for each program in each year). This last variable is itself a choice made by the LDP, as is our dependent variable – spending for the programs in our sample. Thus this last variable is an endogenous variable; we use two-stage least squares to estimate the coefficient for this variable.[18]

Cross section/time series analyses, particularly with nonlinear dependent and independent variables, generally suffer from a number of potential econometric problems; there are many reasons why the errors generated from such a test might not be normal. We tested for and, where possible, corrected a number of these problems such as heteroskedasticity,

[16] We performed the standard F-test for the joint exclusion of all other ministry dummies; i.e., we tested the hypothesis that all other ministry dummies had a coefficient of zero. We reject at conventional levels of significance that the loss of fit due to the restriction is significant.

[17] This choice of specification was based on a simple two-component budget model that is explained fully in McCubbins and Noble (Chapter 5, this volume). Briefly, in a model that explains changes in spending for a particular item, there are two items in the budget: spending for the item being examined, and all other spending. Their approach is similar to a two-good model of an economy, where the point is to examine how changes in the demand or supply of one good affects the price or quantity supplied of the other good.

[18] Standard OLS results do not hold when any one of the independent variables is correlated with the error term, as is the case here. To solve this problem we estimate the endogenous independent variable – total spending for all other items in the budget – by a set of variables that are uncorrelated with the error term. We then use the estimated independent variable in the original regression. By construction, this estimated independent variable is uncorrelated with the error term and standard results apply.

autocorrelation, and general misspecification.[19] In general, our diagnostics lead us to have a reasonable amount of faith in the estimated parameters presented in Table 3.1.

Our regression analysis shows that spending on particularistic programs does indeed increase with the number of LDP members in the Diet. The coefficient on the percentage of the Diet held by the LDP – Percent LDP in Table 3.1 – is significant at well beyond the 95 percent confidence level in a one-tailed test. This allows us to reject the null hypothesis of no effect (a zero coefficient) and the second alternative hypothesis of a negative effect (a negative coefficient). This coefficient implies that a 1 percent increase in the size of the LDP's Diet coalition leads to slightly more than a 1 percent increase in spending for all particularistic programs. This is consistent with our hypothesis that the LDP uses spending on particularistic programs to enable their candidates to develop personal vote coalitions that ultimately reduces intraparty competition and leads to an efficient division of the vote.[20]

The development of a personal vote reduces but admittedly does not eliminate intraparty competition. By controlling the resources available to develop a personal vote, the party manages the size of the personal vote coalition for each of its members in an effort to allow all party members equal access to the party's collective resources. The size of the personal vote coalition for each member may be quite different, but as long as a majority of members in most districts are able to be reelected, differences in the sizes of coalitions are unimportant to the party.[21]

[19] For example, we conducted a number of specification tests. Several of these tests examine the distribution of the residuals generated by the estimation in order to look for evidence of specific kinds of misspecification, the presence of which might lead to incorrect inferences from the parameters estimated for the explanatory variables. We first checked for serial correlation in the errors via a Lagrange multiplier test and were able to reject the presence of first-order autocorrelation at conventional levels of significance. Given that we have annual data, we did not test for higher orders of autocorrelation. We tested for the presence of contemporaneous correlation in errors, common in panel data, by looking for fixed-time effects that would alter all observations in that year. We could not reject the joint test for exclusion of the fixed-time effects at conventional levels – i.e., the explanatory variables that we included in our model seem to pick up substantially all of the fixed-time effects, leaving too little of this kind of correlation in the errors for us to need to further correct our model. We also checked for heteroskedasticity via the Breush–Pagan test (1979). Again we reject the presence of heteroskedasticity at conventional levels, which is to be expected since we are working with partial logs, which minimize the effects of varying size of agency budgets. However, since the power of the Breush–Pagan test is sensitive to the choice of possible explanatory variables affecting the variances, we calculated all standard errors using the White heteroskedasticity-consistent method (1980).

[20] The coefficients on the other variables seem sensible, though we did not find, as McCubbins and Noble did in their study, that the LDP increased spending in election years.

[21] Indeed, a party does not even care if it wins a plurality of votes in each district; it cares only about winning a majority of seats overall. Candidates of the Japan Socialist Party (JSP), for example, were the highest vote getters in 74 out of 130 districts in the February 1990 election, but in the vast majority of these districts the party fielded only one candidate.

What does all this imply? By providing a wide range of services to a large part of the population and weakening the salience of ideological issues, LDP representatives collectively make it harder for politicians of opposition parties to compete. This electoral strategy leaves few niches of support groups unattended and vulnerable to appeals from other parties. It has been extremely difficult for opposition parties to make inroads beyond their traditional support bases, which are organized labor for the Japan Socialist Party and Democratic Socialist Party, the Soka gakkai for the Komeito, and left-wing intellectuals and various fringe voters for the Japan Communist Party. If it is true, as we argue, that the LDP's range of services to local constituents makes it difficult for opposition parties to find new services to provide or to counter with ideological appeals, it follows that robust LDP intraparty competition reduces the risks to the LDP of interparty competition.

As long as rank-and-file party members can discipline their leaders,[22] and as long as party leaders seek to win a majority of seats for their party, the rank-and-file members can get the party to establish policies and institutions to facilitate the development of particularistic policies. The party leadership attempts to hold the line on spending because both government budget funds and campaign contributions are costly to raise. But the leadership must permit at least enough expenditures to ensure a Diet majority and hence their jobs as leaders. The result of rank-and-file pressure is that the vote division in the districts results largely from candidates' abilities to provide particularistic policies.

4. THE PARTY PROVISION OF THE PERSONAL VOTE

Given the importance of facilitation services and pork provision, rank-and-file members need an efficient means to influence bureaucratic and party policy making. Committees of one sort or another are common arenas through which politicians in representative governments oversee and direct policy making. In most parliamentary systems this committee structure is contained in one large committee – the cabinet. However, forums such as caucuses, cabinets, and leadership or ministerially led committees would fail to give the rank and file of the party the ability to

Many LDP candidates won far fewer votes than the Socialist candidate, but the LDP won a majority of seats in most of these districts. In six urban districts, the top Socialist victor won more than twice as many votes than the lowest-placed winner in the district, indicating that the JSP could have increased its seats by six had it been able to divide the vote among two candidates.

22 The recent demise of British party leaders Margaret Thatcher and Neil Kinnock demonstrates that the rank and file hold the ultimate sanction over party leaders, even in supposedly top-heavy British politics.

derive credit from constituency services. In most parliamentary systems such credit claiming seems unnecessary for electoral success, but in Japan, we argue, credit-claiming activities for rank-and-file party members are very much necessary.[23] The leadership serves as a check on the activities of these committees, but policy initiation, oversight, and facilitation services rest with the backbenchers in the committees.

In Japan, as we have argued, the multimember district, SNTV electoral system creates a need for personal support coalitions. The PARC provides such a system. Article 40, paragraph 2 of the LDP constitution requires all bills and policy plans to be examined and approved by the party's Policy Affairs Research Council (*seimu chosakai*) before submission to the cabinet and the Diet.

The PARC consists of a chairman, five vice chairmen, a deliberation council or executive committee (which includes the chairman, vice chairmen, and fifteen other members chosen by their faction leaders), and seventeen committees that correspond to the ministries in the bureaucracy. The chairmanship of the PARC is considered to be one of the four top leadership positions in the party.[24]

LDP Diet members generally belong to four PARC committees, two of which correspond with the representative's membership in a Diet committee (Sao and Matsuzaki 1986).[25] The largest and most popular committees are agriculture, commerce, construction, and posts and telecommunications (Inoguchi and Iwai 1987; *Jiyu Minshuto Seimu Chosakai Meibo* [LDP PARC membership roster] various years). These are also commonly held to be the most particularistic (Fukui 1987; Nihon Keizai Shimbunsha [ed.] 1983). Membership in these committees is limited, by convention rather than written rule, to politicians with at least one completed term in office (personal communication with LDP Diet members).

PARC committees typically meet once or twice a week when the Diet is in session. They hold hearings on legislation, calling in members of the

---

23 Again, we argue that the cause of the difference is to be found in the electoral system. All other parliamentary democracies use proportional representation, STV, or single-member-district plurality systems, in which a vote for a candidate is a vote for a party, rendering same-party competition unnecessary and therefore unlikely.

24 The others are the party president (who, since the party's inception in 1955, has always been selected to be prime minister as well), the secretary general, and chairman of the party's executive council (a group of senior politicians from each of the LDP's five largest factions). Each of these top four positions and the executive committees under them is divided among the factions in rough proportion to the factions' numbers in the Diet (Sato and Matsuzaki 1986).

25 Since faction leaders are said to make appointments to the Diet committees, they appear to control two of the four committee appointments. Although membership in the remaining two committees is in principle self-selective, faction leaders appoint committee chairmen and vice chairmen and thus exert influence on committee members who aspire to leadership positions. Because no data exists on member requests, it is impossible to determine the extent to which any of these assignments are self-selective.

private sector to express their points of view before redrafting the bill. Budget legislation, for example, is not submitted to the Diet until the relevant PARC committees approve the allocations that concern them. But most regulation in Japan is implemented through administrative guidance, only vaguely spelled out in legislation. The primary avenue of PARC influence on policy making is therefore directly through the ministries they oversee. They invite bureaucrats to give account of existing regulatory practices and suggest to the bureaucrats how to adjust regulation to better suit the interests of their constituents.[26]

Finally, LDP backbenchers are popularly dubbed part of a particular "policy tribe" or *zoku* when they have served three or four terms in a PARC committee. The press describes *zoku* as informal groups of committee members who are being groomed for party leadership positions and therefore carry some weight within the PARC's decision-making process. Recent scholarly writing on the LDP, however, has emphasized the degree to which senior party members tend to rotate among cabinet posts, PARC committee chairmanships, and Diet committee chairmanships (Park 1986; Inoguchi and Iwai 1987). From this perspective, *zoku* is largely a descriptive term: It refers to the pool of party leaders within an issue area. *Zoku* overlap a good deal with PARC memberships; but the PARC, because of its institutional formality, is a more useful indicator of product-differentiation strategies.

On some issues such as agricultural price supports, all members from farm districts are likely to take the same position. However, they will differentiate themselves on other issues, and will seek different PARC assignments in order to appeal to distinct groups of voters. Differentiation in PARC affiliations allows LDP members from the same district to build different personal vote coalitions. If members from a single district mirrored each other's PARC assignments, the committee system would not provide a solution to the twin collective-action problems faced by voters and LDP incumbents. Hence, we should observe that PARC committee assignment patterns show evidence that systematic care is taken to separate the committee assignments of LDP members from the same district.

Evidence for such differentiation is readily apparent on inspection of PARC committee assignments. We examined PARC committee assign-

---

[26] It is important to note that just because the party constitution requires PARC committee consideration of legislation before it hits the floor does not mean that these committees are autonomous gatekeepers. The party could always change the rules, and can certainly amend the committee's recommendation. As just discussed, party leadership also engages in screening and selection of committee members. (For a theoretical and empirical discussion of this debate in the American politics literature see Kiewiet and McCubbins 1991 and Cox and McCubbins 1993.) We are not making an argument about decentralized decision making in terms of an abdication of authority by the majority party to its committees. Rather, this is an argument about credit claiming and electoral strategies.

ments for the 1990 Diet session. Under the null hypothesis that committee assignments are made randomly for party members from a single district, it can be shown that the probability of observing no overlap at all in a district's LDP committee assignments falls rapidly as either the district magnitude grows or the number of assignments per member grows, all else constant. For example, assume that members can be assigned to any of seventeen different PARC committees,[27] that district magnitude is two, and that each member gets four assignments. The probability that these two members have no overlap in assignments, assuming a random assignment process, is approximately 30 percent. Increasing the number of assignments to five per member drops the chances of no overlap to 12.8 percent. Further, a simple examination of the combinatorics involved in these calculations shows that much of the weight of the probability distribution function generated by the solution to the problem is tightly clustered around the distribution's central tendency. In other words, with random assignments, we would expect most middle-sized districts to exhibit quite a few overlaps in the assignments for LDP members from a particular district, with very few districts showing either no overlap at all or complete overlap of assignments.

Our test, therefore, is to calculate the probability that a given district will have no overlap under our null model of random assignments, and to compare that probability to the observed proportion of districts that had no overlap. Even with seventeen committees from which to choose, the odds of observing one or fewer instances of assignment overlap drop quickly to near zero with the number of district LDP seats greater than three and average assignments per member also greater than three.

We examined a sample of twenty-six districts, drawn at random, to see how often LDP members from the same district had no overlap in committee assignments.[28] Thirteen of those districts had no overlap at all, while five districts had exactly one overlap between a pair of LDP members. Thus, for eighteen of twenty-six cases, we observed something – no overlap or only one overlap – that we would rarely expect to see if assignments were in fact random. This finding alone allows us to reject the null hy-

---

[27] We are looking at PARC *bukai*, which we translate here as "committees." In addition to the seventeen *bukai*, the PARC also contains forty-six *chosakai* (research committees), and forty-three *tokubetsu iinkai* (special committees).

[28] Of the thirty districts originally chosen for the sample, four (Toyama 2, Fukuoka 1, Oita 2, and Ishikawa 1) were dropped because they did not offer any basis for comparison. This means that they contained either a current cabinet minister, a holder of one of the top four party positions, and/or a parliamentary vice-minister, none of whom receive PARC committee assignments, leaving one or zero PARC committee members in the district. The twenty-six remaining districts were: Hokkaido 5, Kanagawa 3, Aichi 5, Yamaguchi 2, Miyagi 2, Shiga, Nara, Okayama 1, Osaka 6, Nagano 1, Saitama 4, Gunma 1, Wakayama 2, Kochi, Okinawa, Tokyo 10, Chiba 3, Ibaraki 2, Hokkaido 2, Kanagawa 5, Nagasaki 1, Shizuoka 1, Mie 1, Fukui, Niigata 3, and Tokyo 4.

pothesis that assignments are random. Of the twelve districts in our sample that had more than two LDP members, three had no membership overlap and four had overlap between only a single pair. These observations strongly suggest that there is some nonrandom process at work to prevent LDP members in a district from having overlapping committee assignments.

5. CONCLUSION

Japanese parties, if they are to win a majority in the Diet, must on average win more than two seats per electoral district. Because each voter can vote for only one candidate, candidates from the same party compete with each other in each district. The problem for the parties is to find a mechanism for efficiently dividing its supporters' votes. The vote division cannot be left to party voters, who would face a seemingly insurmountable coordination problem subject to all of the classic dilemmas of collective actions (Olson 1965). Neither can the candidates commit to a vote division scheme absent any external enforcement since, as in any prisoner's dilemma, each candidate has a dominant strategy to cheat. If the vote is to be divided efficiently, then, it behooves candidates – who, like all players in a prisoner's dilemma, prefer mutual cooperation if only it can be maintained – to delegate the task of dividing the vote to party leadership.

The leadership has a range of options. It could impose some arbitrary rule (like the phone number example mentioned) that would run the risk of being incentive incompatible for voters and, consequently, ineffective. And any attempt to differentiate candidates using ideological or public-goods criteria would, of course, undermine the party label, presumably the thing that defines the group of "party voters" whose votes are to be divided. The LDP's solution to the problem has been to institutionalize particularistic politics. This keeps the party label intact while simultaneously allowing candidates to differentiate themselves through credit-claiming. By maintaining control over the resources available to individual backbenchers cum candidates, the leadership can encourage candidates to indulge their desire to increase their personal vote coalitions and at the same time ensure that same-party candidates are not stealing votes from each other.

APPENDIX

Methods

McCubbins and Noble (Chapter 5 of this book) defined the following items as particularistic in their data set of expenditures and revenues from fiscal years 1952 (the last budget compiled under the occupation) to 1989:

EXPENDITURE ITEMS

GENERAL ACCOUNT
Prime minister's office
  Science and Technology Agency
  1. Promotion of research into peaceful uses for nuclear power
  2. Science and Technology Agency research laboratory
  3. Science and Technology promotion
  Hokkaido Development Agency
  4. Hokkaido road construction
  5. Hokkaido fishing port facilities
  6. Hokkaido housing construction industry
Ministry of Finance
  Ministry of Finance (internal)
  7. Supplement to People's Finance Corporation
Ministry of Education
  Ministry of Education (internal)
  8. National Treasury subsidies for educational expenses for the handicapped
  9. Supplements to private schools
Ministry of Health and Welfare
  10. Maintenance of environmental health and sanitation facilities
  11. Support for the disabled
  12. Welfare for the elderly
  13. Support for women
  14. Support for children
Ministry of Agriculture, Forestry, and Fisheries
  15. Fishing harbor facilities
  16. Strategic restructuring of agriculture
  17. Agricultural pensions
  18. Silk cultivation and horticulture promotion
  19. Diffusion of agriculture improvement
  20. Strengthening of wet rice agriculture
  21. Sugar price stabilization
  22. Strategic planning of food product distribution
Ministry of International Trade and Industry
  Ministry of International Trade and Industry (internal)
  23. Economic cooperation
  24. Promotion of industrial relocation
  25. Promotion of the computer industry
  26. Industrial plumbing facilities
  Agency of Industrial Science and Technology
  27. Promotion of mining and manufacturing technology

28. Large-scale industrial research and development
29. Agency of Industrial Science and Technology experimental research laboratory

Agency of Natural Resources and Energy

30. Measures for underground resources

Small and Medium Enterprise Agency

31. Measures for small and medium enterprises

Ministry of Transportation

Ministry of Transportation (internal)

32. Subsidies to account of Japan National Railway
33. Subsidies to Japan National Railway Construction Corp.
34. Subsidies for railroad track maintenance
35. Coastline enterprises
36. Subsidies for maritime transportation
37. Stabilization of shipbuilding industry

Ministry of Posts and Telecommunications

38. Integrated Telecommunications Research Lab
39. Local Telecommunications Administration Bureau

Ministry of Labor

40. Career change planning
41. Labor Protection Office
42. Employment Security Office

Ministry of Construction

Ministry of Construction (internal)

43. Strategic planning regarding crumbling of steep inclines and related expenses
44. Coastline enterprises
45. Housing construction
46. City planning
47. Work related to stream and river disasters
48. Restoration of streams and rivers after disasters

Ministry of Home Affairs

Ministry of Home Affairs (internal)

49. Adjustment grants to cities, towns, and villages that are the sites of [defense] facilities

SPECIAL ACCOUNTS

1. Foodstuff control
2. Measures for the improvement of farm management
3. Harbor improvement
4. Airport improvement
5. Road improvement

6. Flood control
7. National pensions

Sources

"General accounts data were taken from official Ippan Kaikei as submitted to the Diet by the Ministry of Finance on behalf of the cabinet . . . these documents are the only place listing all expenditures at the item (*ko*) level (the more commonly known 'important item' [*shuyo keihi*] listed in the *Kuni no Yosan* and elsewhere are too highly aggregated and subject to periodic redefinition). All figures are on an initial budget (*tosho*) basis, that is, before any revisions by the Diet, and before any supplemental budgets. The lack of Diet revisions is not a serious problem, since revisions have been rare in the postwar period, occurring in 1948 (before the period considered here), 1953–55, and in two years since the formation of the LDP (1972 and 1977). Moreover, even in those years revisions covered only a tiny fraction of the budget. Supplementary budgets are also relatively unimportant (in the 1960s the net addition to main budget expenditures was about 4.2 percent, in the 1980s only 3.1 percent), and omitting them greatly simplifies data collection, since in many years there have been two or even three supplemental budgets. Since the composition of items sometimes changes over time, we added and subtracted sub-items as necessary to ensure consistency over time. Generally speaking, we took the item as constituted in recent years and corrected as necessary as we went back through the data. A complete list of descriptions of the item (and other more detailed information) is available on request from the authors.

"Special accounts data came from the semiofficial and widely available *Kuni no Yosan;* in this case there are no problems of excessive aggregation and inconsistent definition. These are also on an "initial budget" basis. For the fourteen special accounts in our sample we measured only subsidies from the general account, since the overall budgets of the accounts include operating and other incomes not derived from national budgets. The *Kuni no Yosan* does not provide a summary figure for subsidies, so we derived them by summing the subsidies to each of the subaccounts (*kanjo*). The transactions between general accounts and special accounts are sometimes complex; in order to avoid any possible double-counting, we never use the two types of accounts in the same equation.

"Economic and demographic data were drawn from the five-volume *Nihon Choki Tokei Soran/Historical Statistics of Japan* and the annual *Nihon Tokei Nenkan/Japan Statistical Yearbook,* both bilingual" (quoted from the appendix to McCubbins and Noble, Chapter 5 herein).

4

The appearance of power: legislators, bureaucrats,
and the budget process
in the United States and Japan

MATHEW D. MCCUBBINS AND GREGORY W. NOBLE

1. INTRODUCTION

In democratic states around the world, legislatures hold a preponderance of formal, constitutional authority to govern. But formal authority is not always manifest authority. Many scholars contend – albeit not without controversy – that in Japan and the United States de facto law-making authority resides outside the national legislature.

Some scholars allege that the executive has usurped policy-making authority from the legislature. Executive officials in the United States and Japan, for example, compile, revise, and audit ministry and agency budget requests and are ultimately responsible for drafting budget legislation. In addition, legislators in both countries appear to defer to the superior knowledge of the executive upon receiving these draft budgets, accepting executive budget proposals without serious review or revision.

Furthermore, when the legislature is actually able to hang onto its formal authority to govern, this authority has often been captured by subgovernments composed of legislators, bureaucrats, and groups interested in a particular policy. The policy that results, then, is often characterized as irresponsible and disjointed particularistic pandering to interest-group pressure, rather than as reflecting some broadly recognized national "good."

In this chapter, we challenge both views of legislative abdication. Previous challenges to this view have been limited largely to the U.S. case and, on the whole, have been policy specific in scope and theoretically rather ad hoc.[1] Our approach, which concentrates on the Japanese version of the delegation/abdication debate, is designed to be both theoretically rigorous and broadly applicable. We challenge the "abdication" view by questioning the logic used to explain general observations such as those just

---

[1] For a notable exception see Ramseyer and Rosenbluth (1993).

described about legislative–executive relations, as well as the validity of the evidence purporting to support these views.

In Section 2, we show the similarity in the arguments about abdication in the United States and Japan. We then demonstrate in Section 3 that the power of bureaucracies and subgovernments is more apparent that real. Our thesis, spelled out in Section 4, is that the observed behavior of legislators and bureaucrats results from managed delegations by the legislative branch to the executive, and from the majority party in the legislature to subgovernments. Moreover, while this managed delegation may lead to the appearance of executive and subgovernment influence, the majority party in the legislature retains real policy-making authority. Our model stands as an alternative to models that emphasize the appearance of power. In Section 5, we address the central contentions about abdication and question the empirical underpinnings of these contentions. We argue that our model can be distinguished from the simple models of legislative impotence so dominant in the Japanese and American literatures, by virtue of its ability to account for more of the functioning and structure of the American and Japanese political systems (e.g., administrative procedures, the Liberal Democratic Party's Policy Affairs Research Council [PARC] system of "divisions," the formal budget processes in both countries, and so forth). The last section concludes.

2. THE END OF DELEGATION

It is widely acknowledged that bureaucratic services are a ubiquitous feature of political development. Weber argued that the bureaucracy was a key facet of the modern administrative state, as "bureaucracy is *the* means of carrying 'community action' over into rationally ordered 'societal action'" (Gerth and Mills 1946: 228). Similarly, in Theodore Lowi's view, the rise of "administration" is "a necessary part of capitalism and capitalist society" (Lowi 1979: 21). For both Lowi and Weber, however, bureaucratic administration poses a threat to the individual freedom that is the promise of modern liberal democracy. Weber argued that the people effectively trap themselves into a rigid, illiberal regime by delegating authority to the bureaucratic machine:

The ruled, for their part, cannot dispense with or replace the bureaucratic apparatus of authority once it exists. For this bureaucracy rests upon expert training, a functional specialization of work, and an attitude set for habitual and virtuoso-like mastery of single yet methodically integrated functions. If the official stops working, or if his work is forcefully interrupted, chaos results (Gerth and Mills 1946: 229).

Inferring power relationships between political actors – for example, whether abdication has occurred – from observed behavior is not a simple task, since we cannot observe people's preferences directly.[2] In terms of government decision making, when we observe a legislature ordering a bureaucratic agency to make policy in a certain issue area and then see that the agency has made policy without further intervention by the legislature, can we conclude that the agency has been given free rein? What else would we have to assume in order to draw this conclusion?

The essence of the abdication hypothesis is that bureaucratic agents can make policy that legislators, if fully informed, would not prefer to existing policy. If a new policy implemented by the bureaucracy is preferred by the legislature to the existing policy, we cannot conclude that the legislature has abdicated its authority, since we cannot demonstrate that bureaucrats have done other than what legislators wanted them to do. Legislators never get something for nothing from their bureaucratic agents, of course – agents must be paid and must be given resources with which to do their jobs. By abdication, then, we mean something more than merely the statement that legislators had to pay more than they would have liked (since this is always the case). We mean that legislators are *actually made worse off* by the actions chosen by their agents than if the agents had not acted at all.

2.1. Bureaucratic dominance

The thesis of executive domination is that Congress actually has abdicated its authority to make decisions: When setting national policy, members of Congress neither choose policy nor influence the choices being made. The U.S. delegation/abdication literature identifies two kinds of democratic failures. First, Congress has abdicated its initiative and authority on most important policy issues to the president and the executive branch. Second, on all other issues, the majority party in Congress has similarly abdicated its rightful role to policy subgovernments.

The first abdication implies that Congress has no effect on the formulation or implementation of policies of broad national interest and, therefore, that congressional elections essentially are meaningless as a tool for implementing the will of the people. The implication of the second form of abdication is that there exists no central agency that can bear responsibility for the conduct of policies that have mostly regional or local impor-

---

[2] A simple example will help to demonstrate this point. Suppose we observe the following scenario. A woman gets into a taxi and gives an address to the driver. The driver starts off and, after a while, stops somewhere in town. Throughout the trip, the passenger has said nothing. When the driver stops, the passenger gets out and pays the driver. The taxi speeds off. Has the passenger abdicated all authority to the driver, leaving the route and eventual destination up to the latter's best judgment? Or, has she delegated the job of driving to the driver in such a way as to ensure herself of a good outcome?

tance, and therefore policy is uncoordinated, often contradictory, and always porcine.

The evidence in support of these claims includes observations that many policy proposals are initiated by the executive and "are not seriously reviewed" by Congress (Sundquist 1981: 12). Further, executive officials make innumerable policy decisions, almost none of which is ever overturned (or even challenged) by Congress. The complaints of individual members of Congress with regard to apparent executive usurpations of legislative authority have also been cited as evidence for this interpretation.

According to this view, a general structural defect in Congress helps to ensure congressional abdication: Members lack the motivation, knowledge, and expertise to conduct adequate oversight (Fiorina 1977). In most policy debates, they defer to the more specialized knowledge of executive agents and subgovernmental actors. These informational and motivational defects, of course, are exacerbated by the general incoherence of legislative activity.[3]

These theoretical currents flow as well through much of the literature on Japanese politics. In Japan, the executive branch comprises the bureaucracy and the cabinet. As the literature points out, the bureaucracy writes nearly all legislation, which, it is claimed, the Diet barely reviews before rubber-stamping its approval (Pempel 1982). According to the standard view, the Diet itself does almost nothing of consequence. It does not draft its own legislation, and its committees do not hold substantive hearings or perform substantive oversight of the bureaucracy. Further, Diet members seem to know little about the issues involved in most policy areas (Kakizawa 1984). These observations have led many scholars of Japanese politics to conclude that "the elite bureaucracy in Japan makes most major decisions, drafts virtually all legislation, controls the national budget, and is the source of all major policy innovations in the system" (Johnson 1982: 20–21).

Abdication is assured as a result of certain defects in the Japanese parliament. First, bureaucrats are a prestigious, elite group in Japanese society (Johnson 1982: 20). Second, because of their abilities and specialized training, Japanese bureaucrats are said to have a large informational advantage over members of the Diet (Campbell 1977: 42; Johnson 1982: 20; see also Inoguchi and Iwai 1987: 35–36; Keehn 1990; Mat-

---

[3] Party leaders in the U.S. Congress are often seen as little more than traffic cops, facilitating the movement of legislation without imposing any programmatic structure (see, e.g., Sinclair 1983: 78–80). A traffic-cop model of leadership underlies most studies of committee assignments in the U.S. House as well. Both Shepsle (1978) and Westefield (1974), while assuming that the party leadership has substantial influence over appointments, argue that the leadership's goal is to accommodate members' assignment requests (see also Goodwin 1970: 77; Masters 1961; Smith and Deering 1984: 240).

suzaki, quoted in Ebato 1986: 177; Schoppa 1991). Third, many analysts believe that the bureaucrats are the only actors in the political system who have the incentive and ability to consider the needs of the whole society. Unlike politicians, they consider the cumulative effect of passing out promises to various groups (Inoguchi and Iwai 1987: 35–36, 281–282, 290–291; Ito 1980: 167). The Budget Bureau of the Ministry of Finance, for example, has been dubbed the "guardian of logic" for the way it protects the national interest against the particularistic demands of politicians and interest groups (Kuribayashi 1986: 10).

Finally, it is argued that the bureaucracy effectively colonizes the entire policy-making system by placing ex-officials in top posts in the ruling party, public policy corporations, advisory councils, private corporations, and so forth (Johnson 1975: 8–10, 22–27). About a quarter of LDP Diet members are former elite bureaucrats. Through the end of the 1960s, top party and government posts such as prime minister, minister of finance, and head of the Policy Affairs Research Council were frequently filled by former top bureaucrats.

2.2. Iron triangles

Representation in the administrative state, for Lowi, reverted from the empowerment of majoritarian political parties within the legislature to a process of government by negotiation – a kind of pluralism that recognizes no boundaries between private civil society and politics. Lowi calls this "interest-group liberalism," in which "the role of government is one of ensuring access to the most effectively organized, and of ratifying the agreements and adjustments worked out among the competing leaders" of interest groups (Lowi 1979: 51). As more and more authority shifted from the hands of elected legislators to executive-branch negotiators, democracy faded away.

Lowi applies his reasoning particularly to the United States, but the basic argument has been applied to Japan as well. Indeed, the popular view in the United States of Japanese politics – of "Japan, Inc." – probably better fits Lowi's story than does the popular view of the U.S. government. A central theme in the Japanese literature stresses the ruling party's inability to control *itself*. This literature, which parallels the literature on "iron triangles" in the United States,[4] argues that subgovernments develop around each policy area, centered around a particular ministry, and composed of officials from the ministry, the interest groups regulated

---

[4] See, for example, Cater (1964); Davidson (1977: 31–33; 1981: 101–111); Davidson and Oleszek (1977); Freeman (1955); Griffith (1961); Jones (1961: 359); Lowi (1972, 1979: 62–63); McConnell (1966); Ripley and Franklin (1984); Schattschneider (1935); Shepsle and Weingast (1987a, b); and Weingast and Moran (1983).

or subsidized by the ministry, and politicians with electoral incentives to specialize in the policy area (Campbell 1977: 40–42, 123–128; 1984).

In keeping with the depiction of subgovernmental policy making, LDP decisions come out of a decentralized process. The position of the party president (who also serves as prime minister as long as the LDP retains its Diet majority) is weak due to factional conflict and instability at the top of the party (Campbell 1977: 165; Fukui 1984: 422; Sakakibara 1991: 75–78). His personal staff is tiny and he has a difficult time getting other influential members of the party to support him. Cabinet meetings are short, ritualistic, and nonconflictual, serving only to ratify decisions made elsewhere (Campbell 1977: 151; Kishimoto 1988: 80–83; Murakawa 1985: 189–190). The General Council, formally the party's highest standing body, plays virtually no part in the content of policy making; at most it orchestrates the timing and Diet deliberation of some controversial bills. The cabinet has little control over the budget and policy making, and there is no "super budget agency" (Murakawa 1985: 93–94, 99, 148, 156–157).[5]

In the absence of adequate leadership and coordination from the prime minister, the cabinet, or the party's General Council, the individual committees of the PARC are said to have virtually unlimited power over their jurisdictions. As a result, the policy process is fragmented, often contradictory, and always conflictual. Where observers of Japanese foreign economic policy once spoke of "Japan, Inc.," authors now title their books and articles "The Unbundling of 'Japan, Inc.' " (Pempel 1987) and *Japan, Disincorporated* (Hollerman 1988).

LDP participation in these subgovernments comes mainly in the form of intervention into policy making by the various *zoku* (tribes) based in PARC committees, particularly the standing committees – "divisions" – corresponding to each ministry. The virtually universal assessment of outside observers is that these *zoku* politicians, while perhaps better informed on the content of policy issues than their predecessors, use that knowledge in the service of ever more effective policy plunder, gathering more resources for their constituents and favored industries no matter what the cost to the budget or to the overall consistency, coherence, and equity of government policy (Nihon Keizai Shimbunsha [ed.] 1983; Pempel 1987: 146, 150; see also Johnson 1990: 82; Sato and Matsuzaki 1986: 84).

---

[5] Some limited reforms were made in 1968, however, in unifying the budget process to include salaries of government employees and decisions on rice prices (Murakawa 1985: 165). For a reprint of the recommendations on the budget of the (first) Ad Hoc Commission on Administrative Reform of the early 1960s, along with extensive commentary, see Kato (1992: 27–61).

3. THE FOUNDATIONS OF ABDICATION: HIDDEN KNOWLEDGE AND AGENDA CONTROL

As we understand it, the abdication thesis rests on two main assertions. The first is that bureaucrats have hidden knowledge, and that politicians are unable to observe all bureaucratic information and activities. This asymmetry of knowledge is partly the result of bureaucrats' elite training, and partly a result of their hands-on experience with the details of regulation and administration. The implication, of course, is that bureaucrats can exploit their advantages to misinform politicians and act in contravention of their "orders," secure in the knowledge that their political bosses will never know.

The second element of the abdication thesis is that bureaucrats exercise agenda control. This assertion stems from the observation that almost all legislation is written by bureaucrats and presented to politicians as take-it-or-leave-it offers. Moreover, it is often claimed that Japanese bureaucrats can circumvent the politicians altogether by means of informal law making ("administrative guidance"; see Johnson 1982).[6]

At first glance, the assertions of the abdication thesis seem quite plausible. The literature is filled with case studies of failed policies. But the thesis of abdication is much stronger than simply claiming that "we can do better" by "throwing the bums out" at the next election. Abdication means that throwing the bums out would have no effect on policy – indeed, that there is nothing the people can do within the prevailing legal framework (e.g., short of revolution) to change policy outcomes. We examine these two assertions in turn.

3.1. Hidden knowledge

It is quite natural to expect that agents will have some hidden knowledge, such as expertise. One of the reasons that principals delegate in the first place is to reap efficiency gains that come from specialization. For example, sick people hire doctors to treat their illnesses in the expectation that the doctor knows something about medicine that the patient does not. Similarly, owners of sick cars hire auto mechanics.

Clearly, in both cases it is possible for the expert agents to take advantage of informational asymmetries in order to make themselves better off at the principal's expense. Both doctors and mechanics can perform unnecessary tests or procedures, or even do nothing while claiming to have

---

[6] There are actually three necessary conditions. The third condition is that the principal must be unable to make enforceable contracts with the agent. In other words, the principal cannot force herself to follow through on a promise to reward or punish the agent for the actions he takes or the outcomes that the principal observes.

solved the problem. For our purposes, then, hidden knowledge means that the principal cannot directly observe everything that the agent knows, and must expend time and effort if she is to have any chance of observing anything that the agent does. Even with oversight, there may be situations in which the principal is unable to uncover the agent's hidden knowledge (Lupia and McCubbins 1993).

Although in theory informational asymmetries may be quite important (e.g., Niskanen 1971; Romer and Rosenthal 1978), there is little evidence to support the assertion that they actually exist. There are two basic problems with the asymmetry arguments in favor of executive dominance. First, legislators have access to many sources of information and expertise on technical subjects outside of the executive.[7] It is reasonable to assume that the intended recipients of government services (voters and other interest groups) know whether or not they are receiving services, and at what level. To the degree that these constituents can inform members of the Diet of the quality and level of services they are receiving, Diet members can keep accurate tabs on policy outputs and on the procedures that bureaucrats are or are not following to achieve those outputs. In policy arenas that demand a great deal of technical expertise – such as environmental regulation, or economic regulation of utilities, industry, and financial markets – the technical expertise used to define standards and to design and implement regulations most is often drawn from the regulated markets and industries themselves, not from the ranks of career bureaucrats (Lowi 1979; Samuels 1987). Even where this is not true, the balance of technical expertise nonetheless often lies with the private sector, not the bureaucracy, and Diet members have as good or better access than bureaucrats to private-sector sources.[8]

Second, it is not obvious that legislators need to master the technical details of policy making in order to approximate full-information decision making (Lupia 1991a, b). Under most circumstances, legislators need only collect and correlate enough technical information to make effective political inferences, and in the field of making *political* inferences from data, it is the politicians who are the experts.

---

[7] In Japan, bureaucrats' superior knowledge is thought to be part cultural, in that bureaucrats are elites. This claim requires that voters and politicians disregard whatever information they actually possess about an issue and defer to choices made by bureaucrats.

[8] The avoidance of noisy, public oversight processes in Japan relative to their prevalence in the U.S. case (Aberbach 1990) is at least partly attributable to the difference between a parliamentary governmental structure and the U.S. model of divided powers. The constitutional role granted the president in the United States often makes direct, less-public oversight techniques infeasible, especially when the president hails from a political party different from that of the majority in the two houses of Congress.

3.2. Agenda control

The second assumption is that the agent has sole control over the legislative agenda. This means that legislators can neither propose legislation on their own nor amend proposals presented to them by their agents. They may only approve or disapprove changes proposed by the agent. In our taxi-driver example, this would mean that the passenger could not order the driver to take an alternate route.

This assumption is much stronger than claiming that legislators do not know enough about a policy issue to propose amendments to a legislative initiative from the bureaucracy (which is an example of the potential effects of hidden knowledge). This assumption says that legislators are bound, either constitutionally or by some self-imposed rule, not to amend proposals or offer any proposals of their own.

The "textbook Congress" literature of the 1950s and '60s emphasized the power and independence of standing committees and their chairmen, in contrast to the relative weakness of the formal hierarchy of the majority Democratic party leadership (see, e.g., Brady 1973; Burnham 1970; Polsby, Gallaher, and Rundquist 1969; Shepsle 1988). A second literature, arising out of Kenneth Arrow's impossibility theorem and out of the study of spatial theories of political processes, added further hand-wringing to this debate (Arrow 1951; Enelow and Hinich [eds.] 1990; Gibbard 1973; Plott 1967; Riker 1980; Sen 1970). Without the partisan discipline of political machines to restrict the feasible set of choices or to permit individuals to make credible commitments to coalitions, these literatures suggested, majority-party rule is all but impossible.[9]

While we accept as true the assertion that in many types of policy decisions bureaucrats have something akin to agenda control, this is not universally true. In the Japanese budget process, for example, there is considerable evidence of active LDP leadership.[10] After the divisive ideological politics of the 1950s, Prime Minister Ikeda led the transition to low-profile policies focused on rapid growth in the early 1960s (Johnson 1982: 201–202, 252). In the early 1970s Prime Minister Tanaka normalized relations with China, boosted public spending, and expanded health and welfare benefits. A decade later Prime Minister Nakasone took the initiative in privatizing public corporations and reforming public finance, leading to the elimination of deficit bonds by 1990.

[9] Since the mid-1970s, however, the intellectual worm has turned. Some scholars have argued that the power of legislative institutions can decline and resurge in generational patterns (Sundquist 1981). Others, such as Brady (1988) and Rohde (1991), argue that the degree to which the majority party acts overtly in the classic, strong Westminsterian party mold varies with the homogeneity of interests represented in the party.

[10] For a similar observation concerning the American budget process, see Kiewiet and McCubbins (1991).

But looking for obvious leadership activities can be quite misleading. We would not expect the leadership of a political party to take the party into uncharted policy waters too often. Dramatic changes in policy will be few if the same party remains in power. Instead, collective responsibility and evolutionary change can be bolstered through structure and process.

Consider an analogy. If we were to look in on a factory, we might see a number of workers welding parts together. Other workers might be painting sheet metal while others lubricate engine parts. Each group is acting independently of the others; each has its own supervisor, its own hierarchy, and its own outside contacts. However, if we were to conclude that there is no collective responsibility in this factory – that each group of workers was its own "subfirm" – we no doubt would be wrong. Each subfirm is doing its job in accordance with schedules, incentives, and procedures designed by those responsible for the factory's output, so that the independent actions of the subfirms eventually fit together for the betterment of all of the factory's employees (and owners). The actions of the factory's leadership – management – can be quite difficult to observe, as its actions largely involve setting up and maintaining the structure and process that coordinates the disparate activities of each subfirm.

We observe the same sorts of structure and process in LDP policy making. According to the standard account, the budgetary process in Japan is supremely bureaucratic (Kakizawa 1984; Noguchi 1991: 122–123). The Ministry of Finance develops guidelines for how much spending ministries can request. Ministries deliver budgetary requests to the MOF by the end of the summer. The MOF reviews them in the fall and announces a draft budget in December. In the revival negotiations around the end of December, the LDP backs reconsideration of a few of the items denied by MOF (mostly pork barrel in nature), but the amounts are small (about 3 percent of the whole budget) and always stay within the MOF's overall framework. After formal submission by the cabinet, and elaborate partisan posturing and frequent delays in the House Budget Committee, the Diet passes the budget. Revisions are rare (none in the past ten years) and never substantial.

The standard account, however, ignores the numerous opportunities that are built into the budgetary compilation process to allow the LDP to oversee, initiate, and veto. All major policy changes must be approved by party leadership. At the beginning of the process both prime ministers and ministers of finance exert powerful influence on the overall composition of the budget, often calling on *shingikai* (advisory or deliberation councils sure to include all interested LDP constituents) for coordination and legitimation. They pushed toward more stimulation from 1960 to the early 1970s, and for more restraint after the early 1980s. Similarly, final decisions in the revival negotiations that effectively cap the budget process are made by the top three or four leaders of the party; virtually all new expenditures are approved in the revival negotiations, usually after receiving support from the party's General Council (Campbell 1977: 185, 194).

Between enunciation of broad principles and conclusion of revival negotiations, party oversight is ubiquitous. The finance minister, always a senior LDP politician, oversees the whole process. The MOF keeps a list of interested LDP Diet members for every single expenditure item and tax provision (Nihon Keizai Shimbunsha [ed.] 1983: 61). Spending ministries report to the relevant PARC divisions before they submit their requests to the MOF, and they keep in constant contact throughout the fall. Within PARC divisions and committees, backbenchers naturally press constantly for expanded spending in their policy areas, but the real decision-making power is in the hands of a relatively small group of chairmen and vice-chairmen (Nihon Keizai Shimbunsha [ed.] 1983: 18, 22; Sone and Kanazashi 1989: 185). And for all the talk of subgovernments, one of the key criteria by which these committee leaders are judged in the contest for top government and party posts is breadth of experience and ability to overcome particularism (Sato and Matsuzaki 1986: 50–51, 216). On the revenue side, the LDP's Tax Commission is in control of yearly tax revisions (Kishiro 1985), while rice prices and government salaries are handled separately from the formal compilation process overseen by MOF, making LDP intervention even more flexible.

The LDP leadership thus provides overall guidance and coordination, as well as structured opportunities for clarifying and transmitting the goals and intentions of the party to the bureaucracy. Proposals, particularly new initiatives, must pass through a whole series of veto gates, all of which are controlled by the LDP, so bureaucrats have a strong incentive to tailor their proposals to appeal to the LDP. The Diet and cabinet appear relatively unimportant only because the LDP has a clear majority and prefers to keep real policy-making authority in-house – the PARC as overseen by top party leadership.

Agenda control comes up again in discussion of subgovernments that are one branch of the abdication side of the debate. Subgovernments, much like executive agencies, are creatures of delegated authority. Committees in the U.S. House, while of venerable origins, must be created anew every two years by a majority vote of the membership – and thus, in practice, they exist at the pleasure of the majority-party caucus, which writes the House rules and imposes them on the entire body.[11] PARC divisions within the LDP arose almost simultaneously with the fusion of

---

[11] Indeed, sometimes committees are abolished. Consider, for example, the comprehensive restructuring of the House committee system accomplished in the Legislative Reorganization Act of 1946, or the abolishment of the Joint Committee on Atomic Energy in 1977.

the Liberal and Democratic parties in 1955, and they exist solely as manifestations of LDP interests. The leadership of the majority party also reviews subgovernmental decisions and holds a veto over the actions of subgovernments through a hierarchy of party-dominated veto gates and through its control of legislative agendas. The full membership of the majority party, in turn, holds a veto over the actions of the subgovernments and reviews the activities of the leadership. These nested veto gates, controlled by the majority party or its agents, establish incentives that profoundly affect the choices of subgovernments (on the U.S. Congress, see, e.g., Cox and McCubbins 1993; Kiewiet and McCubbins 1991).

4. AN ALTERNATIVE VIEW: DELEGATION AND MANAGEMENT

These assumptions impose very stringent conditions on the legislator–bureaucrat relationship. In this section, we will demonstrate in an intuitive fashion that each must hold if abdication is to result. We will do so by demonstrating that the legislature can move policy in a direction it prefers (i.e., can avoid abdication) if any one (or both) of the conditions does not hold. We proceed by assuming, one at a time, that one of the two conditions does not hold (that the legislature *does* possess policy expertise or amendment power or the ability to write binding contracts) and by showing that abdication does not follow.

Recall that we have defined abdication as the situation in which the outcome of a delegation is, from the point of view of the ruling coalition in the legislature, worse than the existing policy. The implication of this section, then, is that legislators can use policy expertise, control over their own agenda, or contracting to avoid outcomes that make them worse off.

First, suppose that the bureaucratic agency has agenda control but no hidden knowledge (and further, that contracting is not possible). This means that the ruling party knows precisely what choices it faces (the status quo versus whatever take-it-or-leave-it alternative the agency offers). The legislative party logically will reject offers it regards as worse than the status quo; hence, abdication is impossible (Romer and Rosenthal 1978).

Second, now suppose instead that the agency's offer is not take-it-or-leave-it (the legislature can amend it), but that the hidden knowledge (and no-contracting) assumption is retained. Agenda control in the hands of legislators rather than bureaucrats can mean two things. First, it can mean that legislators hold veto and amendment powers over particular bureaucratic proposals, such as draft legislation. In this case, if the legislative party knows *anything* about what sorts of policies it prefers to the existing one, it can amend any offer the agency makes to one it prefers to the status quo (such as its own ideal point) and, again, there is no abdication.

Second, legislative agenda control can mean that legislators can choose the scope of a delegation to an agency; that is, how often the agency has to go back to the legislature to ask for more resources. Examples of this aspect of agenda control include annual appropriations bills and so-called sunset legislation, in which an agency's mandate automatically runs out at a predetermined time – so that the agency must obtain legislative approval to stay in existence. Both the Japanese Diet and the U.S. Congress fund most programs on an annual basis.

It follows that a legislature can avoid abdication if it can (1) retain the constitutional ability to amend agency proposals, or (2) uncover at least some of bureaucrats' hidden knowledge through oversight. We turn now to a discussion of the tools that Japanese and American legislators can use to do these three things, allowing them to manage delegations of authority and thereby avoid abdication.

4.1. Controlling the legislative agenda

The simplest management tool available to legislators is the ability to approve, disapprove, or amend proposals emanating from the bureaucracy. No matter who drafts legislation, if legislators can review and amend the draft before it becomes law, they can reject anything that makes them worse off.[12] Thus, any legislature that retains the right to pass judgment on bureaucratic proposals cannot be said to have abdicated its authority.[13]

In parliamentary systems such as that of Japan, legislators introduce relatively few bills; most legislative proposals are instead presented by bureaucrats to the cabinet, which then introduces them as draft legislation to the Diet. Once politicians receive such proposals, however, they are free to change or reject them as they please. One recent example of Diet influence over law making is that of tax reform. The Ministry of Finance introduced reform legislation several times in the 1980s, seeking to impose a general value-added tax to shift the tax burden from corporate and personal income taxes toward greater reliance on taxes on small business. The Diet rejected these proposals time and again, holding out for a tax

---

[12] A legitimate question at this juncture – the one asked by the social-choice literature – is the identity of "they" or "them." We are talking here about the LDP, which, at least until it lost its Upper House majority in 1989, has constituted a stable majority coalition in the Diet continuously since 1955. See McCubbins and Rosenbluth (Chapter 3, this volume) for a justification of discussing the LDP as a stable coalitional actor.

[13] It may choose not to exercise this authority, but there is a fundamental difference between a player choosing not to take a given action and one unable to take an action.

that better protected the interests of small business, one of the LDP's core constituency groups.[14]

In the U.S. system, not only do legislators have final say over the form and content of bills but, further, only legislators can formally introduce a bill. In the course of a typical congressional term, members of Congress will introduce several hundred bills on behalf of the president or other executive-branch agents. During the same period, members of Congress introduce on their own behalf as many as fifteen thousand to twenty thousand bills. Congress may pass as many as two thousand laws in a two-year span, most of which are of congressional origin.

4.2. Police patrols versus fire alarms in Japan

The most straightforward way to eliminate the conditions of hidden action and information would seem to be to institute procedures requiring agents to report whatever relevant information they have obtained and whatever actions they have taken. Every year congressional and Diet committees, regulatory agencies, and executive departments report millions of pages of material on their hearings, investigations, and policy recommendations.

There are costs associated with both the agent's provision and the principal's consumption of information, however (Williamson 1975). If nothing else, the transfer of information deflects time and attention away from other tasks. Best-case reporting requirements would force agents to reveal only enough information to align their incentives with the intent of the contractual agreement between principal and agent (Demski and Sappington 1987). Unfortunately, this is difficult to modulate; that the private sector invests hundreds of millions of dollars annually in the design of information-management systems attests to this difficulty.

A more serious drawback to reporting requirements is the problem of truthful revelation or incentive incompatibility. The agent has incentives to shade his reports or to reveal information in some other strategic manner in order to make himself look good. Employees may discover that energy, skill, and creativity applied to their weekly progress reports pays off much more handsomely than actually doing the job. Even if agents somehow can be constrained to be truthful in their reports, the principal will still not know what they are not reporting. For that reason, principals typically supplement these requirements with what McCubbins and Schwartz (1984) have dubbed "police patrol" and "fire alarm" oversight.

Police patrol oversight includes what we commonly think of as oversight – audits, investigations, and other direct methods of monitoring.

---

[14] Ultimately, the Diet did agree to a tax on final consumption (national sales tax) in 1988. This tax, however, differed substantially from MOF's proposals (Kato 1992).

Fire alarm oversight involves the empowerment of interested third parties – individuals who are not party to the original contract between principal and agent but whose welfare is directly affected by agency action or inaction. An example would be the intended beneficiaries of the agent's actions, such as Social Security recipients or subsidized rice farmers. These affected third parties have an incentive to observe and to attempt to influence the actions of the agent, thus lowering the cost borne by legislators to achieve a given level of agency output. In addition to examining a sample of the agent's activities (or, more typically, the agent's reports about his activities), the legislative principal also obtains information from the affected third parties, who can be expected to report only on agency actions they find disagreeable. Thus fire alarm oversight filters out much of the agency activity on which the principal's interests are being satisfied, and concentrates legislators' attention on the problem cases.

In Japan, affected parties are included in the ubiquitous *shingikai*. The enabling legislation surrounding virtually every ministry or agency mandates the formation of one or more *shingikai*, and many more are formed on an ad hoc basis. Though not legally binding, their reports guide the work of both bureaucrats and politicians. The councils include representatives from affected interest groups, as well as scholars, journalists, and government officials. Often, their composition is set by law to represent a wide range of interests. Four of the five members of the Local Finance *Shingikai*, for example, are selected by associations of mayors, governors, and speakers of local and prefectural assemblies (Murakawa 1985: 176). In other cases, ministries in effect sponsor competing *shingikai*, each dominated by representatives of rival industries. Banking and securities *shingikai*, for example, compete to influence the regulatory framework of the Ministry of Finance (Rosenbluth 1989).

Observers often have dismissed *shingikai* as ineffective, or as or nothing more than the mouthpiece of the ministry to which they report (or of the prime minister). They are particularly criticized for failure to represent the interests of the public at large. (Johnson 1982: 47–48). These criticisms miss the point: *Shingikai* are not intended as democratic clones of the legislature; rather, they give groups that are both interested and important to the LDP an opportunity to provide information, make suggestions, and monitor the policies coming out of the bureaucracy. Information and feedback, in turn, allow politicians to guide the bureaucracy to benefit their important constituents.

4.3. Checks and balances

Most of the problems and remedies we have discussed so far have characterized the principal's problem as one of inducing the agent to expend more effort. The assumption is that the harder agents work, the more they produce. But agents are often in a position to do more harm to the principal than to simply withhold effort; embezzlement, insider trading, official corruption, abuse of authority, and coups d'etat are all testaments to this fact. Whenever an agent can take actions that might seriously jeopardize the principal's interests, the principal needs to impose institutional checks on agency action (Kiewiet and McCubbins 1991: 33–34). Operationally, these require that when authority has been delegated to an agent, there is at least one other agent (or the principal) with the authority to veto or to block the actions of that agent. As Madison observed, ambition is best checked by ambition – that is, agents positioned against each other should have countervailing interests. This is best accomplished by making agents' compensation contingent on different standards, for example by rewarding managers for increasing production but rewarding comptrollers for cutting costs.

Checks are equivalent to what social-choice theorists refer to as the presence of veto subgroups. Similarly, the loss of flexibility that checks induce is the same thing as social-choice stability – difficulty in altering the status quo. Several scholars have analyzed the effects of veto subgroups upon social choice, and their major results are generally intuitive. First, the more veto subgroups there are, the harder it is to change the status quo. The status quo also becomes more difficult to change (a) as preferences within veto subgroups become more homogeneous, and (b) as preferences between veto subgroups become more diverse (Cox and McKelvey 1984). Checks inhibit the ability of agents to take actions that the principal considers undesirable, but necessarily retard agents from taking desirable actions as well; security comes at the price of flexibility. The desirability of imposing checks on delegated authority thus increases with the utility the principal derives from the status quo and with the amount of danger posed by inappropriate agency actions.

Checks are less necessary in Japan, given its parliamentary political system and long-term domination by one party. The LDP can delegate to the bureaucracy without having to worry about elected executive-branch officials with incentives different from those of the legislature, or relying on fire alarms to prevent undesired policies. Even in Japan, though, checks can help to elicit information and to prevent abuses. One of the most common and useful is playing one ministry or bureau against another (Johnson 1975, 1989; Rosenbluth 1989). Within the PARC itself, investigative commissions, which cut across ministerial jurisdictions, help check the narrow biases of the individual PARC divisions (Nihon Keizai Shimbunsha [ed.] 1983: 40).

4.4. Structure and process

Managing agency losses, then, comes down to structuring incentives and choices. The incentive effects of rewards and punishments are universally understood. However, we do not need to see principals reward or punish their agents to know that the promise of reward or the threat of punishment has an effect. Indeed, if the agent has been chosen well and the relationship of actions to rewards and punishments is clear, we would never expect to see the agent punished. That we observe, time and again, executive officials being excoriated before Congress, bears witness to the constitutional fact that members of Congress have little to say about the choice of their executive agents. On the other hand, that Japanese bureaucrats are only very rarely dressed down in public reflects the greater direct control the LDP leadership and PARC divisions have over the choice and promotion of Japanese ministry officials.[15]

Incentives are also shaped through structure and process. Structure refers to who makes what choices when; process refers to the procedures followed in making choices at each stage. The means to manage agency losses – from reporting requirements, to fire alarm systems, to checks – are contained in the structure and process established for executive decision making. In deciding on new program expenditures in Japan, for example, the ministries, in consultation with the appropriate PARC division members, first develop plans for new programs and write requests for the requisite funding. These new expense requests are then submitted to the Bureau of the Budget at the MOF for review by bureau personnel, the finance minister, the prime minister, and, perhaps, the cabinet. MOF and ministry officials then meet to bargain over the funding requests. If an agreement is struck in this meeting, then the new expense request is submitted as part of the budget sent to the cabinet and eventually to the Diet. If not, then a restoration request is submitted and taken up in what is referred to as revival negotiations, attended by ministry and MOF officials, as well as the minister of finance, members of the appropriate PARC division, the LDP secretary general, the chairman of the LDP, and the executive council of the LDP. If agreement is reached at this stage, then the new expense request is submitted in the budget to the cabinet. If not, then a final meeting is held at the prime minister's residence, wherein the prime minister and the LDP leadership meet with the finance minister to decide the ultimate fate of the new expense request. Again, of course, the full cabinet and the Diet have the ultimate authority to approve, amend, or

---

[15] Recall as well our earlier point that such public embarrassments may do little to enhance the reputation of the majority party in a parliamentary system, where no blame for failed oversight can be conferred upon an independently elected executive.

disapprove new expense requests. At each stage of the budget process, the anticipation of actions at the next stage affects the decisions made.

Structure and process exist everywhere. Red tape exists, in all organizations, public and private, the world over. Public hearings are a major part of many administrative procedures in Japan, and notice and comment are often required. Though Japan has no equivalent to the U.S. Administrative Procedure Act (APA), procedures specified in a number of laws were modeled on the APA and the National Environmental Policy Act of 1970 (Upham 1987: 59–61). For example, the Basic Law for Nuclear Power (Genshiryoku kihon ho, P.L. No. 186, 1955) was amended via an order from the Ministry of International Trade and Industry (MITI) requiring public hearings before siting decisions involving nuclear power plants (MITI order No. 250, 1979). Under that rule, MITI must give all relevant "administrative organs" (i.e., local governments) and the general public forty days notice of a hearing (Sec. 2:1). Parties interested in attending or expressing opinions at the meeting must present MITI with a written outline of their comments within twenty days (Sec. 2:3), after which MITI then determines who may attend the meeting and who may speak (Secs. 2:3–2:4).

The appropriate test of whether delegation equals abdication, we argue, is whether there exists a significant causal link between legislative preferences and policy outputs. A growing number of studies indicate that there is such a link. Budget policy in Japan is responsive to shifts in the majority coalition in the Diet. Calder (1988b), for example, gives evidence that the LDP has repeatedly crafted policy initiatives in response to political and economic crises. Further, the literature on Japanese politics is replete with stories of LDP policy initiatives that were passed over bureaucratic objections, from compensating landlords and repatriates to creating toll roads and earmarking gasoline taxes (Campbell 1976; Fukui 1970: 173–197; Nihon Keizai Shimbunsha [ed.] 1983: 64). There are also examples of bureaucratic policy initiatives that failed (Johnson 1982: 255–260). In many cases, bureaucratic initiatives are delayed and modified until they satisfy LDP needs (Muramatsu and Mabuchi 1991).[16]

5. UNDERSTANDING POLITICAL EQUILIBRIUM

To understand political equilibrium, we must first understand what we mean by "equilibrium." The easiest way to define an equilibrium is by example. In playing a card game such as blackjack, the players adopt

---

[16] The story is similar in the U.S. case, where "appropriations decisions depend dramatically upon the party holding the majority in the House and in the Senate" (Kiewiet and McCubbins 1991: 194). Different majority parties emphasize spending in different policy areas.

strategies that depend on the circumstances. For example, they may decide that they will take another card whenever their first two cards total less than thirteen, but pass whenever the total is fourteen or more. If the strategy adopted by each player in a game is a best response to those taken by the other players, then the set of strategies is an equilibrium. This implies that the strategies that each player adopts will be stable. As long as the other players' strategies remain constant, each player individually is best off if he sticks with his strategy.

Within the principal–agent game, the agent and the principal will adopt strategies for dealing with each other. The principal might decide upon a rule to conduct oversight at the sounding of a fire alarm; the agent might decide to take one action as opposed to another depending upon whether or not the principal is monitoring.

The premise of the previous section is that we can view bureaucratic–legislative and party–subgovernment relations as principal–agent games. In the first instance, the legislature delegates its authority to take action – to make law – to appointed officials in the bureaucracy. These bureaucrats are acting on legislated authority, using funds appropriated by law by the legislature, and being paid salaries approved by the legislature. In the second case, party committees (or legislative committees) are making proposals and taking actions for the majority party. The majority party establishes the rules of the legislature that create these committees and define their tasks, that appoint people to them, and that define the rules by which the committees' actions will be considered and rewarded.

Having established these problems as principal–agent games, we can examine the conditions under which abdication is an equilibrium and relate these conditions to the things we observe. We define abdication as meaning that the agent has complete discretion over the policy choices and that the principal has no control. This is an extreme definition, of course, as there may be relative amounts of abdication; but relative amounts of abdication imply that the principal is able to influence the agent's choices to at least some extent.

What do we have to assume so that abdication is the necessary consequence of delegation from the principal to the agent? It is not enough to assume that the agent has agenda control and can make take-it-or-leave-it proposals to the principal, as the principal can still influence the agent's proposals by threat of a veto. Nor is it sufficient to assume that the agent has hidden knowledge that remains hidden, even when combined with the power to set the agenda. In this case, the principal can still influence the agent's proposal (and therefore the policy chosen) as long as the principal can write a contract to influence the agent's actions or can select the agent in the first place in accordance with the principal's interests. Thus, to conclude that abdication is the equilibrium in an agency relationship, we must assume that the agent is a monopoly agenda setter and that the principal is unable to offer incentives to the agent or to learn something of the agent's hidden knowledge. If these conditions hold, then the agent's strategy in choosing a policy is not contingent upon the possible actions (*ex ante* or *ex post*) of the principal.

If, however, the principal can write binding contracts, set up institutional mechanisms such as fire alarms and reporting requirements, or modify the policy proposed by the agent, she can exercise some measure of control over policy. The common effect of each of these tools is that they ultimately affect the agent's utility, causing the agent to incorporate them (and hence the principal's interests) into his calculation about his own move. Thus, in equilibrium, we would expect to see policy at or close enough to the principal's ideal point that the cost of punishing the agent (including the cost in terms of time and money of oversight) outweighs the benefit of bringing policy any closer. We would also expect to see no punishment of agents, no sounding of fire alarms, and no *ex-post* modification of policy by the principal. Again, this is because the agent has anticipated the most he could ultimately get away with and has proposed that as policy.

In terms of our definition of equilibrium, we see that the players' strategies just described meet the test of "best response" strategies. Given the principal's strategy, the agent is best off not shirking; the principal, given the agent's compliance, is best off not altering policy or punishing the agent.

Returning to actual cases of legislative–executive and party–subgovernment relations, what we observe in Japan lends support to our theoretical approach. The power of the LDP to intervene is exercised on occasion, and the structure and process of policy making is rife with fire alarms that occasionally ring, infrequent policy changes, a few vetoes, and rare punishment of bureaucrats or committee members. The fact that out-of-equilibrium behavior does arise every once in a while is a sign that the informational assumptions of the simple model presented here are usually too strong in practice. The occasional *ex-post*, out-of-equilibrium behavior by principals, however, is also the exception that proves the rule, and is totally incompatible with the abdication hypothesis. Inaction by the principal does not imply abdication, but even sporadic action by the principal *necessarily* implies "not abdication."

6. COMPARATIVE STATICS

6.1. Testing the model

In principle, we could extend our model to make it testable. Having defined what an equilibrium is and discussed what things affect the political equilibrium, we can examine how changes in the conditions that gave rise to the equilibrium change it. Political intervention in bureaucratic or subgovernment decision making will be likely in four instances: (1) the majority party is replaced by a new majority coalition with different goals; (2) the composition of the majority party changes, again leading to different goals; (3) the policy is designed to appeal to some central tendency or interest in the enacting coalition, but allows for some wiggle room as it is applied on a case-by-case basis (cf. Fiorina 1977); or (4) the enacting coalition misforecasts the equilibrium bureaucratic or subgovernment response to the structure of the delegation, leading the coalition subsequently to fine-tune the terms of the agency's mandate or procedures. The first two cases suggest comparative statics tests, which would allow us to distinguish our model from the models of bureaucratic dominance (see, e.g., Calvert, Moran, and Weingast 1989; Weingast and Moran 1983).

Cases 3 and 4, however, are classes of "out-of-equilibrium" behavior that have no obvious, consistent interpretation in the abdication models. In the case of individual legislators meddling at the margins of a policy to curry favor for their constituents, what motivations do bureaucratic-dominance models offer for why bureaucrats should ever accommodate such demands? We argue that bureaucrats are likely to be responsive to such demands at the margins because they understand that the members of the enacting coalition expect and demand that they be responsive. In Fiorina's terms, "When a congressman calls about some minor bureaucratic decision or regulation, the bureaucracy considers his accommodation a small price to pay for the goodwill its cooperation will produce" (1977: 43).

The fourth case, that of legislative miscalculation, is perhaps the most interesting of the four classes of legislative intervention, and it is the most difficult for bureaucratic-dominance models to handle. Our model of delegation argues that the enacting coalition delegates in pursuit of a particular policy goal. If the structure and process chosen by the coalition – in anticipation that it will be sufficient to meet the goal – is not sufficient, our model suggests that the coalition will seek to modify the delegation so as to make the goal achievable. This implies, in many cases, that it will apply additional management tools such as institutional checks, procedures, or reporting requirements, to further modulate agency behavior.

6.2. A critical reevaluation of the thesis of abdication

The evidence given to support the abdication thesis is impressive. Yet, we have argued that this evidence is illusory, that the abdication implied by this evidence is more apparent than real. Take, for example, what we know about the budget process in light of the comparative statics just discussed.[17] As discussed previously, in the Japanese budget process there are layers of veto gates controlled by the majority party that lie between MOF budget proposals and final approval of spending figures. These include PARC divisions, the executive board, the cabinet, Diet committees, and the Lower and Upper Houses; each must express approval. Final decisions on budget increments for the "continuing services" budget and all decisions on "revival negotiations" for new project spending, for example, are made by the cabinet and the prime minister.

Further, legislators can be observed to offer their own legislative proposals, as well as to reject, modify, or ignore proposals offered by executive agents. At every stage, politicians can remand or rewrite MOF proposals. At the earliest stage (from April to July of every year) spending ministries consult first with the minister of finance and the prime minister, then with the chairmen and vice-chairmen of the PARC division before announcing the guidelines for budgetary requests. Once the spending ministries have completed their requests, they show them to the PARC divisions before submitting them to MOF (Murakawa 1985: 137–158; Japanese sources also make reference to "gates" – see Sone and Kanazashi 1989: 183). All of this occurs even before the divisions conduct fall hearings, the PARC's Policy Deliberation Committee considers "important items" (around October) and the party's top leaders make the final decisions in the revival negotiations.

In the United States, even with an explicit delegation of authority to the president as in the 1921 Budget Act (see Sundquist 1981), Congress need not even consider the president's proposal.[18] The LDP's PARC, like the

---

[17] Indeed, we find a good deal of evidence in the literature that contradicts the impression of legislative abdication. For example, although it is perhaps not as comprehensive in its coverage of policy areas as the American literature, the Japanese literature provides numerous case studies of LDP oversight and policy making in virtually every policy area, including agriculture, construction, transportation, commerce and industry, science and technology, finance, labor, social welfare, and taxation (Inoguchi and Iwai 1987; Johnson 1989; Nihon Keizai Shimbunsha [ed.] 1983; Rosenbluth 1989).

[18] President Reagan complained, "Every year under the law I submitted a budget program . . . [and] they've put it on the shelf and have refused to even consider it" (*Congressional Quarterly Weekly Report*, October 24, 1987: 2626).

U.S. Congress, almost never acts without a proposal from a ministry. And, after formal introduction by the Cabinet, the legislation finally passed by the Diet usually closely resembles executive proposals.[19] However, it is incorrect to infer legislative abdication or executive dominance from these observations. Indeed, we expect that successful legislation will usually bear close resemblance to executive proposals, regardless of who "dominates" the policy-making process. If executive proposals are to succeed, executive-branch agents must anticipate the reaction of legislators and accommodate their demands and interests. Since they know this, and since making proposals is costly in terms of time and effort, they rarely submit proposals that they expect to fail. This is the well-known law of anticipated reactions (see, e.g., Weingast and Moran 1983, who discuss the disciplinary effect on bureaucrats of congressional committees' "big stick behind the door"; references to anticipated reactions are also common in the literature on Japan, as in Campbell 1977: 126; Murakawa 1985: 104–105; Park 1986: 58). It follows that members rarely make significant changes to executive proposals, because their interests have already been accommodated.

At predictable points, however, there are deviations from the happy equilibrium just described. That is when the power and independent preferences of the legislature are then revealed. This has been particularly true in the United States, with its budget battles and dramatic vetoes and override attempts. In Japan, revision of bills in the Diet is actually fairly common (Iwai 1988; Richardson and Flanagan 1984: 354–356). The LDP's loss of control of the Upper House in 1989 led to defeats or enforced compromises on some bureaucratically drafted legislation, notably the recent failure of a bill to allow Japanese forces to participate in U.N. peacekeeping operations (a watered-down version later passed). We might expect to see more dramatic examples if another party w to gain majority control of the Lower House, only to have to contend with a bureaucracy stocked with agents hired, trained, and conditioned by the LDP. Such examples are lacking due to the LDP's continued dominance of Japanese politics. Only when executive actions deviate from equilibrium, then, is legislative autonomy visible.[20]

Even if it is true that executive agents make uncounted policy decisions subject to only haphazard oversight by the Diet (or the LDP) – and there is substantial evidence to the contrary – these claims are entirely consistent

---

[19] The same could be said for any parliament in a democratic system. In equilibrium, we cannot distinguish from the absence of political intervention whether agencies act so as to make their political chiefs happy, or whether they really do act autonomously.

[20] Fortunately for students of Japanese politics, it appears at the time of this writing as though the idea of coalitional change may not be such a farfetched one for very much longer.

with an alternative interpretation, under which Diet members, in delegating, actually retain all of their authority over policy making.[21] In this alternative view, legislators agree to delegate areas of policy-making authority to executive agents because doing so allows members to make policy on many more areas than they otherwise could. The Diet then uses direct and indirect means to structure the incentives to which executive agents respond when making policy choices.

This emphasis on incentives and oversight does not imply a return to an archaic and artificial separation between politics and administration. As Aberbach and his colleagues (Aberbach, Putnam, and Rockman 1981) have shown, patterns of delegation and oversight vary across countries, and bureaucrats routinely play a political role. Nor, as we have argued, are delegation and oversight perfect or costless. Our point is simply that bureaucrats act from a script written and directed by politicians and parties.

7. CONCLUSION

Social scientists are inclined to infer far too much from appearances. Social-scientific models of policy making often (explicitly or implicitly) exclude those actors in the policy process who appear to be powerless, and model only those who appear to be powerful. But the appearance of power follows most easily from casual observation and, as such, is often deceiving. Parties in the legislature, we argue, can be highly successful in their delegations and yet appear to be very weak in comparison to their agents. Japanese bureaucrats and PARC divisions seem powerful and autonomous vis-à-vis the collective interests of the party rank and file, but they are overseen by senior members of the ruling party. As Johnson (1982) and others have so long argued, the LDP rarely appears to be powerful because we seldom get to see the party publicly contradicting or disciplining its agents.

But models based on the appearance of power – such as those that we have termed abdication models – are incapable of accounting for even a small part of the interactions and connecting structures and procedures we observe between legislators, bureaucrats, and subgovernments. The explanations for abdication itself tend to be ad hoc cultural arguments or teleological arguments about the connection between political development and the "institutionalization" of policy administration. Such explanations carry the explanatory value of the appearance of power to the extreme, ignoring alternative, more parsimonious models in the process.

---

[21] Indeed, stories of subgovernmental power in Japan and the United States themselves challenge the view that legislators cannot affect policy.

We have presented in this chapter an alternative model of Japanese policy making. Although much of our evidence is drawn from the literature on budgeting, our model is much more generally applicable. In our model, the majority party, in organizing its own decision-making processes, delegates authority to make policy decisions to executive officials and subgovernments. This delegation does not result in abdication, but rather is well managed so that in equilibrium we expect a balance between what legislators expect of their bureaucratic agents and what those agents deliver.

Political equilibrium refers in part to a regularity in the expected behavior of legislative principals and bureaucratic agents, given an institutional context, that is, legislative delegations of authority and the terms and conditions of those delegations. That regularity is itself conditioned on a balance between the expectations of political constituents, the governmentally produced goods and services they receive, and the votes they cast. Hence, political equilibrium invokes a kind of iron triangle of its own, between voters, legislators, and bureaucrats. As long as each actor receives from the others what he expects, given his expectations about the likely outcomes under alternative regimes, we do not expect to see significant change, whether in voting patterns in the electorate, in delegations and their associated structures and processes from the legislature, or in policy outcomes from the bureaucracy.

A well-designed delegation is not costless to implement and regulate. Thus, we do not and cannot argue that legislators get exactly what they want from their agents. Instead, we suggest that, given legislators' goals, delegation is likely to be efficient: Legislators can find no lower-cost means to satisfy their goals, all else constant. Our model has the potential to explain more of the bureaucratic and legislative behavior we observe, including the circumstances that give rise to changes in that behavior. Finally, where abdication models are at a loss to explain the observed structure and process of decision making, our model justifies – indeed requires – structure and process as tools to manage delegations.

5

Perceptions and realities of Japanese budgeting

MATHEW D. MCCUBBINS AND GREGORY W. NOBLE

1. INTRODUCTION

Government budgets represent a major component of economic policy in all countries. Governments can make and break domestic markets and industries with their influence over the economy, and government spending decisions can critically affect the behavior of other economic actors. The Japanese government, for example, directs more than 30 percent of the nation's income through the budgetary process.[1]

Despite its importance in shaping the government's policies and in structuring the economy, however, there has been little research on the politics of budget making in Japan. What research there is suggests that there are three key elements to Japanese budgeting. First, changes in spending are incremental. Second, each agency and ministry, once included in the budget, receives a stable or "fair" share of the budget each year thereafter. Third, once a program is in place, spending on it cannot be retrenched. As a first step in understanding Japanese budgeting and politics, we question each of these three stylized facts. We demonstrate, with evidence we have compiled on Japanese spending for the period 1952–89 (see chapter appendix for details on methods and sources), that these "facts" are largely fictions.

The views of the budget-making process that have emerged to explain these fictitious facts have stressed the weakness of the party that has presided over Japan during the past four decades. The ruling Liberal Democratic Party (LDP) is said to be unable to lead and unable to make tough political choices. It has difficulty changing existing budgetary patterns and is virtually incapable of constraining aggregate demands on the budget; thus it is forced to rely on the bureaucracy and on mechanical

---

[1] Of this, 20.6 percent goes through the general account and 10.6 percent through the Fiscal Investment and Loan Program (*Kuni no Yosan* 1990: 1180–81).

rules of budget compilation. As a result, according to the dominant accounts, the pattern of budgetary expenditures tends to be extremely rigid. It lags farther and farther behind developments in Japanese society and constrains the LDP's ability to appeal to new constituencies, particularly in urban areas. Our results suggest that it is time to rethink the LDP's role in policy making.

We proceed as follows. In the next section we review the two branches of the bureaucratic-centric analyses of Japanese budgeting. We first consider the older branch, which argues that the Ministry of Finance dominates the budget process. We then discuss in greater detail the second, more modern, branch of the literature, which emphasizes the predominant role of "iron triangles" in Japanese budgeting. We review the literature on these triangles, or policy "whirlpools" (Griffith and Valeo 1975: 55–56), both from the view that they are driven by ministry desires and from the view that they are highly responsive to the LDP's *zoku* (particularistic policy cliques). These two views, we point out, are largely contradictory. In Section 3 we outline the policy expectations derived from these variations on the bureaucratic-centric school and contrast them with program-, agency-, and ministry-level data for the years 1952–89. Section 4 concludes.

2. THE JAPANESE ADMINISTRATIVE STATE

One major theme of studies of policy making in Japan is that the LDP is unable to control and direct the bureaucracy. Tsuji, for example, argues that the Japanese bureaucracy

has held a paramount position in the government structure since the beginning of the Meiji period [1868]. . . . In the postwar period, just as in the prewar period, the National Diet and the political parties, though clad in their new, gorgeous gowns, have danced on a stage synchronized by a complex bureaucracy (1964: 92; see also Tsuji 1969).

Tejima (1976: 126–127) argues that this constitutes a sort of technocratic "administrative state" in which the bureaucracy controls input as well as output functions. This view is common in American interpretations of Japanese politics as well: "The elite bureaucracy in Japan makes most major decisions, drafts virtually all legislation, controls the national budget, and is the source of all major policy innovations in the system" (Johnson 1982: 20–21).

In most accounts, four factors are adduced to account for the superiority of the bureaucrats in policy making. First, they are a highly elite group, attracting "the most talented graduates of the best universities" (Johnson 1982: 20). Higher-level ministry positions are widely considered to be among the most prestigious jobs in Japan. Second, bureaucrats are said to have a near monopoly on the knowledge and skill necessary to operate the complex budgetary system (e.g., Campbell 1977: 42). Even those who focus on the role of LDP politicians in policy matters agree that bureaucrats have a decisive edge in information (Inoguchi and Iwai 1987: 35–36; Matsuzaki, quoted in Ebato 1986: 177).

Third, many analysts believe that bureaucrats are the only actors in the political system who have the incentives and ability to consider the needs and interests of Japan as a whole (see, e.g., Inoguchi and Iwai 1987: 35–36, 281–282, 290–291). Unlike politicians, the argument goes, bureaucrats consider the cumulative effect of passing out promises to various groups (Ito 1980: 167). The budget bureau of the Ministry of Finance, for example, has been dubbed the "guardian of logic" for the way it protects the national treasury against the particularistic demands of politicians and interest groups (Kuribayashi 1986: 10). Fourth, the bureaucracy is seen as effectively colonizing the entire policy-making system by placing ex-officials in top posts in the ruling party, public policy corporations, advisory councils, private corporations, and so forth (Johnson 1975: 8–10, 22–27; Kuribayashi 1986: 148).

While there is something of a consensus that the bureaucracy is in charge of the actual conduct of policy making in Japan, there is considerably less agreement as to which bureaucrats actually make policy, particularly budget policy. The traditional argument is that the budget bureau of the Ministry of Finance has ultimate control. An alternative argument focuses on the tight links between individual ministries, groups of LDP politicians, and interest groups – the Japanese version of "iron triangles." We will discuss each of these views in turn.

2.1. The Ministry of Finance (MOF)

Several top Japanese scholars have made the claim that the MOF compiles and coordinates the budget and is therefore the most influential policy-making organ in Japan. "Nowadays, Ministry of Finance officials have come to exercise leadership not only over budget compilation, but over the whole policy-making process" (Ito 1980: 159, 161). And in a recent overview, Noguchi argues that despite the increasing prominence accorded to politicians in recent years, "the MOF still controls the essential parts of the budget by various technocratic means. . . . Consequently, political factors . . . play a minor role in budget making in Japan" (Noguchi 1991: 140–141).[2]

---

[2] This interpretation is also common among journalists and other analysts (Ando 1984). Japanese newspapers' exhaustive coverage of the final stages of the annual budget-

These assertions of MOF dominance, however, are difficult to test directly. Knowing that the MOF sets the budget does not help us to formulate expectations about how much money will be spent on specific budget items and programs. We would still need to know the MOF's spending priorities. It may well be true that the MOF cares more than other budget participants about minimizing the size of the budget, eliminating waste, and implementing appropriate fiscal policies as well as, perhaps above all, preserving its own autonomy and status (Campbell 1977: 111), but it is difficult to operationalize these goals and test the degree to which the MOF attains them. In any case, it flies in the face of evidence that budget deficits are quite frequent in Japan to argue that the MOF is both powerful and concerned with balancing the budget (see *Zaisei Seisaku Kenkyukai* 1985: 176 for a comparative overview of the ratio of budget deficits to GNP in Japan).

Thus, we do not test the thesis of MOF dominance directly. Rather, we merely note in passing that the recent findings of the "iron triangles" literature imply that the MOF-dominance view cannot be correct, as the MOF cannot dominate budget politics if there is in fact no central coordination to the spending of the iron triangles. It is to this more recent literature that we now turn.

2.2. Iron triangles

A more widely held version of bureaucratic dominance argues that bureaucrats are individually powerful, but not centrally coordinated. Each ministry, and sometimes each bureau within a ministry, is a power unto itself. Responsibility for initial preparation of ministry budgets naturally devolves to the individual ministries and agencies and, the argument goes, it is difficult or impossible for the MOF to scrutinize each item in these budgets.

While many analysts agree that MOF oversight of the spending ministries is weak, the currently dominant view holds that an individual ministry is not so much an independent center of power in contention with the MOF, but rather one vertex of an iron triangle (on the U.S. literature, see Cater 1964; Freeman 1965; Griffith and Valeo 1975). A second vertex arises from a decentralized network of *zoku* – literally "tribes" or "clans" – groups of middle-level LDP politicians headquartered in the committees of the ruling party's Policy Affairs Research Council (PARC) (Inoguchi and Iwai 1987; Nihon Keizai Shimbunsha [ed.] 1983). *Zoku* politicians use specialized knowledge (gained from PARC committee ser-

compilation process focuses overwhelmingly on the way the Ministry of Finance makes a few strategic concessions to politicians and spending ministries in order to hold the budget together.

vice) in the service of increasingly effective policy plunder, gathering more resources for their constituents and favored industries regardless of the cost to the budget or to the overall consistency, coherence, and equity of government policy. The third vertex consists of the constituents of the first two groups.

The iron-triangle interpretation of bureaucratic dominance suggests that there is no "responsible" party government in Japan because there is no coordination of *zoku* influence on the separate policy clusters. It stresses that the reason the LDP cannot exercise direction and leadership over the bureaucracy, and the budget and policy making more generally, is not so much the inherent superiority of bureaucrats as the ruling party's inability to control *itself* (cf. Schoppa 1991).[3] As Johnson (1990: 82) summarizes the situation, "The result [of the rise of *zoku*] was the appearance of . . . the 'headless chicken' or the 'truncated pyramid' – the 'headless monster' for short – meaning a Japanese system in which no one [is] ultimately in charge."

This inability of the party to control itself is said to arise from three sources. First, the recruitment of LDP Diet members is not subject to LDP management and is dominated by ex-bureaucrats. About one-fourth of LDP Diet members are former bureaucrats who thoroughly dominated top party and government posts through the end of the 1960s.

Second, the leadership of the LDP is not given the resources to enforce discipline and to coordinate policy making. Most analyses stress that the party president (who is also prime minister as long as the LDP retains its Diet majority) is institutionally weak (e.g., Campbell 1977: 165; Sakakibara 1991: 75–78), with a minuscule official staff and few institutional tools with which to control party affairs. Further, the cabinet is said to wield little control over the budget (Campbell 1977: 151; Kishimoto 1988: 80–83; Murakawa 1985: 189–190), and there is no "super budget agency" empowered to enforce policy coordination (Murakawa 1985: 93–94, 99, 148, 156–157).[4] Similarly, it is argued, the General Council

---

[3] The weakness and indiscipline of the LDP has been a staple feature of accounts by the bureaucratic-dominance school (see, e.g., Ito 1980: 166–167). But academic analyses of the LDP's indiscipline have taken on more importance in the past decade or two as scholars have come to agree that politicians play an important role in policy making. To proponents of the bureaucratic-dominance view, such as Johnson (1990), the LDP simply supplements a system built around bureaucratic units. Contrast this with Murakawa (1985: 1–2, 116–117, 136, 170–171), who emphasizes that bureaucrats consult their political masters at each stage of the process. There is more agreement over the basic cause of this increase in LDP influence: Political stability and the LDP's long-term majority in the Diet have led to the growth of policy expertise within the party (Sato and Matsuzaki 1986). The *zoku* are the embodiment of that new expertise.

[4] Some limited reforms were made in 1968, however (see Murakawa 1985: 165). For a reprint of the recommendations on the budget of the (first) Ad Hoc Commission on Administrative Reform of the early 1960s, along with extensive commentary, see Kato (1992): 27–61.

(formerly the Executive Council, and formally the party's highest-standing body) and the Policy Deliberation Commission (the PARC's executive committee), play essentially no part in the content of policy making (Sato and Matsuzaki 1986: 99; for a contrary view, see Murakawa 1985: 100–101).

Third, the LDP is said to be nothing more than a persisting logroll among a set of special interests. In the absence of adequate leadership and coordination from the prime minister, cabinet, General Council or Policy Deliberation Commission, the individual PARC committees gain virtually unlimited power over their respective jurisdictions (Noguchi 1991: 131, 133; Sakakibara 1991: 53, 69, 75, 78).

3. PERCEPTIONS AND REALITY

The central message of the iron-triangle model of budget politics is that policy is made independently, issue by issue. However, strictly interpreting the logical implications of this view, independent issue-by-issue budget policy making implies that there is no politically imposed overall budget constraint restricting the growth in government in Japan. The only possible budget constraint must arise from the individual preferences of the actors in each policy whirlpool. Each iron triangle is in charge of only a slice of the overall budget. Members of this iron triangle, therefore, can restrain overall budget growth only by restraining spending in their own areas. Since members of any one group cannot be assured that other groups will likewise restrain themselves, it is easy to show that the iron triangles are themselves caught in a prisoners' dilemma: No set of interest groups wants to slash its spending programs in the name of balanced budgets when others do not follow suit. The implication is that the overall budget will grow explosively.

The adherents to the bureaucratic-dominance view are unwilling to follow the full logical implications of their theory. They recognize that overall budgets typically do not show explosive growth in real expenditures, nor do budgets appear to tend toward absorbing all of a country's gross national product. Therefore, there must exist some coordinating mechanism that helps these hypothesized iron triangles to overcome the prisoner's dilemma they face. Since (by assumption) there is no enforcement mechanism that impels each iron triangle to stay under a particular budgetary target, it follows that the coordinating mechanism must be decentralized and must satisfy some generally acknowledged norm of fairness, so that it does not create overt, zero-sum conflicts between iron triangles over how overall budget cuts or increases should be distributed. These iron-triangle adherents have further argued that Japanese iron triangles, through repeated budgetary bargaining with one another over the years, have developed norms of behavior that govern how budgets are to change in each policy area. Spending for each agency and ministry changes only "incrementally" from year to year, and each agency's or ministry's share of the budget is stable, or "fair."

Agency and ministry budgets are then included in a gigantic omnibus logroll. This logroll has been protected institutionally by the creation of government ministries and PARC committees, each out to protect and expand its respective turf and budget. The budget process, therefore, has become increasingly rigid. Competing demands can be reconciled only by relying on precedent and mechanical rules of allocation. If the alliance of bureaucrats, politicians, and interest groups in each policy area is bound with ties of iron, retrenching the budget even of obsolete areas becomes difficult or even impossible. The persistent bias toward public works and the countryside, despite the massive shift of population out of agriculture, has been a continuing theme in the literature (e.g., Noguchi 1980b, 1982; Sakakibara 1991). The pattern extends beyond the countryside, however: "Much of the party's weight has been thrown on the side of the status quo, protecting programs and ministries which the Ministry of Finance, for one, would prefer to cut back. . . . its net effect has been to diminish responsiveness" (Campbell 1977: 142).

These implications of the iron-triangle model of Japanese budgetary politics can thus be boiled down to three simple concepts, labeled in the literature as "fair shares," "incrementalism," and "nonretrenchment." We discuss and test each of these concepts in turn.

3.1. Fair shares

By far the most commonly cited terms in Japanese budgeting are "balanced," "fair," or "equal shares." Wildavsky (1964) defines fair shares in terms of the budgetary "base" for a ministry, agency or program.

The base is the general expectation among the participants that programs will be carried on at close to the going level of expenditures. . . . "Fair share" means not only the base an agency has established but also the expectation that it will receive some portion of funds, if any, which are to be increased over or decreased below the base of the various governmental agencies (1964: 17).

Campbell (1975: 72, 76) argues that Japanese budgeting fits the "fair shares" paradigm.

Japanese budget allocations do not fluctuate very much. It is as if the new revenues that become available each year are shared out more or less evenly so that each ministry gets about the same proportion of the new as it had of the old. The equilibrium of the previous year is maintained; no "unbalance" is introduced. . . . Balance . . . is *not* setting an expenditure level by assessing how important a program is to national priorities, how effective it has been in the past, or even how much political support it has attracted.

87

This balanced outcome, he argues, is most observable at the level of ministries, but also applies to bureaus and specific programs within ministries (Campbell 1975: 77–78). As a norm undergirding interactions among the elites involved in budgeting, it is both a value (evenhandedness, equity) and an aid to calculation ("add together and divide by two" – Sato and Matsuzaki 1986: 161–162).

If the norm of balance is so widely used, however, the problem becomes balancing what with what. As Campbell (1975: 77) notes, "balance is not a tightly defined administrative rule." One possibility is that budgeters try to balance and equalize the benefits given to different groups, or to the individuals within them. Campbell (1975: 75–76) cites former MOF vice-minister Kono Kazuyuki as pointing to health care benefit levels for different demographic groups in Japan as one example of balance. Evidence suggests, however, that balance across benefit groups does not explain budgetary outcomes. If one looks at the budget allocations for health care and pensions before the reforms of the mid-1980s, for example, the picture that emerges is quite different from the one highlighted by Kono. The Japanese government subsidy for health insurance contributions was 100 percent for the elderly, 50 percent for farmers, 32 percent for the self-employed and workers in small businesses, 16.4 percent for employees of big companies, and zero for various government-sector employees and teachers in private schools. This pattern has little to do with balancing benefits, but correlates very well with the degree to which the groups support the LDP. Precisely the same political logic could be observed in government contributions to various pension programs (Zaisei Seisaku Kenkyukai 1985: 100, 95).[5]

The fair-shares notion expounded in the literature predicts that all agencies and ministries share proportionately changes in the full budget. Thus, if the budget increases by 10 percent, then each agency and ministry expects to receive a 10-percent increase. Such an expectation would imply that a randomly chosen Japanese agency should receive a percentage spending increase equal to the increase for the budget as a whole. However, we found that it is *never* true in our data on Japanese spending that

[5] It should be noted that Kono was writing in 1957, whereas these figures reflect the situation in 1985; since then, as part of the broader movement to reform administration – and shift the LDP's constituency base – both health care and pensions have been rationalized somewhat. The actual allocation formulas for health care in the mid-1980s were in a couple of cases slightly more complicated than the simplified summaries given in the text, but they do not change the overall pattern. It should also be noted that benefits (as opposed to contribution subsidies) were actually lower for the self-employed: 70 percent vs. 100 percent. There was little difference in treatment of dependents, however, and full benefits were provided to the self-employed once costs exceeded 57,000 yen per month. Moreover, even in the various employees' health insurance schemes, a 10 percent copayment was introduced after October 1984, further decreasing the gap. *Kuni no Yosan 1989,* pp. 89–90. See also Fujii and Reich (1988).

the percentage change in an agency or ministry budget (from one year to the next) exactly equals the percentage change in the overall budget. Clearly, the "fair shares" argument is not literally true. We therefore need a less stringent test of the basic notion underlying "fair shares."

An alternative test begins with the premise that random shocks might cause a given agency's budget share to move away from its usual level, but that the overall budget process is governed by a norm of constant fair shares. We would expect, then, that once the emergency had passed, the budget share for the agency would return to its historic level. If after some time this did not occur – that is, if the shock caused a lasting increase or decrease in the agency's share – we would be inclined to reject the fair-shares hypothesis.

The empirical problem is to choose a time frame that is long enough such that any shock can be fully neutralized, but not so long that overall budget priorities will have changed. We choose to examine agency budget shares over moving five-year periods (for example, for an item introduced in 1952 we examine the periods 1952–56, then 1953–57, etc.) to look for fair shares. The actual test regresses each agency's or ministry's net share (the agency budget divided by the total budget net payments on the national debt) on a time trend. If the time trend is found to be significant, then on average the share for the agency was either increasing or decreasing over the five-year period. This would be contrary to what the fair-shares model would predict.

Thus our test of the fair shares hypothesis is performed by running the regression

$$\text{Share}_{it} = C_i + B_i \text{ Time} + e_{it}, \ (1)$$

where Share_{it} is the net share for agency i in year t, C_i is a constant, and e_{it} is a random error. We test the null hypothesis of fair shares that B_i equals zero (there is no time trend in the agency's or ministry's share) against the alternative hypothesis that B_i does not equal zero (there is a time trend) with a standard t-test on B_i. If B_i is not statistically different than zero, we cannot reject the fair-share hypothesis. Since we are estimating the model over such a small time frame, we are biasing the results of the test in favor of the fair-shares model because the confidence intervals for B_i will be fairly large and will likely include zero.

Before we present our test results, it is helpful to get some intuition for our test by examining some examples of budget shares. Figures 5.1 and 5.2 present the net share of the budget for two ministries from 1952 to 1989. Let us look first at agriculture, a critical constituency for the ruling party. Figure 5.1 plots the net share of the budget allocated to the Ministry of Agriculture, Forestry and Fisheries (MAFF); the ministry's budget jumped from 11 percent to a peak of 16 percent in the 1950s and then

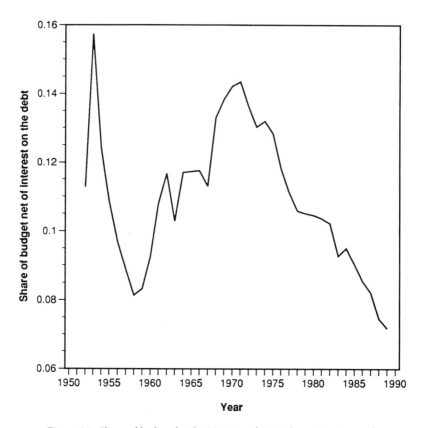

Figure 5.1. *Share of budget for the Ministry of Agriculture, Forestry, and Fisheries, 1952–89*

dropped, in only four years, to 8 percent of the net budget. MAFF's share of the budget then climbed to more than 14 percent by 1970, before sinking again into single digits (7 percent by 1989).

While the data shown in Figure 5.1 appear on the surface to be inconsistent with the idea of stable shares, our test might still fail to reject the null hypothesis that the overall budget shares are constant for many subperiods because there appears to be little or no overall trend in MAFF's share of the budget. Figure 5.2, however, presents a pattern of spending shares that would lead us to reject the null hypothesis in favor of the alternative hypothesis that budget shares are *not* constant. In Figure 5.2, although the budget share for the Ministry of International Trade and Industry (MITI) oscillates wildly, it nonetheless evinces a general increas-

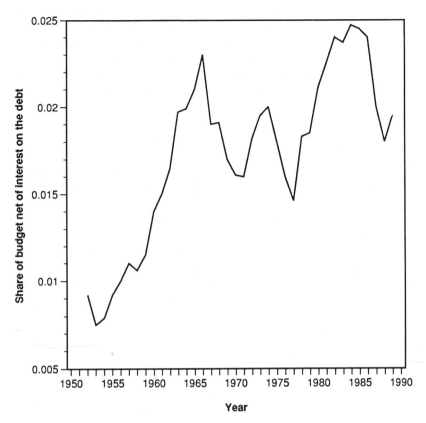

Figure 5.2. *Share of budget for the Ministry of International Trade and Industry, 1952–89*

ing trend (from less than 1 percent to almost 2.5 percent of the net budget).

The evidence in Figure 5.2 foreshadows the findings from our statistical test. We estimated the budget-share trend equation (equation 1) separately for 92 items and 15 ministries in the Japanese budget from 1952 to 1989 (this entailed up to 34 separate regressions for each item or ministry). In every instance we were able to reject the fair-shares null hypothesis that the trend coefficient was statistically indistinguishable from zero, at the .05 significance level. Thus we found no evidence at all that Japanese budgets conform to a fair-shares notion of budgetary stability.

This result is quite intuitive upon a little reflection on the fair-shares hypothesis. The hypothesis states that each agency or ministry garners a near-constant share of the total budget over time. This implies that programs cannot be added to (subtracted from) the budget without a compensating subtraction (addition) of another program, since any new program receiving a nontrivial budget, relative to the whole, necessarily reduces every other program's share. Further, fair shares implies that budgeting priorities cannot change, either, because changes in programs and the program mix within ministries – such as often occur – would make balance difficult or impossible to maintain.

3.2. Incrementalism

3.2.1. Conceptual ambiguities. The concept of incrementalism is closely related to that of budget balance: "Each year most budget items receive a small increment of additional funds above what had been received in the previous year" (Campbell 1977: 16; but note Campbell's definition on p. 63, which could have very different implications). Conventional incrementalism exercises have asked "Does last year's budget predict next year's?" and they usually conclude that it does (see, e.g., Wildavsky 1964). Incrementalism as an analytical approach suffers from a number of limitations. By itself, the concept is vacuous, telling us nothing about budgeting changes across or within spending categories, or about rates of change. If rates of increase were not exactly the same in all areas – for example, steady increments of 1 percent in one area, 6 percent in another area, and 12 percent in a third, as shown in Figure 5.3 – budget shares would, of course, diverge quite substantially over time. In Figure 5.3, we simply project the budgets of three hypothetical agencies, all of which begin with equal shares of the overall budget in the first year, but grow at different "incremental" rates thereafter.

Contrary to the expectations in the incrementalism literature, the hypothetical example illustrated in Figure 5.3 is easily matched from our sample of Japanese agencies. Figure 5.4 plots spending (in current yen) from 1961 to 1981 for budget items from the MAFF, the Ministry of Transportation, and the Ministry of Labor, respectively. Spending for each agency started at roughly the same level in 1961, and each agency grew at a different rate during the succeeding twenty years. As a result, spending for the strategic restructuring of agriculture ended up at three times the level of the Meteorological Administration, which in turn was almost twice as high as unemployment countermeasures. It should be obvious from this figure that incrementalism does not tell us much without auxiliary assumptions about when to include what in the base and about the political motivations behind the rates of change for particular budget items.

3.2.2. Tests of the basic model. We can test also incrementalism more formally. If budgets are incremental, then "the largest determining factor

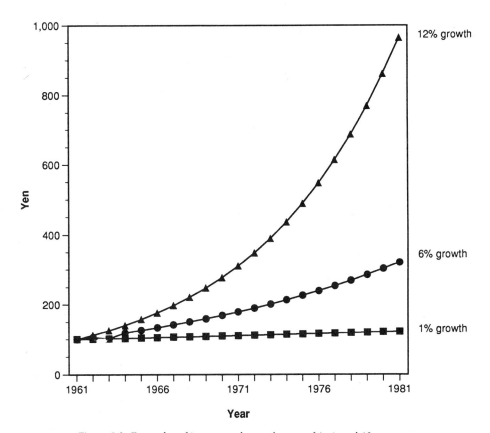

Figure 5.3. *Examples of incremental growth rates of 1, 6, and 12 percent*

of the size and content of this year's budget is last year's budget" (Wild-avsky 1964: 13). This implies that last year's budget is a good forecast for this year's. The usual test, performed on U.S. budget items by Davis, Dempster, and Wildavsky (1966) in pathbreaking work using regressions similar to equation 2 below, is to forecast this year's budget as a simple, linear function of last year's budget and test whether or not the coefficient on last year's budget, B_i is positive and significant. Davis et al. judge that if B_i is positive and significant, then spending for agency or ministry i is incremental:

$$y_{it} = a_i + B_i \, y_{it-1} + e_{it} \ (2)$$

where y_{it} is the budget in constant (1970) yen for agency or ministry i in year t; a_i is a constant term for agency or ministry i; B_i is the coefficient for the previous year's budget; and e_{it} is an error term.

93

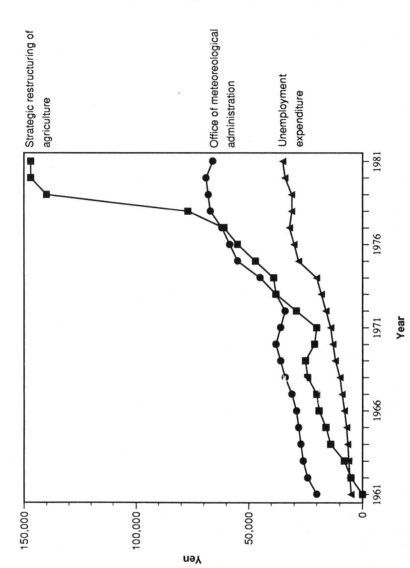

Figure 5.4. *Spending for three agencies in the Japanese General Account budget, in nominal yen, 1961–81*

There are several critiques to be made of this approach. As we have already noted, a finding that B_i is positive and significant does not itself tell us anything about "incremental" budgeting per se. Also, inferring from an estimated B_i that the true B_i is significantly greater than zero, as Davis et al. do, depends on equation 2 being the correct or "true" specification of the model, that is, that there are no explanatory variables left to the error term that also significantly affect y_{it}. In a later test Davis et al. acknowledge that equation 2 is not the true specification. Moreover, even if equation 2 did accurately portray the true model, it does not follow that a large t statistic for B_i means that last year's budget is the "largest determining factor" of y_{it}. Such a finding merely implies that y_{it-1} has a statistically significant effect on y_{it}. The largest systematic component determining spending could well be the constant term, c_i. Or, the "largest determining factor" might not be either systematic component (c_i or y_{it-1}) at all, but rather the stochastic component of budget choice (the error term).

More important, such a test puts no bounds on the range of B_i for which incrementalism would be supported. Does a $B_i = 2.3$ (implying that the budgets for agency i grow by 230 percent per year on average) qualify as incremental? What about $B_i = 1.5$, or $B_i = 0.6$? Indeed, the range of estimated values of B_i for our sample of ninety-two Japanese agencies is from less than 0.5 to greater than 2.5.

Finally, nearly all economic time series satisfy the condition that in a regression such as proposed, the coefficient on the lagged independent variable, B_i, will be positive in equation 2 (i.e., that the series is positively serially correlated; Harvey 1990). Typically, however, we do not interpret regressions on sales of refrigerators or housing prices or income to imply anything about incremental decision making on the part of consumers, producers, or wage earners. Rather, we observe that the economy has grown, which implies that consumers have more income and are able, therefore, to purchase more and better goods. Unless our theory about the relationship between government services and household income tells us that government services are inferior goods (demand decreases as income increases), we have no reason to expect anything but a positive B_i, regardless of our theory about how budget makers think, given that we have not controlled for changes in the size of the economy. The simple linear forecasting equation based on last year's budget, therefore, does not provide a direct test of the incremental hypothesis.

The task of empirically testing the incrementalist model is difficult, in part because nowhere in the literature is the full model of budgeting explicitly stated, nor are all of the necessary consequences of such a model discussed. The central tenet of the incrementalist model, however, is clear in a colloquial sense: Budget decisions are "small." Politicians and bu-

reaucrats, according to the incrementalists, lack the faculties and resources necessary to make fully "rational" decisions in a highly complex
environment. This claim has two important corollaries. First, decision
makers facing great uncertainties in the world prefer to change from
existing policies to new policy goals only bit by bit, and in ways that are
easily reversed. For example, suppose a newly elected policy maker wishes
to change the budget to enhance his own reelection chances. The best
budget choice to reach this goal is not clear. The decision maker therefore
might choose to experiment – to reallocate a small amount of money (or
slightly increase or decrease a particular budget item) and see what happens. If things work out well, he then slightly increases the allocation. If,
on the other hand, things go awry, he can easily reverse his initial policy
choice, since very little has been invested.

Second, to further reduce the degree of complexity that a budget maker
need consider, incrementalists argue, he will tend to accept without question most of the existing relationships between budgetary items and programs and most of the decision rules used by the previous budgetary
officer to make policy (i.e., standard operating procedures). Hence, the
incrementalist policy maker addresses only a "small" number of policy
questions at any one time and risks only "small" changes from the status
quo in those policy areas.

Thus, we can derive two clear hypotheses from the incrementalist theory of budgeting: First, changes in agency budgets will tend to be small
from one year to the next; second, since budget makers can handle only a
small number of issues at a time, most budget items will tend to move
together in any given year. However, since budgetary changes are subject
to a collective-choice mechanism (perhaps in the form of the omnibus
logrolling process discussed earlier) where individual iron triangles are
responsible for justifying budget proposals in each policy area, it is not
obvious why incrementalists would believe that budget makers would be
incapable of adjusting budgetary priorities across the board every year.
Hence, this form of incrementalism is itself inconsistent with the larger
thesis of bureaucratic influence on budgeting. Incrementalist theory cannot have it both ways: Either budgeting decisions are made by a central
agent that suffers from cognitive limitations (and hence moves cautiously
and "incrementally"), or they are not. If, on the other hand, the individual
iron triangles are in a divide-the-budget-yen competition with one another, as implied by the logrolling story, virtually any division of the
budget pie could arise from annual negotiations. A strict interpretation of
the budgeting-through-logroll thesis, then, implies that we cannot make
any predictions about the outcome of the process with any real confidence, beyond perhaps a "don't rock the boat" kind of prediction, which

would be equivalent to the fair-shares hypothesis that we rejected in the previous subsection.

Nonetheless, the "small" and "few" implications of incrementalism are widely held to apply to Japanese budgeting. We might be able to test these incrementalist claims by collecting budget data and assessing whether or not changes in annual allocations are in fact small and few in number. Doing so raises a number of methodological questions, such as what are the appropriate level of analysis, the proper specification of the dependent variable, and so forth (see, e.g., Natchez and Bupp 1973). For example, at what level of budgeting – ministry, agency, or line item – should we look? The higher the level of aggregation, it stands to reason, the higher the chances that budget policy will appear stable in the fair-shares and incrementalist senses, since many divergent trends for different agencies may cancel each other's effects on the aggregated budgetary unit.

Allowing that these methodological questions can be addressed satisfactorily, the next question is how we decide what cutoff makes a change small. We might agree that 1 percent is small, but what about 10, 15, or 20 percent? Are percentage changes appropriate when comparing changes in programs of radically different sizes (what if a 1-percent change in outlays for a program corresponds to a change of more than one billion yen, while in another, the same change counts for only a few million yen)? Testing "how small is small" is a hopeless task, in that we cannot nail down a "fair" test that would be accepted widely as addressing the appropriate question.

The basic incremental model presumes a great deal of stability in budgeting. Hence, we want to find tests of the "stability" notion, beyond the results we presented in Section 3.1, where we rejected "fair shares." The most common stability concept used by incrementalists is the one used by Wildavsky. Annual budgets, he suggests, are composed of two parts – a base defined by the previous year's budget, plus an "increment," a deviation from last year's budget that reflects changes in the world (Wildavsky 1964: 17). To test for incrementalism, we must assume that the changes in the world that influenced budgetary decisions last year are independent of those affecting this year's increments. This follows from Davis et al., who state that they "have chosen to view the special events of each year for each agency as random phenomena that are capable of being described by a probability density or distribution" (1966: 533). In other words, "we may represent the sum of the effects of all such events by a random variable that is an increment or decrement to the usual percentage of the previous year's appropriation" (1966: 533). What follows from this claim is that the errors from a regression of this year's budget on last year's budget will be white noise – as Davis, et al. put it, "The random variable [will be] normally distributed with mean zero and an unknown but finite variance" (1966: 533).

In its simplest statement, therefore, modeling this year's budget involves estimating a coefficient on last year's budget under the assumption that the error process is correctly specified (e.g., in equation 2, this requires us to assume that no significant explanatory variables are omitted). What do we expect of the relationship between last year's budget and this year's? Davis, et al. argued that the requests in a given year should be, on average, greater than the appropriation for the previous year (1966: 533). Hence, they expected the coefficient on last year's budget, y_{it-1}, in this regression to be greater than 1. This test differs somewhat from the more simplistic notion of incrementalism discussed above (as described in equation 2), where the incrementalists found support for their hypothesis in a finding that the coefficient on last year's budget was significantly greater than zero (B_i was positive). But, as we have mentioned, Davis et al. were modeling nominal budget figures, and they did not control for general growth in GDP and the overall budget. Hence their test was biased in favor of their hypothesis that coefficients for each spending item are greater than 1. This bias becomes apparent once we make the observation that there is in general a positive relationship between government spending and underlying trends in the economy. Indeed, they found only two "exceptions" (Davis et al. 1966: 539) to this expectation for a data set including fifty-six U.S. agencies from 1947–63.

But, as Davis, Dempster, and Wildavsky recognized, a coefficient greater than 1 in their simple model implies an explosive growth process (1966: 546). It is hard to reconcile the stability of the budget base with the "explosive growth rates" that characterize Davis et al.'s findings. Strictly speaking, if the budgetary base is stable, the coefficient on last year's budget in a regression on this year's budget should equal 1. For Japanese budgets in the postwar period, we test the hypothesis that the incremental process is "stable" – in other words, that the coefficient is equal to 1 or that the incremental process is explosive, that is, that the coefficient is greater than 1 as predicted by Davis et al. – against the alternative hypothesis that the coefficient is less than 1. Davis et al. argue that if the process is incremental, then the coefficient must be greater than or equal to 1 (1966: 539). Therefore, if we can reject the hypothesis that the coefficient is greater than or equal to 1, we can reject Davis et al.'s version of incrementalism for Japanese budgets.

We therefore would like to test the following basic model:

$$Y_{it} = B_i Y_{it-1} + e_{it} \quad (3)$$

where Y_{it} is spending for budget item i in year t and e_{it} is some small (random) deviation from the base, Y_{it-1}, last year's budget. The coefficient B_i is the subject of our test.

However, we can test the incremental hypothesis in this manner only if equation 3 is correctly specified. For example, if there are excluded variables that are correlated with Y_{it-1}, these will bias our estimate of B_i. We would not be able to interpret the results of such a regression as evidence for or against the null hypothesis (that budgets are incremental). That equation 3 is not correctly specified was recognized by Davis et al. themselves, in that they later estimated a model that also included political and economic explanatory variables in the regression (Davis, Dempster, and Wildavsky 1974).

An important excluded factor in estimating government spending would be the general growth in population and the economy that countries such as the United States and Japan have experienced over the past two or three decades. Governments have also grown, both in real terms and as a percentage of GDP, for most countries in the twentieth century. We should expect this general growth in government to be positively correlated with spending in any particular budget item; thus, not including a general-trend term in the regression will result in the estimated coefficient, B_i, being larger than the "true" coefficient B_i. We also need to include a constant term in the equation. Not including a constant will also bias the estimates of B_i (Maddala 1977).

In estimating economic time series, it is well known that many such series exhibit serial correlation. Failure to correct for serial correlation leads to estimated standard errors for B_i that are too small, leading us to incorrectly accept the null hypothesis that the process is incremental too often, especially when the estimated coefficients are positively biased. We corrected for this by also including the lagged first difference of the dependent variable, $Y_{it-1} - Y_{it-2}$. Like Davis et al., we will leave any other economic and political effects to the error term, as we assume that they are uncorrelated with the included variables (an assumption with which we are admittedly not too confident, but it simplifies our exposition here and, furthermore, biases our test in favor of the null hypothesis). Note that we do adjust for inflation by using constant yen values for budget items.

Thus, we estimated the following equation:

$$Y_{it} = a_i + B_i Y_{it-1} + D_i TREND_{it} + G_i(Y_{it-1} - Y_{it-2}) + u_{it} \quad (4).$$

where $TREND_{it}$ is a sequential counter starting at 1 for the first year in our data set, 2 for the second, and so on for program i (typically, the first year is 1952). This counter increases year by year, mimicking the effects of an annual trend in spending. The data set used to estimate equation 4 is described in the appendix to this chapter. The test is then on whether B_i is

99

greater than or equal to 1 (the incremental model) or, alternatively, less than 1.[6]

In this estimation, under the null hypothesis that the process is incremental, the distribution of the test statistic on B_i (the usual t-statistic from an OLS regression) does not have a student's t distribution because, fundamentally, the process assumed by Davis et al. is explosive – that is, the errors from the regression have infinite variance. Instead of a simple t-test, therefore, we employed a Dickey–Fuller test (Dickey and Fuller 1979; see also Fuller 1976; MacKinnon 1991). This test statistic has a distribution that accounts for the infinite variance of the errors (if the null hypothesis is true that the underlying process is nonstationary, i.e., B_i is greater than or equal to one). Coincidentally, this test statistic also biases the test results *in favor* of the null hypothesis, that is, toward finding that the process is incremental (Simms 1988).

We found that we can reject the null hypothesis that B_i is greater than or equal to 1 for more than 90 percent of the cases in our data set (for 99 of 108 Japanese budget items over the period 1952 to 1989, the coefficients were positive, but less than 1). Given the results of this test, we find almost no evidence for the Davis et al. incrementalism hypothesis for Japanese budgeting. Given that Japan has a parliamentary system, and that a single party (the LDP) has dominated postwar Japanese politics, Japan should have been one of the strongest cases for the incrementalism theory. Hence, our results also suggest that the incrementalist budgeting theory may have little utility.

3.2.3. Testing piecewise incrementalism.   Not satisfied that these results will completely convince adherents to the incrementalist approach, we conducted yet another test of incrementalism. Davis, Dempster, and Wildavsky argue that if budgeting is incremental, changes in agency budgets will tend to be "smooth." This means that the *budgeting rule* used to determine year-by-year changes for an individual agency *does not itself change* from year to year. In other words, the budget base is stable even though there may be large deviations from year to year in an agency's budget. Thus Davis et al. imply that for most agencies a single, linear regression line will well fit the entire data series – that is, that there are no kinks or discontinuities in the spending trend for the agency. Recognizing that this claim is testable, Davis et al. conducted a test for structural breaks by dividing each agency time series into two parts (breaking at "the

---

[6] Equation 5 is really just the test for a unit root in the series Y_{it}, which has been studied extensively in the econometrics literature. See White (1980), MacKinnon and White (1985), and MacKinnon (1991) for a thorough review of the problems associated with such tests and for more accurate tables for the distribution of the test statistic.

probable year of change"; Davis, Dempster, and Wildavsky 1966: 547), fitting a separate regression line to each part. They then used Chow's F-statistic to test whether or not the regression lines for the two parts were significantly different. In their simple case with only a single regressor, the test tells whether or not the coefficient on the single explanatory variable is significantly different for the two subperiods. They reported for their U.S. budget data set that "a substantial majority of cases fall into the not temporally stable and temporally unstable categories" (Davis, Dempster, and Wildavsky: 538).

Although this in itself is evidence against the incrementalist hypothesis, Davis et al. interpreted their results as indicating something akin to piecewise incrementalism. They argued that the breaks they observe often can be explained by referring to "political" events (1966: 540–543). While budget making is disturbed occasionally by exogenous events, between shocks it reverts to a characteristically "incremental" process. Of course, this implies that their original model was misspecified, and that incrementalism is at best only part of the story.

Our intent here is not to critique Davis et al. Their work provided a great advance for the field of budgetary studies in the 1960s. We return again to what they said and how they tested their model because they present the clearest statement of the incrementalist model of any we have found in the literature. We agree that a test of incrementalism should look for structural breaks (Davis et al.'s "shift points") in the estimation of agency spending parameters. The incrementalist model, strictly speaking, predicts that there should be no structural breaks. Apparently, one structural break per decade is not enough to get those who have put forth the incremental model to reject that model. We are willing to accept the Davis et al. hypothesis of piecewise stability and test for it. The piecewise incremental hypothesis, therefore, is simply that there will not be more than one structural break per decade per agency. The alternative hypothesis is that structural breaks occur more often than once in ten years.

Testing this is not as simple as running a regression for two time periods and using a Chow statistic to test whether the estimated parameters differ significantly. This test is appropriate only when the "shift point" is known (Beck 1983). An alternative method is provided by Brown, Durbin, and Evans (1975). The idea behind this test is to estimate the regression for some subperiod and use the results of that regression to forecast the next year's budget. If there are no structural breaks, the forecasts should be "good"; that is, the forecast errors will be statistically small. Conversely, if a structural break occurs in the year being forecast, the error will be large. The statistic suggested by Brown et al., called CUMSUMSQ, resolves the problems that invalidate the Chow test when the "shift point" is not known a priori.[7] Basically we are looking to see if the test statistic stays within upper and lower bounds derived by Brown et al. (for statistical tables, see Harvey 1990; for a discussion of the test, see also Beck 1983). Examples of the test statistic and the Brown, Durbin, and Evans upper and lower bounds are given in the following two figures. In Figure 5.5, we show an example of a program for which there were no significant structural breaks, *"Expenditure for Atomic Bomb Victims."* At no point in the series did the CUMSUMSQ statistic exceed its upper or lower bound (denoted by parallel lines in the figure). In Figure 5.6, we show a similar figure for the much-studied Ministry of Finance. In contrast to the *"Expenditure for Atomic Bomb Victims"* program, MOF expenditures failed the CUMSUMSQ test for most years, including every year from 1962 to 1983.

Unfortunately (or fortunately, depending on your patience), we cannot present graphs for all 107 agencies for which we conducted the test. Therefore, we simply summarize the results of the CUMSUMSQ test. We found that the vast majority of the cases show clear evidence of multiple structural breaks each decade in the budget time series: 85 of 107 agencies or programs showed three or more statistically significant structural breaks.[8] Of the remaining twenty-two cases, seven had one or two statistically significant breaks. Thus, again, very few of the Japanese budgetary items we examined exhibited the fundamental characteristics that would allow us to accept the hypothesis that they were generated by an incremental process. Here too, then, our results indicate that we can, with a high degree of confidence, reject the incrementalist budgeting model for Japan.

3.3. Nonretrenchment

The third basic concept in the existing literature on Japanese budgeting is the difficulty of retrenchment: imposing cutbacks on existing beneficiaries of budget programs, particularly when those beneficiaries are strong supporters of the LDP. Even Calder, who argues that political choice and responsiveness shapes budgetary outcomes, says that pressure groups exercise "near veto power over change in entitlement programs" (1988b: 375). If some programs are allowed to grow faster than average under a fixed total budget, others necessarily are squeezed.

[7] The CUMSUMSQ statistic for each agency is a vector with T elements (one for each subperiod, starting from year k+1, where k is the number of parameters in the model) calculated as follows: for each subperiod $(1, \ldots, t)$, we calculated and summed a series of forecast errors (first forecasting the t_kth observation based on having observed periods 1 through t_{k-1}, then adding t_k to the observed data and forecasting t_{k+1}, and so forth up to year t. That sum is then divided by the sum of forecast errors for the same iterative process for the entire period through year T.

[8] We dropped one item because its time series was too short for our test.

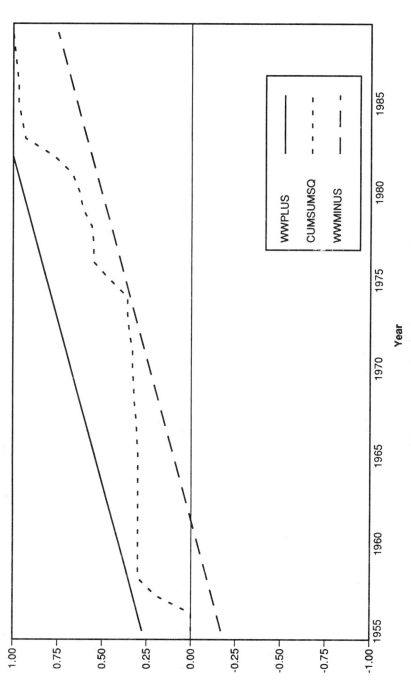

Figure 5.5. *CUMSUMSO test for expenditure for atomic bomb victims*

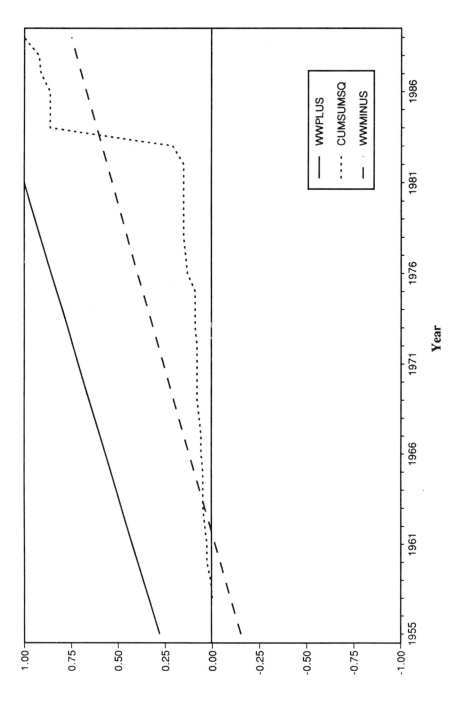

Figure 5.6. *CUMSUMSO test for Ministry of Finance*

Cutting existing benefits and entitlements is difficult in any democracy, of course. The evidence from our detailed study of budgetary outcomes suggests that it is no more difficult in Japan than elsewhere. Indeed, it appears that it may even be easier: From the end of the 1970s, when the budget deficit suddenly expanded, the LDP in fact cut back on the benefits supplied to several old support groups as it worked to bring the budget deficit under control and diversify its constituency base.

Spending on public works was cut drastically in the 1980s, even though this hurt building contractors, who had become a crucial source of electoral support for the politicians of the ruling party (see, e.g., Curtis 1988: 69–70). From a peak of 16.9 percent in 1979, the share of the general account budget going to public works was cut nearly in half, declining to 9.9 percent by 1990 (*Zaisei Tokei* 1990: 208–217). Noguchi's seemingly ad hoc explanation that "politicians are more interested in the geographical allocation of the public works budget than in its total size" (Noguchi 1991: 136–137) is of no solace to the politician who cannot get a dam or old folks' home built in his or her district because some other politician has received the only project available.[9]

Other examples of cutbacks abound. For instance, agricultural price supports were reduced beginning in the late 1970s (Noguchi 1991: 136; but see also, *Kuni no Yosan* 1986: 920; 1989: 908, 916; cf. Curtis 1988: 58); the level of central-to-local government subsidies was drawn down throughout the eighties (*Kuni no Yosan* 1989: 244–245; *Zaisei Seisaku Kenkyukai* 1991: 111, 121); and increases in government spending on health care and pensions lagged behind the growth in eligible beneficiaries (Fujii and Reich 1988; *Kuni no Yosan* 1989: 98; Reich 1990; *Zaisei Seisaku Kenkyukai* 1985: 95; and see, in general, Noguchi 1991).

The argument that politics made cutting of benefits to old programs and beneficiaries impossible while economic and demographic factors alone explain increased spending is untenable. As we have seen, many policy changes have been made, including cuts and shifts in the costs and benefits of programs. Nor are economic and demographic effects, important though they are in all countries, automatically translated into outcomes: A number of efforts have been made to counteract the effects of Japan's aging population, and more will undoubtedly be made in the future. Japanese budget makers can change programs, and are able to retrench even in the face of opposition.[10]

---

[9] It should be noted that the experience of the 1980s also contradicts Noguchi's earlier (1979, 1980a) arguments that public works expenditures are allocated in an apolitical way to optimize social-overhead capital and counteract business cycles.

[10] While Noguchi's (1991) argument that retrenchment is well-nigh impossible in Japan is untenable, he is on target in pointing out that much of the reduction in the deficit in the 1980s came about through increases in corporate and individual income taxes and social

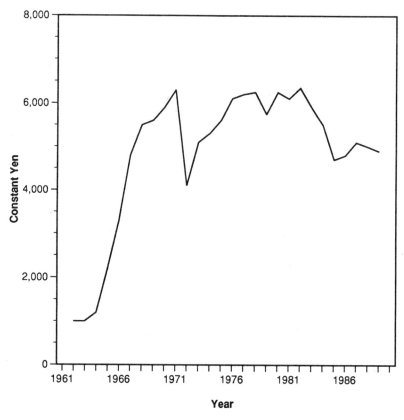

Figure 5.7. *Expenditures for the Agency of Natural Resources and Energy, in constant yen, 1961–89*

It is worth noting that successful retrenchment is not just a novel phenomenon made possible by the administrative reform movement of the 1980s. Despite the prognostications of the iron-triangles model, retrenchment has been a common occurrence in Japanese budgeting. Figures 5.7 and 5.8 offer two examples of agencies whose budgets (in constant 1970 yen) have been retrenched at least twice each. In Figure 5.7, we show that the Natural Resources and Energy Agency in MITI was cut severely in the early 1970s and then again in the 1980s. The budget for the Ministry of Construction, illustrated in Figure 5.8, shows a similar pattern.

security contribution rates. These are hardly apolitical acts, however, and the ability of the LDP leadership to resist tax-cutting pressures from backbenchers and interest groups has been notable. See Muramatsu and Mabuchi (1991).

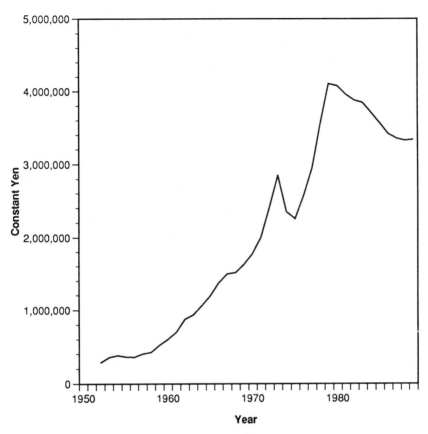

Figure 5.8. *Expenditures for the Ministry of Construction in constant yen,*
1952–89

Evidence of retrenchment can be found even well before the 1970s.
Sixty-four of the items in our sample of Japanese agencies and ministries
had their budgets cut in the 1950s.[11] Many of these agencies and ministries were scaled back for several years in a row. For example, *personnel*
supply management in the Defense Facilities Administration Agency was
cut in 1954, 1955, 1956, 1958, and 1959. Spending for weapons and
vehicles in the Defense Agency was cut in 1954 and from 1957 to 1959.
The MOF itself was scaled back from 1954 to 1956; agricultural promotion in MAFF was retrenched in each year from 1956 to 1958; and subsidies for maritime transport were cut every year from 1955 to 1958.
Similar cutbacks occurred in the sixties, and in the 1970s, 84 items of 110

[11] All comparisons refer to 1970 constant yen amounts.

in our sample were cut at least once. Moreover, almost every item in our sample was retrenched year after year in the eighties. The cuts were most widespread and steepest between 1983 and 1986, showing the very real impact of the administrative reform movement.

4. CONCLUSION

Existing accounts of the Japanese budgetary process stress the inability of the LDP to make political choices, especially its inability or unwillingness to impose burdens on existing constituents. In some accounts, the main sources of resistance are the elite bureaucracies, either the Ministry of Finance or an alliance of it with spending ministries.

Many accounts of the budget process stress that the Ministry of Finance plays the central role in budget-making decisions. We made little effort in this chapter to test the claim of MOF dominance since, in its usual form, the argument is almost impossible to falsify. It is undeniably true that MOF has been delegated many budget-making functions and duties. If some policy is enacted over the opposition of particular politicians or subgovernments, it is easy to claim that MOF is responsible.

An examination of the degree to which the MOF has been able to enact its key preferences, however, provides a better handle on this question. The MOF is said to have resisted the trend toward ever-increasing deficit spending from 1965 to the late 1970s; yet it failed. It tried to persuade the LDP to introduce a new value-added tax in 1979; again, it failed. A resurrected VAT was then watered down into the consumption tax under further electoral pressure, finally achieving passage in 1989. And the defense and foreign aid budgets increased rapidly in the 1980s, despite MOF conservatism.

Further, the MOF-dominance thesis gives us little insight into the timing of various policy changes. The MOF strove throughout the 1980s to reduce the issuance of bonds, yet the deficit-reduction account decreased in the mid-1980s before increasing in the late 1980s. In some years strong tax receipts led to large supplementary budgets; in other years, the extra revenue was used to retire government bonds. It is difficult to explain these differences by looking at the MOF alone.

This is not to say that the MOF never wins any battles; clearly, it does win some. But if subgovernments (spending ministries backed by interest groups and rank-and-file politicians) sometimes lose the battle for budgetary resources to the MOF, it may behoove us to ask why. The Ministry of Finance is clearly a crucial player in the budgetary system, but it does not act on its own, and it is not free to follow its own objectives at the expense of the goals of the ruling party, whether particularistic or collective. It is the LDP, through its parliamentary majorities, that has the constitutional authority and the electoral incentive to govern budget making.

Particularly in recent years, the dominant interpretation of Japanese policy making has stressed the strength and resilience of subgovernments, or iron triangles, of bureaucrats, politicians, and interest groups in each policy area. These subgovernments, it is said, tenaciously resist efforts to impose spending limits or coordinate policy across subgovernmental boundaries. Given the absence of political leadership and coordination, the only way to write the budget has been to rely on various mechanical rules – balanced budgets, equal shares, zero ceilings – whether imposed by the MOF or the administrative reform movement. Nobody actually makes choices: Only inertia, mechanical rules, economic fluctuations, and demographic trends can explain how the budget is made.

These explanations, however, "explain" the wrong outcomes. Closer examination of Japanese budgetary expenditures and related policies reveals that changes in items, programs, and shares are much more dynamic than existing accounts allow. Clearly, as Campbell (1977) and others have shown, politicians, bureaucrats, and interest groups form subgovernments in Japan just as they do in the United States and elsewhere. Such specialization is rational and understandable. The crucial question is whether the triangles are really made of iron. Our evidence on the Japanese budget suggests not. We tested a variety of "stability" notions, including fair-shares budgeting, incremental budgeting, and the rule of non-retrenchment, that we drew from the existing literature on Japan. In each case, we were able to reject soundly the stable-budgeting hypotheses.

Existing explanations for Japanese budgeting, therefore, cannot account for the dynamism we have found in the budgetary data. The most promising avenue for such a new approach is to reexamine the influence of party politics. Recent work by Calder (1988b) on the way the LDP has historically paid off valued constituents whenever it gets into electoral trouble; by Kohno and Nishizawa (1990) on the timing of public works projects; and by Mabuchi (1989) on the impact of the partisan composition of the Diet on budget expenditures, all suggest that politics and partisan influences exert a major impact on budget outcomes in Japan.

Of course parties try to help their constituents. To do so, they seek to acquire and allocate governmental resources. And, of course, policy making is messy and conflictual. That does not mean, however, that choice and leadership are impossible. If it did, it would be difficult to explain how the LDP has remained in power as long as it has, and how it managed the transition from the political decline and budgetary chaos of the 1970s to the austerity, fiscal reconstruction, and political recovery of the 1980s. The important issue is how parties balance their diverse constituencies, conflicting demands for particularistic and collective goods, the desires of various groups for spending versus popular resistance to taxation, and so forth. To go beyond the current myths about the Japanese budgetary process requires a model of party organization that incorporates these tensions.

APPENDIX

Methods

We selected data to cover two major flows of funds in the complex Japanese budgetary system: expenditures in the general account, which is funded by tax and bond revenues, and subsidies to the various special accounts from the general account.

In selecting individual items, whether items in the general accounts (*ko*), or special accounts receiving subsidies from the general account, we followed the following principles: (1) In order to ensure statistical robustness, we eliminated item, special accounts, or public agencies covering less than ten consecutive years; most items existed throughout the whole period, or started in the 1950s or 1960s and then continued through 1989. (2) We picked at least one item from each ministry or agency; for most ministries we picked between four and ten items. (3) We tried to include virtually all of the major spending items in the budgets, as well as a sample of medium-sized and smaller items. (4) We tried to include a broad range of substantive types, including some items that are clearly public in nature (Board of Audit, Meteorological Agency, national pensions), others that seem to be "pork barrel" in nature (Hokkaido fishing port facilities, industrial plumbing facilities), and some "semipublic goods" in between (industrial relocation promotion, career change planning).

The number of items in the annual general account budget has ranged from 400 to 500, increasing somewhat over time; in 1986, for example, the number was 484. Our sample of eighty-eight individual items thus accounted for about one-fifth of all items. The total spending accounted for by our item was nearly 100 percent of total general account spending in 1986.

In the time period we studied, sixty-two separate special accounts appeared; twelve either lasted less than ten years (most less than five) or were transferred to other accounts, leaving fifty long-lived accounts. The special accounts are extremely diverse, and many are essentially accounting conventions. Our sample covers fourteen of the more substantively important special accounts, including six of the thirteen special accounts with gross expenditures greater than one trillion yen in 1991.

110

Sources

General Account data are taken from the basic official *Ippan Kaikei* documents as submitted to the Diet by the Ministry of Finance on behalf of the cabinet. These documents are highly detailed (850–900 pages each) and hard to acquire. To our knowledge, no previous academic study of the Japanese budget has used these primary documents. These documents offer a crucial advantage over all other sources: They are the only account of all expenditures at the item (*ko*) level (the more commonly known "important item" [*Shuyo Keihi*] listed in the *Kuni no Yosan* and elsewhere are too highly aggregated and subject to periodic redefinition). All figures are on an initial budget (*tosho*) basis, that is, before any revisions by the Diet, and before any supplemental budgets. The lack of Diet revisions is not a serious problem, since revisions have been rare in the postwar period: 1948 (before the period considered here), 1953–55, and two years since the formation of the LDP (1972 and 1977). Moreover, even in those years, revisions affected only a tiny fraction of the budget. Supplementary budgets are also relatively unimportant (in the 1960s the net addition to main budget expenditures was about 4.2 percent, in the 1980s only 3.1 percent), and omitting them greatly simplifies data collection, since in many years there have been two or even three supplemental budgets. Since the composition of items sometimes changes over time, we added and subtracted subitems as necessary to ensure consistency over time. Generally speaking, we took the item as constituted in recent years and corrected as necessary as we went back through the data. A complete list of descriptions of the item (and other more detailed information) is available on request from the authors.

Special Accounts data come from the semiofficial and widely available *Kuni no Yosan;* in this case there are no problems of excessive aggregation and inconsistent definition. These are also on an "initial budget" basis. For the fourteen special accounts in our sample we measured only subsidies from the general account, since the overall budgets of the accounts include operating and other incomes not derived from national budgets. *Kuni no Yosan* does not provide a summary figure for subsidies, so we derived them by summing the subsidies to each of the subaccounts (*kanjo*). The transactions between general accounts and special accounts are sometimes complex; in order to avoid any possible double-counting, we never use the two types of accounts in the same equation.

Economic and demographic data come from the five-volume *Nihon Choki Tokei Soran/Historical Statistics of Japan* and the annual *Nihon Tokei Nenkan/Japan Statistical Yearbook*, both bilingual.

EXPENDITURE ITEMS

GENERAL ACCOUNT
Total Expenditures
A. Imperial Household
B. Diet
    1. House of Representatives
    2. House of Councillors
C. Court of Justice
D. Board of Audit
E. Cabinet
F. Prime minister's office
    Management and Coordination Agency
    1. Pensions (veterans; also MPs and government officials)
    Hokkaido Development Agency
    2. Hokkaido road construction
    3. Hokkaido fishing port facilities
    4. Hokkaido housing construction industry
    Defense Agency
    5. Weapons and vehicles
    6. Aircraft
    7. Shipbuilding
    8. Facilities maintenance
    9. Research and development
    Defense Facilities Administration Agency
    10. Facilities operation and related expenses
    11. Personnel supply management
    Science and Technology Agency
    12. Promotion of research into peaceful uses for nuclear power
    13. Science and Technology Agency research laboratory
    14. Science and technology promotion
    Okinawa Development Agency
    15. Okinawa education promotion
    National Land Agency
    16. Coordination of national comprehensive land development
G. Ministry of Justice
    Justice Agency
    1. Office of Administrative Reform
H. Ministry of Foreign Affairs
    Ministry of Foreign Affairs (internal)
    1. Economic cooperation
    2. International allotments and other expenditures
    3. Operating expenses for international cooperation organizations

I. Ministry of Finance
Ministry of Finance (internal)
 1. Economic cooperation
 2. Supplement to People's Finance Corporation
 3. Ministry of Finance (internal)
National Tax Administration
 4. Tax Administration Office

J. Ministry of Education
Ministry of Education (internal)
 1. National treasury subsidies for educational expenses for the handicapped
 2. Promotion of school education
 3. Maintenance of public educational facilities
 4. Scholarship expenses
 5. Supplements to private schools
 6. Science promotion

K. Ministry of Health and Welfare
Ministry of Health and Welfare (internal)
 1. Research and development
 2. Expenditure for atomic bomb victims
 3. Public health and sanitation
 4. Lifestyle protection
 5. Support for the disabled
 6. Welfare for the elderly
 7. Support for women
 8. Support for children
 9. National supplement to Social Insurance Fund
 10. Subsidy to National Health Insurance Plan
 11. Aid to bereaved families and families of internees
 12. Maintenance of environmental health and sanitation facilities

L. Ministry of Agriculture, Forestry, and Fisheries
Ministry of Agriculture, Forestry, and Fisheries (Internal)
 1. Agricultural promotion
 2. Strategic restructuring of agriculture
 3. Agricultural pensions
 4. Silk cultivation and horticulture promotion
 5. Diffusion of agriculture improvement
 6. Strengthening of wet rice agriculture
 7. Promotion of animal husbandry
 8. Sugar price stabilization
 9. Strategic planning of food product distribution
Forestry Agency
 10. Promotion of forestry

Fisheries Agency
11. Promotion of fisheries
12. Fishing harbor facilities
M. Ministry of International Trade and Industry
Ministry of International Trade and Industry (internal)
1. Economic cooperation
2. Promotion of industrial relocation
3. Promotion of the computer industry
4. Industrial plumbing facilities
Agency of Industrial Science and Technology
5. Promotion of mining and manufacturing technology
6. Large-scale industrial research and development
7. Agency of Industrial Science and Technology Experimental Research Laboratory
Agency of Natural Resources and Energy
8. Measures for underground resources
Small and Medium Enterprise Agency
9. Measures for small and medium enterprises
N. Ministry of Transportation
Ministry of Transportation (internal)
1. Subsidies to account of Japan National Railway
2. Subsidies to Japan National Railway Construction Corp.
3. Subsidies for railroad track maintenance
4. Coastline enterprises
5. Subsidies for maritime transportation
6. Office of meteorological administration
7. Stabilization of shipbuilding industry
8. Promotion of employment for deckhands
O. Ministry of Posts and Telecommunications
Integrated Telecommunications Research Lab
1. Integrated Telecommunications Research Lab
Local Telecommunications Administration Bureau
2. Local Telecommunications Administration Bureau
P. Ministry of Labor
Ministry of Labor (internal)
1. Unemployment countermeasures
2. Career change planning
Labor Protection Office
3. Labor Protection Office
Employment Security Office
4. Employment Security Office
Q. Ministry of Construction
Ministry of Construction (internal)

    1. Strategic planning regarding crumbling of steep inclines and related expenses
    2. Coastline enterprises
    3. Housing construction
    4. City planning
    5. Work related to stream and river disasters
    6. Restoration of streams and rivers after disasters

R. Ministry of Home Affairs
  Ministry of Home Affairs (internal)
    1. Subsidies for principal and interest on local debt
    2. Subsidies to cities, towns, and villages that are the sites of nationally owned and operated facilities
    3. Adjustment grants to cities, towns, and villages that are the sites of [defense] facilities

SPECIAL ACCOUNTS
    1. National Forest Service
    2. National land improvement
    3. Harbor improvement
    4. Airport improvement
    5. Road improvement
    6. Flood control
    7. Welfare insurance
    8. Sailor's insurance
    9. National pensions
  10. Laborer's insurance
  11. National hospitals
  12. Foodstuff control
  13. Measures for the improvement of farm management
  14. Coal, petroleum, and alternative energy

PART II

Politics and policy

6

Telecommunications policy: structure, process, outcomes

ROGER G. NOLL AND FRANCES MCCALL ROSENBLUTH

In all nations, telecommunications is among the most heavily regulated industries. Until the 1970s, most nations had publicly owned telephone companies, operating either as part of a ministry that included the post office or as a quasi-independent, government-owned corporation that was extensively regulated by such a ministry. A few democracies permitted telephone companies to be private, for-profit corporations, but in these cases the industry was an extensively regulated monopoly.

During the 1980s, the structure of the telecommunications industry and its regulation underwent massive reorganization in most Organisation for Economic Cooperation and Development (OECD) countries, and even in many developing nations. The reasons for this transformation are many, and their full explication is beyond the scope of this chapter.[1] In brief, amazingly rapid technological progress in telecommunications and in the entire microelectronics and information sector made traditional methods of providing and regulating telecommunications obsolete. In response to these changes, most countries have adopted policy changes that are broadly similar. Although the details of the reforms vary among countries, two important generalizations are accurate. First, the emerging consensus is that private ownership is superior to public ownership in producing efficient, low-cost, technologically progressive telecommunications systems. Second, most governments have come to believe that in some parts of the industry, competition is superior to monopoly.

Japan and the United States are not exceptions to these generalizations, although they have adopted very different approaches to reform. Liberalization of telecommunications policy began in the United States during

---

[1] For a discussion of the reasons for change in the United States, see Peltzman (1989) and Joskow and Noll (1993). These essays reflect the general consensus in the scholarly literature that the regulatory reforms of the 1970s and 1980s were not the result of an ideological shift to neoconservatism, but instead were brought about by changes in technology and the economic conditions of regulated industries.

119

the 1960s, through a series of decisions by the Federal Communications Commission (FCC) – the federal regulator of telecommunications – and the federal courts, that introduced competition into long distance service and terminal equipment.[2] American policy makers now are debating the last logical step in liberalization, the highly controversial commitment to competition and, eventually, deregulation in local service. In Japan, liberalization began in 1986 with the privatization of Nippon Telegraph and Telephone (NTT) and Kokusai Denshin Denwa (KDD), and the introduction of both value-added and facilities-based competitors shortly thereafter. Unlike the United States, Japan's liberalization started at roughly the same time as other advanced industrialized democracies adopted similar policies. And, while Japan, like the United States, has introduced structural competition in to almost every component of the industry, the Japanese system remains heavily regulated and only partially privatized. U.S. policy, by contrast, has been to deregulate whenever a market is structurally competitive.

This chapter explores the similarities and differences between Japan and the United States in the structure, process, objectives, and consequences of liberalization. Japan and the United States profess to have the same basic objectives in telecommunications policy, but in practice their policies are very different and produce different consequences for both users of telecommunications services and manufacturers of equipment. In our view, these policy differences arise from variations in the political structures of the two countries. In the United States, the regulatory system "stacks the deck" in favor of end users, especially rural consumers and information-intensive business customers. In Japan, the structure and process is designed to favor firms that manufacture telecommunications equipment and, among end users, rural customers and information-intensive industries.

Which policy orientation is "better" depends on debatable value judgments as well as cause–effect economic relationships; however, objectively, the main differences in outcomes are that the Japanese system charges substantially higher prices and provides less service, but generates proportionately greater sales revenues for Japanese makers of telecommunications equipment. One purpose of this chapter is to compare the industry's performance indicators in some detail, and to explain why the policy institutions in each country lead to these differences in outcomes.

---

[2] The liberalization process in the United States actually began in 1959, when the "Above 890" decision by the Federal Communications Commission allowed companies to build microwave networks for their own private use. Then, between 1968 and 1970, a series of decisions by the FCC and the courts permitted competition in terminal equipment, long distance, and value-added services. For details, see Noll (1979) and Noam (1983b).

1. POLITICS, ECONOMICS, AND TELECOMMUNICATIONS

The centerpiece of our analysis of telecommunications policy in Japan and the United States is the political process, and the policy objectives of elected political officials. The two main premises of our argument are as follows. First, a nation's political institutions, such as the organizational structure of the government and the electoral system, have an important influence on the policy objectives of elected governments. Second, technical and economic reality are most productively viewed as establishing limits and creating trade-offs that constrain the attainment of the policy objectives of a government. The main burden of this section is to explain the implications of both premises for telecommunications policy making in Japan and the United States.

1.1. Politics and Policy

Chapters 1 and 2 provide the basic theoretical framework for our analysis of the policy significance of the differences in political structure between Japan and the United States. Here we seek to expand and embellish these points to focus on their implications for telecommunications policy. The key differences between Japan and the United States that are the focus of our analysis are as follows.

1.1.1. Federalism. In Japan, all power to regulate infrastructural industries like telecommunications resides in the national government, whereas in the United States policy authority is divided between the state and federal governments.[3] The importance of this difference is immediately apparent from the analogy between states in a federal structure and nations within an international trading system. In a federal system, each state seeks to advantage its own citizens at the expense of citizens of other states and nations. Basic access and other local services are consumed almost exclusively by residents of the community that contains the local exchange. In contrast, on average half of long distance customers reside

---

[3] The U.S. federal government is constitutionally entitled to assert jurisdiction over all aspects of the regulation of infrastructural industries through its power to regulate interstate commerce. Because interstate services share the use of local-exchange systems, the latter is in interstate commerce and so could be federally regulated. But historically, the states were the first to engage in regulation, and the first federal statute on economic regulation, the Interstate Commerce Act, was passed in part to reassert the right of states to regulate after the Supreme Court ruled in the *Wabash, St. L. and Pac. Ry. v. Illinois (1886)* case that states could not regulate intrastate railroad service if the railroad also provided interstate service. All subsequent federal economic regulatory statutes have preserved a role for state regulation, including the Communications Act of 1934, which gives states the exclusive right to regulate local access and intrastate long distance telephone service.

elsewhere, and far less than half of the telecommunications equipment that is used within a state is actually manufactured there. Likewise, a local-exchange company is more closely identified with a state than are long distance carriers and national information-service suppliers, which are more dispersed. Hence, all else equal, state regulation will be prone to biases in favor of local services and local-exchange carriers, whereas national regulation will give greater weight to interstate services and equipment manufacturing. By the same logic, national regulators are more likely to favor domestic services at the expense of international service, but less likely to favor local service at the expense of national services and equipment manufacturing.

1.1.2. Government structure. The main differences in the organization of government between the United States and Japan are the role of the courts and the relationships between legislative bodies and executive institutions. Concentration of most authority in a single parliamentary body composed of members elected from different constituencies, as in Japan, makes decision making easier and more flexible, but it also enhances the influence of particularistic interests. An important implication of the U.S. system, with bicameralism and an independent, nationally elected executive leader, is that it leads to more explicit conflict among elected officials, which in turn creates a more formalized relationship with the bureaucracy, and a greater reliance on the courts to review bureaucratic decisions and to resolve policy disputes. In telecommunications, U.S. regulatory decision making is procedurally complex, and is carefully scrutinized – often reversed – by the courts.[4] By contrast, regulatory procedures in Japan are informal, confidential, and with few exceptions unlikely to be scrutinized by the judiciary.[5]

1.1.3. Electoral system. In the United States, both state legislatures and the federal House of Representatives are elected from single-member districts, with the winner chosen by plurality in almost all cases. The U.S.

---

[4] The nature and scope of judicial review in the United States is governed by the constitutional guarantee (Fifth Amendment) that a person cannot be deprived of the use of property without due process, the Administrative Procedures Act of 1946, procedural provisions of substantive laws like the Communications Act of 1934, and court decisions that embellish these provisions. The court has actively supervised state and federal regulation since the beginning of the nineteenth century. States, too, are subject to the constitutional protection (Fourteenth Amendment) of due process and their own administrative legislation. To a first approximation, standing is granted by the courts to anyone who is materially affected by a regulatory decision. See Shapiro (1988: 45).

[5] Judicial review is governed by the Administrative Case Litigation Law of 1963. In most cases, standing is given only to the person or company that is the subject of a ruling, and even then, if a statute confers broad authority on an agency, the court normally grants discretion to the agency in interpreting its statutory authority and mandate. For more details, see Upham (1987) and Tanakadate (1986).

Senate has dual-member districts (states), but each senator is elected in a separate election, again nearly always on the basis of a plurality of the votes.[6] In Japan, the electoral system is in the process of being redesigned; however, during the period of liberalization in telecommunications policy, the members of the more powerful Diet branch, the House of Representatives, represented multimember districts, with the winners being the leaders in an election based on a single nontransferable vote (SNTV). In this system, some Diet members were elected with as little as 10 percent of the popular vote in their districts.

Both electoral systems give candidates an especially strong incentive to advocate narrow, special-interest policies in return for campaign contributions. These contributions can be used to engage in extensive advertising and to provide personal favors for constituents, thereby increasing an officeholder's electoral security through the development of a personal vote through name recognition. Moreover, candidates can use campaign contributions to increase their personal welfare, through either personal expenditures or expenditures on behalf of other candidates that increases the power of the legislator who provides them. The incentive to engage in such behavior is present in any system in which voters choose from among individual candidates rather than parties, but it is stronger in a system of multimember districts with SNTV. In this system candidates can succeed electorally by focusing their attention (and expenditures) on much narrower interest groups. Hence, they can advocate policies that benefit a small proportion of the population and still achieve electoral security. Of course, whether politicians will respond to these incentives depends on the systems of controls on campaign expenditures, including the vigor with which they are enforced. While both countries have relatively ineffective controls on campaign finance, the Japanese system, at least through the 1993 election, had much weaker enforcement than the U.S. system. Consequently, although in both countries legislators raise substantial campaign contributions for both electoral success and personal welfare, the amount raised by Diet members, especially members of the LDP, was substantially larger than the contributions received by members of the House of Representatives. In Japan, important sources of these contributions are the large trading combines that, among other things, have affiliates that manufacture telecommunications equipment and provide various communications services.

To summarize, the legislative systems of both countries accord greater political power to organized particularistic interests with significant economic stakes in government policy decisions. The structural bias in favor

---

[6] States determine the details of their election systems for House and Senate, and in a few cases a runoff system requires that the winner obtain an absolute majority of the votes cast.

of organized groups is somewhat greater in Japan for several reasons: (1) The absence of a formal, open policy-making process and extensive judicial review makes policy deals with particularistic interests more difficult to detect; (2) Japan lacks the checks and balances that arise from an independent executive and a small, coequal legislative branch, both of which have larger, more heterogeneous constituencies; (3) The Japanese electoral rules in force until 1993 (multimember districts with SNTV) forced the LDP to divide the vote among multiple candidates in most districts, which was partly accomplished by having candidates specialize in different policies in order to cater to different interests; and (4) The concentration of authority in the national government is inherently less favorable to consumers and other localized interests because they are less well organized in national policy making than in state/prefectural or local politics.

The regulatory-policy implications of these core differences in the political system are straightforward. Both countries are likely to care about the efficiency of their infrastructural industries, but their policies will also reflect their distributive objectives. In pursuing both goals, their regulatory systems and policy outcomes should reflect the differences in their political systems in three ways.

First, when the ruling coalition in Japan wants to change policy, it ought to be able to do so more quickly because it has fewer checks and balances. Moreover, the Japanese policy-implementation process ought to be more flexible because the close connection of the ruling party to the bureaucracy in a one-house parliamentary system removes the need for formal process in the bureaucracy. Because the Japanese governmental system contains fewer veto points and procedural requirements, Japan can move more quickly in making major alterations in policy, such as decisions to introduce competition, to privatize, to adopt network standards, or to change pricing methods.

Second, because the administrative process in Japan is more flexible and more easily controlled by the parliamentary majority than is the case in the United States, Japanese political leaders should be more prone to use regulation for distributive policies that benefit organized economic interests. Moreover, in Japan the absence of federalism should advantage national service and manufacturing companies at the expense of local service. The local-service bias in the United States means not just lower prices to consumers, but also prices that reflect distributive politics in a state: a bias in favor of rural communities and local industries that use information services intensively, such as financial services, especially in comparison to customer groups, national service providers, and equipment companies located outside a state. In Japan, the distributive bias should reflect national politics, which favor rural interests (as in the

United States) and manufacturing exports, especially in high-technology industries, at the expense of the purely domestic economy and consumers.

Third, elected political officials in Japan should find it easier to benefit personally from telecommunications policy because the same informal, largely invisible administrative system that accords flexibility also makes political corruption more difficult to detect. Thus, the Japanese regulatory system, all else equal (including the integrity of political officials), is likely to be more scandal ridden and more all-encompassing. A larger, more comprehensive regulatory system creates greater opportunities for political leaders to exercise gatekeeping roles, through which they can obtain personal or electoral favors, and a more informal, less visible system makes the costly and even corrupt aspects of such a policy less likely to have negative political consequences.

1.2. The economic constraints

Telecommunications policy involves three types of economic issues: structure, prices, and fiscal status. Structure refers to decisions about entry and exit in markets: whether the players are government entities or private firms, and which players can own which types of telecommunications facilities, can provide which services, and can sell which types of equipment. Price policy has two elements: setting a ceiling on a firm's total revenues, and hence on average prices; and determining the price structure, or the relative prices for different services and customer classes.

Fiscal status refers to the connection of telecommunications services to direct expenditures and revenues by the government. In telecommunications, structural and pricing policies are the primary means for achieving the political objectives of government officials. Obviously, these policies allocate economic burdens and benefits among the players in the industry, including its customers, and so are essential to the distributive objectives of the government. Pricing policies are also closely tied to a government's fiscal objectives, for a company cannot provide revenue for other government activities unless its prices accommodate the transfer.

An important factor affecting telecommunications policy is the nature of demand. For most citizens and all businesses, the demand for basic access – installation plus the monthly fee before any call charges – is highly inelastic, whereas the demand for calling and information services is elastic.[7] This economic reality sharply constrains a stated policy objective in almost all nations: universal service, which means that service is univer-

---

[7] Demand is inelastic if a change in price causes a smaller percentage change in the quantity of service that is purchased. In advanced economies, the best estimates of demand elasticity are that a doubling of access price reduces the access by only a few percent, but that a change in the price of calling causes a larger percentage change in usage.

sally available and affordable, so that anyone who wants it can have it. Inelastic demand makes achieving universal service through subsidies very expensive – large subsidies are required to achieve small gains in the number of subscribers. Thus, the main effect of subsidizing access is re-distributional, whereas an implicit tax on usage to finance this subsidy imposes social costs through reduced efficiency because it discourages calls that consumers would buy at a price that exceeds the cost of supplying them.[8]

Although telecommunications policy is a playing field for distributive politics, three factors enhance the standing of efficiency considerations in the policy-making process. First, like other infrastructural industries, tele-communications derives political salience from its ubiquitous economic linkages. All industries and nearly all consumers use communications services, giving the entire society an economic stake in a well-functioning system.

Second, telecommunications, like most but not all infrastructural industries – for example, not like freight shipping – is a relatively homogeneous consumer good with approximately the same price everywhere. Hence, citizens, the press, and political officials can easily and cheaply use the performance of the telecommunications sector as an index of the state of the economy and government economic policy, giving the industry a political visibility and importance that extends beyond the stakes of individuals and interest groups in any particular policy decision. As a result, telecommunications policy is somewhat less likely to be completely controlled by the narrow interests with a large stake in the industry than is the case for many other economic regulatory policies.

Third, of all infrastructural industries, telecommunications has the most substantial linkage to high-technology manufacturing. Telecommunications service providers and their customers constitute a large fraction of the market for microelectronics-based products. Because the information sector is experiencing extremely rapid technological progress, a moribund telecommunications industry can handicap a nation's economic growth.

The tension in telecommunications policy arises from the fact that economic constraints force conflicts among the political objectives of elected officials. Specifically, distributive objectives, short-term cost minimization, and economic growth are not fully compatible. As one example of trade-offs among these objectives, in choosing policies about pricing and facilities ownership, a government must strike a balance between short-term cost minimization and technological progress, in that the latter is

---

[8] For an explanation of how and why state regulators nevertheless try to cross-subsidize access from toll tariffs, see Noll (1985).

induced by letting innovators set prices above their production costs. Likewise, regulators who choke off low-cost bypass of local telephone companies may keep access prices lower, but harm the competitiveness of information-intensive industries. Or, if regulators introduce price competition among carriers, they undermine the ability of service providers to subsidize a favored group. A government that wants to subsidize favored groups must keep some prices above costs, which in turn usually requires protecting a monopoly or managing a cartel.

1.3. Implications for performance

By combining political and economic analysis, we can make several predictions about differences between Japan and the United States in the performance of the telecommunications sector. To summarize the main conclusions: Both nations should care about technical progress and economic efficiency, but their distributive biases should produce different policies. Japan should focus more on the implications of telecommunications policy with respect to the health of its high-technology manufacturing industries, reflecting the priority accorded these interests in national politics. The United States should focus more on telephone prices and service quality. Thus, in the United States, not only do we expect prices to be lower, but we expect to find that businesses will face fewer roadblocks against constructing their own systems and bypassing the public network.

We also expect Japanese telecommunications service companies to spend more on equipment, using higher service prices to pay for more equipment at higher procurement prices from the telecommunications equipment industry. Moreover, we do not expect to find that the decision to permit multifirm participation in a market will be accompanied by one to permit competition to occur, for true competition would undermine the process by which telecommunications service firms support the profits of equipment companies through procurement. We expect large businesses – equipment manufacturers and intensive users of telecommunications – to derive more of the benefits of liberalization and multifirm participation in Japanese compared with U.S. industry.

2. APPLYING THE THEORY: POLITICS AND PROCEDURES

The preceding section provides several predictions about the differences between Japan and the United States in telecommunications policy during the liberalization period. This section examines the processes and outcomes of telecommunications policy during the liberalization period to determine whether the differences between the countries conform to these predictions.

2.1. Regulatory structure and process

The structure and process of regulatory agencies are the organizational and procedural aspects of decision making. The elements of structure and process that are important here are the institutional arrangements of telecommunications regulation that enable an elected government to retain control over policy while delegating its day-to-day implementation to civil servants.[9]

The nature of the delegation problem differs substantially between Japan and the United States. In parliamentary systems like Japan's, the ruling party or coalition in the legislature runs the government and resolves policy disputes. The American system of federalism, bicameralism, and an independent executive makes the resolution of conflicts in policy implementation far more difficult. Consequently, in the United States, political officials are more likely to rely on the design of implementing agencies as a means to assure compliance with the general policy agreement that is embodied in a statute. Thus, U.S. regulatory statutes define more clearly the methods to be used to make decisions. U.S. legislators, knowing that they are likely to have policy conflicts between legislative branches and with the independent executive, are more likely to rely on formalized decision-making processes and judicial review to police the decisions of agencies than are legislators in Japan.

2.2. Legislative mandate

In both Japan and the United States, the core of the structure and process of telecommunications regulation is statutory; however, the nature and origins of the statutes that have governed the liberalization process are very different. In Japan, the NTT Corporation Law and the Telecommunications Business Law, which were enacted in April 1985, authorized the privatization of NTT and established the basic regulatory structure for the domestic industry. In the United States, the sections of the Communications Act that deal with telecommunications have not been significantly amended since the act was passed in 1934. Indeed, the basic approach to federal regulation has not changed materially since the Mann–Elkins Act of 1910, which instructed the Interstate Commerce Commission to regulate interstate telephone service in the same way it was regulating the railroads, a procedure that itself was enacted in 1887. Thus,

---

[9] For an explanation of how structure and process influence the policy outcomes of agencies, see McCubbins, Noll, and Weingast (1987, 1989).

Japan's liberalization has taken place under a statute designed for that purpose, whereas the U.S. liberalization has been under the authority of a statute designed to regulate nineteenth-century railroads.

2.3. Structure

In the United States, most regulatory authority is delegated to the Federal Communications Commission (FCC), a quasi-independent regulatory commission. The FCC has five commissioners, each of whom is appointed for a fixed five-year term. Appointments to the commission are nominated by the president and confirmed by the Senate. A new president can pick the chair of the FCC, but unless a position is vacant, must select a chair from the existing membership. In practice, the chair usually resigns when the presidency changes, so that the new president is free to nominate anyone as the new chair; however, a new government does not acquire a voting majority of commissioners until three members have resigned or finished their terms, which typically takes about two years.

The chair of the FCC is more influential than the other commissioners because the job carries two important powers. The chair is in charge of the staff and can pick the primary bureaucratic officials, who do not hold fixed-term appointments. The second powerful role of the chair is to set the agenda of the commission, which makes decisions on the basis of simple majority rule.

In addition to the FCC, the Department of Commerce plays some role in telecommunications policy by sponsoring research and development joint ventures in high-technology industries, and through the planning function of the National Telecommunications and Information Administration. However, the antitrust division of the Department of Justice is probably the most important player other than the FCC.[10] The Department of Justice, not the FCC, has the primary authority to police anticompetitive activities in the telecommunications industry. The jurisdiction of Justice includes all operations of the industry that are part of interstate commerce. Because the network is fully integrated, this jurisdiction includes local service, even though the FCC is precluded by statute from regulating intrastate services.

The structure of state regulation varies considerably. Most large states have organizations that are broadly similar to federal regulatory agencies, headed by multimember commissions having fixed terms. In some states, the commissions are elected, rather than appointed by the governor. In

---

[10] Justice has been involved in telecommunications since it divested Western Union from AT&T in 1908 and negotiated the Kingsbury Agreement in 1913. The latter permitted AT&T to acquire local-service monopolies in return for providing long distance interconnection for other local companies.

still others, regulation is a branch of the state attorney general's office. Whatever their structure, these organizations also regulate other utilities, typically including electricity, gas, water, and transportation.

Because the jurisdictional boundary between state and federal authorities is blurry and constantly in dispute, several bodies have been created to coordinate national regulatory activities. The most important is the National Association of Regulatory Utility Commissioners, which is an organization of state regulators that, among other things, sponsors studies of jurisdictional issues, participates in federal regulatory proceedings, and organizes joint federal–state meetings about common issues. In addition, periodically the FCC organizes special conferences with state regulators to make joint decisions about jurisdictional matters.

In Japan, responsibility for telecommunications policy is vested almost exclusively in the Ministry of Posts and Telecommunications, headed by a cabinet appointee serving at the pleasure of the prime minister. Before liberalization, NTT was part of the government, and no formal mechanisms were needed to make policy. Pricing issues were studied in the MPT, but price changes and investment budgets had to be approved by a vote of the Diet. With liberalization came a more complex regulatory system, adopted by statute, that set up a structure and process for resolving disputes among participants in the industry and between the now-privatized industry and the government. The MPT controls prices, investments, and service offerings by facilities-based carriers, entry for all types of service, and all telecommunications-sector standards.

In the new regime, the minister is advised by the Telecommunications Business Advisory Council. As of October 1992, the Advisory Council had twenty-two members, all of whom were otherwise fully employed (Table 6.1). Of these, four were university professors, one was a leader of the Japanese Federation of Housewives, one was a labor leader, and the rest were executives from businesses with a stake in the industry.

The only other Japanese agencies with a role in telecommunications policy are the Ministry of International Trade and Industry (MITI), and the Ministry of Finance (MOF). MITI sponsors research consortia for developing telecommunications equipment. MPT and MITI sometimes find themselves with overlapping interests when MPT policies about entry and standards create conflicts with MITI's preferences regarding the directions new technology should take.[11] MOF has responsibility for managing the sale of NTT equities during the privatization process. MOF's potential conflicts with MPT arise over the decisions by the latter concerning prices and market structure, since lower prices and more competition

---

[11] For a lively account of the jurisdictional battles between MPT and MITI over telecommunications policy, see Johnson (1989).

Telecommunications policy

Table 6.1. *Telecommunications Advisory Board (October 30, 1992)*

Name	Title and organization	Industry stake
Chair		
Watanabe, F.	Advisor, Tokyo Fire and Marine Insurance	Investor, user
Vice-chair		
Asao, H.*	President, Japan On-Line Equipment	Supplier
Members		
Akiyama, M.	Professor of Engineering, Tokyo U.	
Arai, A.	President, Nihon Keizai Shimbun	Information services
Funada, M.	Professor, Rikkyo U.	
Hamawaki, Y.	Chair, BMW Japan	User
Honoki, M.*	President, Captain Service	NTT affiliate
Horiuchi, K.	Professor of engineering, Waseda U.	
Ichiriki, K.	Vice-chair, Association of General Type II carriers	Information services
Ishii, C.	President, Printemps Ginza	User
Ito, M.	Professor Emeritus, Kyoto U.	
Iwayama, M.	Vice Chair, Japan Labor Federation	Union employees
Kato, M.	Federation of Houswives	Consumers
Kitajima, Y.	President, Japan Ink	Information services
Kosai, Y.	Director, Japan Economic Research Center	Information services
Mita, K.	Chair, Hitachi	Supplier, investor
Mitomi, Y.	Advisor, Japan NCR	Supplier
Miyazaki, I.	Director, Daiwa Research Center	Information services
Monden, H.	Director, International Development Center	Information services
Sakai, M.	Advisor, Japan Long-term Credit Bank	User
Shinohara, S.	Director, Contemporary Information Research Center	User
Sonoyama, S.[a]	Chair, Cellular Center	Supplier

Note: [a]Indicates former Ministry of Posts and Telecommunications official.
Source: Ministry of Posts and Telecommunications Secretariat, internal memo, October 20, 1992.

reduce NTT profits and hence the revenues derived from privatization. As in the U.S. Congress, in Japan agencies with different policy responsibilities serve somewhat different groups of Diet members (and hence constituencies), and so frequently favor somewhat different policies; however, in most cases MPT is the most influential agency because of its control of licensing, investment, and prices for facilities-based carriers.

The main significance of the structural differences between Japan and the United States is that the American system reflects greater concern that telecommunications policy might be implemented by an appointee who will not carry out the policy agreement in a statute. The advantage of America's multimember, specialized commission and further division of policy responsibilities among agencies is that this structure minimizes the problems associated with a single appointment, perhaps orchestrated by a president with superior information who wishes to implement a policy that the legislature would never approve. Of course, this safeguard is not without costs, because security from a maverick appointment is purchased at the cost of making policy nonresponsive to changes in the preferences of elected officials.

2.4. Process

The formal procedures for making regulatory decisions differ markedly in the two countries. The Japanese system has very few formal procedural requirements, whereas the United States is procedurally complex.

In Japan, a distinction is made between policy and regulatory functions, which are procedurally simple, and enforcement and punishment, which are more complex. Regarding price and entry issues, the new Japanese Telecommunications Business Law establishes three types of business activities that require a license. Type I businesses are facilities-based carriers; Special Type II consists of domestic information services that are offered to "many and unspecified persons" and all foreign value-added services. General Type II refers to other value-added services.

Type I services are the most extensively regulated. To receive a license to build new facilities or to offer new services on an existing facility, a carrier must receive a "permission" from the MPT. Permissions can be granted only to companies in which Japanese nationals hold a controlling equity interest (at least two-thirds, although NTT and KDD, the international carrier, must have 80 percent Japanese ownership). The Telecommunications Business Law (Article 10) stipulates that the request for permission be evaluated on the basis of a description of the facilities to be constructed and the services that will be offered, a business plan that demonstrates financial viability, a market assessment showing that demand justifies the service and that the new facility will not create excess capacity, and engineering information proving compliance with technical standards as promulgated by the MPT. Type I carriers also must have their tariffs approved by the MPT, which must be cost-based, "fair and reasonable," and not "unfairly" discriminatory (Article 31). The Telecommunications Advisory Council must be consulted about new or amended permissions, changes in tariffs, changes in regulatory rules regarding the definitions of the types of carriers, and changes in regulations pertaining to the interconnection requirements between networks, between types of carriers, and between networks and terminal equipment.

132

Special Type II carriers apply for a "registration," and need only supply information about the service to be offered, the facilities to be used, and their business plan (Article 24). Registration can be denied if the proposal is false or incomplete, or if the prospective licensee is deemed to lack financial and technical competence. Special Type II carriers must submit tariffs to MPT, but there are no further requirements about their levels and they are not technically subject to an approval process. General Type II carriers submit a "notification," which requires only the specification of the service offered and the facilities used (Article 22). No approval is required, and no tariffs need to be submitted.

The Japanese Telecommunications Business Law makes no special provisions for judicial review of any MPT decisions, and requires only a hearing for enforcement actions against licensees. MPT is required to hold a formal hearing to revoke a permission or a registration, to issue an order to improve business operations, to order interconnection by a Type I carrier, and to revoke a designation to a private entity to test terminal equipment for compliance with technical standards (Article 94). In addition, compulsory arbitration can be invoked to resolve disputes over rights of way for telecommunications facilities (Articles 75–77). Denials of license applications and tariff proposals do not require a hearing, nor does the promulgation of the rules on which these decisions will be based.

Judicial review of MPT decisions is available through Japan's Administrative Case Litigation Law. This statute, and its interpretations by the Japanese Supreme Court, provide a far narrower basis for judicial review than in the United States. With few exceptions, standing to appeal is limited to the company that is the subject of a regulatory decision. Thus, a carrier can appeal a decision about its prices, investment plan, standards compliance, or license application, but judicial review is not available for the company's customers, suppliers, or competitors. Administrative law requires that MPT follow the procedural guidelines in its organic statute and demonstrate a reasonable basis for a decision. As a practical matter, the court almost never rejects ministerial decisions, but instead defers to an agency's interpretation of its statutory powers and requirements. In any case, the standing limitation stacks the deck in favor of regulated firms, for only they can pose even a slight threat to cause judicial reversal of a regulatory decision.

In the United States, the FCC, like other regulatory agencies, is subject to complex procedural guidelines for licensing carriers and regulating rates. One set of procedures flows from the Administrative Procedure Act and related case law that applies to all regulatory agencies. These procedures require the agency to give affected parties the right to submit evidence in regulatory proceedings, to take into account all relevant evidence in reaching a decision, and to make decisions that are consistent with the agency's legislative mandate and that are rationally based on the evidence before them. A further procedural distinction is made between general rule making and case adjudication. The former is less complex and rule bound, but it does require that the agency offer parties the opportunity to submit evidence pertaining to its proposed rules. Adjudication includes both the enforcement activities that require hearings in Japan and the investigations into pricing and entry if the agency is going to deny an application. These hearings closely resemble court procedures and are presided over by an administrative law judge. The judge's opinion, together with the evidence collected in the process, is then submitted to the commission.

A second set of constraints on U.S. regulation arises from judicial interpretations of the federal Constitution. For example, the constitutional prohibition against uncompensated takings has been interpreted as requiring that a regulated firm must be permitted to set prices high enough to earn approximately a competitive return on capital investments. In addition, the "due process" protection in the Constitution has been interpreted to give standing to parties affected by a decision other than the regulated company.

The FCC's decision making is also constrained by the details of the Communications Act. In essence, the FCC bears the burden of proof that a license or a rate proposal should be denied, and that it has jurisdiction (rather than the states) to decide an issue. Moreover, a proposal by a common carrier to change rates or to post a tariff for a new service automatically goes into effect after a brief waiting period unless formally challenged by the FCC. The agency's decisions about standing to participate, the evidentiary basis of decisions, and the compatibility of the decision with the statute are all subject to judicial review, which is often searching and occasionally extremely important. In both terminal equipment and long distance message toll service, the courts played an important role in liberalization by ruling that the FCC had not met this burden of proof when it denied permission to a prospective competitor of the regulated monopoly.[12] Likewise, the court has prevented the FCC from

---

[12] In Hush-A-Phone, the court reversed an FCC decision banning an attachment to telephones that enabled the user to speak into a telephone without being heard by others in the same room. (See *Hush-A-Phone Corporation v. FCC*, 238 F. 2d 266 [D.C. Circuit Court 1956]). This decision led to *Carterfone*, in which the FCC authorized radio telephones that were not manufactured by AT&T. (See 13 FCC 2nd 420 [1968]). In *Execunet*, the court reversed an FCC decision to deny MCI authority to compete with AT&T in interstate long distance toll service. (See *MCI Telecommunications Corporation v. FCC*, 561 F.2d 365 [D.C. Circuit 1977] and *MCI Telecommunications Corporation v. FCC*, 580 F.2d 590 [D.C. Circuit 1978], cert. denied 461 U.S. 938 [1978].) See Noll (1989) for further discussion of the role of the courts in liberalizing U.S. telecommunications policy.

requiring uniform accounting practices (such as depreciation allowances) for both interstate and intrastate services.

Unlike the Japanese legislation, the Communications Act does not specify the standards for setting prices and granting licenses. Instead, the FCC is given considerable latitude in both areas, including the freedom not to regulate.[13] Thus, most important policies are specified in rules issued by the FCC or decisions by the courts in reviewing these rules, not in statutes. In practice, the FCC has not regulated the activities of any of the competitive facilities-based carriers since the Execunet decision of 1978, and has never regulated value-added services. Indeed, the FCC has never engaged in extensive regulation of facilities construction even by the dominant carrier and former monopolist, AT&T. The primary focus of FCC regulation is the tariffs charged by AT&T for long distance services and the tariffs and service characteristics of local exchange carriers for interconnection to long distance networks. The FCC is not bound by statute to be concerned about the adequacy of demand for new facilities and services, and as a practical matter has ignored these issues since 1978. Thus, the agency regulates far less than MPT regulates in Japan; however, what the FCC does regulate must be accomplished through its highly formalized process.

The procedures in the United States serve two functions that are not needed in Japan. First, they are necessary for a system that relies upon judicial review to assure that agency decisions are consistent with the policy preferences expressed in a statute. Second, formalized procedures make decisions depend on information, much of which can be supplied only by groups having a stake in a policy. Procedures, then, empower some groups at the expense of others, by determining the extent to which agency decisions are constrained by the information that these groups provide (or do not provide).

The U.S. procedures serve a third function that is performed in another way in Japan. Legislative delegation of policy implementation requires "oversight" – some means of monitoring the development of policies in the bureaucracy to assure that mistakes are not being made. A common form of monitoring, attractive because it is not very costly and avoids mistakes before they occur, is fire alarm oversight.[14] In this form of monitoring, the interests that are supposed to be served by a policy are given formal roles in its development, which allows them to detect policies that they oppose before they are adopted. In Japan, the Telecommunications Advisory Council provides a "fire alarm" to the interests represented on

---

[13] For an analysis of the Communications Act, see Paglin (1989).
[14] See McCubbins and Schwartz (1984).

it. In the United States, the formal processes of the FCC perform a similar function. In both cases, affected parties can not only voice concerns directly to the relevant regulatory body, but also pull the "fire alarms" in the offices of political representatives if their intervention is deemed necessary and desirable.

Finally, structure and process in both countries serve to stack the deck in favor of certain policy orientations and interest groups. The U.S. federal system stacks the deck in favor of local service. The more cumbersome U.S. decision process slows changes in policy, and in so doing advantages incumbents and dominant firms at the expense of entrants and smaller competitors; however, the fact that the FCC's regulation of individual firm decisions is discretionary has strongly benefited competitors, since their proposals are rarely reviewed. By contrast, because in Japan an entrant must receive a license before entering a market, the Japanese system is more heavily stacked against entrants and competition. This situation applies with greatest force to facilities-based carriers, which bear a burden of proof that their services are desirable.

2.5. Political sources of liberalization

In both Japan and the United States, telecommunications liberalization arose because important user and supplier groups were dissatisfied with ubiquitous regulated monopoly and managed to achieve policy change. The way change came about, however, differs substantially between the countries, due to differences in their political structures.

2.6. Reform in the United States

Prior to liberalization, AT&T, which provided all long distance service and about 85 percent of local service, was vertically integrated with Western Electric, an equipment manufacturer. AT&T purchased virtually all of its equipment from its own affiliate, and required that its subscribers use only Western Electric telephone instruments. The largest independent local telephone company, GTE, was also vertically integrated and practiced the same procurement policies.

Vertical integration of telephone companies was always a matter of sharp controversy in the United States.[15] When the Communications Act of 1934 was passed, there was intense floor debate about whether to prohibit vertical integration. Republicans and conservative Democrats blocked language that would have led to divestiture, but the latter joined

---

[15] For a history of telecommunications policy from the invention of the telephone until the liberalizing changes of the 1970s, see Brock (1980).

their liberal colleagues to block attempts to sanctify vertical integration and horizontal monopoly in the statute. Eventually, Congress settled for a statute that did not designate an official national carrier, that did not excuse the industry from antitrust (as other regulatory statutes had done for other infrastructural industries), and that required the FCC to embark on a study of the vertical integration issue and propose an appropriate policy. By the time the study was completed in 1939, the government was occupied by World War II, and took no action.

After the war ended, the FCC report, which had been critical of vertical integration into manufacturing, became the basis of a 1947 antitrust lawsuit against AT&T, seeking divestiture of Western Electric. The Truman administration took the position that legislation was unnecessary because the Communications Act accorded regulated telephone companies no antitrust exemption. In practice, liberal Democrats faced the same blocking coalition in Congress that they had faced in 1934, so that a legislative solution probably was not feasible.

The rationale for the suit was that many companies in the electronics industry were excluded unfairly from sales to telephone companies because of the latter's procurement policies. But the case never went to trial. When the Republicans regained control of the White House in 1953, they quickly moved to settle the antitrust case. The settlement required that AT&T license its technologies broadly and stay out of any businesses other than selling telecommunications services and equipment. However, reflecting the Republican position when the 1934 act was passed, the settlement permitted AT&T to remain vertically integrated and to continue its sole-source procurement policy.

The settlement did not satisfy the firms that wanted to sell telecommunications equipment, and they continued to work for relaxation of the procurement rules. But the means to break the monopoly switched from antitrust litigation to pleadings before the FCC and, when unsuccessful, appeals of these decisions to the courts.

World War II generated another rival against the established monopolies. Rapid technological progress had made feasible the use of microwave technology, rather than cables, as a means of transmitting telecommunications messages. Many large companies preferred to build their own private microwave systems rather than to buy service from telephone companies, and some even sought to provide microwave-based connections for others. Immediately after the war, both types of companies began to lobby the FCC for licenses to build microwave systems.

For the most part, the FCC resisted requests for entry from potential competitors of AT&T. But two key decisions eventually caused the entire system to unravel. One was "Above 890," which permitted a company to build a microwave system for its own use. The other, deriving from the settlement of the antitrust case, allowed a customer of a telephone company to own a computer that was attached to the telecommunications system, even though a customer could not own a telephone. These exceptions to the system of ubiquitous monopoly created new demands for further relaxations, as well as irrefutable common experience that a hybrid system was workable and, to some, desirable.

Eventually, in 1969 the FCC decided to allow owners of private systems to sell dedicated lines to others, and also let competitors sell services that the authorized monopoly carrier did not offer, such as high-speed data connections and value-added services. But the FCC did not authorize competition in ordinary long distance toll service. Initially, the agency took the position that entry was permissible only for services that AT&T was not providing, or for which the company was not meeting all demand. In a 1976 decision, the FCC explicitly ruled that long distance toll calls were adequately supplied by AT&T, and so were off-limits to competitors. But this decision was overturned by the court in *Execunet*, which stated that the agency had failed to bear the burden of proof that competition was undesirable.[16]

The most cataclysmic liberalizing event was yet another antitrust case, filed by a Republican administration in 1974. Although the FCC supported the suit, the regulators played very little role in developing and prosecuting the case. Once again, the case was in response to complaints from equipment manufacturers and new service providers that AT&T was unfairly handicapping them in their attempts to compete. The 1974 case was far more ambitious than the 1947 complaint, for it sought to separate local telephone service from all other elements of the industry: terminal equipment, long distance, network equipment, and value-added services.

As before, the Department of Justice sought no legislative action. But the legislature became involved in the case nonetheless. Between 1976 and 1981, AT&T and supporters of the status quo lobbied intensively for a revision of the 1934 Communications Act that would at least preserve

---

[16] A similar sequence of events took place in terminal equipment. The FCC tried to ban all terminal equipment that was not owned by the telephone company, but this decision was overturned by the courts. Moreover, the settlement of the 1947 case, not an FCC decision, prevented AT&T from owning computers that made use of telephone lines. In responding to the loss of control over terminal equipment, the FCC gave AT&T the right to test "foreign" attachments and, if it saw fit, to deny them the right to be used unless they conformed to company standards or used an expensive interface device manufactured only by AT&T. The effect of this policy was to prevent significant competition, because AT&T found that all competitive equipment failed its tests. The abuses from this process eventually led the FCC to set up its own testing and licensing system, and to deregulate terminal equipment.

AT&T as an integrated enterprise, and hopefully reestablish ubiquitous regulated monopoly in the industry.[17] The two most important sources of support for AT&T were state regulators and the Department of Defense (DOD). State regulators perceived correctly that federal liberalization threatened the flow of subsidies from federal to state services, and would put pressure on them to liberalize as well. They supported re-establishment of the status quo ante through legislation as a means to preserve the orientation of the old system toward their primary concern, local telephone service. The Department of Defense saw liberalization as a threat to an integrated national network and the research capabilities in AT&T, both of which were valuable for defense purposes.

As before, Congress did not act, as moderates blocked legislation that would have given AT&T what it wanted. The final showdown came in late 1981, when legislation that would have put an end to the antitrust case was narrowly defeated; within a few weeks, AT&T proposed a settlement that gave the Department of Justice most of what it sought without the need to litigate the case to conclusion.[18] The settlement led to the separation of AT&T into eight companies, seven regional companies that provide local-access and local toll service, and AT&T, which continues to provide long distance service, value-added services, and telecommunications equipment. The seven regional companies are precluded from manufacturing and long distance, and until 1990 were precluded from most information services as well.

The purpose of divestiture was to assure that a local-access carrier had no ownership interest in companies that supply it or its customers with equipment, long distance service, and value-added services. The theory is that prohibiting vertical integration promotes competition. It does this by eliminating the incentive of local-access carriers to pay too much for equipment and services from sister companies or otherwise advantage them through discriminatory practices.

Through divestiture, the federal government has succeeded in introducing competition into all markets within its jurisdiction. The states still regulate local access and the shorter toll calls that local-exchange carriers are permitted to provide. The nation has been divided into 165 "local access and transmission areas" (LATAs). The least-populous states are a single LATA, but some large states have ten or more. Most states have (sometimes reluctantly) copied federal policy and permitted largely unregulated competition in this segment of the industry. But states have not

---

[17] For a history of these attempts, see Temin and Galambos (1987).
[18] For a description and analysis of the divestiture agreement and its economic rationale, see Noll and Owen (1988).

copied the federal lead within the LATAs. Most states prohibit or severely limit competition for local access and intra-LATA toll calls.[19]

The final irony in the history of liberalization in the United States is that by the mid-1980s, the Department of Justice had reversed its position about vertical integration in telecommunications, but could do very little about it. When the Reagan administration came to power in early 1981, many of its top officials expressed traditional Republican opposition to the antitrust case. However, most of the Reagan officials were recused from decisions about telecommunications because they had business ties to AT&T. Hence, the antitrust division of the Department of Justice continued to prosecute the case vigorously. But general skepticism about it prevailed in the administration, notably in DOD, and in appointments to the FCC, the Department of Commerce, and eventually even the Department of Justice. Although none of these officials espoused a return to the predivestiture world, they did advocate permitting the seven regional companies to enter manufacturing and long distance services.

The structure of the industry and the nature and scope of its regulation continue to be unsettled.[20] All participants continue to jockey for favorable position, and the presence of numerous policy-making institutions continues to produce inconsistencies and conflicts. Seven years after divestiture, the local-access carriers succeeded in getting the court to permit them into information services, and local carriers still seek entry into other prohibited areas. But the steadily increasing reliance on competition rather than regulated monopoly is unlikely to change. Court and FCC decisions that have allowed multiple entities in facilities-based services such as private lines, long distance, local private networks, and radio telephones have created an enormous, well-organized constituency that will oppose a policy reversal. And the fragmented policy structure – including the court – virtually guarantees that these players can always find a decision maker who will thwart an attempt to seriously roll back the liberalization process. In essence, procompetitive statutes, judicial review, and the jurisdictional conflicts between federal and state regulators provide structural protection for competition once it has been established.

The history of the reform process in the United States can be interpreted in an implausibly Japanese way. Specifically, while elected officials in Congress and the executive stood passively by, bureaucrats in the FCC

---

[19] The extent to which states inhibit local service and intra-LATA toll competition varies enormously. In some states, toll carriers are allowed to place intra-LATA calls, but are not allowed to tell their customers that they do! In a few large cities, significant access competition has emerged, especially for multiline access service to large businesses. For a detailed discussion of these developments, see Huber (1987).

[20] For a review of the pending issues, see Lehr and Noll (1991), Noam (1983a, b), and Noll (1989).

and the antitrust division proceeded to unravel the status quo. The major un-Japanese element to the story is the proactive role of the courts, which were at least as responsible for liberalization as the bureaucrats. But this interpretation is superficial, for the failure of the elected political officials to take action as the story unfolded is also consistent with the view that policy was developing in a manner that was compatible with the original statutory policy, structure and process, and the policy preferences of key veto players in the political process.

Like other quasi-judicial independent regulatory agencies, the FCC was set up procedurally to favor the status quo. Its procedures are complex, and the agency depends on industry for the information necessary to reach decisions. But anyone could ask to enter any market – and they did, frequently. Thus, the FCC was not set up to prevent entry and competition, although it was sure to retard it by virtue of its structure and process.

The process of judicial review, in a generally procompetitive statutory environment, was stacked in favor of competition. Because the agency had to prove its actions were correct if it did not grant the wishes of a potential entrant, but could grant an entrant's wishes as long as it had a rational basis for doing so, judicial review normally could only reverse anticompetitive decisions. Moreover, the judiciary was not structurally tied so closely to the incumbents as was the FCC. Hence, a process in which the court acts to liberalize more rapidly than the FCC prefers is predictable from the structure that was established by the 1934 legislation.

2.7. Reform in Japan

Liberalization in Japanese telecommunications began in earnest not long after the momentous 1982 settlement of the AT&T antitrust case in the United States. But the different regulatory paths the two countries have taken reveal a great deal about how the structure of decision making shapes both the policy-making process and policy outcomes. Two features are most notable about Japan: the small number of veto points in the policy-making structure, and the systematic policy bias in favor of producers.

In Japan, prefectures have no effective role in most aspects of economic regulation, including telecommunications. Japanese courts were also silent in telecommunications liberalization, deferring instead to the bureaucracy's interpretation of the law. But Japan's telecommunications reform was not engineered by central bureaucrats largely insulated from dissenting views and therefore free to pursue their own vision of Japan's technological development and economic growth. The liberalization of Japan's telecommunications markets – to the extent it has occurred – has been a highly political process, coordinated by the top echelons of the

Liberal Democratic Party. The struggles over policy choices have not been principally between the LDP and its rivals or agents, but within the party itself.

Telecommunications liberalization in Japan took place roughly simultaneously with the liberalization of two other industries, surface transportation and tobacco. The context in which the liberalization movement arose was a general dissatisfaction with the efficiency of government-owned companies, and telecommunications reform quite plausibly would not have taken place in the absence of strong sentiment to reform other nationalized industries, especially the Japan National Railroad. Nevertheless, the inclusion of telecommunications in the reform process arose because the practices of MPT and NTT had become controversial.

The first significant demand for liberalization dealt with the equipment market, and it came from abroad. In the late 1970s and early 1980s, NTT's closed procurement patterns came under U.S. scrutiny. U.S. trade representative Robert Strauss threatened to take action against Japan,[21] noting that NTT was buying huge amounts of equipment, virtually all from Japanese suppliers, at higher prices than those of U.S. suppliers. Japanese export industries were alarmed, knowing that their large stake in foreign trade made them vulnerable to retaliation by the United States. Consequently, the LDP was eager to ward off a trade war, but without making large enough concessions to hurt important constituents – including the privileged NTT suppliers. The LDP was chagrined, then, when NTT president Akigusa fanned the flames of U.S.–Japan rancor when he announced, "The only things NTT will procure from U.S. suppliers are mops and buckets."[22]

A second impetus for telecommunications liberalization in Japan came from the most intensive and largest business users of telecommunications services – financial institutions, trading companies, and manufacturers with far-flung operations. These industries had watched w ch interest the antitrust proceedings in the United States, and warned the government that substantial telecommunications price cuts in the United States without comparable changes in Japan would leave them saddled with a competitive disadvantage in international markets. Not satisfied to lobby only for price reductions in long distance and high-volume services, these businesses argued that the entire regulatory edifice was increasingly untenable. Without competition from other sources, the nationally owned monopoly, NTT, had too little incentive to innovate new kinds of telecommunications services.

Joining the telecommunications users in the swelling chorus for change

---

[21] Curran (1982).
[22] Yayama (1982: 126).

were electronics firms not already part of the NTT "family" of suppliers. NTT procured almost all of its equipment (1.7 trillion yen in 1980) from four firms – Nippon Electric (NEC), Fujitsu, Hitachi, and Oki Electric – and their seventy or so subcontractors.[23] The family firms also benefited from NTT's large R&D budget, through privileged access to the NTT research institute's policy results.[24] Toshiba, Matsushita, Kyocera, and other nonfamily firms were outside of the loop.

At the prompting of the Keidanren, Japan's largest and politically most influential business organization, in which firms that supplied NTT and other Japanese parastatals were outnumbered, in 1980 the Diet passed legislation establishing an Ad Hoc Administrative Reform Council.[25] The Diet ordered the council to examine the government's fiscal and regulatory policies and to recommend reforms that would "reduce the government budget deficit and make economic policies more efficient."[26] Prime Minister Nakasone appointed former Keidanren chairman Toshio Doko – who also had been Toshiba's chairman – to spearhead the reform efforts. The Administrative Reform Council's Fourth Committee, led by Keio University economist Hiroshi Kato, immediately took up the question of privatizing nationally owned enterprises, including NTT, Japan National Railways, and the tobacco and salt monopoly.[27]

The Administrative Reform Council encountered mixed enthusiasm in the LDP. The party leadership accepted the business community's charge that certain areas of economic regulation, including telecommunications, were antiquated and inefficient – or at least not to their liking. Ranking members of the party's Policy Affairs Research Council (PARC) telecommunications committee were staunchly opposed to change. These party backbenchers benefited richly from NTT's cozy relationships with insider firms, accepting large donations from the "family" in exchange for supporting the regulatory status quo.[28]

---

[23] In 1980, for example, NEC sold NTT 130 billion yen in equipment, accounting for 17 percent of NEC's total sales that year. NTT did not place orders on the basis of competitive bids, but on the basis of friendly deals with these "family" companies. Friendly, in fact, may be too weak a word. Fujitsu had been selling switching equipment to NTT at $560 per port and exporting the same equipment at half that price. Similarly, the insider firms were selling standard black telephones to NTT for about twice the price of the same telephones in export markets. Ohmae (1979: 259); Yayama (1982: 127).

[24] See Ohmae (1979: 259), and Yayama (1982: 126). Sixty percent of the executives in the top ten family firms were from NTT, either on loan or as retirees (*Asahi shimbun*, February 4, 1982).

[25] The members of the Reform Council, hand-picked by Prime Minister Nakasone, were mostly business executives and academics who favored budget reductions and regulatory reform.

[26] Yamamoto (1983: 160).

[27] Hirose (1981: 248).

[28] Yamamoto (1983: 160).

In January 1981, before the Administrative Reform deliberations had gotten very far, Prime Minister Nakasone replaced NTT president Tokuji Akikusa with a reform-minded outsider and Doko protégé, Hisashi Shinto. Nakasone made this appointment over the objections of the PARC telecommunications group members, who were pushing instead for NTT vice-president Yasusada Kitahara to succeed Akikusa.[29] Kitahara had risen to NTT's top ranks by nurturing ties with the PARC telecommunications committee members, helping to funnel in their direction large and continuous donations from the NTT suppliers.[30]

NTT's new president, Shinto, was more amenable to the LDP leadership's plan to revamp telecommunications policies along the lines that the Keidanren wished. In February 1982, for example, Shinto disclosed NTT's secret list of technical standards for NTT procurement in order to widen the circle of suppliers.[31] But Shinto's action was a small step, and the Administrative Reform Council sought far greater changes when, in July 1983, it recommended privatization and the breakup of NTT.[32]

The cabinet responded swiftly to the council's proposals, deciding on August 10, 1982, to submit privatization legislation by the next Diet session. But the party leadership had to work out a scenario that was acceptable to the PARC Telecommunications Division in order to obtain a parliamentary majority for reform. Mindful of the necessity to retain an LDP majority to continue to control the government, parliamentary leaders are careful not to undermine too drastically the constituency base of any group of LDP members. As a transitional measure, according to a compromise worked out by party leader Shin Kanemaru, NTT would first be turned into a stock company that was owned by the government. Eventually, the government would adopt a plan whereby half of the stock was to be sold in a series of offerings spread over four years.[33] The law also required that the government retain at least one-third of the shares permanently.[34] Because share placement did not go well, by 1992 national and local government entities still owned 65 percent of the shares.[35] Thus,

---

[29] Watanabe (1985: 20–22).

[30] Kitahara was known in the business community as NTT's "political bureau chief," although there was no such post (Nishii and Nishimae 1989b: 16). An informal group of business leaders known as "the Committee to Establish a New NTT" backed Nakasone's decision to appoint Shinto the new NTT president. Members of this committee included Hiroki Imazato of Seiko, Sohei Nakayama of the Industrial Bank of Japan, and Ryuzo Sejima of Ito Chu trading company. The PARC telecommunications committee apparently launched a brief but abortive campaign to oust Shinto soon after he was appointed (Nishii and Nishimae 1989b: 16; Yayama 1982: 128).

[31] *Asahi shimbun,* February 4, 1982.

[32] Yamamoto (1983: 162).

[33] Takano (1992: 27).

[34] NTT Corporation Law of 1985, Article 4.

[35] Takano (1992: 36).

the protectors of the status quo – led by the PARC Telecommunications Division members – succeeded in preventing real privatization of NTT for several years.

Another task for the LDP was to establish criteria for entry into telecommunications services. The LDP's Commerce Division represented the interests of businesses outside the family, taking up where the party's Administrative Reform Task Force left off. It argued in favor of free entry for telecommunications carriers and for firms providing value-added services on leased lines.[36] The Commerce Division went so far as to invite Clyde Prestowitz, a former U.S. Commerce Department bureaucrat, to speak to it about the dangers for U.S.–Japan relations of not opening those markets to foreign competition.[37] MITI, reflecting its greater concern about trade relations and the efficiency of Japanese export industries, strongly supported a less restrictive regulatory system. The PARC Telecommunications Division – which represented NTT and its suppliers – and MPT disagreed, arguing that MPT should retain strict control of new entry into all facets of telecommunications, from facilities-based carriers to value-added networks.[38]

As had been the case with NTT privatization, LDP leaders brokered the details of the entry rules. The top four officers of the LDP – the party president (also the prime minister), the secretary general, the PARC chairman, and the Executive Council chairman – hammered out a deal by April 6, 1984, that was eventually incorporated into the Telecommunications Business Law. Strict entry controls, as advocated by MPT and the Telecommunications Division, were applied only to facilities-based carriers. For General Type II carriers (offering value-added services to a restricted group), entry controls were minimal, as advocated by MITI and the Commerce Division. A compromise was found for value-added carriers offering services to the general public, with MPT succeeding in retaining entry regulation but less-firm controls than it had sought. However, MPT would not be allowed to turn down a request for entry, or issue software or hardware adjustment orders, without first consulting MITI. Moreover, MITI's administrative vice minister would have a voice on the Telecommunications Advisory Board, where final decisions about market entry were to be made.[39]

Embedded in the maddeningly opaque licensing system was a rather subtle compromise between the PARC Telecommunications Division (representing the status quo providers), and the Commerce Division (representing users and potential entrants). The status quo would be altered to

[36] *Asahi shimbun,* December 21, 1983.
[37] *Asahi shimbun,* March 9, 1984.
[38] *Asahi shimbun,* March 13, 1984.
[39] *Asahi shimbun,* March 28, 1984; April 3, 1984 (evening); April 6, 1984.

meet the new demands of the business community. But change would be gradual, and would take into account the interests of the status quo firms. By the time the cabinet voted to submit the telecommunications bills to the Diet in April 1984, both sides seemed satisfied that they had done as well as the system allowed.

2.8. Comparisons

In both countries, the political pressure for reform came from users, manufacturers, and potential entrants in telecommunications services who were excluded from the vertically tied, regulated monopoly system. But the methods used by these interests differed dramatically.

The Japanese advocates of reform focused on the ruling party in the Diet because legislative change was required to undo a government-owned statutory monopoly. Reformists were forced to compromise with defenders of the status quo to protect all interests represented in the LDP so that the ruling party would not risk its majority in undertaking regulatory reform. The U.S. reformers, operating under statutes that permitted competition, focused instead on the FCC, repeatedly asking permission to compete with the ubiquitous regulated monopoly. The FCC's structure and process led the agency to proceed slowly, but nevertheless it gradually liberalized on its own. Moreover, the U.S. system of easy and extensive judicial review pushed the process faster than the FCC was willing to go.

The process began earlier in the United States because the legal technology of telecommunications policy had not clearly decided whether the industry should be monopolized or competitive, regulated or not, as it had in Japan. Hence, as each new technical innovation opened a new opportunity for competitive entry, the issue was brought to the FCC. In Japan, the legal technology firmly established government-owned monopoly as the preferred state, so that technological and economic change had to cumulate in order to build a strong enough coalition to overturn the reigning statutes and bring dramatic, discontinuous change. Even then, the change was structured as a compromise between entrenched interests and their challengers because both groups were highly influential within the ruling LDP.

2.9. Policy flexibility and speed of change

The speed of reform clearly varied dramatically between Japan and the United States, largely because of the legal environment of the policy process. U.S. telecommunications policy has been a matter of controversy since the Bell patents expired in the mid-1890s, and no regulatory regime has survived for more than twenty-five years without significant change.

In essence, the regulatory process was constructed in a manner that allows each new potential entrant to be partially accommodated in the system without a major disruption. By the time of the 1984 divestiture, the commitment had already been made to liberalize most of the system, so that the event itself was not disruptive of the industry. Thus, the U.S. system is highly flexible and inherently procompetitive, but designed to make change go slowly.

The legislative system in the United States is, by contrast to the regulatory process, inflexible to the point of ossification. As in Japan, the major players all have champions in the government, but unlike Japan, the U.S. process for changing legislation requires running a gauntlet of veto gates. Negotiating an accord when a change would worsen the lot of any interest that controls a veto gate is very difficult, requiring the identification and implementation of a statutory "side payment" to the losers that, because it would have to be visible, would also have to be legal and nonscandalous. In Japan, few players actually possess vetoes. And, because agreements are negotiated behind the scenes, with cash used for side payments, a legislative deal need not reveal all of its terms, and so is easier to reach. Thus, in Japan, the ruling party could completely rewrite its underlying statutory basis for telecommunications policy in less than three years.

The nature of telecommunications liberalization in Japan was also dramatically different from that in the United States. First, Japan's parliamentary and unitary (nonfederal) system of government gives the majority party in the Diet unfettered influence over the bureaucracy and over the regulatory process at every stage of implementation. Second, because during the liberalization period the LDP had a stable Diet majority that was likely to govern for the foreseeable future, it could rely on the Diet to resolve implementation disputes as they arose in the liberalization process, and had no interest in granting the judiciary an independent role to stabilize policy through possible changes in the government. The effect of these features on regulatory institutions was that the lines of authority in the policy-making process were clearer and more predictable than in the United States. By the same token, because the LDP controlled both legislative and executive functions, it could easily adjust one to suit the needs of the other, and so tended to write statutes that more completely specified the policy direction than is the case in the United States.

Despite the flexibility inherent in the Japanese system, the government is not able to make sweeping regulatory changes in a short time. True enough, once the LDP made a decision on the basis of the party's overall interests, party discipline ruled, and backbenchers had to go along with the party's decision. But before decisions were made, the party had to deal with serious sticking points if not vetoes – from within: the groups of backbenchers with vested interests in various aspects of the status quo.

The LDP leadership could not simply steamroll these backbencher interests, because the electoral system and the consequent need to divide the vote made backbenchers and the interests they represented important for maintaining the party's Diet majority.

In telecommunications, party leaders concluded that it was important to respond to the changing interests of businesses not in the NTT family, but they met with fierce and effective resistance from the PARC Telecommunications Division. So long as the LDP had to compete electorally in the framework of multimember districts and single nontransferable votes, the party leadership was reluctant to eliminate any important source of campaign contributions to an important group of LDP members. Rather, the party was likely to strike bargains, balance competing interests, and cut new players into old deals.

The ultimate effect of the Japanese system was that change of any kind had to wait until several interests coalesced to form a power base that mattered for the LDP's future. When this occurred, change was more sweeping than a single reform event in the United States, but represented a carefully crafted compromise between the upstart challengers and the defenders of the status quo. The Telecommunications Business Law and the NTT Corporation Law are more sweeping than any single reform decision that was made in the United States; however, these laws also did not liberalize the industry as much as the cumulative effect of the many separate, and individually less sweeping, telecommunications decisions in the United States.

The 1993 Diet elections and subsequent reform activities raise an important issue regarding the future of telecommunications policy in Japan. The most likely permanent outcome of the Japanese political reform appears to be a system combining proportional representation and single-member legislative districts, as in Germany. This system will reduce the special-interest orientation of members of the Diet, and will increase party competition and the instability of single-party control. Most likely, these changes will make regulatory policies in Japan somewhat more favorable to consumers, and less favorable to equipment suppliers, than has been the case in the past. But reform will not eliminate the unification of the legislative and executive functions and will not bring a federalist structure. Consequently, these changes are not likely to lead to the form of procedurally complex regulatory policy making with extensive judicial review found in the United States. For example, administrative systems in the United Kingdom and Germany do not exhibit the procedural complexity of the U.S. system.

Similarly, this type of reform will not eliminate the importance of the personal vote in the electoral success of many Diet members, and so will retain the incentive to trade favors for campaign contributions. Only if reform includes substantial restrictions on campaign financing for individual candidates is the special-interest orientation of the Diet likely to be radically reduced. But, as in the United States, significant reform of campaign financing seems unlikely because it clearly conflicts with the long-term electoral security of individual Diet members. Hence, reform may moderate, but probably will not substantially reduce, the role of organized interests in policy making. The implication for telecommunications policy is that the general pattern of reform is not likely to change dramatically when the new system is firmly in place.

3. POSTLIBERALIZATION PERFORMANCE

Because the political forces motivating and orchestrating reform differ between the two countries, the effect on the performance of the industry is also expected to differ. In this section, we examine the postreform record of both countries according to several economic performance indicators – entry, prices, and costs – as well as by a measure of political performance, that is, the extent to which the postreform industry has given rise to political scandals.

3.1. Scandal and corruption

The U.S. government has been involved in its share of scandals, but the public record tells of none in telecommunications.[40] The presence of multiple veto points in the U.S. system, including the Congress, the president, and the multimember FCC, makes coordinated corruption among them all quite difficult – and prone to disclosure. The problem is exacerbated by the empowerment of numerous conflicting groups in the formal regulatory and judicial review processes, not just the regulated industry.

In Japan, corruption is endemic to telecommunications policy. Prior to NTT's privatization, as one might imagine from the close relationships among NTT, its suppliers, and politicians, sweet deals were commonplace. The ostensible reason for Shinto's replacement of Akigusa as NTT president in 1981 was the revelation of wrongdoing at the top in NTT. NTT management had apparently faked accounts, claiming to have taken business trips and hosted golf tournaments when they had in fact routed substantial sums to LDP politicians.[41] Akigusa was forced to resign in the face of this scandal, although Nakasone already had his reasons

---

[40] The record is not so happy in the FCC's other domain, broadcasting. During the late 1940s and 1950s, the FCC assigned most of the nation's VHF television stations, many of which went to politicians – among them, eventual president Lyndon Johnson.
[41] Nishii and Nishimae (1989a).

for shaking up NTT personnel. At about the same time, a similar scandal also rocked the international carrier, KDD.[42]

Lest NTT privatization and telecommunications reform seem to have expunged corruption from the regulatory process, think only of Recruit. The Recruit affair, which caught more politicians in its sticky net than any other postwar Japanese scandal, stemmed from telecommunications regulation in the new regime. Recruit was an upstart employment-information company, and its chairman, Hiromasa Ezoe, was eager to lease lines from NTT to transmit its employment data base (as a value-added service), as well as to resell high-speed digital transmission service to small companies that could not afford their own lines.[43] In 1985, Ezoe gave tens of thousands of Recruit shares to NTT president Shinto, a host of politicians (allegedly including Prime Minister Nakasone), and a smattering of other business executives and well-placed academics in exchange for their "goodwill."

Although much is still unknown about the Recruit affair, the motive for Ezoe's generosity apparently was that he expected regulatory difficulties in MPT and the PARC Telecommunication Division.[44] He was ensuring that the LDP would look out for him. The Recruit scandal suggests that the pattern of regulatory favors from the preprivatization days has not been eliminated, but rearranged.

3.2. Market structure

Before liberalization, the structures of telecommunications markets were similar but not identical in Japan and the United States. In the United States, AT&T, a private company, accounted for about 85 percent of local-access customers and equipment sales, and enjoyed almost a complete monopoly in long distance. Western Union had a monopoly in telegraph services. GTE had about half of the remaining local-service market and was a monopoly supplier of its own equipment. Approximately fifteen hundred other companies had small fractions of local service. The U.S. international market was divided among several companies, including AT&T, RCA, Comsat, Western Union, and ITT, with regulation

---

[42] The timing of the scandalous disclosures was probably not mere happenstance. This kind of money politics is common in Japan, and the Japanese system does not provide any incentive for an insider to blow the whistle on LDP officials. The split within the LDP over reform, however, would create a reason for revealing scandal involving the defenders of the status quo.

[43] Nihon keizai shimbunsha (ed.) (1989: 20–22).

[44] See, for example, Nihon keizai shimbunsha, ed. 1989: 69–73. The close relationship between Recruit and the LDP leadership is also a plausible explanation for the willingness of Recruit to buy two Cray supercomputers, allegedly to help the government placate U.S. complaints about NTT procurement practices (Nishii and Fujimori 1989: 14–17, and Nihon keizai shimbunsha [ed.] 1989: 65–67).

rather than competition allocating traffic among them. In Japan, NTT enjoyed a monopoly in all domestic services, and KDD, which had been privatized in 1952, was a monopolist in international services. Four consortia of electronics firms supplied virtually all equipment to these carriers. In both countries, this picture had changed radically by 1990.

3.3. Entry in the United States

In the United States, the initial liberalization in long distance in 1969 induced important but limited entry. Probably the best measure of the number of firms in the long distance toll market is the number of companies with carrier identification codes. These three-digit numbers enable a local-access customer to dial into the network of the associated carriers.[45]

By December 31, 1982, approximately when the divestiture settlement with AT&T was announced, eleven long distance providers had carrier identification codes.[46] A year later, when divestiture formally took place, forty-two companies had carrier ID. By mid-1991, this number had jumped to 597. Of these, 327 provided "equal access" long distance service.[47]

Market share data show considerable concentration in toll calls (Table 6.2). At the time of divestiture, AT&T accounted for approximately 85 percent of total interstate toll minutes, and 99 percent of "premium minutes" – equal-access calling at standard long distance toll tariffs. Not until 1986 was equal access provided to a majority of telephone lines, and this fraction did not pass 90 percent until late 1990. AT&T's market share has steadily fallen as equal-access provision has increased. By 1992, its share of both premium and total interstate switched-toll minutes was

[45] No distinction is made between facilities-based and resale carriers; however, in the U.S. system this distinction is unimportant. Carriers in either category can enter the other, and most are hybrids, owning transmission facilities along the most heavily used links in their network, and sharing or leasing use of facilities elsewhere to provide greater geographic coverage.

[46] The data about the number of carriers and their market shares come from the FCC's annual publication, *Statistics of Communications Common Carriers*. As the industry had become more competitive and less regulated, the quality and scope of the FCC's data have diminished. In sad realization of this state of affairs, telecommunications expert Bruce Owen has remarked, "If I had known deregulation meant that they were going to stop collecting the data, I would have been against it."

[47] Equal access means that a customer can choose to make the carrier the long distance company that handles all inter-LATA toll calls that are dialed without a carrier ID code. In the United States, local-access customers select a primary long distance carrier, but can gain access to other carriers by dialing the carrier ID code before dialing the long distance number. In some cases, a customer using a carrier ID would also have to dial an account number, for the local-access carrier does not provide billing services for many carriers. A customer can switch primary carriers by simply informing them and paying a small fee.

Table 6.2. *U.S. toll service market structure*

Item	AT&T	MCI	Sprint	Other Toll	Bell LECs	Other LECs
Toll revenues ($ billion)						
1981[a]	28.6	0.4	0.2	0.4	6.9	2.6
1984	34.9	1.8	1.1	1.1	9.0	3.4
1991	34.4	8.3	5.4	7.2	10.1	4.0
Long distance market shares						
1981[a]	96.3	1.3	0.7	1.3	na	na
1984	90.1	4.5	2.7	2.7	na	na
1991	62.2	15.0	9.7	13.1	na	na
Total toll revenue share						
1981[a]	72.9	1.0	0.5	1.0	17.6	6.6
1984	68.3	3.4	2.1	2.1	17.7	6.6
1991	50.6	11.0	7.5	8.7	15.8	6.4

Note: [a]Data for 1981 are estimates for AT&T and LECs. Prior to divestiture, the division of toll revenues among AT&T and local carriers was much different than after divestiture. The 1981 estimates divide total revenues approximately as they would have been divided by divestiture had it occurred prior to 1981. Long distance market shares for Bell LECs and other LECs is not applicable (na).
Sources: Federal Communications Commission. 1991. *Statistics of Communications Common Carriers, 1990–91 Edition*. Washington: U.S. Government Printing Office, p. 6; and FCC. 1992. *Preliminary Statistics of Communications Common Carriers*. Washington: FCC, p. 6.

around 60 percent. Its share of presubscribed lines was higher, about 75 percent.[48]

International telecommunications has not changed as dramatically since divestiture. In 1982, the United States had six telephone carriers and six record carriers serving international markets. By 1990, four new telephone carriers and two new record carriers had entered; however, exits and mergers kept the number of telephone carriers at six and reduced the number of record carriers to five, one of which had shrunk to almost nothing. The problem, of course, is that international carriers are governed by international regulatory rules, which are anticompetitive.

[48] Although these market share data indicate that long distance service is still quite concentrated, they probably overstate AT&T's actual market power. Virtually everywhere it operates, AT&T faces competition from several carriers, including three with nationwide networks and marketing efforts. Although AT&T's rates continue to be regulated by the FCC, the rates of the other carriers are not.

Table 6.3. *Revenues of U.S. common carriers, 1991 ($ million)*

Local exchange carriers	
Basic access	26,710
Network access[a]	25,718
Total access	52,428
Toll[a]	13,846
Leased circuit	1,027
Public telephone	1,890
Mobile services	204
Directory	2,941
Customer premises	132
Other	12,037
Total other services	32,077
Total revenues	85,505
Long distance carriers	55,260
Total all carriers	140,765

[a]Network access charges are the monthly charges to customers for access to the long distance network. Carrier access charges are included as part of toll revenues.
Source: Federal Communications Commission. 1992. *Preliminary Statistics of Communications Common Carriers.* Washington: FCC, pp. 6, 39–40.

Intra-LATA toll is still largely monopolized by local-exchange carriers (LECs), and as shown in Table 6.3, accounts for about one-sixth of LEC revenues. The extent of competition in this service is growing, because some states have relaxed prohibitions against intra-LATA toll competition; however, the extent to which the recent decline in LEC toll revenues (and growth in interexchange carrier revenues) is accounted for by intra-LATA competition is unknown because these data are not collected.

Market shares in telecommunications equipment reveal a pattern that is similar to long distance.[49] In terminal equipment, AT&T experienced precipitous sales declines after divestiture, with shares falling to 20 percent of previous level or less, in several markets. In central-office switches, AT&T has retained about 60 percent of sales; however, as with long distance, the better indicator of the degree of competitiveness is the magnitude and speed of lost sales – a decline in market share of more than 20 percent in three years. The main beneficiary has been Northern Telecom-

[49] For more details, see Noll and Owen (1989).

153

munications, the manufacturing affiliate of Bell Canada. Japanese and European switch manufacturers have not been successful in gaining a major foothold in the U.S. market except, in the case of Siemens, through acquisition of an American company, Rolm.[50]

In local-access service, despite the rapid growth of cellular telephone usage, local wireline access monopolies account for well over 90 percent of access. Since the federal government began to encourage competition in the 1960s, state regulatory policy has been significantly less procompetitive than federal policy. The stated reason is to maintain a pricing policy that cross-subsidizes residential access prices; however, recent studies of the economics of telephone service conclude that the actual pattern of subsidies is from business customers in larger cities to all customers, business and residential, in rural communities.[51] To date, access competition has been limited to the relatively minor overlap between mobile telephones and wireline access, the possibility of providing an independent local service among telephones in a large company or a large building, and the presence of a few alternative access providers that have been allowed to enter into the central business districts of a few large cities.

Nevertheless, even this last bastion of protected monopoly is beginning to erode. On April 16, 1993, Ameritech, the Bell operating company serving the Great Lakes states, submitted a proposal to the FCC to sell separately all components of local-access service, to allow resale of all of these components, to advocate the elimination of regulatory barriers to entry in all unbundled elements of local service, and to introduce "number portability" – the ability of a customer to retain the same telephone number when switching to another access provider – in return for permission to offer long distance service.[52] Eventual adoption of the plan is certainly several years away at best, in part because it is controversial among other local-access providers and long distance carriers, and in part because many of the implementation details remain to be specified. Nevertheless, several state regulatory commissions, including four that regulate Ameritech, have formally supported Ameritech's proposal.

---

[50] The reason for the lack of success of foreign firms in the U.S. switch market is still a matter of controversy. The old Bell companies, AT&T and Northern Telecommunications, are arguably the most efficient switch manufacturers in the world; however, some observers believe that the lack of success of foreign firms in the United States arises for basically the same reasons that U.S. firms are not very successful in Japan and Western Europe: Traditional procurement patterns and different national technical standards create high indirect trade barriers. See, for example, Fransman (1992), who cites the lack of success of ITT, a U.S. switch manufacturer with substantial foreign sales, in penetrating the U.S. market after divestiture because it could not adapt its high-quality switch to U.S. standards at a reasonable cost.

[51] See Crandall (1992) and Noll and Smart (1991).

[52] The details of the proposal, and the responses and counterproposals of others, can be found in Federal Communications Commission docket DA 93–481.

In mobile telecommunications services, the market contains literally thousands of firms, but competition has been limited (although it is growing).[53] All seven regional Bell operating companies, GTE, and several independent companies provide cellular telephone service, and in 1993 AT&T bought the largest independent supplier, McCaw. Actual competition is limited, however, because the FCC has licensed only two cellular telephone systems in each geographic area. But the FCC has also created a very large number of "private land mobile" systems, categorized by type of business user and technology. One category, Specialized Mobile Radio (SMR), which was originally intended for fleet services, has been permitted to be connected to the telephone network for more than a decade, but historically, regulatory restrictions have prevented SMR companies from selling services broadly that compete with cellular systems.

The historical limitations on radio telephony are rapidly eroding. Recently, the FCC relaxed restrictions on some providers of private radio services, enabling them to reconfigure their systems to offer mobile telephony. In 1993, several companies responded by announcing their intentions to convert specialized radio services to multiuse systems, including mobile telephones; one such company, Fleet Call, has already received FCC permission to enter the cellular business. In March of 1993, the House of Representatives joined the parade by passing a bill adopting a proposal by President Clinton that would transfer the spectrum now reserved for the government to new radio telephone technologies.[54] The FCC began implementing this legislation that September by announcing plans to allocate this spectrum to allow the entry of three to six national personal-communications service providers.[55] Through these policies, the FCC is gradually introducing real competition into the mobile telephone business; however, the agency officially maintains that the purpose of these policies is not to create a competitive radio-access alternative to ordinary telephone service.

The FCC's hesitancy to advocate publicly a competitive local-access policy is comprehensible only within the context of U.S. regulatory federalism. States are the principal authorities for regulating local access and all other local common carrier service. The FCC creates categories and restrictions in radio communications in part to avoid having the courts declare that these services are local common-carriers and, therefore, outside the FCC's regulatory jurisdiction. This enables the FCC to retain the authority to license numerous providers and to eschew price regulation in these technologies. The use of radio telephony for basic

---

[53] For a detailed analysis of competition in cellular telephone and other forms of mobile radio, see Rosston (1993).

[54] Andrews (1993).

[55] *New York Times*, September 20, 1993, p. 1.

access to the national telephone system is a common-carrier service, and so within state jurisdiction. Many states have subjected it to rate regulation, in part in fear that if its prices were too low, it would siphon business from local-exchange carriers.

Obviously, the FCC's reluctance to create structural competition in common-carrier services is understandable if the end result is not real competition, but state-regulated cartels. Nevertheless, recent events indicate that many states are now willing not to regulate if competition emerges, encouraging the FCC to relax its restrictions and to pursue an avowedly procompetitive access policy. These events indicate that radio telephony not only will become more competitive in the near future, but may become a serious access competitor to wireline companies within a few years.

Finally, one of the more controversial issues in the United States is the state of value-added or information services. The public debate rages over whether the United States is rich or poor in the availability of enhanced services. On the one hand, the United States has extensive private data networks, and a very large number of companies offering bulletin boards, electronic mail, answering service and voice mail, and specialized videotext (such as catalogs and electronic delivery of news). The United States also has by far the most extensive cable television system in the world, with over sixty national networks providing programming to more than 50 percent of homes, and more personal computers with modems than any other nation. On the other hand, the United States does not have anything like France's Minitel, extensive switched video, or many other services that are imaginable. The only generalization about which there is widespread agreement is that computer-based information services that use ordinary telephone lines face no entry barriers from regulators or telephone companies for the simple reason that neither organization even knows why any given business orders local-access lines. The controversy arises because only ordinary telephone lines are available in all but a few areas. More technologically advanced means of interconnection are essentially available only over private systems.

Procompetitive policies in the United States have made almost all components of the telecommunications industry more competitive. Only in local access and intra-LATA toll has competition not become significant, and even here there is a growing prospect as state regulation becomes less restrictive and radio technologies claim more of the access business. Whereas all of these trends began in the early 1970s, clearly divestiture was a major event. Only in low-end customer equipment did competition become vigorous before divestiture. In all other areas, most of the increase in competition has taken place since the breakup of AT&T into eight independent companies.

Table 6.4. *Entrants in Japan, 1992*

Type of carrier	Number of Carriers							
	1985	1986	1987	1988	1989	1990	1991	1992
New Type I								
National	0	3	3	3	3	3	3	3
Regional	0	0	3	4	7	7	7	7
Satellite	0	2	2	2	2	2	2	3
Mobile telephone	0	0	0	3	5	13	16	19
Paging	0	0	0	2	2	2	2	2
International	0	0	0	2	2	2	2	2
Total	0	5	11	35	43	60	66	70
New Type II								
General	85	200	346	512	668	813	912	996
Special	0	9	10	18	25	28	31	37

Type of Type I service	Number of carriers in 1992
Domestic long distance	4
Domestic leased circuit	13
Domestic data transmission	2
Mobile telephone	19
Mobile data transmission	1
Paging	36
Ship communications	2
International telephone	2
International data transmission	1

Source: Ministry of Posts and Telecommunications. July 1992. "An Outline of the Telecommunications Business."

3.4. Entry in Japan

Entry into telecommunications in Japan has also been substantial since the implementation of the reform legislation in 1985. Table 6.4 shows the number of new companies entering each major category of service since then. As in the United States, the focal points of competitive entry have been interexchange services, value-added services, and mobile communications. In all cases the absolute numbers are far lower in Japan than in the United States. Nevertheless, in the absence of other constraints, the numbers would be sufficient to produce a competitive market.

In long distance, three national terrestrial networks and three satellite systems are available; in the highly populated area surrounding Tokyo, Osaka, and intermediate points (the Tokyo–Osaka corridor) regional car-

157

Table 6.5. *Telecommunications markets in Japan*

Service	1985	1987	1990	1991
Revenues (trillions of yen)				
Domestic telephone	4.20	4.50	4.88	4.94
Domestic leased circuits	0.25	0.30	0.44	0.46
Mobile telephone	0.02	0.05	0.25	0.30
Paging	0.07	0.09	0.13	0.15
Other domestic	0.39	0.42	0.36	0.45
International telephone	0.14	0.19	0.21	0.23
International leased circuits	0.01	0.01	0.02	0.02
Other international	0.06	0.05	0.04	0.04
New competitor market shares				
Domestic telephone		0.3	4.7	6.5
Domestic leased circuits		0.0	11.0	13.6
Mobile telephone		0.0	28.7	35.6
Paging		1.1	29.2	32.3
Other domestic		0.0	2.6	2.8
International telephone		0.0	12.6	20.7
International leased circuits		0.0	11.4	16.8
Other international		0.0	0.0	0.0

Sources: Ministry of Posts and Telecommunications, "Type One Telecommunications Market," internal memo, July 6, 1991, and "An Outline of the Telecommunications Business," internal memo, July 1992.

riers are also active. Mobile telephone service is much like that in the United States. Whereas numerous companies participate, the number is limited to two in each geographic area, except for three in Tokyo. International facilities-based entry has been minimal, as in the United States.

Table 6.5 contains a summary of the size of various Japanese telecommunications services markets and the aggregate market shares of the competitors. In addition to these data, another indicator of the penetration of competitors is market shares of interprefectural calls, which are roughly comparable to inter-LATA calls in the United States. In 1990, the new entrants had captured 16 percent of these calls, and 46 percent of interprefectural calling in the Tokyo–Osaka corridor.[56] These data are not strictly comparable to U.S. data; however, the combined share of AT&T plus all local-exchange carriers in total telephone revenues (including leased circuits) is about 85 percent, compared to NTT's 93 percent, indicating that competitive entrants are about twice as important in the

[56] InfoCom Research (1992: 31). These data apply to only the prefectures where new entrants provide service. Only NTT serves some of the more remote areas.

United States as in Japan. Of course, because AT&T competes with LECs for leased access and in some cases for intra-LATA tolls, and because the LECs compete outside their service territories in radio telephone and information services, this comparison understates the greater development of structural competition in the United States. Nevertheless, the new entrants are growing rapidly in Japan, and these differences primarily reflect the fact that the key event in the United States – divestiture – took place nearly three years before structural competition was first licensed in Japan.

An important part of the story about entry in Japan is the identity of the companies providing common carrier services (Type I and Special Type II). In the United States, these companies are generally strictly telecommunications services companies, whereas in Japan they tend to be joint ventures among families of companies that have a strong presence in the electronics industry. Table 6.6 provides a road map to the complex world of Japanese industrial combines – which companies are aligned with which. Table 6.7 shows the largest investors in Type I carriers, and Table 6.8 presents the same information for the Special Type II carriers.

The data in these tables indicate that the number of independent entities is far smaller than the number of total entrants shown in Table 6.4. For example, Mitsubishi is a major investor in two of the three national long distance carriers, one of the three satellite carriers, five of the seven regional carriers, one of the two international carriers, seven of the sixteen mobile telephone carriers, and ten of the thirty-six Special Type II carriers. Many of the carriers are associated with other infrastructural firms, such as electric utilities or railroads, which in turn are part of industrial families that include equipment suppliers. Moreover, the general pattern of ownership is overlapping joint ventures. Sometimes Mitsubishi will venture with Mitsui, sometimes with Sumitomo, and so on. The end result is a complex tapestry of interrelated companies. This pattern is consistent with the view that the purpose of entry has been primarily to give more large companies and combines a share of the telecommunications business, and less to provide real competition to users.

When cross-ownership is taken into account, the new facilities-based companies cannot be regarded as competitors with each other. As Table 6.7 shows, all of the national and regional entrants are a joint venture involving Mitsubishi and Mitsui. Likewise, all of the cellular companies are a joint venture involving Daini Denshin-Denwa Inc. (DDI), which in turn is a joint venture among the same two families, three other *keiretsu*, and electronics firms Kyocera and Sony. All three new digital carriers are owned in part by Japan Telecom, which is a joint venture involving Mitsubishi, Mitsui, and Sumitomo. Thus, the apparent entry boom in Japanese facilities-based telecommunications is more accurately seen as the

Table 6.6. *Japanese corporate groupings*

Name	Member companies (a partial listing)
Mitsubishi	All Mitsubishi companies, Meiji Life, Tokyo Fire and Marine Insurance, Asahi Glass, Kirin Brewery, NYK Line, Chiyoda Chemical, Japan Construction Metal Products, Hokoku Cement
Sumitomo	All Sumitomo companies, Nippon Electric, Toyo Kogyo, Satellite Telecommunications, Sanyo, C. Ito, Wakayama Kyodo Power, Takeda Chemicals, Asahi Chemicals, Kajima Corporation
Mitsui	All Mitsui companies, Sakura Bank, Taisho Marine and Fire Insurance, Onoda Cement, Fuji Film, Fuji Xerox; loosely affiliated with Toshiba and Toyota
Fuyo	Fuji Bank, Yasuda Fire and Marine Insurance, Oki, Yasuda Trust and Banking, Hitachi, Nissan, Marubeni, Nippon Kokan, Seiko, Canon, Sapporo Breweries, Showa Denko, Dai Nippon Printing, Daiichi Cement, Nisshin Four, Keihin Electric Express Railway, Toa Railway, Yokogawa Electric, Yodogawa Steel
Daiichi Kangyo	Daiichi Kangyo Bank, Asahi Mutual Life, Taisei Fire and Marine Insurance, Fujitsu, Fuji Electric, Furukawa Electric, Isuzu, Kanamachi Rubber; loosely affiliated with C. Ito and Nissho Iwai trading companies
Sanwa	Sanwa Bank, Nippon Life, Nippon Fire and Marine Insurance, Koa Fire and Marine Insurance, Toyo Trust and Banking, Daido Mutual Life, Hitachi, Osaka Cement, Kobe Steel, Maruzen Oil, Fujisawa Pharmaceutical, Kansai paint, Toyo Rubber, Toyo Construction, Toyo Information Systems; loosely connected to Nomura Securities

Note: Hitachi is affiliated with both Fuyo and Sanwa, and C. Ito is affiliated with both Sumitomo and Daiichi Kangyo.
Sources: *Handbook of Japanese Financial/Industrial Combines.* 1972. San Francisco: Pacific Basin Reports; *Japan Company Handbook.* 1993. Tokyo: Toyo keizai shimposha.

creation of a second large rival to NTT by business alliances that have a significant presence in the electronics industry but that were not part of NTT's procurement family.

The final important structural feature is that NTT remains largely un-privatized. NTT is also a partner in several of the Special Type II carriers. Because the government owns most of the stock, it faces a conflict in regulating the industry. More vigorous competition will reduce its net

Table 6.7. *Type I carrier entrants, 1992*

Carrier	Domestic Keiretsu (1) (2) (3) (4) (5) (6)						Other Domestic (partial)	Foreign
Inter-city carriers								
Daini Denden (DDI)	*	*	*	*	*		Kyocera, Sony, Ushio Electric, others	
Japan Telecom	*	*	*				JR East, West, Tokai	
Teleway Japan (TWJ)	*	*	*				Toyota, Road Fac. Assoc.	
International carriers								
ITJ	*	*	*	*			Matsushita, Nissho Iwai, Bank of Tokyo	
IDC							C. Itoh, Toyota	Cable & Wireless, Pacific Telesis
Regional carriers								
TTNET	*	*					Tokyo Electric Power, Nissan	
Osaka Media Port	*	*	*				Osaka Municipal Gov't, Kansai Electric Power	
Chubu Telecom.	*	*					Chubu Electric Power	
Shikoku Information and Telecom.	*	*					Shikoku Electric Power	
Kyushu Telecom.	*	*					Kyushu Electric Power	
Hokkaido Telecom.	*	*					Hokkaido Electric Power	
Mobile carriers								
IDO							Teleway Japan, Toyota, Tokyo Electric, Nissan, Chubu Electric	
Tu Ka Cellular Tokyo	*	*	*	*			Nissan, DDI, Sony, KDD, LTCB,	Motorola BritTel. GTE NYNEX, U.S. West, Rogers
Hokkaido Cellular							DDI, Hokkaido Electric	
Hokuriku Cellular							DDI, Hokuriku Electric	
Chugoku Cellular							DDI, Chugoku Electric, Mazda	
Kansai Cellular							DDI, Kansai Electric	
Kyushu Cellular							DDI, Kyushu Electric	
Shikoku Cellular							DDI, Shikoku Electric	
Tohoku Cellular							DDI, Tohoku Electric	
Digital carriers								
Tokyo Digital							Japan Telecom, JR East, Toyota, KDD, Nippon Steel	PacTel, C&W
Tokai Digital							Japan Telecom, Toyota, KDD, Toho Gas	PacTel, C&W
KDP							Japan Telecom, JR West, Toyota	PacTel, C&W

Notes: Groups of companies: (1) Mitsubishi, (2) Sumitomo, (3) Mitsui, (4) Fuyo, (5) Daiichi Kangyo, (6) Sanwa. See Table 6.6 for members.
* other shareholder

Roger G. Noll and Frances McCall Rosenbluth

Table 6.8. *Special Type II entrants, 1992*

Carrier	Domestic keiretsu (1)	(2)	(3)	(4)	(5)	(6)	Other Domestic	Foreign
Intech	#	*				*	Daiwa Securities	
Fujitsu	*	*		#		*	IBJ	
JCRI		#						
NEC	*	#				*	Daiichi Life	
Hitachi							Hitachi[a]	
Kyodo			*					
Japan ENS					*		IBJ, Hitachi, KDD	AT&T
Oki	*	*		#			Daichi Life	
NIS			*	#			Bank of Tokyo	Brit Tel
NTT Internet			*	*	*		NTT, Nikei, Hitachi	
Japan Info							NTT	IBM
Int'l VAN							Matsushita, TEPCP, Bank of Tokyo, Intech, JAL	
Nomura							Nomura	
Mitsui Info			#					
Japan IBM								IBM
Nikkei							Nikkei	
Toyo Info						#		
INES	*						Kyoei Life, Daiichi Life	
NI&C							NTT	IBM
NTT Data							NTT	
Mitsubishi Info Net	#							
Dentsu Int'l Info							Dentsu	GE
Kennet	*	*					KDD, Osaka Gas, Kansai, Matsushita	Brit Tel
Recruit							Unknown	
Toshiba	*	*	*				Daiichi Life, LTCB	
Bitel							Bitel	
Sprint								Sprint
Unisys	*		*	*				Unisys
New Japan Steel Inf							New Japan Steel	
Daiwa Res		*					Daiwa	
DEC							DEC	
First Net							Canon, NTT, DHL	
Matsushita	*	#	*				Matsushita	
Fairway						#		C&W
Syncordia							Unknown	
Fax Int'l							Unknown	
Total	10	9	7	4	3	5	Daiichi Life 4, Daiwa 2, NTT 5, Hitachi 3 Bank of Tokyo, KDD Matsushita, IBJ all 2	IBM 3, Brit Tel 2

Notes: Groups of companies: (1) Mitsubishi, (2) Sumitomo, (3) Mitsui, (4) Fuyo, (5) Daiichi Kangyo, (6) Sanwa. See Table 6.6 for members.

Largest shareholder

* other shareholder

[a]Hitachi is affiliated with Fuyo and Sanwa.

revenues and its prospects for selling the remaining stock that is to be privatized.

The conclusion from these facts is that the raw nose-count data vastly overstate the extent of structural competition. Overlapping ownership patterns reduce the likelihood that most of the new companies will actually compete.

NTT continues to procure much of its equipment from its "family firms," as Table 6.9 suggests. The government's aim in allowing new entry was not to make carriers adopt a more diverse procurement policy, but through new carriers to give more equipment suppliers access to the industry.[57] The one possible exception was foreign suppliers, for pressure from U.S. trade negotiators led to assertions by Japanese leaders that privatization and structural competition would be part of a strategy to make equipment markets more open to U.S. firms. In some ways, this has occurred, for several American firms have secured ownership positions in various new carriers (this being the distinctly Japanese way to securing access to equipment procurement). Hughes, for example, has an interest in one of the new satellite carriers, and AT&T, IBM, General Electric, Sprint, and Unisys have interests in Special Type II carriers. NTT has also dramatically increased its procurement from foreign firms, from $19 million in 1981 to $603 million in 1991 and $784 million in 1992. These figures are clearly more than "mops and buckets." In some areas, foreign purchases have become a large fraction of total procurement, most notably in information-processing systems, where foreign suppliers accounted for 40 percent of procurement in 1992. Nevertheless, for all NTT procurement, purchases from foreign firms are still less than 5 percent of NTT's annual investments.[58]

Not surprisingly, the thrust of liberalization policy in Japan is not to create what Americans would call competition. The pattern of overlapping ownership and vertical integration makes the number of distinct decision-making entities far smaller than the number of legal entities. Nevertheless, the magnitude of the change in the industry is far from trivial, in that the growth of new entrants in Japan is broadly similar to the growth in the United States. The government service monopoly has clearly

---

[57] In April 1993, the MPT announced intentions to lay an extensive fiber optics network with government funds, rather than rely on investment by the carriers themselves. According to an executive with whom we spoke at a new long distance carrier, this reflects the government's desire to bolster NTT's ability to continue subsidizing equipment suppliers in the face of long distance competition. See also Aizu Izumi, April 16, 1993.

[58] Data on NTT procurement from *NTT Procurement Activities 1992*, NTT, pp. 5, 43, and *NTT Procurement* (no date), NTT America. Procurement of U.S. and Canadian products accounts for about 95 percent of total purchases from foreign firms (private communication from Koichiro Hayashi, president, NTT America), but only recently did NTT buy its first U.S. switches. See Bradsher (1993).

Table 6.9. *Dependence of electronics firms on NTT procurement*

	NTT procurement as percentage of sales	Equipment sold to NTT	Corporate group (shares held)
"Big Four" suppliers			
Hitachi	1–2%	Digital switches, etc.	
Nippon Electric (NEC)	10-20%	Digital switches, etc.	Sumitomo Group
Fujitsu	9%	Digital switches, etc.	Fuji Elec. (15%)
Oki Electric	28.5%	Digital switches, etc.	Fuyo Group
Subcontractors and other suppliers			
Toshiba	1%	Telephones, switches	Mitsui Group
Kanda Telecommunications	43%	Telephones	Fujitsu (12%)
Nittsuko	23%	Telephones, switches	NEC (34%)
Meisei Electric	50%	Telephones, switches	NEC (9%)
Daiko Electric	50%	Telephones, switches	Oki (20%)
Takamizawa Electric	7%	Telephones, switches	Fujitsu (37%)
Tamura Electric	37%	Telephones	NEC(16%), Oki(16%)
Nakayo Telecommunications	33%	Telephones, switches	Hitachi (20%)
Hasegawa Electric	na	Telephones, switches	Fujitsu (55%)
Iwasaki Electric	28.5%	Telephones	
Matsushita Telecommunications	1%	Telephones, car phones	Matsushita Electric (61%)
Anritsu	20%	Public telephones, switches	NEC (26%)
Northern Telecom	na	Digital switches	
Kokusai Denwa	5%	Car phones, pagers	Hitachi (21%)
Mitsubishi Electric	1%	Car phones	Mitsubishi Group
Nihon Cordless	13%	Car phones	Nissei Textile (22%)
Motorola	na	Car phones	
Toyo Electric	8%	Pagers	NEC (40%)
Matsushita Denso	na	Facsimiles	Matsushita (60%)
Canon	na	Facsimiles	Fuyo Group
Tamura Machines	na	Facsimiles	
Ricoh	na	Facsimiles	
Brother	na	Facsimiles	
Origin Electric	16%	Power supply equipment	Fuyo Group
Sanken Electric	7%	Power supply equipment	
Kyosan	5%	Power supply equipment	Mitsubishi Group
Tamura	2%	Power supply equipment	Sumitomo Group
Shin Dengen Kogyo	10%	Power supply equipment	Fujitsu (8%)
Sanyo Electric	10%	Power supply equipment	
Nippon Electric Machinery	na	Power supply equipment	NEC (35%)
Fujitsu Denso	na	Transmission equipment	Fujitsu (70%)
Ogura Denki	30%	Transmission equipment	NEC (10%)
Denki Kogyo	na	Antenna	NEC (6%)
Ando Electric	11%	Electronic measuring equip.	NEC (51%)
Tohoku Metals	7%	Telephone cards	NEC (43%)
Yuasa Batteries	na	Batteries	Mitsui Group
Furukawa Batteries	na	Batteries	Furukawa (53%)

Source: Koichi Nemoto, "Denki tsushin jigyo to tsushin meekaa no kankei to tenkai [The Relationship Between the Telecommunications Industry and Equipment Makers, and its Development]," *Tohoku daigaku keizai gakkai* 53,(no. 3(1992):142.
na = Not available

been broken while government still possesses most of the ownership in the dominant domestic carrier; formerly excluded industrial combines have gained an important foothold in the industry; and even several Japanese divisions of large U.S. firms have become members of the families of firms involved with several new entrants. American equipment manufacturers have had modest but important success in selling some high-technology products in the formerly closed Japanese network equipment market. While this is not open and free competition in the American sense, it is most definitely liberalization within the Japanese context.

3.5. Service prices, usage, and costs

Because the political objectives of telecommunications reform differ considerably between Japan and the United States, patterns of pricing in the two countries can be expected to differ, with consumer prices relatively lower in the United States. Likewise, to the extent that telecommunications carriers are regarded first as protected markets for equipment suppliers, costs and prices in Japan can be expected to be higher than in the postdivestiture United States. Finally, differences in the level and structure of prices should produce corresponding differences in patterns of use. In particular, higher costs and prices in Japan should result in less usage, and the Japanese policy of charging for use for all calls (not just long distance) should reduce local-exchange usage relative to the United States.

The long-term general price performance of telecommunications is broadly similar in Japan and the United States. Historically, prices of all telecommunications services have increased less rapidly than the consumer price index (CPI). In Japan, the CPI increased fivefold from 1960 to 1990. Between 1962 and 1990, basic access prices doubled in larger cities and tripled in smaller ones, and the price of a local call rose from seven yen to ten yen (about 40 percent).[59] Long distance calls during weekdays remained largely unchanged, although prices fell slightly for the longest calling distances in the last two years of the period. In the United States, the average annual increase in the CPI between 1935 and 1991 was 4.2 percent, and for telecommunications services the average increase was 2.1 percent.[60] Thus, in both countries there has been a steady long-term decline in the real price of telephone service of approximately the same magnitude.

In recent years, the pattern of price changes and relative prices have not been the same in the two countries. Table 6.10 shows several relevant price increases in various categories of services in the United States since

[59] Historical data on postwar NTT prices are from internal documents provided by staff of the Ministry of Post and Telecommunications.
[60] Federal Communications Commission (1992: 7).

Table 6.10. *Recent trends in U.S. telephone prices (percent change in price indexes)*

Year	CPI	CPI–all telephone services	CPI–all local charges	PPI–monthly service charges	CPI–toll: interstate	CPI–toll intrastate
1978	9.0	0.9	1.4	3.1	-0.8	1.3
1979	13.3	0.7	1.7	1.6	-0.7	0.1
1980	12.5	4.6	7.0	7.1	3.4	-0.6
1981	8.9	11.7	12.6	15.6	14.6	6.2
1982	3.8	7.2	10.8	9.0	2.6	4.2
1983	3.8	3.6	3.1	0.2	1.5	7.4
1984	3.9	9.2	17.2	10.4	-4.3	3.6
1985	3.8	4.7	8.9	12.4	-3.7	0.6
1986	1.1	2.7	7.1	8.9	-9.4	0.3
1987	4.4	-1.3	3.3	2.6	-12.4	-3.0
1988	4.4	1.3	4.5	4.6	-4.2	-4.2
1989	4.6	-0.3	0.6	1.9	-1.3	-2.6
1990	6.1	-0.4	1.0	1.5	-3.7	-2.2
1991	3.1	3.5	5.1	2.1	1.3	-1.5
1992	3.2	0.6	1.2	0.6	0.0	-1.9

Note: All data are for calendar year except 1992, which shows the July–July change.
Source: Federal Communications Commission. 1992. *Trends in Telephone Service*. September, pp. 7–8.

1978. Because of the nature of the regulatory process, telecommunications price changes lag by a year or two changes in the general rate of inflation, which is revealed in the late 1970s and early 1980s in Table 6.10. The 1978–81 CPI inflation hit telecommunications in 1980–82, with the latter increasing a little more than half as fast as the former. Divestiture on January 1, 1984, led to a major increase in telecommunications prices. Given a background inflation rate of a little less than 4 percent during the period just before and after divestiture, the expected price performance would have been for telecommunications prices to increase by about 2 percent per year. The excess price increase attributable to divestiture was about 10 percent for 1984 and 1985. Since divestiture, however, the price performance has been substantially better than historical experience. From 1986 through 1991, telephone prices have increased by about half a percent per year, on average, while the CPI has increased at about a 4.4 percent annual rate. This below-trend performance in telecommunications prices has now offset the immediate price increases after divestiture.

Table 6.11. *AT&T rates, 1984-1992*

| Distance | Charge for five minute call ($) | | | | | |
| | January 1984 | | | July 1992 | | |
in miles	Day	Eve.	Night	Day	Eve.	Night
<10	0.96	0.57	0.38	1.00	0.65	0.55
11-22	1.28	0.76	0.51	1.10	0.65	0.59
23-55	1.60	0.96	0.64	1.10	0.65	0.59
56-124	2.05	1.22	0.82	1.10	0.70	0.59
125-292	2.14	1.28	0.85	1.10	0.70	0.65
293-430	2.27	1.36	0.90	1.15	0.70	0.65
431-925	2.34	1.40	0.93	1.15	0.75	0.65
926-1,910	2.40	1.44	0.96	1.19	0.75	0.65
1,911-3,000	2.70	1.62	1.08	1.25	0.77	0.65
3,001-4,250	2.80	1.68	1.12	1.50	1.04	0.80
4,251-5,750	2.91	1.74	1.16	1.65	1.10	0.85

Source: Federal Communications Commission. 1992. *Trends in Telephone Service.* September, p. 11.

The four leftmost columns of Table 6.10 indicate that telephone prices were dramatically restructured in the United States during the 1980s. Between 1980 and 1986, real basic monthly service charges for both residential and business customers rose sharply. The average price (including taxes) for residential basic access with unlimited local calling rose from $8.32 in 1980 to $16.13 in 1986, an annual rate of increase of about 11 percent. The same service then rose to $18.64 in 1991, an annual rate of increase of less than 3 percent (and so more like the historical pattern).[61]

Interstate telephone calls, except for the inflation year of 1980, rose much more slowly in the early 1980s, and after divestiture fell dramatically. Table 6.11 shows the changes in AT&T's federally regulated long distance tariffs from 1984 to 1992. For calls during the day and early evening exceeding fifty-six miles (ninety km), prices have fallen, in most cases by more than 40 percent. These price reductions have tracked price cuts by the essentially unregulated competitors, who remain a few percent cheaper than AT&T. Since 1987, intrastate toll rates have also been falling, although not as dramatically as federal rates. Intra-LATA toll rates are regulated separately in each state, but generally they are lower than the

---

[61] Federal Communications Commission (1989: 16), and FCC (1992: 10). For a more complete discussion of local access prices after divestiture, see Noll and Smart (1991).

rates for comparable inter-LATA distances.[62] As an example, in California in 1992, the rate for calls to adjacent calling areas was ten cents for the first three minutes, plus four cents for each additional minute, so that a three minute call in the lowest AT&T rate distance category would be 18 cents, not $1.00, if made within a LATA. For distances of twenty to seventy miles, California peak rates for three minutes varied from 66 cents to $1.02, for evening rates from 46 to 72 cents, and for night rates from 27 to 40 cents, all of which are below the comparable AT&T rates.[63] Again, the price per minute is higher for the first minute, so that calls of longer duration are still less expensive than the AT&T rates. Because almost all short distance toll calls are placed within LATAs, these prices are the better indicator of the U.S. price structure.

We have not been able to locate telephone price indexes for Japan; however, NTT's historical pricing data since 1953 reveal distinctly different patterns than those in the United States. Since 1977, the nominal price of basic monthly service has remained virtually unchanged in Japan, although it has been unbundled, as in the United States, into separate charges for basic access, inside wire maintenance, and telephone instrument rental. As in the United States, customers are free to provide their own terminal devices, but unlike in the United States, inside wire maintenance must still be procured from the local-access provider. The monthly rental for telephones in Japan has fallen slightly, while the other prices have not changed.

To compare Japanese and U.S. prices requires selecting an appropriate dollar value for the yen. All of the calculations in this chapter assume that a dollar is equivalent to 130 yen, which is at the high end of the value of the dollar during the entire reform period and is higher than the average exchange rate during the early 1990s. At the average exchange rate for the early 1990s, the dollar value of Japanese telephone services prices would be about 10 percent higher than the figures reported here.

Tables 6.12 and 6.13 compare October 1991 U.S. prices and January 1992 Japanese prices for various residential and business access services. Both tables break down prices by size of local calling area; however, the table for Japan is a complete representation of the NTT price system, whereas the U.S. table averages prices for selected local areas for Bell operating companies across all states. Because all states have different local-access pricing systems, one cannot construct strictly comparable

---

[62] The main reason for this phenomenon is that inter-LATA carriers are required to pay usage-based "carrier access charges" for the portions of calls between the inter-LATA carrier's points of presence in each LATA and the ultimate origin and destination of the call. This amounts to paying two local toll calls as part of each intra-LATA call.

[63] These prices are taken from the local-calling prices in the *Pacific Bell White Pages,* May 1992. Because the data appear as prices between specific calling areas, maps were consulted to determine approximate distances.

Table 6.12. *U.S. access prices*

Basic monthly access charge, 1991 (including excise taxes)	
Residential	
Unlimited local calling	$18.64
Lifeline	11.11
Local measured service (50 calls)	14.36
Touchtone	1.27
Installation	44.17
Business	
Unlimited local calling	37.59
Local measured service (200 calls)	36.93
Touchtone	1.98
Installation	77.19

Monthly access	Size of local calling area (000 terminals)				
charge (1988)	1	5	50	500	1,000
Residential	10.76	1.11	12.40	13.56	12.98
Business	25.87	6.99	31.74	38.33	36.33

Sources: Federal Communications Commission. 1992. *Trends in Telephone Service*. September, p. 10; National Association of Regulatory Utility Commissioners, *Bell Operating Companies Exchange Service Telephone Rates.*

Table 6.13. *Access prices in Japan (NTT), 1985–1992 (130Y = $1)*

Monthly	Size of local calling area (000 lines)				
basic access	<0.8	0.8–8	8–50	50–400	>400
Residential	$5.78	$7.32	$8.86	$10.40	$11.94
50 local calls	3.85	3.85	3.85	3.95	3.85
Total bill	9.63	11.17	12.71	14.25	14.79
Business	8.86	11.17	13.48	15.79	18.10
200 local calls	15.40	15.40	15.40	15.40	15.40
Total bill	24.26	26.57	28.88	31.19	33.50

Other basic services (business and residential, all areas)

Initial installation	$560
Subsequent installation	73
Touchtone service	3

Source: NTT. 1992. *Summary of Charges for Telecommunications Services.* January, pp. 1, 8.

169

tables for the United States and Japan. Likewise, in Tokyo, TTNet (a regional carrier) also sells local access according to a different price structure than NTT's.

The first important fact that stands out from these tables is that local-access prices are not very different. In particular, for large cities, local measured service in Japan costs $11.94. Adding the fifty calls per month that are included in the U.S. rate, the comparable Japanese price is $14.79. This price is a little lower than unlimited service in the U.S. and a little higher than U.S. local measured service, with the gap between large and small communities greater in Japan. Although Japan has really not yet started the process of bringing prices more in line with costs in its less-populated areas, average access prices are broadly similar in the two countries.

The second important fact is the dramatic difference in installation fees. The initial subscription fee in Japan is $560 per line, with an additional $73 every time a subscriber moves. There is no differential between residential and business users. This phenomenal difference in the initial installation fee, which is the equivalent of about $4 per month in the basic access charge, makes telephone access in Japan more expensive than in the United States. After adding the monthly equivalent of the difference in installation fees, the residential rural rate becomes $13.63, which is only slightly below the average U.S. rate for measured service. The large city rate becomes about $19, which exceeds the price of unlimited local-calling service in the United States.

Third, the cost per call for measured service is lower in the United States. For example, in California, the measured-service local-calling rate is 4 cents for the first minute, and 1 cent per minute thereafter, whereas the Japanese rate is 7 cents for each three minutes, so that for calls exceeding three minutes, the U.S. charge is much cheaper. Moreover, Japanese local tolls have been remarkably stable, at least until 1993. NTT has always charged for local calls.[64] This price was 7 yen per three minutes in 1953, and was increased to 10 yen in 1976. In 1993, NTT proposed doubling this rate to 10 yen per ninety seconds. This increase will make the price of a three minute local call about 15 cents, which is more than twice the U.S. charge and approaches the U.S. price for calls from pay telephones.[65]

Fourth, long distance tolls have not been affected by liberalization as much as have U.S. long distance rates. NTT introduced direct-dial long distance calls in 1962, and the prices established then, which distinguished

---

[64] The other access provider, TTNet, has a different price structure: $650 for installation for installing a single line, plus $37 a month for service that includes fifty hours of call duration for all calls up to twenty km, plus $19 for each additional twenty-five hours of local calls. InfoCom Research (1992: 37).

[65] *Financial Times of Japan*, March 16, 1993, p. 24.

Table 6.14. *Toll prices in Japan, 1987–1992 (130Y = $1)*[a]

	Distance (km)								
	<20	20–30	30–40	40–60	60–80	80–100	100–160	160–320	320+
1984: NTT									
Peak	23	38	46	69	92	108	138	200	308
Shoulder	23	38	46	69	69	69	77	115	185
Trough	23	38	46	69	69	69	77	115	169
1992: NTT									
Peak	15	38	46	69	92	108	138	154	154
Shoulder	15	38	46	69	69	69	77	92	92
Trough	15	31	38	54	62	62	69	85	85
1992: NCC									
Peak	38	38	38	62	69	108	108*	154*	154
Shoulder	31	31	31	38	38	54	54*	77*	77
Trough	31	31	31	38	38	54	54*	77*	77

*The distance break for the NCCs occurs at 170 km, rather than 160.
[a]Price in cents for three minute call
Note: Japanese prices are expressed in the number of seconds allowed for 10 yen, so that the entries in the table are based on the number of ten = yen charges necessary to allow 180 seconds of connect time. In nearly all cases, the price would enable the caller some additional time beyond three minutes.
NCC = new common carriers
Peak = 8 a.m. to 7 p.m. weekdays
Shoulder = weekdays 7–11 p.m, other days 8 a.m to 11 p.m.
Trough = 11 p.m. to 7 a.m.
Source: NTT, "History of Rates for Direct Dialed Calls"; and InfoCom Research. 1992. *Information & Communications in Japan 1992*. Tokyo: InfoCom Research, p. 36.

between day and evening calling, remained unchanged until 1980, when a lower late night rate (9 P.M. to 6 A.M.) was introduced. In 1981, a further distinction was made between weekdays and Sundays and holidays, with prices cut for daytime calls in the latter times. In addition, price cuts of about 15 percent were adopted for the longest long distance category (over 320 km). But for all other price categories, NTT prices were the same in 1988 as they had been in 1962.

The changes in toll prices during liberalization are shown in Table 6.14. Since 1988, NTT toll prices have dropped for the shortest and longest categories, but for calls between 40 km and 160 km, prices for weekday daytime and evening service remain exactly the same as in 1962. Because well over 90 percent of telephone calls in Japan are for distances under

160km,[66] the implication of these changes is that for nearly all calls, NTT prices have not changed in three decades. For the competitive carriers other than TTNet, the prices shown do not include the charges by NTT for local access. For customers without private lines, NTT local access charges are at least 10 yen per three minutes on each end. The exact amount is determined by the distance of the call over NTT lines from a competitive carrier's points of presence to the points where the call begins and terminates. Thus, from the customer's perspective, the prices charged by NTT and its competitors are essentially the same. The conclusion to be drawn from both the historical stability of long distance prices and the parallel pricing between NTT and its competitors is that the entrants have been brought in under a price umbrella at the old monopoly tariffs.

Tables 6.11 and 6.14 illustrate a very important difference between toll prices in Japan and the United States. Note that AT&T's prices are insensitive to distance. As a result, AT&T's prices are much higher than Japanese prices for short distances, but at longer distances are much lower. Prices are about the same are in the range of fifty to sixty miles. In the United States, these shorter calls would be mostly intra-LATA toll calls provided by local-exchange carriers, with substantially lower prices than AT&T's. The longest distances in Japan fall into the AT&T category of 926–1,910 miles, which has a peak price of $1.19 for AT&T compared to $1.85 for NTT and $1.54 for the new Japanese carriers. For shorter distances, the comparison with the California intra-LATA rates produces a similar result. The California price for calls to adjacent local exchanges is 18 cents for three minutes, compared to NTT's fifteen cents for less than twelve miles (twenty kilometers); however, beyond three minutes the California price is lower because of the lower prices of additional minutes. For longer calls, California intra-LATA rates are about the same as NTT below thirty-six miles (sixty km), but are 10 to 30 percent below the NTT rates beyond this distance. Perhaps the most striking differences between Japan and the United States emerge for cellular telephone service. In the United States, cellular prices not only vary among states and carriers, but most carriers offer customers a menu of pricing plans, each with a different basic monthly hookup charge and a price per minute of use in peak and off-peak periods. For the pricing plan with the lowest monthly charge (and the highest per-minute charges), the average price in the United States in 1990 among a sample of sixty-five systems was $20.59, and the average per-minute charge was 55 cents.[67] In Japan, the monthly charge varies depending on the type of telephone used (auto, shoulder phone, or hand held), but not by geographic area. The unweighted average across tech-

[66] InfoCom Research (1992: 21).
[67] Rosston (1993: chapter 5).

nologies and carriers was approximately $100, and the unweighted average per-minute charge was about 61 cents.[68] But in addition, Japanese subscribers face an initial subscription fee that averages about $350, for which there is no counterpart in the United States.

Price comparisons clearly show that most telecommunications services are substantially cheaper in the United States than in Japan. Moreover, Japanese pricing penalizes both usage and long distance calling relative to shorter toll calls. The overall effect of this pricing structure should be to reduce utilization; moreover, because in both countries the profits of the dominant carriers are limited by regulation, the main explanation for higher prices in Japan should be higher costs. In particular, based on the conclusion that the Japanese political system should bias telecommunications policy in favor of equipment manufacturers, we hypothesize that the Japanese system should have higher capital costs and less-efficient usage of capital than the U.S. system. Data pertaining to all of these issues are summarized in Table 6.15.

One striking performance indicator is the overall penetration rate of telephone service. The high installation charge in Japan holds down the number of lines to levels usually associated with less wealthy, less technologically advanced economies. In 1991, the United States had 51.4 lines per 100 population, whereas Japan had 42.0, nestled comfortably among Italy (40.0), New Zealand (43.4), and the United Kingdom (44.4).[69] Likewise, in cellular telephone service, where both installation and monthly access charges are much higher in Japan, Japan had an estimated 1.6 million subscribers in 1992, compared to about eleven million in the United States, amounting to a penetration rate that is more than three times higher in the United States.[70]

Another striking comparison is the extent of usage. High calling prices hold down calling in Japan. Japan has almost exactly half the population of the United States; however, Americans make more than six times as many telephone calls. More amazingly, Americans spend twelve times as many minutes using the telecommunications system, and almost fifteen times the amount of time on local calls.

Given the differences in usage, the Japanese pay a great deal more per unit of service than do Americans. Japanese pay slightly less per telephone line in total charges; however, NTT's revenues per telephone call are double the figure for the United States.

Finally, as expected from the analysis of the political forces at work in Japan, the Japanese system is more capital intensive: Revenues per dollar of capital investment are more than 10 percent higher in the United States,

[68] InfoCom Research (1992: 46–47).
[69] Salomon Brothers, Inc. (1992).
[70] Salomon Brothers, Inc. (1992) and *New York Times*, March 3, 1993.

173

Table 6.15. *Comparative performance data, 1992*

Item	Japan	U.S.
Subscriber lines		
Residential (millions)	37.3	88.4
Business (millions)	16.8	35.4
Total (millions)	54.1	123.8
Total (per 100 population)	51.4	42.0
Domestic calls (billions)	72.6	463.2
Local	49.9**	400.3
Short toll*	9.4**	20.1
Long distance*	13.3	42.9
International (in & out) calls	.32	.57
Calls per line	1,342	3,742
Minutes of use (billions)		
Local	122.6	1,828.9
Toll	78.6	599.9
Total	201.2	2,429.0
Minutes per line	3,719	19,620
Minutes per call	2.77	5.24
Total telephone revenues (billions)	40.9	108.9
Revenues per Line	756.01	879.64
Revenues per Call	.56	.24
Revenues per Minute of Use	.20	.05
Net plant (NTT vs. AT&T + LECs) (billions)	70.10	166.80
Total All Revenues	43.50	117.40
Total Revenues/Net Plant	.62	.70
Net Plant per Line	1,296	1,347
Net Plant per Call	.97	.36

Sources: InfoCom Research. 1992. *Information & Communications in Japan 1992*. Tokyo: InfoCom Research, Inc.; and FCC. 1992. *Statistics of Common Carriers*. NTT documents.

and capital investment per call in Japan is nearly three times as high as in the United States. Investment per line is about the same; however, Japan's far lower usage rate should make their investments lower in the part of the system that is usage-sensitive. Moreover, the higher population density of Japan should lead to shorter access lines, on average, which in turn should produce lower investments in the usage-insensitive aspects of telephone service provision.

Apparently NTT has actually become more capital intensive since privatization. Although its ratio of the value of capital investments to sales fell in the years before privatization, since 1985 this ratio has actually increased about 7 percent.[71] Employment has declined since privatization. While total personnel expenses have increased by about 15 percent, revenues per employee have grown nearly 40 percent. Hence, NTT's high prices and costs are attributable to its investment activities, not its employment practices.

A final feature of NTT is that privatization has actually led to greater, not smaller, payments to government. In fiscal year 1985, the net payments to government by NTT were only $660 million, but this rose to $1.75 billion in 1990.[72] Interestingly, the dollar value of dividends to all stockholders remains unchanged since one-third of NTT was privatized. All of the government's increase in revenues from NTT comes from higher taxes. Together with the expenditure data, these facts indicate that the beneficiaries of NTT privatization have been its equipment suppliers and the government, not stockholders or customers. These effects provide considerable insight into why the price of NTT stock has fallen by two-thirds since the end of 1987, and why the government has been unable to complete its privatization plans on schedule.

4. CONCLUSION

Telecommunications liberalization clearly does not mean the same thing in Japan as in the United States. In the United States, liberalization was for the purpose of introducing more competition into the industry, which in turn had the effect of bringing prices more in line with costs and, on balance, reducing prices by forcing service suppliers to be more efficient. The effect has been to open service provision and equipment procurement, but as a means of reducing costs and prices. In Japan, the intensely politicized telecommunications industry has been influenced by the politics that is common to Japanese industrial policy. Consumers are heavily taxed to support industrial suppliers, and the regulation of firms has been a patronage system that supplies favors to the stalwart supporters and contributors of the ruling party. The resulting system is remarkably expensive and underutilized for a nation that prides itself on being a world leader in information technology. The implicit differences in technology policy that lie behind the performance data are quite interesting. The United States is clearly relying on domestic market competition to force improvements in both equipment and services. By taxing domestic markets, Japan is relying on implicit subsidization in both service and equipment to generate funds for innovation. To the extent that demand pull and market competition have a role in Japan, it is in the international market, in which the biggest customer is the United States.

[71] Takano (1992: 48).
[72] Ibid., 106.

The Japanese approach gives its information-technology sector a clear advantage: a large domestic market in which they are insulated from competition, but a large U.S. market in which they compete and, to succeed, must be responsive to customers. Although one can question why the Japanese pursue a policy that undermines living standards in Japan, the policy seems to give Japan's companies the best of both worlds. But it also makes them very vulnerable, for a weakly performing domestic telecommunications system may inhibit the ability of Japan's information-technology companies to remain competitive in world markets.

In both nations, one commonly expressed reason for liberalization was precisely this: to induce performance improvements in the domestic network that would cause telecommunications services to support the communications needs of a world-class information-technology sector. The same firms that are benefiting from equipment sales to carriers in the Japanese system are also going to be harmed as customers of the network by the corresponding low efficiency and high prices. As the data show, high usage prices deter the development of information services and the equipment and software that goes with them because they discourage the long connect time that is necessary for interactive use over the network. Hence, information services in Japan, compared to the United States, will be biased in favor of simple data delivery (e.g., electronic publishing) but against systems that require on-line interactions between users and information suppliers (e.g., electronic shopping).

Meanwhile, the Japanese telecommunications system reveals clearly the major drawback of the Japanese political system that prevailed until 1993. Policy in Japan has not been oriented toward providing low-cost, widely available consumer service, and the measures of consumer welfare indicate that telephone customers are substantially better off in the United States than in Japan.

7

The politics of nuclear power in Japan and the United States

LINDA COHEN, MATHEW D. MCCUBBINS, AND
FRANCES MCCALL ROSENBLUTH

1. INTRODUCTION

Japanese and American electric utilities have pursued sharply different nuclear energy policies since the mid-1970s. U.S. utility companies have all but abandoned nuclear power. They have ordered no new nuclear power plants since 1978. Moreover, they have canceled all plants ordered after 1974 as well as one-third of those ordered before 1974. While nuclear power continued to grow as a percentage of both total electricity generation and installed capacity throughout the 1980s, that growth rate slowed markedly as the number of plants in the construction pipeline dwindled. Nuclear's share of power production is expected to begin declining as older plants are decommissioned without any new plants to take their place. All this is occurring despite evidence that utilities had formulated ambitious plans in the 1960s and 1970s for its development.[1] Total net nuclear power design capacity (i.e., units licensed for operation, under construction, or on order) declined from 163 gigawatts electric in 1980 (169 reactor units, 70 of which were then in operation) to 121 GWe (130 units) in 1985 and only 113 GWe (120 units, 111 of which are in operation) in 1990 (*World Almanac* 1992: 196).

In contrast, Japanese nuclear capacity has mushroomed. Utilities currently operate forty-one nuclear-powered plants (32.2 GWe capacity) generating 26 percent of electricity supply, up from five plants (1.8 GWe) in 1973. Japanese utilities also have another eleven plants (10.6 GWe) under construction, and Japanese policy makers expect nuclear-generated electricity to make up 35 percent of capacity by the year 2000.

---

[1] Policy makers in the United States anticipated that American utilities would eventually bring as many as five hundred light-water plants on line, generating enough cheap power to render electricity "too cheap to meter."

Linda Cohen, Mathew D. McCubbins, and Frances M. Rosenbluth

Economists have argued that the difference between United States and Japanese use of nuclear power plants follows from differences in construction and operating costs in the two countries. This is undeniably part of the explanation. Much of that cost difference can, however, be attributed to differences in government policy, which are a matter of choice. This chapter offers an explanation for why nuclear power *policies* in the United States and Japan have diverged since the 1970s.

In assessing policy choice, regulatory economists have observed that bureaucratic processes (such as the licensing of power plants) impose compliance costs on regulated industries and can change relative prices in an economy. To the degree that utilities cannot shift the costs of nuclear regulation to other parts of the economy, it follows, demand for nuclear power will be reduced. Both economists and political scientists have remarked on the myriad bureaucratic hurdles that utilities must overcome to build new nuclear power facilities in the United States (implying high compliance costs), whereas their Japanese counterparts face relatively few such impediments (implying relatively lower compliance costs). Simply put, the Japanese face less red tape, so their licensing process is cheaper than ours. It follows, all else equal, that Japanese utilities will place greater emphasis on new nuclear capacity than will American utilities. What is not explained is why government policies toward nuclear power differ in the two countries.

We argue that the policy differences largely follow from different constitutional structures (a federal, Madisonian system in the United States versus a parliamentary system in Japan) and different electoral systems (Japan's single nontransferable vote – SNTV – system versus the United States's single-member-district, plurality elections). In the United States, the nuclear power plant construction industry is dead for two complementary reasons: First, environmentalists and not-in-my-backyard (or NIMBY) citizens' groups gained a say at many levels (local, state, and federal) in policy making. These groups' interventions slowed to a crawl the regulatory process in approving the siting, planning, construction, and operation of nuclear power plants, and forced costly modifications of plant designs to reduce thermal and radiation pollution emissions and increase plant safety. Second, at a time when real incomes in the United States were stagnant or declining, political opposition to new, expensive generating capacity and congressional passage of the Public Utilities Regulatory Policies Act of 1978 (PURPA) gave utilities in high demand-growth areas strong incentives to abandon plans to build new capacity. Instead, they turned to policies to promote the more efficient use of existing capacity, including the creation of a nationally integrated electrical grid to wheel power from areas of excess capacity, and a variety of demand-management policies intended to conserve energy and smooth power use.[2] These two factors – political opposition to new facilities and the availability of alternative supplies through wheeling and demand management – sharply reduced utilities' short-term requirements for new generating capacity in the United States, both nuclear powered and conventional (Joskow 1974).

Japanese utilities faced a much different environment. At the time of the first oil shock in 1974, more than 50 percent of installed generating capacity in Japan was oil fired. Policy makers responded to the economic crisis caused by the oil embargo by encouraging the diversification of the base generating capacity, including nuclear power.

Japan also has an environmentalist movement and NIMBY activists who oppose the development of nuclear power (Donnelly 1991; Krauss and Simcock 1980; McKean 1981). However, Japan's regulatory process offers many fewer points at which opponents of nuclear power can intervene to stop or delay development of nuclear power (see Figure 7.1). This is a matter of political choice, however; the Japanese legislature can create as many (or few) checks on bureaucratic decision making as it desires. Nuclear regulation could have become as complex in Japan as it is in the United States, but it did not. We argue that this difference in policy choices reflects not just a different constitutional system, but also the interplay between Japan's SNTV electoral system and the Liberal Democratic Party's electoral strategy. Major industrial supporters of the LDP demand policies that favor large construction projects; nuclear power plants are among the largest such projects. The potential opposition to nuclear power in Japan, on the other hand, consists of environmental groups, who tend to support opposition parties and thus are of little consequence in LDP electoral calculations; and NIMBY constituents, such as farmers and fishermen, whom the LDP placates with further side-payment policies.

The plan of the chapter is as follows: In Section 2 we present the arguments and evidence regarding the relative costs of nuclear power plant construction and operation in the United States and Japan. Critical differences between the two countries include demand characteristics, the structure of utility rate regulation and risk factors faced by utilities in the two countries. The evidence clearly supports the claim that nuclear power is competitive (vis-à-vis alternative generating capacities, such as oil, gas, coal, and conservation) in Japan but not in the United States. We present our explanation for this divergence in Section 3, where we trace the differences in the two countries' nuclear power market and regulatory structures. Section 4 concludes.

---

[2] Among other requirements, PURPA requires electric utilities to purchase the output of qualifying cogeneration and alternative energy generation facilities at rates no lower than the utility's incremental ("avoided") costs. This requirement raises the risk to utilities that any new power plant it might build would contribute to excess capacity.

PROCEDURES FOR A NUCLEAR POWER PLANT
(FROM SITE SELECTION TO PLANT COMMISSION)

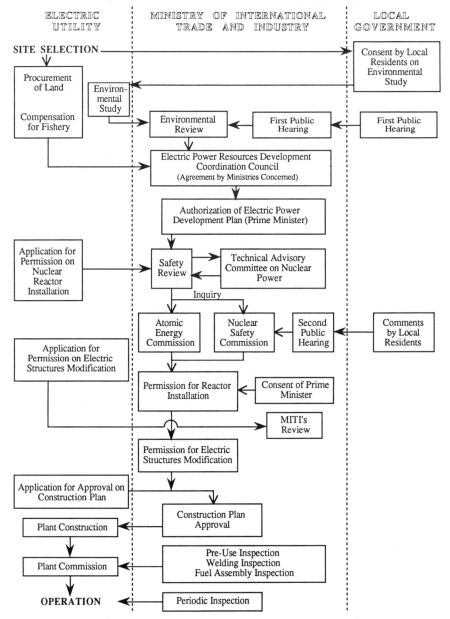

Figure 7.1. *Nuclear plant licensing process in Japan*

2. COMPARATIVE ELECTRICITY ECONOMICS: JAPAN AND THE UNITED STATES

Why is Japan seemingly so successful at building and operating nuclear generating capacity, while in the United States nuclear economics no longer glows? In explaining the divergent records of nuclear programs in the United States and Japan, the economics literature has focused on construction costs for reactors in the two countries. Costs are indeed lower in Japan today. Japanese construction costs relative to U.S. costs dropped from rough comparability in the early 1970s to less than half of U.S. costs in the 1980s (on a per-megawatt basis, based on comparisons of published U.S. figures with proprietary data obtained from Japanese utilities; see, e.g., Hinman and Lowinger 1987). Stated operating costs in Japan are approximately one-half U.S. operating costs (on operating costs see, e.g., Navarro 1988, 1989). Because of different nuclear cohorts, these comparisons overstate the cost differential. In particular, the Japanese did not begin building nuclear plants in earnest until just before the United States gave up. Therefore, the oldest Japanese plants are the same cohort as the newest American plants. The construction and operating costs of similarly sized and aged plants are roughly similar in the two countries. Newer Japanese reactors, however, have no counterparts in the United States, rendering comparisons of construction costs impossible and of operating costs problematic. Nevertheless, economists have argued that these cost differences arise from construction delay, learning, management structure, and financing. We will deal with each of these in turn.

Much of the construction cost difference between U.S. and Japanese nuclear power plants is attributed to differences in construction lead times (the time required to build a plant). Plants that came on line in Japan in the first half of the 1980s had a construction lead time averaging 5.3 years; in the United States, the figure was 11.2 years (Hinman and Lowinger 1987). Longer lead times increase charges for borrowed capital. In the United States, it is not uncommon for 40 percent of the cost of a nuclear power plant to consist of interest charges on debt. Furthermore, unexpected delays involve additional charges, including contract penalties and substitute power purchases.

The learning and management differences in plant construction are apparent in the structures of both the utility industry and the construction industry. In Japan, there are only three vertically integrated vendors of nuclear plants serving only nine utilities. Japanese nuclear plants are standardized to a much greater extent than those in the United States, as Japanese utilities buy nuclear facilities under turnkey contracts (in which the facility is to be delivered, ready for operation, at a set time for a set price). U.S. vendors, in contrast, ceased selling turnkey reactors in 1966

181

(Burness, Montgomery, and Quirk 1980; Montgomery and Quirk 1978). Thereafter, utilities assumed the risk of cost overruns for plants in which the multiplicity of vendors (architects, engineers, construction firms, and balance-of-plant companies) resulted in an extraordinary degree of customization (Cohen 1979: 69). Since 1975, increased standardization has headed the list of every set of policy proposals intended to enhance the safety or economic competitiveness of nuclear power in the United States, reflecting the belief that customization has imposed a crushing penalty on the attractiveness of the technology.

Finally, the financing issue represents a fundamental difference between the two countries. The Japanese Development Bank subsidizes loans for nuclear power development. Utilities pay the lowest interest rate that the JDB offers, which is on average about a percentage point lower than the long-term prime rate offered by commercial banks.[3] By contrast, American utilities have had to compete for financing in the capital markets. This has resulted in relatively higher costs for loans and a higher risk burden for utilities.

A closer examination of these three cost components – lead times, standardization, and financing – reveals their connection to policy choices. Administrative obstacles – that is, red tape – is often as costly as economic ones (see U.S. Department of Energy 1980: 145, Table 10).

The licensing requirements in the two countries diverged appreciably in the mid-1970s. On one side, the Japanese government streamlined its licensing procedures in 1977, dropping the potential number of required licenses from 160 down to only 66, stemming from thirty-three different laws.

As outlined in Figure 7.1, in Japan, after a utility selects a location, it submits its application for a site license, including an environmental impact report, to the prime minister. The Ministry of International Trade and Industry (MITI) then holds a public hearing to give notice to and hear comments from the local community.[4] The application then goes to the (popularly elected) prefectural governor for approval, after which the Electric Power Development Coordinating Council (EPDCC)[5] offers a recommendation to the prime minister, who has the final word.

---

[3] For example, the average long-term prime rate offered by private banks in June 1989 was 5.7 percent, while the rate at which utilities could borrow from the JDB for investment in nuclear capacity was 4.85 percent. In June of 1990, the figures were 7.6 percent and 6.4 percent, respectively.

[4] The administrative guidance governing these public hearings gives MITI a veto over who may attend and what issues they may address.

[5] EPDCC is an "independent" ministerial body attached to the Economic Planning Agency, composed of representatives of eight ministries and eight outside members (usually academics); the prime minister is ex officio chair. The eight ministries and agencies represented are: MITI, the ministries of Finance, Home Affairs, Construction, and Agriculture; and the Economic Planning, Environment, and Land Agencies.

Once siting has been approved, the Atomic Energy Commission and the Nuclear Safety Commission – panels of academics and industry representatives reporting to the Science and Technology Agency – undertake safety examinations.[6] MITI, with the approval of the prime minister, may then grant separate licenses for construction, testing, and operation. MITI also inspects post construction safety. It is important to note that all of the veto gates just described are subject to the continued pleasure of the majority party in the Diet.[7] Should a majority of the Diet so choose, any or all of these stages could be eliminated, modified, or replaced. We will return to this point in Section 3.

Compare this relatively streamlined Japanese process to the dozens of local, state, and federal agencies, as well as multiple levels of federal and state courts, whose approval is needed in the United States to build and operate nuclear plants. The San Onofre plant on southern California's coast, for example, had to obtain more than two hundred separate licenses before it could go on line.

Power plant siting and utility generating capacity planning in the United States are subject to state and local regulation, whether the plant is to be nuclear or conventional. Several states, including California, Minnesota, Oregon, and Vermont, have legislated special restrictions on nuclear power plant construction on radiological health and safety grounds. In addition, the National Environmental Policy Act (NEPA), the Federal Water Pollution Control Act (FWPCA) – as amended in 1972 – and Housing and Urban Development (HUD) 701 comprehensive planning assistance all give the states powerful tools to check plans for development of nuclear power generating capacity, even to the extent of duplicat-

---

6 The Diet altered the mission of the NSC in 1978 following a radiation leak in the Japanese self-defense force's nuclear-powered ship, the *Mutsu*. The Diet's intent was for the NSC to provide a "double check," along with MITI's check, on the safety of new plants (see the 1978 Amendment to Nuclear Power Commission and Nuclear Safety Commission Establishment Act of 1955, Law No. 188).

7 The Japanese judicial system hypothetically serves as an avenue for challenging the siting and operation of nuclear power plants. A person opposed to an administrative decision to license a nuclear power plant may file suit in court under the Administrative Legislation Act, pursuant to Section 7 of the Nuclear Regulation Act. But in practice, no legal suit brought against a plant has ever prevailed, which is just as one would expect. Since the LDP's constituents can press their claims directly to the governing party, those who resort to the legal system tend to be outside the LDP electoral coalition. As is typical of parliamentary systems, Japan's judiciary (by being deliberately inhospitable to citizens with grievances) acts as a sort of screening device. The courts limit standing to residents in the neighborhood of the proposed plant site who can demonstrate damage to their person or property. Furthermore, courts limit their own scope for reviewing administrative action (Haley 1978; Upham 1987; Young 1985). Refusing to comment on scientific and technical issues of plant safety, the courts ask only whether the administrative agency granting a plant license met the procedural standards prescribed by law. The courts have found in favor of the agencies in all eight cases brought to date (unpublished internal MITI document). See also Schoenbaum and Ainley (1988).

183

ing and perhaps challenging Nuclear Regulatory Commission (NRC) reviews (U.S. Dept. of Energy 1980: 35).

What makes the American system especially sticky is that federal licensing agencies and regulations all accord some form of participatory rights to parties (from state governments to local residents of proposed nuclear plant sites) with an interest in the license. At the Nuclear Regulatory Commission (and its predecessor, the Atomic Energy Commission), for example, legal standing in the licensing process is virtually unlimited. Any individual or group that files the appropriate papers receives intervention status. The only limit on standing is the extent of the commission's own legal jurisdiction (for example, prior to 1969, potential environmental intervenors had almost no hope of gaining standing before the AEC). Intervenors may be eligible for federal financial assistance in order to hire legal counsel, and they can introduce evidence, interrogate other parties, cross-examine witnesses, and present their own witnesses (Atomic Energy Act of 1954, P.L. 83–703, as amended). Finally, if unhappy with the initial permit or licensing decision they can appeal the whole business to the review levels within the NRC and from there to the federal courts and to Congress. With the construction permit process at the NRC, for example, there are six review stages, four appeals stages, and six separate federal agencies (as well as state and local agencies) involved in making the permit decision.

Opponents of nuclear power have often complained that this structure and process is ineffective because construction and operating plans almost always are approved. Cohen (1979), for example, found that 92 of 116 AEC/NRC construction permit application cases initiated between 1966 and 1974 had been resolved by 1977; all received approval by the commission. Out of 103 "substantive" issues raised in these licensing cases, Cohen found that applicants prevailed 87 times, intervenors only 16 (Cohen 1979: 86, Table IV). But intervenors were much more successful on "procedural" issues, for example, whether a particular topic could be discussed at the hearing or the granting of a delay for further preparation.

More important from our perspective are the dual effects of delay and anticipated response by utilities. Whether or not plant construction ultimately is approved, the effect of all this structure and process is to increase the cost of bringing a nuclear power plant on line. Following the 1971 Washington D.C. circuit court decision in the Calvert Cliffs case, which forced the AEC (later, the NRC) to require permit applicants to comply with NEPA and file environmental impact reports (EIRs), all licenses were held up for more than twelve months as applicants backtracked to complete environmental reviews. One of the effects of NEPA was to incorporate public concerns about the potential consequences of low-probability accidents into the licensing process. While the Atomic Energy Act allowed the AEC to ignore such events, NEPA required an environmental impact statement that characterized all residual risks and included them in an overall cost-benefit analysis.

In effect, the application of NEPA to the nuclear industry slowed by as much as two years the licensing of reactors (Cohen 1979). The timing was particularly unfortunate for American utilities (which, as we noted above, bore most of the risk of construction delays and cost overruns following 1966), as inflation and interest rates rose sharply in the late 1970s. Consequently, the procedural due process accorded opponents wound up imposing far greater costs on utilities than anyone had anticipated in the early 1970s. The Congressional Budget Office estimated in a 1979 study that financing problems were directly responsible for as much as 19 percent of total construction delay time at nuclear plants. A share of these financing problems probably resulted from previous delays from regulatory activities. The CBO attributed another 19 percent of delay time directly to regulatory compliance (see U.S. Dept. of Energy 1980: 145, Table 10).

Why didn't the United States follow Japan in streamlining its regulatory process? This is especially interesting in light of the fact that in the early 1970s, utilities were still interested in building nuclear plants (as can be seen in the bulge in construction permit applications filed in 1973 and 1974), and were complaining vociferously about licensing delays. As Weingast (1980) observed, Congress, which passed NEPA, could have acted to amend it if members of Congress had become unhappy with how the act was applied after the circuit court handed down the 1971 Calvert Cliffs decision. But to conclude from its inaction that Congress was antinuclear in 1972 is incorrect. The largest federal energy research and development program ever was concurrently getting underway at the AEC to develop breeder reactors, a technology that makes sense only if the country has a big light-water reactor industry in need of fuel; indeed, the breeder program was justified on this basis (Cohen and Noll 1991). Further, public opinion polls indicate that the general population continued to support nuclear power development right up to the accident at Three Mile Island in 1979 (Fort and Hallagan 1991).

Congressional ambivalence about nuclear power is apparent in the history of legislative efforts in the mid-1970s. First, the AEC was abolished in 1974, and a new regulatory institution, the NRC, was established that, divorced from the enormous nuclear weapons laboratory establishments of the AEC, was far more likely to be antinuclear than its predecessor.

Second, instead of streamlining, the United States government added layers into the licensing process, creating new avenues into the regulatory process for opponents of nuclear power. Since the dissolution of the Joint Committee on Atomic Energy (JCAE) in January 1977, attempts to

185

streamline the regulatory process have failed to generate any steam. The JCAE had been established in 1946 as a joint House and Senate committee charged with overseeing the development and promotion of nuclear power. At the opening of the Ninety-fifth Congress, a coalition of anti-proliferation and environmentalist Democrats was able to include the demise of the JCAE in the rules of the House, passed by a straight party vote.[8]

The differences between standardization, financing, and lead times all lend credence to the claim that the gross costs to utilities of building nuclear plants are lower in Japan than in the United States. But in large part the costs of constructing and operating nuclear plants themselves are the results of policy choices. In Japan, for example, the government chooses to subsidize interest expenses, and quells potential opposition by compensating farmers, fishermen, and local governments.[9] Japan also streamlined its licensing process in 1977, the same year that the Congress dissolved the JCAE, and at the same time that the United States placed further licensing and legislative obstacles in the way of nuclear power development. Ease of financing is one component of lead-time determination, so that financing policies have a double effect on construction costs. Finally, a probable cause for the lack of standardization in the United States is the overall slowdown in nuclear orders – had the industry continued to expand in the 1980s, U.S. utilities would probably have pushed toward more standardized designs, as has happened in Japan. Thus, rather than telling us about the actual costs of building nuclear power plants, cross-national cost comparisons reflect government policies toward nuclear power development.

More fundamentally, cost is not the determining factor for the success or failure of a nuclear energy program. Utilities in both countries are governed by rate-of-return regulation. This means that cost, as long as it can be included in the rate base, actually adds to a utility's profit and makes relatively costly nuclear plants potentially more attractive than,

---

[8] In the Ninety-fourth Congress, the JCAE was moribund. It reported virtually no important nuclear legislation: Dozens of bills were introduced calling for a curtailment or streamlining of regulation, dealing with nuclear waste policy, and considering international implications of the fuel cycle. The only nuclear power–related bill to pass (other than continuing authorizations) was an extension of the Price–Anderson Act, which limited utility liability in the event of a nuclear accident.

[9] The *dengen sanpo* [three electricity generation laws] for compensation of communities that host power plants were passed in 1974. The laws provide funds that a host town can use for projects such as the construction of roads, schools, and civic centers. The money is raised through the assessment of a small tax (445 yen – about $3.50 now – per 1000 KWh) on all electricity consumption in Japan (Hatsuden yo shisetsu shuhen chiiki seibi ho [The Law for Compensation of Areas Surrounding a Plant Site]; Dengen kaihatsu sokushin zei ho [Electric Power Development Tax Law]; and Dengen kaihatsu sokushin taisaku tokubetsu kaikei ho [Electric Power Development Special Account Law]).

say, smaller oil-fired plants. What costs will be allowed into the rate base is, of course, a matter of policy choice. Note that U.S. utilities were already canceling nuclear reactor orders from 1974 to 1978, when estimated construction costs in the United States were roughly similar to those in Japan. Construction-cost differential alone, therefore, is not a sufficient explanation of the different outcomes in the two countries. Subsequently, the relative cost of building a plant in the United States rose to about twice the (per-MW) cost of a comparable plant in Japan. The cost increase was after the plant cancellations had begun, however, and not before.

We have shown that the supply-side differences between the U.S. and Japanese nuclear power industries are not sufficient to explain those industries' divergent results since the 1970s; we turn now to the demand side. Since 1975, electricity markets in Japan and the United States have experienced divergent patterns of demand growth and price regulation. The differences explain some of the discrepancies in nuclear plant construction schedules and costs in the two countries. In addition, they suggest that very different incentives exist for utilities to invest in new capital-intensive generating capacity, making nuclear power a more attractive investment in Japan than in the United States. In the next subsection, we give an overview of the critical contrasts, finding that the evidence suggests the standard view of the nuclear productivity gap between the two countries should be modified.

2.1. Demand for electricity

In the past two decades, average annual real growth in total megawatt-hours in Japan was 48 percent higher than in the United States (3.45 percent per year versus 2.33 percent per year). Furthermore, as shown in Figure 7.2, for most Japanese utilities demand doubled from 1975 to 1990. The chart indicates that all Japanese utilities have experienced consistent growth in demand, marred only by two blips immediately following the first and second oil shocks.

At the same time, growth in peak summer demand (a measure of maximum demand) in the United States dropped. As shown in Figure 7.3, peak demand in the United States was growing at more than 8 percent prior to 1973; after 1973, growth averaged less than 3 percent. Thus, the need for new capacity has fallen by over half in the United States since 1973.

Moreover, as can be seen in Figure 7.4, U.S. projected growth in demand exceeded actual growth in demand by roughly 100 percent between 1978 and 1987. A dramatic falloff in demand growth and persistently optimistic demand-growth forecasts meant that utilities undertook far more capacity additions from 1970 to 1976 than proved necessary. Thus,

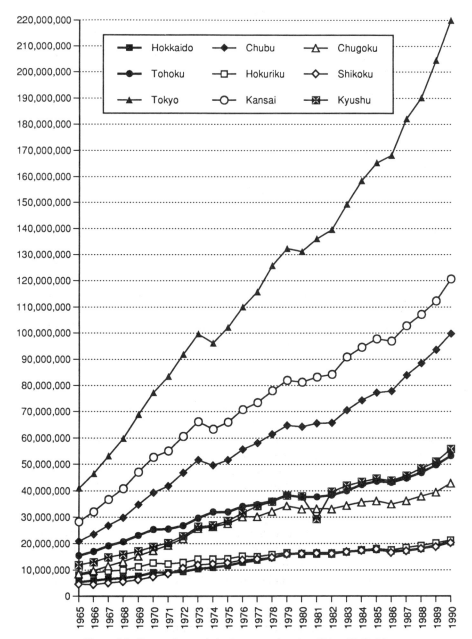

Figure 7.2. *Demand growth for Japanese electric utilities, 1965–90*

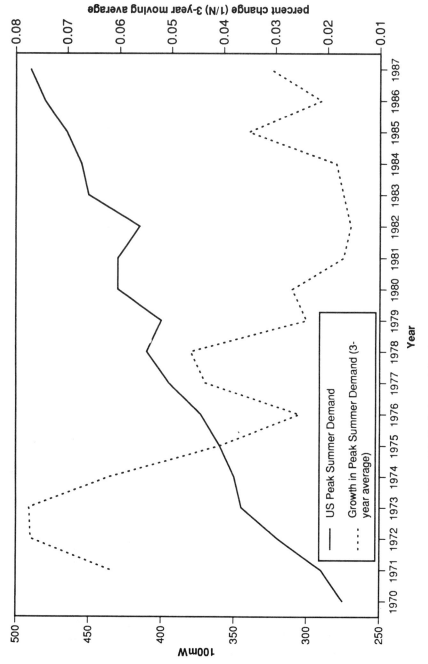

Figure 7.3. Peak demand for electricity in the United States, 1970–87

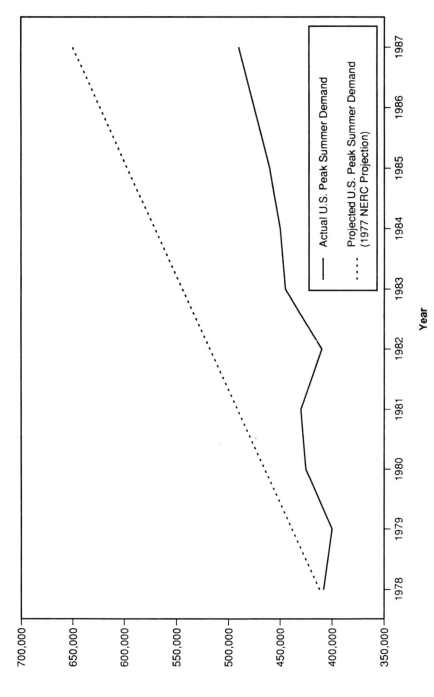

Figure 7.4. Comparison of projected and actual U.S. peak summer demand for electricity, 1978–87

as shown in Figure 7.5, as new plants came on line, U.S. capacity reserve margins grew from the 1970s into the late 1980s. Prior to 1974, utilities maintained on average 16 percent more generating capacity than they needed to meet their highest annual demand for electricity (the summer peak). When demand failed to materialize in the mid-1970s, additional capacity continued coming on line, and reserve margins increased to 25 percent. In Japan, by contrast, capacity reserve margins average about 13 percent.

The result of slackening demand in the United States was that virtually all new capacity under construction was delayed or abandoned and new orders were unnecessary. Indeed, utilities cite demand considerations as a cause in over one-fourth of the construction delays during this period (U.S. Dept. of Energy 1980: 145). Of course, increases in delays lead to higher costs, especially interest charges, which make up about 25 percent of all costs for American utilities.

2.2. Rate regulation

In both countries, in setting electricity rates utilities are guaranteed a specified rate of return on their capital investments. The sum of the capital investment on which profit is made is called the rate base. Japan and the United States differ on what capital expenses can be included in the rate base, when they can be included, and for how long.

Japanese rate base calculations allow 50 percent of projected construction costs to be placed in the rate base at the beginning of construction (MITI n.d.: 9). Allowing such projected costs into the rate base is known as using "construction work-in-progress" (CWIP) allowances.[10] In the United States, twenty-three of fifty state public utilities commissions (PUCs) allow some CWIP, although the amount is typically quite limited. Ohio, for example, allows 20 percent of previous expenditures on plants at least three-fourths complete. In general, U.S. utilities get an "allowance for funds used during construction." This means that interest charges during construction are added to other construction costs and included in the rate base after the plant is placed in service, to the degree allowed by the state PUC. The dramatic differences in rate-setting practices between the two countries makes cost comparisons, which are already skewed by subsidies and financial practices, all the more problematic.

---

[10] Actually, the rate base does not change automatically every time a utility makes an investment. A utility must petition MITI when its profits have been squeezed by increasing costs, but MITI has proved generous in granting increases. Naturally, a major capital investment will cause such a squeeze and lead to a revision of the rate base before too long. The interval between rate-base revisions has averaged about three years in the period under consideration (personal communications with MITI officials, 1992).

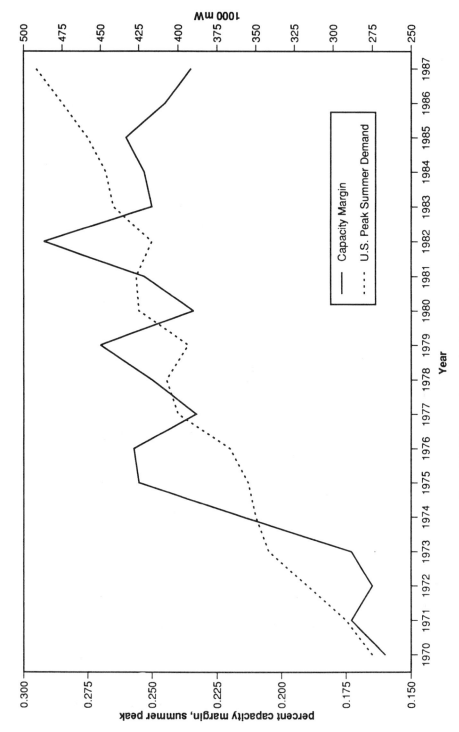

Figure 7.5. U.S. capacity margins for electricity, 1970–87

2.3. Regulatory risk

In Japan, utilities commission the construction of nuclear reactors based on turnkey contracts. They purchase a reactor whole from the vendor, so they are quite certain from the outset of what it is they are buying and what it costs.[11] Also, utilities in Japan are blessed with certainty as regards rate making. They know that all capital expenditures can be included in the rate base, when each portion of CWIP will be included, and for how long each will be counted.

In the United States, many utilities have had part of their expenses disallowed at the last minute. In some cases, such as the Shoreham plant on Long Island, a working reactor was not allowed to operate. In others, such as Diablo Canyon in California, operation was delayed for years. Such delays sometimes lead to canceling the project altogether; for example, construction on the Cherokee Nuclear Station in Gaffney, S.C. was halted and its half-finished reactor containment vessel was converted into a gigantic swimming pool used to film the movie *The Abyss*.

Thus, in Japan there has been sufficient demand to warrant expansion of base-load capacity and, because of the form of utility regulation, such expansion is profitable and virtually risk-free. In the United States, by contrast, utilities were hit from both sides of the electricity supply equation. On one hand, growth in demand did not meet projections, so it was not as profitable to build new base-load plants as it had been in previous decades. On the other hand, changes in the regulatory process and the decline in congressional support made it more expensive and riskier (with respect to the likelihood that the utility could earn a return on its investment) to build nuclear plants.

3. POLITICAL DETERMINANTS OF MARKET AND REGULATORY STRUCTURE

While Japanese utilities continue to order nuclear reactors, U.S. utilities do not. Furthermore, because of the regulatory atmosphere, even as the demand for electricity is again picking up in the United States utilities are still unwilling to order new nuclear capacity. We have identified four pertinent critical differences between the United States and Japan: (1) cost, (2) demand, (3) utility regulation, and (4) risk with regard to rate and profit. The question is, why do these differences exist?

---

[11] When the rate of return exceeds the interest rate (and by definition any "fair" rate of return allows a real return on capital) then the utility winds up ahead on any debt that can be accounted for under CWIP. From a financial viewpoint, lengthy construction schedules will not detract from company profits.

Linda Cohen, Mathew D. McCubbins, and Frances M. Rosenbluth

The United States has a system of separated and federated powers. Authority is divided among the House of Representatives, the Senate, the president, and the corresponding branches of state governments. Moreover, the constitutional structure of the United States was constructed on the principle that "Ambition must be made to counteract ambition" (*Federalist* 51). Not only is decision-making authority shared, it is shared by people who are elected at different times, from different constituencies, and by different rules, so that they often (and by design) have contrasting and conflicting incentives and goals. Each added player, responsive to his own electoral constituency, in the policy-making process implies, *ceteris paribus,* that fewer policy compromises will be reached. The multiplicity of such players collectively implies an increase in both the number of opportunities and the diversity of strategies available for access to and influence on policy-making processes by the opponents of any prospective policy choice.

From a social choice perspective, all else constant, the greater the number of veto players and the greater the diversity of preferences among them, the less likely there exists a policy that is satisfactory to all players (Cox and McKelvey 1984; Hammond and Miller 1987). From a transactions-costs approach, we learn that as the number of veto players increases so too do the transactions costs involved in striking deals among the players and, all else constant, the less likely it is that policy compromise will be reached. Thus, in policy areas such as nuclear power that have significant federal and state involvement, agreements will be difficult to strike and nearly impossible to maintain.

This multiplicity of veto gates means that the reversionary outcome – that is, the policy that prevails should no agreement be reached, is privileged.[12] Prior to 1969 and the passage of NEPA, the U.S. policy-making apparatus was biased in favor of promoting nuclear power. Environmentalists and prospective neighbors had few grounds on which to challenge proposed new plants; pro-nuclear members of Congress populated the JCAE; and both electricity demand, and demand expectations, were growing, while the real cost of electricity to consumers was plummeting. Thus consumers wanted new capacity and hardly noticed the bite of paying for it, while utilities wanted to build new nuclear power plants. The worm turned with NEPA and Calvert Cliffs. Suddenly, environmentalists and NIMBY activists had a seat at the table. The costs of buying these opponents off in the U.S. system quickly outstripped utilities' desire to build new nuclear-powered capacity.

---

[12] For example, the reversionary outcome could be the maintenance of a program at the levels prescribed in the last voted budget, as in the cases of Social Security and agricultural subsidies, or, alternatively, it could be the termination of the program.

Japan, on the other hand, has a system of unitary and fused powers, where executive and legislative authority reside in the same body, the Diet, which is sovereign at all levels of government. This means that the majority party in the Diet controls all levels of government, and that only one bargain need be struck for a policy decision to be reached. Naturally, since policy is relatively easy to make, it is also easy to change. This contrasts with the United States, where the same gauntlet of veto gates that renders original policy choice an arduous process awaits later attempts to change reversionary policies. So, with respect to the long-term continuity in Japanese nuclear energy policy, it is highly relevant that the majority party in Japan has remained the same for the entire period under consideration. Indeed, the LDP has held the reins of government continuously since 1955.[13] With this background in mind, we proceed to an explanation of the four crucial differences between U.S. and Japanese nuclear regulatory policy.

3.1. Cost

In the United States, numerous distinct government authorities, each with a veto, establish regulatory processes for nuclear power. Because ambition is pitted against ambition, the regulators' interests often conflict. Conflict and delays increase with the number and diversity of interests represented in the process. Thus, costs to utilities – primarily interest payments and foregone revenue – are large and increasing. Such site-specific costs as environmental impact assessment and safety-related expenses are also larger, as there are more and more hoops through which the utilities must jump.

In Japan, there are many fewer veto gates and licenses, all of which are controlled by the same party. Although the description of the regulatory process represented in Figure 7.1 listed several government agencies, our point is that all of these bureaucrats serve one political master – the majority party in Parliament. Once "party approval" is given, the remaining licenses should be pro forma. Thus regulatory costs are relatively small, as are site-specific costs.

A final word can be said about the different subsidies in the regulatory processes of the two countries. In Japan, we observe side payments that

---

[13] The LDP lost its majority in the Upper House for the first time in 1989, but because the Lower House is sovereign on budgetary decisions and the choice of the prime minister, this is not as important as it would be in the United States. In contrast to the United States, Japanese rules with respect to nuclear plant licensing do not require explicit actions by anyone other than ministry officials, the prime minister, and the prefectural governor, all of whom in many prefectures remain under the control of the LDP. Further, since basic geographic and geologic facts constrain nuclear power plant siting to only a few areas in Japan, only a few of the prefectural governors are relevant to nuclear power policy.

grease the wheels of regulation and administration. The "Three Laws" (see note 9) are but one example. In Japan, electricity rates are structured to favor industrial users, whereas in the United States, rates favor residential consumers, who are not generally considered to be a specific constituency group. The explanation for this discrepancy can once again be found by looking at the relevant institutional structures. Since in the United States there are so many veto players without overlapping preferences, we expect the range of feasible alternatives to be quite limited. Further, as we expect fewer deals to be struck under the American than under the Japanese system, we also expect less compensation (fewer side payments) to be allocated.

3.2. Demand

In the United States, the response to the inflationary and environmental concerns of the 1970s was to discourage demand for electricity. In most states, increasing block rate structures were established for all users of electricity. Further, many states set up redistributive rate structures, so that industrial users paid a far greater share of the per-unit costs than was true in Japan. Combined with PURPA policies, overconstruction in the early 1970s, and a recessionary economy, utilities were therefore able to put off the need to build new electric generation capacity and allay some of the environmental concerns with regard to electricity generation.[14]

It is not clear that Congress could have encouraged the use of nuclear power by subsidizing it, even if it had wanted to do so. The actions of state legislatures and PUCs to increase prices and to dampen the demand for electricity meant that utilities would not have been able to earn a return on investments in nuclear power plants. States like California and Texas, where demand for electricity was still growing, would have found it tough to encourage the building of nuclear power plants because support for nuclear power at the federal level had evaporated. Air, water, and waste-disposal regulation, as well as other nuclear regulation, would have made it impossible to meet increased demand using oil, coal, gas, or nuclear energy. Moreover, opposition to nuclear power at the federal level had become firmly entrenched in the regulatory process via NEPA and the Calvert Cliffs decision; and in the House and Senate committee systems, as jurisdiction over nuclear power issues was distributed to several committees in each chamber. Nuclear power advocates lost their privileged

---

14 PURPA also helped in this regard, by creating large regional markets for electricity. Areas such as San Diego, in which the demand for electricity has actually grown over the past two decades, have met their increased demand by buying surplus electricity off the grid from other states and even other countries.

institutional position for good when House Democrats unilaterally dismantled the JCAE in 1977.

In Japan, oil was the issue (Eguchi 1980; Samuels 1987). At the time of the first oil shock, more than 50 percent of electric generating capacity was oil-based. By contrast, the United States relies very little on oil-fired electricity generation – it was only 5.7 percent of net generation in 1989 (U.S. Department of Commerce 1991: 579, Table 972). The Japanese government sought to resolve its uncertainties with respect to energy supplies by reducing oil consumption. The question is, Why? There were many policy options available, from electricity conservation (as in the United States) to the purchase of long-term contracts for oil. The answer lies in the politics of LDP decision making.

In elections to the Lower House, the Japanese use a single nontransferable vote (SNTV) system. Each district sends up to six representatives to the Diet; each voter gets only one vote to cast for an individual, and the top six *individual* (as opposed to party) vote-getters are elected; it is thus possible for a party to win almost all the votes cast but take only one seat, if all those votes were to go to a single candidate. In contrast, the United States uses a single-member-district system, in which the candidate with the most votes wins.

The SNTV electoral system requires any majority-seeking party to run more than one candidate per electoral district.[15] Consequently, the party must engage in some form of vote division in order to spread the "party vote" optimally among its many candidates in each district. The particular solution used by the LDP is to subsidize its candidates' pursuit of personalistic votes while simultaneously marketing the party label as a public good for all endorsed candidates. Each candidate caters to a distinct bloc of voters, and dispenses various regulatory and budgetary favors as well as large sums of money to build up personal loyalty as a supplement to party loyalty (McCubbins and Rosenbluth in Chapter 3 of this volume).

In Japan as elsewhere, a heavy reliance on particularistic politics implies the need for massive amounts of money. Indeed, election campaigns in Japan are four to eight times as costly as in the United States. For the LDP, a large share of campaign financing comes from domestic industry, the biggest consumers of electricity. Earlier, we suggested that one possible response by Japanese utilities to the oil shocks of the 1970s could have been a turn toward longer-term contracts for oil. However, MITI approved rate increases averaging 56.8 percent in June 1974, essentially passing through the oil price increases. A second major rate increase, averaging 21 percent, was approved in 1976 (Samuels 1987: 163). The

---

[15] The 512 members of the Lower House in Japan are elected from 130 two- to six-member districts. Therefore, a majority of 257 implies an average of two seats per district for the majority party.

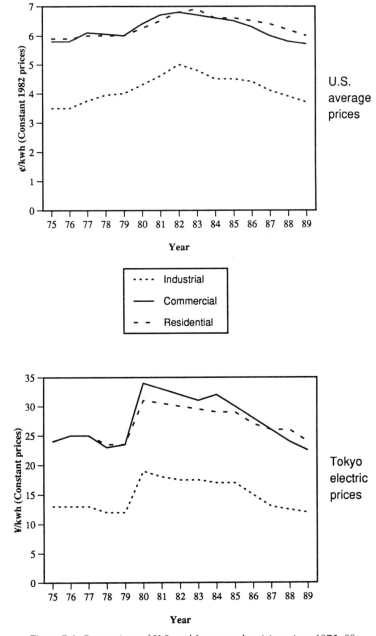

Figure 7.6. *Comparison of U.S. and Japanese electricity prices, 1975–89*

brunt of these increases was borne by small businesses and residential customers, however, thanks to the use of a diminishing block rate structure and utility side payments to major customers (for example, when the utilities garnered windfall profits in 1986 due to changes in the exchange rate, they kicked back $6.2 billion to industrial customers; see Samuels 1987: 225).

Thus, it was relatively painless for the LDP to substitute away from oil. For electricity, the move has been to coal, gas, and nuclear power, as well as some price-induced conservation for small (residential) users. In keeping with the LDP's tradition of favoring its big contributors, the Japanese government also established a pricing system that discourages residential consumption and encourages industrial use of electricity with a declining block rate structure. Indeed, as shown in Figure 7.6, in some years, residential consumers subsidize business users.

3.3. Regulation

In the United States, PUCs are established and appointed by state governments and have long favored residential interests over those of the utilities. Prior to the advent of inflationary and environmental concerns after the 1973 oil shock, PUCs had quite cozy dealings with utilities that sought price decreases. Electoral competition in the states caused the PUCs to be opened up to consumer and environmental interests after the mid-1970s (Joskow 1974).

These new interests succeeded in establishing new regulatory requirements. The addition of new requirements to the regulatory process necessarily implies the creation of new potential bottlenecks, points at which the licensing process can grind to a halt. Furthermore, insofar as these new veto gates are placed in regulatory, political, or judicial arenas, they increase the number of points at which opponents of nuclear power may access the process and exert pressure for the exercise of one veto or another. It comes as no surprise, therefore, that utility regulation has become increasingly hostile to the utilities as new structure and process has been added to regulatory decision making.

The LDP's continuous domination of Japanese politics suggests that there has been no electoral pressure to change policy away from producers and big customers and toward residential consumers. Because the LDP's electoral strategy depends heavily on providing private goods, they are not seen as being as concerned with public-goods issues as their opposition. The out parties, which are unable to provide particularistic goods, concentrate their electoral rhetoric on classic public-goods issues, such as nonproliferation or environmentalism. Unitary government, parliamentarism, and majoritarianism combine to allow for only one access point to government decision making: the majority party. If Japanese opponents of commercial nuclear power cannot get a hearing with the LDP, they are out of luck. Japan's political-institutional structure has allowed the LDP to ignore politically unimportant opponents of its policies.

It is understandable, then, that utility regulation has remained quite favorable to the utilities (and to industry in general), and that the costs of favorable treatment are not borne by the LDP's other important constituents. Industry does not subsidize residential consumption; rather, residential customers bear most of the costs of nuclear development. And farmers and fishermen, also traditional bastions of LDP support, are actually compensated by the LDP (see note 9); once again, residential consumers pay for these subsidies.

3.4. Risk

Finally, differences in profit risk follow from the differences in rate regulation and regulatory cost. PUCs and courts in U.S. states cannot commit years in advance to allow part or any of a utility's expenditures into the rate base. Because the numerous veto gates are controlled by institutionally distinct and often politically opposing agencies, the receipt of one license has no implications for success or failure in receiving other licenses farther down the line. These battles will be fought at a later time by sides yet to be determined. In other words, intervening elections at any level of government could alter the partisan control of certain veto gates, rendering prediction about probabilities of success a risky game. In Japan, as long as the LDP rules, there is no uncertainty. Of course, utilities and other beneficiaries of the regulatory structure do their best to ensure that LDP does in fact continue in power.

4. CONCLUSION

Electrical generating capacity in Japan has grown over the past fifteen years, with roughly equal contributions from the development of new capacity in gas and coal as well as nuclear power. In the United States, in contrast, electrical generating capacity has stagnated: Part of the untold story of the demise of the nuclear power plant construction industry in the United States is that no new capacity has been added in coal, gas, or oil either. The number of licenses required to site, build, test, and operate a nuclear power plant in the United States is much higher than in Japan. Since each license requires an administrative decision, each is a veto gate.

All else equal, the more veto gates there are, the greater are the costs of nuclear power, and the higher is the risk that the utility will not earn a return on its investments.

Indeed, the evidence shows that before nuclear power development in the United States ground to a halt, the lengths of delays at virtually every step of the process were growing, at great cost to the utilities in terms of interest charges and revenue foregone. Fully built plants have not been allowed to operate, and utilities did not know how much of their capital outlays would be included in the rate base by state PUCs. By contrast, the Japanese system is streamlined. Uncertainty is reduced, and utilities know that all of their costs will be allowed into the rate base.

This characterization, while accurate as far as it goes, begs the question of why the licensing procedures in the two countries are so different. Again, the answer lies in their different institutional structures. The large number of distinct, constitutionally defined players in the United States makes for a multitude of veto gates, often with contradictory goals and preferences. If one player or, alternatively, any number of players with identical preferences were in charge of issuing the more than two hundred licenses required to generate electricity in the United States, the number of steps would not necessarily imply long delays and uncertainty. Any proposal that survived the first step would not subsequently be stymied. This is basically the system in Japan, where all licenses are controlled by a single veto group – the majority party. Only one gatekeeper need be satisfied for a proposal to go forward. Thus we find that the constant increasing trend of growth in nuclear capacity coincides with the continuance of LDP supremacy in the Diet.[16]

Nuclear power plants are more attractive investments for Japanese utilities than for their American counterparts. This is unsurprising given the lower costs – including subsidized financing, lower risk, a streamlined regulatory process, and a more favorable demand structure for electricity – in Japan. All of these aspects of the cost–benefit analysis are endogenous to the political systems of the two countries, however. The Japanese and American governments decide what may be included in the rate and when, who will bear the risks, and whether to encourage or discourage demand. These governments are made up of a greater or smaller number of veto players, as determined by their respective constitu-

---

[16] Additionally, almost all prefectures with nuclear power plants had LDP governors at the time of siting. Ultimately, though, the majority party in the Diet has the power simply to eliminate the prefectural governor's veto from the licensing process. Although other officials – elected or not – may have formal decision-making authority, all power under the constitution resides in the Diet. The same cannot be said about the U.S. House of Representatives.

tions, with more or less contradictory incentives. The divergence of policy with regard to nuclear power generation is the consequence of political choices made by actors in radically different institutional environments, and the decisions themselves are equilibria induced by those different structures.

8

The politics of foreign policy
in Japan and the United States

PETER F. COWHEY

A sound theory of foreign policy requires a strong theory of domestic politics. The collective-goods dilemmas posed by international politics are no different in principle than the ones posed by taxation or civil liberties at home. If the stakes can sometimes seem dramatically higher in foreign policy, as in the threat of war, this should produce specialized adaptation of government institutions to manage the collective-goods problem. This is how governments manage comparable risky domestic problems, as witnessed by the creation in most countries of specialized central banks to handle the national money supply. Neither the creation of central banks nor the intricate institutions of diplomacy repeal the laws of domestic politics, however. Their terms of power and missions remain responsive to the political leadership that created and maintains them.

This chapter examines how the rules governing elections and the division of powers within a government shape the politics of military security commitments and economic security policies in the United States and Japan. Differences in political institutions, by creating divergent political priorities and bargaining problems for policy making, have fostered sharply contrasting strategies for national security.[1]

Military security commitments are promises to assist other countries through the potential use of force. These promises vary, of course, with respect to their breadth and depth, their credibility, and the degree to which they are made conditional on performance in other areas. The United States' political system has permitted an extensive range of commitments with relatively low conditionality and high levels of credibility after 1945. In contrast, Japanese politics has led to narrow, noncredible, and extremely conditional international commitments.

Economic security policies embrace the linkages between policies for industrial promotion and weapons acquisition, particularly the use of

[1] This paper draws materially from Cowhey (1993a, b).

203

military procurement to enhance civilian technological capabilities. Can the government commit to target particular contractors for military procurement in order to create these linkages? I argue in this chapter that Japan under the LDP could make such commitments far more easily than could the United States.[2]

1. THE ARGUMENT

World War II left a powerful political legacy in the United States and Japan. The U.S. voting public feared the dangers of appeasement; the Japanese public feared resurgent militarism. Many analysts explain policy differences between the two countries largely in terms of international power and this political legacy (e.g., Bobrow 1993: 432; Chapman et al. 1982; Katzenstein forthcoming). But the essential question should deal with when, why, and how this political legacy translates into particular political outcomes, as the U.S. difficulty in responding to its widely deplored budget deficit shows. Political institutions shaped how the legacy of war became national security strategy in both nations, and the manner in which institutions did so precisely fit the logic of other policy choices described in this book. There is nothing unique about security policies and politics.

The electoral system shapes policies because it influences the incentives of political leaders.[3] As Cox and Rosenbluth show in this volume, a first-past-the-post system in a single-member district (the highest vote getter goes to Congress) favors the two-party system built around pursuit of the median voter to build a majority of voters.[4] It encourages parties to build their reputations with voters by providing collective goods (such as the fruits of a sound currency or a strong national defense). In a single-nontransferable-vote system (SNTV) with multimember districts, as in Japan, a candidate wins by developing a very loyal minority coalition of voters, accomplished by showering targeted favors and services on them rather than emphasizing the provision of collective goods.[5] Rosenbluth (1993: 125) notes that the "electoral system only minimizes, but does not obliterate entirely the political salience of broadly based issues." As a

---

[2] There are many other types of economic security policy. This paper does not evaluate the policy's net economic benefits.

[3] Bobrow's analysis (1993: 427) of how institutional variables explain Japanese security choices does not systematically treat electoral law as a variable that interacts with the division of power.

[4] The median voter is the range of policy preferences where most voters cluster.

[5] Japan elects Diet members in multimember (two to six seats) districts, and each voter can vote for only one candidate. A party can win a majority only by running several candidates in each district. No party wanting majority status can run on broad policy issues because members of the party could undercut each other in the same district. Instead, candidates cultivate a minority block of voters by lavish patronage politics.

result, the LDP allocated a larger percentage of government funds to pork-barrel spending and loan guarantees to business than found in most parliamentary systems (McCubbins and Rosenbluth in Chapter 3 of this volume).

Governments also vary according to the division of powers. In parliamentary governments a single party (or coalition) controls the executive and the legislature. This makes it easier to agree on how to target collective goods as a reward for party supporters. In addition, a parliamentary system is more likely to grant extensive delegation of power to a single executive bureaucracy because there is no rivalry between the executive and legislature. A unified bureaucracy makes it easier to coordinate claims of rival firms (Rosenbluth 1993). Moreover, especially when one party constantly controls the government, policy making becomes less transparent because the ruling legislators know that they have firm control over the political rewards of policy. This is the case in Japan.

In contrast, legislatures in presidential systems (i.e., divided powers) tilt more toward distributional (e.g., pork-barrel) and constituency-service politics because it is harder for the different branches to allocate credit for the creation of collective goods than for building roads. Divided powers, especially when reinforced by differences in election cycles and districts, either curtail the delegation of power or require more detailed contract-and-reward systems to oversee new delegations of power. Major initiatives in American foreign policy were possible only because Congress redesigned executive agencies to reconcile the management of foreign policy with the division of power. The tensions between the branches of government also increased transparency in policy making because the legislature had an interest in forcing disclosure by executive bureaucracies.

Parliamentary governments also have fewer obstacles (veto gates) to initiating new policies or to reversing old ones than do systems with divided powers. Thus, all else being equal, it is easier to make and break foreign-policy commitments in a parliamentary system than in a system of divided powers.

To illustrate, from 1945 through the 1970s the electoral system and concerns of voters in the United States gave incentives to both parties' presidential and congressional wings to sponsor innovative collective goods through foreign policy. By design, provision of these collective goods entailed distribution of targetable, particularistic benefits. These particularistic benefits, built into the very fabric of policy, foster support constituencies for individual policies. Thus, once a commitment is made, the division of powers and electoral competition together make reversal extremely difficult. Moreover, there has been enough transparency in the policy process to permit allies to monitor and judge the direction of American policy on their own, thus enhancing their trust in U.S. commitments (Cowhey 1993b). The net result was innovative and credible security commitments. In contrast, defense procurement to boost particular firms and regional centers was difficult because the politics of budgeting restrict credible promises of this type (McCubbins 1991).

The story was just the opposite in Japan. Given voter suspicions of militarism after 1945, the conservative LDP had to tread carefully on security issues, and the SNTV electoral system offers few incentives for an LDP politician to attempt to build political power by becoming the Sam Nunn of Japan. The LDP successfully used its control of the Diet to create self-imposed limits on the military that were so politically charged as to be difficult to reverse. It then used these political pledges as bargaining leverage to convince the United States of the political dangers of larger defense efforts. In short, the LDP created a two-level game (Putnam 1988) of domestic political pledges to reassure voters about its military policies that simultaneously limited American bargaining room. At the same time, the LDP equated national security with economic development. Japan's parliamentary system, combined with the internal political structure of the LDP, made it possible to offer sustained commitments to targeted firms and regional production centers.

Sections 2 and 3 analyze the institutional constraints on security policy in the United States and Japan. Sections 4 and 5 show their differing impacts on security commitments and economic security policies. Section 6 reviews the findings and briefly discusses future dynamics.

2. U.S. POLITICS

The conventional wisdom about U.S. foreign policy holds that the division of power between a cosmopolitan president and a parochial Congress favor bureaucratic politics and political paralysis. When the executive branch's influence wanes, foreign policy is in trouble (Krasner 1978a). However, the conventional wisdom fundamentally misunderstands electoral incentives and the implications of the division of power for foreign policy.

2.1. Electoral incentives

The U.S. electoral system influences the ability to make foreign policy commitments. On the one hand, the concern over party identity provides incentives for parties to take consistent stands on major issues of foreign policy. It also makes it risky to reverse these positions. On the other hand, the differences in electoral incentives for the president, the Senate, and the

House lead to diverging approaches to foreign policy, with Congress in particular emphasizing the distributional aspects of goods tied to foreign policy.

Of course, electoral systems will affect policy commitments only insofar as voters care about foreign policy. The traditional literature on voting and U.S. foreign policy has held that voters' low level of information on international affairs means that foreign policy is not important. Newer theories of voting argue that voters care about many issues, even if they do not have detailed information about them.[6] Foreign policy may not be a daily concern for most voters, but forays into foreign policy issues can ignite powerful retrospective punishment by voters (Aldrich et al. 1989; Nincic 1990). While members of Congress may know little about foreign policy, they delegate power to members who are willing to pay attention and accommodate the political dictates of the party (Cox and McCubbins 1993).

Brand name identities mean that parties have a tough time reversing positions once they have made a major public commitment.[7] Unless voter preferences have changed radically, a major shift in party position leaves significant openings for the opposition.

The importance of collective goods does not end distributional politics or constituent services to win voter support, however. Elected officials choose policies that disproportionately favor their supporters and emphasize particularistic benefits for which they can take clear credit when designing collective goods. The distributional imperatives of the executive and of both chambers of the legislature differ. Thus, foreign policy commitments like the defense commitments of the United States depend on reconciling diverse distributional preferences. Policy often trades off efficiency against this distributional imperative. In the postwar period, the creation of a potent national defense in the United States came at the expense of a bloated national budget.

2.2. The division of powers

In a system of separated powers, it is often hard to agree on policy even when a single party controls both branches of the government; this is due

---

[6] Voters make judgments on issues where they have little information (including many domestic issues) in ways that make sense given that limited information. Party identification is an important cue on issues that voters care about when they lack other information. This is especially true in congressional races. Party identification in turn depends on retrospective assessment of performance, which can change rapidly. Because attributable benefits are one key to a politician's success, presidents traditionally like foreign policy because they have clear claims to control (Popkin 1991).

[7] Other models of foreign policy overlook this issue (Bueno de Mesquita and Lalman 1990; 1991).

to differences in the electoral base of the executive and legislature. Yet even Republican control of the Senate did not stop Truman from making dramatic changes in U.S. foreign policy, thanks to the electoral salience of isolationism and communism. The election of 1944 showed that the isolationists had lost at the ballot box, and both parties knew it (Barone 1990: 167–181). The question was how to stake out an internationalist position consistent with each party's specialized base of voters.[8]

Divided powers increase the number of veto gates in the policy process. This makes new initiatives considerably harder than in a parliamentary system but it also makes the reversal of major policies harder. For example, congressional rebellions against a standing commitment require new legislation that the president can veto.[9] The tug-of-war between the branches also leads to more systematic disclosure of information about policy making. This increases the transparency of foreign policy choices both to voters at home and foreign allies. Thus, the division of power can increase the continuity and credibility of foreign policy commitments.

Executive bureaucracies are also subject to tighter controls than in a parliamentary democracy because each branch of government guards its interests against the other. Moreover, the different electoral incentives for the president, the Senate, and the House lead to diverging approaches to foreign policy. House members are the most parochial and have the shortest time horizons for judging programs, Senate members less so, and the president least of all – because he is directly identified with broad swings in national well-being. Accordingly, the House member should most strongly view foreign policy through the lens of local distributional impacts and specialized voter groups in her district (Jacobson 1990).

Congress benefits less directly than the president from diffuse national benefits, and is always more sensitive than the White House about imposing costs on individual congressional districts to win national collective goods. This leads to institutional innovations for major new commitments (e.g., the Federal Reserve system for central banking) to reconcile different time horizons and size of constituencies.

Institutional innovations were prerequisites for delegating new foreign policy powers to the executive. These innovations included: (1) institutional "fire alarms" (devices making it easy for the disgruntled to get

---

[8] When the Republicans controlled Congress in 1946, they chose Vandenberg as chair of the Foreign Relations Committee even though he had become committed to an internationalist order. Vandenberg defined the terms by which the Midwest wing of the Republican party joined the eastern wing in accepting multilateralism championed by Democrats. Despite reservations by Republican conservatives, Truman could count on thirty Republican senators as supporters on foreign policy (Cowhey 1993a; Reichard 1986). The voter consensus lasted until at least the early 1970s (Barone 1990).

[9] In general, it requires a shift in both the presidential party and the majority congressional party to get a major reversal of a commitment.

information and complain); (2) "trip wires" (requirements for explicit authorization of certain uses of a general authority) to satisfy critics about contingent dangers of an innovation; (3) "time limits" on authority to force executors of the policy to pay attention to critics; (4) "customized tailoring" of agency personnel and powers to facilitate certain outcomes, including creation of specialized new agencies and fragmentation of bureaucratic jurisdictions; (5) "self-binding behavior" by the executive branch whereby the head of government has to make prominent declarations of intent and responsibility (as in requiring the president to "certify" that China is in compliance with human rights rules); and, (6) "stacking the decision process" to make sure that all key interests get represented (Kiewiet and McCubbins 1991; McCubbins and Schwartz 1984).

The executive and legislative branches used these methods to make foreign policy innovations more consistent with the electoral imperative. For example, to curb excessive diplomatic generosity, Congress insisted on the independence of the Marshall Plan from the State Department, a short life cycle for the agency, and leadership by a corporate executive from Indiana sympathetic to protecting the interests of the industrial Midwest. In general, institutional innovation under divided powers leads to greater fragmentation of authority over policy to cater to diverse specialized constituencies and increase executive accountability. This fragmentation also makes it harder to coordinate distributional benefits among claimants who are in direct competition with each other for the same prize. Thus, the United States could maintain a general commitment to certain security promises, but it had a hard time marrying military-procurement policy to regional industrial policies in the manner of Japan (see section 5.1).

3. JAPAN

In comparison to the United States, it is easier to undertake major policy initiatives in a parliamentary system under control of a majority party. Because there is no division between the executive and legislature it is easier to target benefits for long-standing supporters, as happened in economic security policy. However, there are also no built-in checks on reversals of policy promises. This poses problems when trying to limit foreign or domestic demands for politically risky policies. So, the LDP invented a mixture of institutional constraints and self-binding political pledges to manage the political and diplomatic bargaining risks of foreign policy. At the same time, prolonged LDP rule permitted extensive delegation to the bureaucracy. This delegation created a significant veil over the Japanese policy process to foreign allies that reduced the transparency and credibility of foreign policy promises.

3.1. The division of powers

The main checks and balances on policy were within the LDP itself, where Diet backbenchers and faction leaders customarily require consensus on controversial initiatives such as security issues. The LDP constitution requires all legislation and policy initiatives to be approved by the pertinent Policy Affairs Research Council (PARC) committees. The PARC committees specialize by subject and provide LDP Diet members with their closest counterpart to the policy expertise and patronage opportunities of congressional subcommittees. They also permit the LDP to let individual Diet members claim personal credit for policies relevant to their constituents. Together with party leaders who specialized in particular policy areas, the *zoku,* and the heads of the factions (the rival party power groupings that provide campaign funding for their members and vie for control of the LDP) they provided a thorough set of checks on any unwanted initiatives by the cabinet (such as daring moves on security policy).[10] As a further safeguard, the LDP organized the government so as to limit the resources available for independent initiatives by the prime minister (Kernell 1991).[11]

Once it has set a policy, the Diet can delegate extensive authority to bureaucracies because there is no rivalry between the legislature and the executive. Unified control lets political leadership design quiet but effective controls over the bureaucracy. If policy preferences are clear and stable, the bureaucracy can then reliably target benefits to interested parties. If important constituents later complain, politicians can intervene. Political leaders also settle major ministerial feuds over turf because the choice of the lead ministry implies which types of policy preferences (and constituents) will prevail.

3.2. Electoral incentives

In comparison to the United States, the Japanese electoral system rewards cautious leadership built on distributional politics.[12] Even though the LDP's electoral identity positioned it as the conservative party of economic growth and global competitive success (Inoguchi 1990), foreign policy had few attractions for LDP politicians because it demanded limits on attractive distributional politics (e.g., protecting Japanese firms from imports) in order to preserve such collective goods as a defense pact with

[10] The *zoku* is an informal club (or "tribe") of members of the LDP who are recognized leaders in a particular policy. Leadership in the relevant PARC is usually a requisite for becoming part of a *zoku. Zoku* include members of all the political factions in the LDP.
[11] Calder (1988a) argues that the only political force capable of backing systematic policy reform was the American diplomatic establishment.
[12] See Cox and Rosenbluth in this volume and Calder (1988b: 63–70).

the United States. As a result, when tough foreign choices on behalf of foreign policy were necessary, it fell to the heads of the LDP factions to pull together a collective policy response that went beyond routine politics.[13] Even then, there was no political incentive to do anything more than the minimum necessary to appease foreign allies (Bobrow 1993: 429).[14]

Military security was especially unattractive in part because there was less patronage to distribute than the rest of economic policy, and in part because of general public skepticism about the military.[15] Therefore, the LDP wanted to manage the U.S. relationship while finding ways to limit electoral exposure on defense choices. Internal checks within the LDP constrained controversial policy departures on security while permitting continuity in those with strong support, including long-term commitments to distributional benefits when beneficiaries were small in number, stable in identity, and important to the party. However, in the case of defense, the relevant PARC committees were not very popular for many years, and LDP Diet members blocked efforts by prime ministers to increase spending on defense at the expense of other priorities.[16] The defense PARC committee became more popular only in the 1970s, when a traditional clientele of aerospace and electronics firms came to value defense funding more highly. The LDP then created new budgetary and military procurement rules to assist them.

4. THE DOMESTIC POLITICS OF MILITARY COMMITMENTS

This section examines the selection of military commitments that define the contours of defense and diplomatic relationships. While balance-of-power considerations influenced national strategies, each country's policy approach also reflected its political structure.

---

[13] The factions are relatively cosmopolitan and representative of the party as a whole (Kohno 1992). Faction leaders are senior politicians who rise by raising money and bargaining skillfully across issues; they value the privileges of majority rule more than particular issues so they have an incentive to compromise to save the party.

[14] Even when the leadership intervened to reduce barriers to foreign competition in order to solve a trade crisis, it still favored continued administrative regulation of markets in order to collect political rents from all market participants. These measures significantly reduced the market's transparency and increased the nontariff obstacles to foreign entry (Encarnation and Mason 1990; Kohno 1992, note 30).

[15] Foreign policy and defense were among the worst specialties for electoral security or advancement in the party because they did not generate large flows of campaign monies (van Wolferen 1989).

[16] Military spending was more popular with conservatives before they unified into the LDP in 1955 (Calder 1988b). The 1955 merger made it easier to target benefits for civilian spending.

4.1. The United States

After World War II the United States had little choice about global leadership. Its international power was unprecedented in modern history. International systemic pressures meant that limiting Soviet influence was important to the United States, which in turn meant that it had to organize international security and economic arrangements. Moreover, the United States was necessarily both an Atlantic and Pacific power, and no American policy could avoid the growing importance of nuclear weapons for defense strategy. Nonetheless, beyond these considerations the political structure of the United States shaped many important strategic choices.

After 1945, the United States attempted to use multilateralism (arrangements stressing nondiscrimination and indivisibility among a group of nations), as opposed to bilateralism, emphasizing strict reciprocity, as the basis for its distinctive strategy for world security and economic order (Ruggie 1992). This meant the United States committed itself to protect Western Europe as a whole (as long as a country was willing to join NATO) rather than just favor a few special client states. Multilateralism was politically attractive because it avoided domestic political problems that would have plagued other internationalist solutions (Cowhey 1993a).

This sensitivity to domestic politics was predictable because the division of powers gives each branch of government a veto over policy. Differing electoral incentives mean that Congress will be more sensitive than the White House about ethnic voters' sensibilities in individual legislative districts.

Multilateralism in Europe solved a fundamental political dilemma for both political parties because it potentially included the homelands of all American voters of European descent, not just a favored few. For example, Irish Americans always resented relying primarily on Britain as a European partner, and German Americans had favored isolationism because internationalism traditionally had been defined as anti-German until the Marshall Plan and NATO. In recognition of these political realities Dean Acheson ordered the end of all internal State Department studies organized around a special relationship with Britain (Acheson 1969: 387; Cowhey 1993a).[17]

In short, multilateralism was not simply the dream of diplomats, but also bore the strong imprint of America's political leadership. But politics

---

[17] American voters in 1945 were mainly of European ancestry, and so was the practical thrust of the multilateral innovations. Although the United States proposed multilateral security arrangements in Asia, it accepted Japan's refusal to back such an approach (Pyle 1993). It was easier to accept Japanese claims for special treatment because there was far less American voter sensitivity to bilateralism favoring any one power in Asia.

need not be the enemy of policy creativity. Congress wanted to avoid the draft (which it did until the Korean war), counteract popular worries that international commitments would simply drain American wealth while foreign nations shirked, keep tight rein on any executive-branch thinking that might threaten war, and hold down spending. The early emphasis on saving Europe by a NATO that entailed no troop commitments reflected both strategic thinking and political dickering. Similarly, casting NATO as a "mutual aid" institution responded to fears in U.S. politics of foreigners "bleeding the U.S. dry."[18] The growing centrality of nuclear weapons to national military strategy posed the problem of rapid choices that would have enormous consequences. Therefore, Congress resorted to more *ex ante* controls that limited presidential choices.

For example, it tinkered with the force structures available to the president (and thus the types of escalation and war fighting strategies). The congressional budget process forced disclosure of information on strategic options by fostering interservice rivalry and favored those initiatives designed to fight large-scale battles in Europe rather than smaller wars elsewhere. Congress largely denied the president other tools (including control over personnel) to redefine the grand strategy of the professional military (Avant forthcoming).

Other *ex ante* controls focused on restructuring decision-making processes to make certain types of choices less likely. Some involved approval procedures for military actions. The NATO accord included a "trip wire" – the right of each member country to follow its own constitutional processes in determining how to fulfill its commitment to mutual defense. Another set of checks restructured the national security institutions. Congress changed the laws governing how foreign security policy got made to increase the fire alarms and to "restack the decision process." The National Security Council (NSC) was partly an effort by a set of senior officials representing diverse constituencies to hem in Truman (and raising the chances of disclosure of plans upsetting those constituencies) (Destler, Gelb, and Lake 1984; Leffler 1993).[19] This act followed the approach of the Administrative Procedure Act of the previous year; it regularized the process of decision making, including intelligence operations for the first time, to make it accountable to Congress (Koh 1990).

---

[18] Vandenberg cast NATO as an organization stressing "mutual aid and self help" precisely to assure Congress that NATO was not a one-sided bargain (Ireland 1981). Multilateralism also addressed concerns over internationalism possibly bleeding America while other countries shirked. Collective public institutions (e.g., NATO or the World Bank) with conditions on access to their benefits provided standardized criteria for resolving the endless possibilities for disputes on burden sharing.

[19] This was one reason for Truman's coolness toward the NSC. Congress also authorized the head of the newly created Joint Chiefs of Staff to bypass the administration and report directly to Congress.

In short, the division of powers led to institutional tinkering to reconcile differing incentives of the legislature and executive. These controls took two forms. One was the design of decision making to enhance accountability to the legislative branch, and to improve the chances for disgruntled constituents to complain. The other was the design of the program mandate to preclude (or discourage) projects contrary to the priorities of Congress. In addition, under divided powers the difficulty of reversing commitments and the transparency of the policy process enhanced the credibility of American commitments.

4.2. Japan

The international position of Japan, like the United States, influenced the options for security policy. As a defeated power in a bipolar nuclear world, Japan could not easily check its closest geographic threat, the Soviet Union, on its own. So, the U.S. defense connection was essential (unless Japan opted to gamble on some version of neutrality). The main question about strategy and capability was the structure of the security relationship to the United States. There were two key questions: Would Japan have a firm security guarantee from the United States, including tangible deployment of forces; and how much could the United States press Japan to take an extended perimeter defense (how narrowly would Japan constitute its theater of self-defense operations) and develop massive military assets (Hellmann 1969; Mochizuki 1983–84).

If the alliance with the United States was the cornerstone of policy, then would Japan bow to American pressure for an extended defense perimeter? Although conservative in its politics, the government found defense politics especially unrewarding and wanted to minimize the scope and prominence of defense issues (Pyle 1988).[20] This task was easier because neither Washington nor Japan's Asian neighbors wanted a Japanese military resurgence. Nonetheless, the United States had a constant temptation to ask Japan to undertake more security tasks. For example, the price for the end of the American occupation included the creation of a Japanese military force and a treaty giving the United States rights to military bases (Schaller 1985).

The Japanese leadership developed preemptive security policy commitments to fend off both political opposition at home and the United States.

---

[20] In the 1950s the Socialists recruited militant unions to an alliance that attacked the LDP by rejecting the U.S.–Japan Security Treaty. Military issues were potentially the left's strongest suit. The treaty's revisions of 1960 provoked the largest mass protests in contemporary Japanese history and forced the prime minister to resign (Ishida and Krauss 1989: 11–12; Packard 1966).

Political leaders stacked the political cards against the development of force capabilities that could invite U.S. pressure (or claims by the Japanese military) for extended obligations. They interpreted Article 9 of the constitution as a trip wire to limit commitments and used "customized tailoring" of the defense agencies to limit capabilities. LDP leaders also found it useful to employ "self-binding behavior" to limit their political dilemmas.

On the face of it, the Japanese constitution preempted U.S. claims for an extended security perimeter. "The 'no war' clause (Article 9) of the 1947 constitution would seem, according to a literal interpretation, to render armed forces . . . illegal" (Stockwin 1989: 105). Moreover, the opposition and some parts of the LDP blocked the two-thirds majority necessary to amend Article 9. Nonetheless, Article 9 left considerable maneuvering room. For example, it did not prevent the creation of the Self Defense Force and its subsequent development into a sophisticated military force.

However, the LDP did not wish to interpret Article 9 too liberally (Pyle 1993). Its restrictive interpretation of Article 9 always let the LDP say to the United States that the constitution limited its options, and that the United States would create a political imbroglio if it were to demand much more. The LDP was using a tactic similar to the one employed by the United States in the bargaining game over exchange rates that Fukui and Weatherford discuss in this volume. It created a series of prominent political pledges concerning defense that blunted attacks by political opponents on the left. At the same time, as Johnson (1992) notes, the U.S. government always deemed LDP rule to be vital to U.S. security interests. Therefore, when the LDP created a political game in which U.S. pressure for more-forthcoming Japanese actions on security could create a dangerous electoral backlash, the United States had to tread lightly.

For these tactics to work at home and abroad they had to be pursued vigorously. Half-hearted and little-publicized actions would convince no one. So the LDP honed the art of making prominent political declarations of policy against acquiring controversial military capabilities. In 1957 it declared against the acquisition of a nuclear weapons capability. It further reiterated and passed legislation to this effect in 1968 and 1971.[21] In 1968, after controversy arose about the use of Sony photo technology by American bombers in Vietnam, the LDP introduced legislation that affirmed the principle of no exports of military technology, and of the three nonnuclear principles (no possession, no manufacturing, and no transit of nuclear weapons in Japan) (Calder 1988b: 439).

Another indication of the political grip on military strategy was the 1

---

[21] The United States approved of Japan's rejection of nuclear weapons and its ban on arms exports (Johnson 1992).

percent limit on defense spending. During the Vietnam era there was considerable criticism of Japanese support for the U.S. effort. Would-be leaders of the LDP had to balance the defense relationship with the United States against the political risks. The response was a 1969 pledge to limit Japanese defense spending to no more than 1 percent of GNP that evolved into a formal doctrine by 1976.

The 1-percent pledge was a classic case of self-binding behavior by executive leadership. It was a political invention, faithfully reiterated by a string of prime ministers to LDP backbenchers, to show that there would be strict limits on any expansion of Japanese capabilities. It was precisely the kind of device one needs when there are no institutional checks in government institutions on foreign policy commitments. It was prominent, easy to monitor, and preempted much of the strategy debate within Japan and with the United States. Even after its repeal, following long negotiations between Prime Minister Nakasone and the senior leadership of the LDP, the LDP created new pledges to limit total spending (Katahara 1990: 281–287).

These strategies also let the LDP exercise effective civilian control over the military even though there was far less active civilian review (e.g., independent think tanks for military strategy) than one normally associates with such control (Van Evera 1985). A narrow interpretation of Article 9 plus the nonnuclear principles constituted *ex ante* controls for military strategy. Diet members must give full prior approval to even a limited military effort, and the military has no direct access to the prime minister or the Diet.[22] It even lost a bid to have the military report directly to the minister of defense rather than a civilian vice-minister.

The Japanese problem in participating in the Gulf War with Iraq signaled how small the Japanese role was likely to be in any global security system unless there was a change in political institutions. The Kaifu government had to substitute large financial contributions for military action because the Diet rejected military participation. The diplomatic embarrassment over the Gulf War tarnished the LDP's reputation as the party of international success. Japan's inability to join peacekeeping forces even threatened acquisition of a permanent seat on the U.N. Security Council, a big setback to rising Japanese public expectations.

The political embarrassment finally prompted LDP backbenchers to propose a modest change in security policy to reduce international criticism. The Policy Committee of the LDP, backed by the defense *zoku*, suddenly declared in 1992 that Article 9 did not block extensive participa-

---

[22] In 1986, the LDP created a new cabinet-level organization, the Security Council of Japan, in order to smooth out embarrassing fights over security policy, not to foster new policy thinking (Katahara 1990: 106–117). The Japanese military leadership is very careful to avoid political controversy (Bobrow 1993; Katzenstein forthcoming).

tion in U.N. peacekeeping forces.[23] However, Prime Minister Miyazawa deemed this revisionist view too controversial for consensus in the LDP, much less in the Upper House of the Diet where Miyazawa needed some votes from centrist opposition parties for any legislation.[24] The final legislation permitted Japanese troops to participate solely at the request of the United Nations after a cease-fire was in place. Japanese peacekeepers could make only minimal use of weapons. Moreover, it forbade Japanese participation in any mission to separate warring parties forcibly (e.g., Bosnia) without prior approval of the Diet. In practice, Japan can field only small-scale logistical and medical assistance for less-violent UN missions.

In short, Japan's limited commitments on security showed little chance of changing despite single-party control in a parliamentary system until mid-1993. Electoral incentives favored the status quo.[25] Political leaders did not benefit significantly (nor did the LDP as a whole) from dwelling on foreign policy. So, the LDP built self-binding commitments to win two-level games by making prominent pledges to voters at home that also lowered U.S. bargaining latitude. No Japanese prime minister could abandon these principles without approval from the LDP leadership.

5. WEAPONS CHOICE AND ACQUISITION

Weapons acquisition has implications for economic development – the "economic security" dimension of military procurement. Analysts have noticed a striking difference in U.S. and Japanese approaches that appears symptomatic of how the two countries handle national economic strategy (Sandholtz et al. 1992). The respective approaches – "spin-off" and "spin-on" – have two components: the approach to linking civilian and military technology and the policy for supporting regional production centers tied to particular industries.

The United States defines security as the ability to execute military missions and spends money to develop technologies to that end. The link to economic development comes from the process of spin-off, whereby military technologies coincidentally bolster the civilian technology base. This was the story of semiconductors, for example (Flamm 1988). In

---

[23] Ichiro Ozawa, who later was a leader in the defections from the LDP in 1993, and the defense *zoku* (not faction leaders) endorsed this position. Hisao Takagi, "LDP Panel Backs Active Role for Troops," *Nikkei Weekly*, February 29, 1992, p. 2.

[24] The LDP lost control of the House of Councillors (the Upper House) by a narrow margin in 1989, thereby giving the opposition the power to block some legislative actions.

[25] The only hint of broader commitments was in Asian security. Even here LDP government officials ruled out formal military arrangements. For alternative scenarios, see Inoguchi (1989) and Johnson (1992).

217

contrast, Japan's security doctrine assumes that, apart from the country's safety from attack, security entails the indigenization, diffusion, and promotion of advanced technology as the key to national safety and prosperity (Friedman and Samuels 1993; Samuels 1991, 1994; Vogel 1992).[26] LDP members found this to be an appealing twist on their security strategy.

Samuels and Whipple (1989) have dubbed Japan's distinctive pattern of weapons acquisition and design "spin-on." Japan adds value to its weapons by enhancing them with advanced civilian technologies. These enhanced weapons in turn justify a preference for Japanese designs and suppliers, rather than those from the United States. This also feeds the growth of civilian industries designated as national priorities because it supports the development of key technological skills. The explicit goal of spin-on is a two-way enhancement of technology through civilian–military flows, including a commitment to support specialized regional production communities for key industries.

How does one explain these differences, particularly the commitment to regional industrial centers? The international structure of power certainly mattered. Operating under the U.S. security umbrella, Japan had more luxury than the United States in picking its priorities, including importing weapons technology from allies when development did not fit its needs. Nonetheless, Noble (1992) has shown that the United States government was not blind to economic security issues. Electoral incentives and the divisions of power in the two countries explain the policy differences.

5.1. The United States: spin-off

The United States recognized the need for, and understood the commercial consequences of, maintaining the national technology base for national-defense projects. However, politics also restrained the U.S. approach to nurturing industry through military procurement. The electoral incentives of Congress, along with the division of powers, tilted policy toward national logrolls for defense procurement that minimized picking winners from among companies and regions.

To begin, congressional power over weapons programs means that every program has to win a sustainable majority coalition in Congress over many years of appropriations. The overall political problem fits Noll and Shimada's (1991) analysis of research and development and infrastructure polices. Only industries that are geographically ubiquitous

---

[26] Samuels (1991) argues that the creation of the SDF provided the mechanism for getting American technology that was only available through military cooperation programs.

and visible to most voters are good candidates for promotion by congressional appropriations. Infrastructure projects (such as highways) are the best candidates; but cleverly parceled-out defense contracts are not a bad second (both infrastructure and defense also can be packaged as collective goods – good transportation and a sound defense – that appeal to voters).

Ideally, a project should not benefit just a few companies at the expense of many others. Otherwise, highly motivated losers may work against the program (Cohen and Noll 1991). Thus the government may have to forgo a project rather than appear to favor companies with special help.[27] In addition, divided powers often lead legislatures to divide bureaucratic jurisdictions to check executive power and give particular constituents champions within the executive branch. Fragmented administration of defense policy reduces the ability of the executive branch to coordinate and harmonize competing corporate claims.

Of course, U.S. defense procurement necessarily picks winners in the sense that a few firms dominate the largest awards, but each allocates a large share of the contract to a vast array of subcontractors who blanket the United States (Mayer 1992). The appeal of spin-off as a doctrine for the commercial connection is that it is theoretically neutral. The U.S. government does not pick who will profit most in the commercial realm from military projects; that is up to the skills of individual firms.

American policy also does not maintain regional production centers, a major goal of Japanese policy. U.S. aerospace contractors pass many of the risks and financial pressures of their business on to subcontractors who cannot meet stiffer terms in hard times. As a result, subcontracting for the major U.S. aerospace companies flies out of traditional production centers in the Pacific Northwest or Southern California (Friedman and Samuels 1993). The U.S. government does not bail out the subcontractors; the federal budget for financial guarantees to smaller businesses is much smaller than in Japan. Moreover, an important financial support for spin-on policies in Japan comes through profits inflated by collusive bidding procedures. In the United States, where the political opposition has an incentive to emphasize big-policy issues, largess to business is always fair game for criticism. As a result, however imperfectly, competitive bidding procedures have significantly cut profit margins (McMillan 1992).

Could the United States have a system that explicitly maintained a system of regional production centers? An independent legislature elected by local districts makes it hard unless a regional commitment is part of a bigger package (e.g., a regional park is part of a package of many new national parks). Moreover, under divided powers, there are many veto

---

[27] Moreover, federalism in the United States led to a strong antitrust policy that makes it difficult to create projects that are simply all-inclusive, as happens in Japan.

points over policy and many institutional checks on bureaucratic discretion. For example, the Congress requires annual reapproval of projects. This means that multiple opportunities exist for specialized blocking coalitions to thwart programs. In addition, changing party control of the branches of government means that it is not easy to bind future decisions by current choices.

As a result, the overtones of a zero-sum competition (some companies lose, and awards for major weapons systems do not neatly fall into concurrent packages) create pressure for each project to distribute rewards on a broad geographic basis. Therefore, no major contractor will credit promises of sustained government assistance for preferential treatment of regional subcontractors. There are too many blocking coalitions unless the project has widespread geographical support, and there are no credible institutional guarantees of a continuing majority for the project (Cohen and Noll 1991). The net result is a system loaded with pork, but less able to undertake regional development goals or more proactive policies to commercialize military technology.

5.2. Japan: spin-on

Why can Japan support spin-on policies? While electoral considerations limit the military budget, within those totals SNTV leads the LDP to support both big and small businesses. A parliamentary government under continuous control can delegate power to expert bureaucracies to do much of the policy work, including preparing initiatives. Political leadership then "stacks the deck" of the decision process to require consultation with key interests and their political advocates (McCubbins, Noll, and Weingast 1987). If there is a consensus on a political objective there are ways to make these promises believable by designing the process to favor the outcome. This is what makes the bureaucratic standing and budgetary procedures of the Self Defense Force and Japan Defense Agency so striking.

The JDA does not have full ministerial status, and a member of the Ministry of Finance, not a JDA bureaucrat, is the budget chief. This arrangement makes sure that JDA does not get too expansive in its demands early in the process. The JDA can boost its share of the government budget only at budget reconciliation talks directed by the prime minister and LDP leaders (who often prefer other political priorities) (Calder 1988b, 425–426).

Defense spending was a lower priority partly because business has offered only measured support for defense projects. Defense procurement is not as important for Japanese defense contractors as in the United

States.[28] High rates of civilian growth even divert the interests of smaller firms who might otherwise become hooked on defense spending (Bobrow and Hill 1991).

Nonetheless, the doctrine of spin-on calls for a tight integration of military procurement and industrial-promotion policies. A single JDA office, the Equipment Bureau, does all procurement. The director of the bureau is a MITI official, and MITI thinks of weapons development as part of its industrial-promotion program.[29]

There is a question as to whether the LDP could easily reach a consensus on whom to target for benefits. It is not easy for the Japanese government to succeed in picking winners. The optimum opportunity exists if the industry is relatively concentrated and suffers a competitive disadvantage against the rest of the world (Noble 1989; Samuels 1987). This is precisely the case for Japan's military contractors; ten firms receive 67 percent of the government contracts and traditionally sought to reduce reliance on foreign partners for technology (Chinworth 1992: 190). The situation is particularly telling in aerospace.

Unlike most Japanese weapons suppliers, Japanese aerospace firms rely on government procurement for 80 percent of their revenues. Moreover, the biggest firms jointly own subsidiaries for participating in the aircraft and jet engine industries.[30] Cooperation in the Japanese aerospace industry resembles *dango* (bid rigging) in the construction industry; it exceeds collusion levels in the aerospace industry in other countries (Friedman and Samuels 1993). Procurement policies have raised weapons costs and impaired their effectiveness, but the policies have built a stronger national technological base (Bobrow 1993: 417).

Japan not only embraces indigenization and sharing of technology, it also nurtures regional production centers (Friedman and Samuels 1993). This distinctive approach creates a collective association of regional subcontractors to raise financing collectively (they sign each other's loan applications), bargain collectively with the prime contractor on acceptable contracting practices, and create political support at the local, regional, and national levels for their practices. Political success has given

---

[28] Whereas defense constituted over half the sales of the top ten U.S. contractors, it was a small fraction for the major Japanese suppliers (Vogel 1992).

[29] JDA challenged MITI's control in the early 1950s but was turned back (Katzenstein forthcoming). Japanese weapons procurement also had to pay attention to American sensibilities. Therefore, the Ministry of Foreign Affairs has a prominent voice in reviewing these choices.

[30] Mitsubishi, Kawasaki, and Fuji Heavy Industries are joint partners in the Japan Commercial Transport Development Corporation, which is the Japanese partner in making Boeing 767 components. The Japanese group received grants and loans from government to cover up to 50 percent of development costs. The Japan Aero Engines Corporation is a consortium of Mitsubishi Heavy Industries, Kawasaki Heavy Industries, and Ishikawajima–Harima Heavy Industries (Mowery 1988: 80,93).

these smaller firms the strength to bargain successfully with prime contractors and win favorable treatment from specialized regional financing institutions.

The policies to support regional production centers may reflect Japanese ideology about economic security, but why doesn't the political structure produce countervailing incentives? To begin, SNTV gives the LDP a strong interest in handing out particularistic benefits to constituents that individual Diet members can claim as a result of their specialized efforts (McCubbins and Rosenbluth in Chapter 3 of this volume). Guaranteeing small-business loans is especially popular and the loans command a large share of the national budget. The LDP also has no serious policy conflicts over market arrangements that win the support of most industrial participants.

Moreover, Japanese industrial practices make it easier for the members of an industry to coordinate side payments within their own ranks (Noll and Shimada 1991: 228). The key industry association, the Defense Production Committee (DPC) of Keidanren, has about eighty industrial companies and roughly a hundred financial institutions. It promotes higher domestic production, indigenous weapons development, and increased military R&D.[31] Executives are members of all the key *shingikai* (advisory committees) to the JDA, and the companies advise on which weapons system to embrace among alternative candidates (Chinworth 1992, 24–25). Thus, the potential for well-coordinated targeting of benefits exists due to high concentration in the industry and extensive interfirm coordination.

The next question is whether the government is willing to take special measures to lock in benefits; the answer has been yes. The LDP took extraordinary steps by making special provisions for military procurement projects in the budget process. The Defense Agency begins the procurement process through development-program contracts involving research that is largely funded by the contractors. Unless a firm is part of the preliminary research it cannot bid. The JDA's Equipment Bureau awards all the contracts, a tremendous concentration of budgeting authority compared to U.S. practices. Most strikingly, about 85 percent of all procurement (measured by expenditures) is awarded by noncompetitive bidding and another 14 percent is done through bidding restricted to two or three firms (Chinworth 1992). Firms bidding on the quasi-competitive contracts almost certainly will get at least a share as a subcontractor, and the

---

[31] The chair of DPC, usually from Mitsubishi Heavy Industries, is also the head of Keidanren's science and technology subcommittee. The DPC operates under an informal agreement with other companies that it will not advocate a bigger military budget (Katzenstein forthcoming).

same is true for those who work under development contracts on projects leading up to noncompetitive awards.

Thus, the JDA can make informal selections of prime contractors, and their subcontractors, years before the award of the procurement contract.[32] In addition, the Diet has elected to take procurement contracts out of the annual budget. Instead, the "budget as approved by the Diet represents full appropriation levels" (Chinworth 1992: 49) and the appropriation covers a five-year cycle of spending.[33] In short, the contractor can count on predictable funding over a prolonged cycle. This budgetary stability makes it easier to sustain a regional base of subcontractors.[34] Moreover, unlike that in the United States, Japanese policy permits contractors to run military and civilian production lines side by side (Katzenstein forthcoming).

The LDP could also more readily make credible promises than its American counterparts. Believable promises about future conduct mean that contractors and subcontractors bargain within a framework where a third party (a government ministry) has promised that it will offer continued support and discipline for complicated bargains to share risks and costs. A parliamentary government under one-party rule can easily delegate powers to bureaucracies with authority to broker collective action problems among firms. For example, a major problem in sharing information among firms was the possibility that some firms would cheat. The Technical Research and Development Institute of JDA personnel "monitors commercial and dual-use technology through routine contacts . . . [it] acts as an honest broker among Japanese firms" (Chinworth 1992: 46).

Moreover, the LDP has internal institutional arrangements to enforce these promises. The most important are the *zoku* for defense and the PARC committees – the Research Commission on Security, the National Defense Division, and the Special Commission on Military Bases (Katahara 1990: 359) – that have to approve all budget proposals. There was little evidence of struggle for control of the defense PARC committees among LDP factions. Moreover, the *zoku* reflected all major LDP factions. Commitments backed by the *zoku* were difficult to reverse because

---

[32] Holding down government funding of the initial research and development also reinforces the hand of industry. If government had firms pick up the research tab, then chose another firm, companies would soon start cutting back on their research efforts.

[33] The government further assured budgetary stability in 1986 when it declared JDA planning documents were "official government programs, thereby committing the government and Finance Ministry to achieve as many as possible of the objectives outlined in the five-year programs." (Chinworth 1992: 49).

[34] "Once this informal selection is made, companies will begin limited infrastructure and/or personnel investments in anticipation of a contract, even though a formal signing might still be two to three years ahead. . . . Companies also begin subcontractor arrangements" (Chinworth 1992: 61).

it took a consensus to change policy. Absent a major change in the constituency of the LDP there was little reason why the *zoku* and PARC committees would approve a significant reshuffling of distributional benefits, especially when all significant social interests were satisfied.[35]

6. CONCLUSION

This chapter shows how electoral competition and the division of power influence military security commitments and economic security policies. Many analysts have considered U.S. politics poorly suited to innovations in grand public policy but very good at doling out pork. Japan is supposedly the epitome of public purpose, not pork. This chapter shows that U.S. political institutions have made it possible to create extensive innovative commitments for military security while restricting the options for the use of military procurement to advance civilian industrial goals. Japan's political structure has worked against military commitments while facilitating the targeting of military-procurement benefits to particular industries, firms, and regions.

The first-past-the-post electoral system in the United States gives political parties a continuing reason to campaign on major foreign policy choices. This strengthens the possibility for making security commitments. But the differences in electoral districts and cycles among the legislative chambers and the president make it hard to target economic benefits to support spin-on policies for economic security. The SNTV system of Japan discourages electoral attention to public policy issues and permitted the LDP to dominate politics by finessing uncomfortable issues. As a result, the LDP embraced strategies to take security off the policy table at home and with its principal ally, the United States.

Divided powers in the United States have further reinforced the divergent fortunes of military and economic security policies. Divided powers make it harder to initiate major new policies, but harder to reverse them because the large number of veto points favors the status quo. The rivalry between the legislature and executive further influences policy by encouraging divisions of bureaucratic power and the disclosure of information to ease monitoring by the legislature. On the one hand, once established, military commitments are more credible because it is hard to reverse policies, and the transparency of the American political process makes it easier for U.S. allies to judge American good faith. These factors increased the credibility of U.S. military commitments. On the other hand,

---

[35] The LDP can also be more patient than its American counterparts in waiting for returns on these policies. Japanese elections are less frequent and called at irregular intervals by the LDP. Thus electoral timing allows a slightly longer start-up period before returns are necessary.

the quarrels spawned by divided powers made it harder to make believable promises to foster regional production centers because political interests over distributional policies differed and numerous blocking coalitions were possible in the annual appropriations process. The fragmentation of bureaucratic control over procurement also made it harder to broker an agreement among the proposed beneficiaries of economic security policies.

The story was very different in Japan. The checks within a parliamentary system under one-party rule existed mainly within the ranks of the LDP. The party constitution required consultation with the PARC committees that blunted most temptations for prime ministers to respond fully to American requests about military security initiatives. The LDP further used its command of a parliamentary government to tailor "self-binding behavior," prominent pledges, and Diet bills continually reaffirming the limits on acceptable military security capabilities and promises. By elevating the political visibility of these promises the LDP could argue to the United States that it would be politically dangerous to bow to American wishes. The United States had to moderate its demands because it feared the security policies of the LDP's rivals.

At the same time a parliamentary system allowed the LDP to target military benefits to advance economic security goals. The cabinet and the Diet shared the same constituent concerns and so could agree on distributional priorities. The LDP then delegated power to bureaucracies to coordinate the requests of constituent firms and engineered special budgeting and procurement procedures to support these companies.

9

Coordinating economic policies: a schematic model and some remarks on Japanese–U.S. exchange rate policies

HARUHIRO FUKUI AND M. STEPHEN WEATHERFORD

1. INTRODUCTION

In September 1985, the finance ministers of the Group of Five (G-5) nations – England, France, Germany, Japan, and the United States – signed an accord to intervene in the foreign exchange markets so as to drive down the value of the American dollar, primarily against the Japanese yen. This was for many reasons a historic event, not least for the fact that the largest beneficiary of the then current state of affairs, Japan, committed itself to the voluntary destruction of a major source of its comparative advantage in the international market. Japan's government representatives did this with the full knowledge that the country's exporters and domestic producers alike would suffer (at least in the short run) from increased competition at home and abroad.

Even if we limit our analysis to the policy choices of just the two main players – Japan and the United States – two questions spring immediately to mind. First, why did the United States settle on exchange rate adjustment as the preferred method to reduce its massive trade deficit and to rectify its businesses' loss of competitiveness? Other, unilateral options were certainly available. Trade protection for ailing industries was one alternative. Major fiscal or monetary adjustments were also possibilities. Why did the United States choose to pursue coordinated manipulation of the foreign exchange markets?

Second, and perhaps more puzzling, is the decision of the Japanese government not only to acquiesce in the inflation of its currency, but to participate actively in the process. If the traditional story of Japan, Inc. is to be believed, then the deliberate effort to impose costs on the huge export firms and their small subcontractors is surely a conundrum calling out for explanation. All things equal, we would expect Japan to have preferred the status quo to any change, and assuredly to any change in the direction of an inflated currency.

226

The thesis of this chapter is that the final outcome – the signing and implementation of the so-called Plaza Accord – can be understood as an equilibrium induced by the structure of decision making in Japan and the United States, respectively, operating within an international framework of economic interdependence (see Shepsle 1979 on structure-induced equilibria). Contemporaneous journalistic accounts and scholarly post-mortems show that the key decision makers in the Japanese government believed that the expected result of no agreement to realign foreign exchange rates, or the "reversionary outcome," was not "no change," but rather a unilateral protectionist move by the U.S. Congress. Thus, the options they weighed were between low protection and a high yen on the one hand, and high protection and a passive exchange regime on the other.

Our approach follows the logic of Putnam (1988), who proposed the image of a two-level game to represent the interplay between domestic and international goals and constraints.[1] Focusing on the tension between the bargaining power of each of the countries and the likelihood of successfully completing an agreement, the two-level game image calls attention to the fact that international agreements must be approved in two different arenas – once when they are struck between national representatives, and again when each negotiator must return home to secure ratification for the agreement in the domestic political process. As negotiators, therefore, national representatives not only must act in light of the offers "across the table" at the international meeting, but also must attend to the domestic interests and coalitions arrayed "behind the chair."

Each country's domestic institutions and politics outline the parameters of a "win set," comprising those internationally negotiated outcomes that could secure ratification in the domestic political process. The greater the overlap between different countries' win sets, the greater the likelihood that an agreement can be negotiated. In terms of the relative power of each country in the negotiations, the smaller a given country's win set the more limited the range of negotiated outcomes that will be able to gain ratification, and hence the greater the power that country's representative has in the negotiations.[2] The spatial model of Figure 9.1 depicts a final version of the two-level game that resulted in the Plaza Accord.

In Figure 9.1 the vertical axis in the figure refers to the amount of trade protection imposed by the United States, while the horizontal axis measures the extent of exchange rate adjustment (think of it as the value of the yen relative to the dollar). The origin of the graph represents the current policy (CP) – no protectionism and no exchange rate adjustment. It is also

---

[1] Putnam's perspective complements the leading theories in international relations by providing a common metaphor that has the potential for uniting theory building about causal impulses from both the international and the domestic side.

[2] For other examples see Evans, Jacobson, and Putnam (1993).

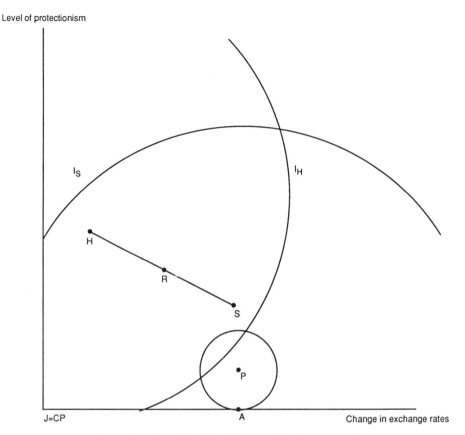

Figure 9.1. *The political foundations of the Plaza Accord*

assumed to be the ideal point (i.e., the most-preferred outcome) of the Japanese government (J). We will justify the assumption of a unitary national preference below. The points H, S, and P represent the ideal points of the U.S. House of Representatives, Senate, and President, respectively.

We can use the tools of spatial modeling to find equilibrium outcomes from this array of preferences.[3] Assume first that the choice (contrary to the above statement) is between the current policy (CP) and some change. Indifference contours can be constructed by drawing circles centered on each player's ideal point and passing through the point CP. The "win set,"

[3] For a discussion, see Enelow and Hinich (1984) and Ordeshook (1986). Mathew McCubbins and Peter Cowhey have provided valuable advice that helped us to apply this model to our case.

or set of points that are preferred by J, H, S, and P, is then the area of intersection of the indifference contours of all four players. It is clear that if the reversionary outcome were indeed CP, no policy shift would occur. The win set would be empty. Close examination reveals that this result obtains because Japan prefers nothing to CP; it will therefore "veto" any proposed change and the United States will go home empty-handed.

We will argue here that the U.S. administration credibly threatened Japan with trade protection in the event of deadlock at the Plaza talks. The set of possible legislative acts by the U.S. government is outlined by the triangle connecting points H, S, and P (the Pareto Set).[4] The figure illustrates that the U.S. Congress and President Reagan could have moved unilaterally (i.e., without Japan's agreement) to change the existing policy from CP to some other point like R. This would entail an increase in U.S. tariffs and some unilateral change in the exchange rate. Note that in Figure 9.1, R is preferred by H, S, and P to the current policy, CP. This potential alignment is what would make the American threat of protectionism credible.

The Japanese decision makers, then, were faced with the following choice: make a deal with the Reagan administration (that would not require legislation and could therefore avoid a congressional veto) or else sit by and watch the U.S. Congress and the president raise tariff barriers to Japanese goods. If, for example, Japan were to agree to an exchange rate adjustment as large as that represented by point A, they could preempt congressional action to change policy to a point such as R, thus making a move from A to R impossible. We would expect that the House and Senate would be able to agree to some point on the line segment connecting H and S, (both want some protectionism) but that the president would prefer to veto such a change from A to R. This is demonstrated by the fact that the president's indifference curve through A does not intersect the H–S line segment. Thus, we argue, Japan avoided congressionally inspired protectionism by signing the Plaza Accord.

We develop the detailed logic of this argument in four parts. Section 2 explains why our emphasis on domestic politics and the politics of bargaining over the exchange rate is the correct way to frame the issues posed by the Plaza Accord. Section 3 justifies our definition of the players in the international-level bargaining game depicted in Figure 9.1 by examining the structure of decision making in the two countries. Section 4 demonstrates the model's validity by showing the empirical justification for the placement of the players' preferences in this two-dimensional space, and shows how the domestic bargaining game shaped international bargaining. Section 5 summarizes our argument.

---

[4] See McCubbins, Noll, and Weingast (1987) for a similar illustration.

2. INTERNATIONAL ECONOMICS AND
DOMESTIC POLITICS

Our model emphasizes the role of domestic politics in shaping the international bargaining over exchange rates. There are two possible objections to this approach. The first, and more traditional, critique is that international choices about consequential choices can be explained purely by the logic of how international politics shape the national interest. The second objection is that our analysis of the choice of exchange rates wrongly assumes that exchange rates are subject to political manipulation. Some economists argue that the real question is why governments invest so much political attention on a policy choice that has no plausible impact on economic activity. This section explains why both objections are not persuasive.

2.1. International explanations

There is little dispute that increasing volumes of foreign trade, the easy movement of international capital, and floating exchange rates have a growing impact on domestic employment and prices, especially because they can transmit the effects of one nation's domestic economic disequilibrium to others (Cooper 1968, 1985). Conforming economic policy to circumscribed national capacities poses painful challenges for governmental processes and national politics.[5]

Many analysts assume that the logic of national positions in response to interdependence can be straightforwardly deduced from the logic of the distribution of power in the international system. Thus, an analysis of domestic politics is of secondary explanatory importance. However, the Plaza Accord is an anomaly in terms of power-based theories of international cooperation.

The content of the accord itself is historically notable because outside of the dollar-exchange system in the later years of Bretton Woods, there are few examples of surplus countries assisting with the correction of current account imbalances. The Bretton Woods experience is taken as evidence confirming the importance of a powerful international hegemony for

---

[5] This challenge is especially pointed in the United States and Japan, where mirror-image changes in relative economic power have most dramatically altered familiar constraints and responsibilities. The research reported in this paper is part of a larger project that seeks to contribute to such a perspective, by analyzing how the United States and Japan have worked toward resolving three salient policy problems during the 1980s. The larger project also focuses on the controversy over government policy toward trade in semiconductors and on the dispute over joint development of the FSX, the next-generation fighter plane for the Japanese defense forces. A preliminary report on the larger project appears in Fukui and Weatherford (1990).

global financial cooperation. As the dominant power not only in the monetary system (where the dollar was the reserve currency and the primary transaction medium) but also in trade, finance, and military security, the United States could afford to accommodate its trading partners as their own markets developed. But this dominance had been significantly dissipated by the mid-1980s, and no other country had risen to a position of equal prominence, thus ruling out the explanation of Japanese cooperation based on relatively static distributions of international power resources.[6] Our explanation focuses instead on a combination of domestic and international factors, giving special weight to the structure of policy making and the immediate alignment of domestic political interests in the two key countries involved in the Plaza negotiations.

More generally, international-power explanations of national positions pose the danger of taking the notion of the national interest as an analytical primitive, an unambiguous "given" against which international bargains can be compared. Usually more than one policy option can be seen as consistent with some valid formulation of the national interest. For instance, how should short-term outcomes be weighed against the long term? A country that set out to maximize short-term gains might see it as rational to engage in hard, uncompromising bargaining, even at the risk of alienating others in the longer run. Or how should competing domestic interests be weighed? Few international bargains affect all societal groups identically, and this raises the question of whose claims should count for more in aggregating domestic interests into an overall national preference. The strong dollar, for example, made it easy for American consumers to buy imported products, but made it extremely difficult for U.S. exporters to compete in foreign markets. In short, even defining the objectives of national diplomacy requires an explanation of domestic political factors.

2.2. The exchange rate as a policy instrument

One school of economic theory would argue that our analysis of the Plaza Accord is in error because exchange rates cannot be influenced by governments. The theory argues that the exchange rate is nothing more than the price of a nation's currency, and that like any price it is completely determined by the market. An exchange rate under a system of floating currencies simply reflects international currency traders' views of the relative purchasing power of the different currencies available in the market at a given time. If true, then the real puzzle is not why Japan accepted an

---

[6] For perceptive analyses of U.S. and Japanese financial power and the literature on power and cooperation, see Strange (1988).

outcome that it did not particularly like, but rather why governments exerted great effort on such a futile exercise.

The more general view, which we accept, is that governments influence the exchange rate at which their currencies trade in international markets. Even under an international monetary regime of floating exchange rates and vast amounts of freely circulating private capital, most economists agree that the governments of the major powers (e.g., the G-3, Germany, Japan, and the United States) can, particularly if they act in concert, influence the levels of their exchange rates.[7] Governments can buy a particular currency to bid up the price when its value appears too low, or sell to drive its value downward. A government can also make declaratory statements of its evaluation of the currency's desirable level (backed by a credible commitment to intervene in the market), where the "announcement effect" of imminent intervention will lead rational speculators to trade the currency in the intended direction.

The U.S. and Japanese central bankers and finance ministers who have been most closely involved in recent attempts at coordinated intervention for exchange rate policy believe in its efficacy. (See, e.g., Volcker and Gyohten 1992: 231–32, 248.) Of course, one might argue that central bankers and finance ministers want to appear to be efficacious agents working to promote the national interest, and that this might lead them to exaggerate the influence of government policy on one or another occasion. Even granting this, however, it would be irrational for agents to persist in such an exaggeration, since that would lead their political principals to expect more from them than they could deliver.

Government decision makers recognize that the concept of exchange rates as solely market determined rests on the incorrect assumptions that capital movements are completely free of any restrictions and that market actors form rational expectations on the basis of all available information. Free-market theorists may be right that the exchange rate of a national currency simply reflects international currency traders' judgments of its relative value at a given time. However, those traders' views are shaped in large measure by actions, and even mere statements, of governments, and by the official judgments underlying those actions and statements. In other words, currency traders, like traders in commodity and futures markets, take cues from authoritative government actions as well as from other indicators of the relative values of their commodities, that is, currencies.[8]

---

[7] See, for example, Hamada and Patrick (1988); Mayer and Taguchi (1993); Taylor (1982). We are grateful to our colleague Benjamin J. Cohen for conversations about this issue.

[8] A recent empirical study of seventeen coordinated exchange rate interventions by the G-3 countries since 1985 provides broadly grounded empirical evidence that the exchange rate instrument can effectively serve government policy aims (Catte et al. 1992).

3. THE STRUCTURE OF DECISION MAKING IN JAPAN AND THE UNITED STATES

This section examines the actors in the choices about the Plaza Accord. The exchange rate policy system traditionally has been depicted as an unusually centralized and clearly bounded one, insulated from societal pressures and interest group politics. Two sorts of arguments are offered in favor of this characterization. The first cites the complexity of international monetary relations, arguing that this makes it difficult for domestic groups to identify their particular interests in exchange rate policy, and that the expertise required by the subject matter lends the process a symbolic aura that made it seem "above politics" (Krasner 1978b: 65–66; Odell 1982: 347). The second refers to the difficulties of collective action: "For those groups hurt by the rise in the effective exchange rate of the dollar – whether under Bretton Woods or the subsequent floating-rate system – a dollar devaluation was a distinctly non-excludable good: no individual could be prevented from benefiting from the change, whether or not he had contributed to it" (Gowa 1988: 26).

To the extent that the exchange rate policy system matched this description, it would be, in essence, a "one-level game," in which each country could be depicted as a unitary actor. As Figure 9.1 shows, we regard such a depiction as appropriate for Japan during the mid-1980s but inappropriate for the United States. Moreover, societal pressures on the exchange rate policy system were quite strong in both countries. In Japan, these took the form of persistent disputes between separate bureaucratic agencies, especially the Bank of Japan and the Ministry of Finance, and they were finessed only by the exertion of unified control by elected politicians. In the United States, they appeared as different patterns of constituency pressures on the president and on members of the House and Senate.

How did the structure and process of decision making in Japan and the United States lead to the Plaza Accord? Our model (represented by Figure 9.1) centers on the strategic choices of four players – Japan, the U.S. House, the U.S. Senate, and the U.S. president.[9] Although the basic insights that enable us to model this international game as including just these four players are developed more fully elsewhere in the volume, this section

---

[9] Although we compare policy-making institutions and processes only in Japan and the United States, concentrating on these two arguably provides a fair overview of the background and the agreement, given these two countries' key roles in the premeeting negotiations that set the agenda for the Plaza meeting (Funabashi 1988a, b), as well as their disproportionate share in the adjustments that followed. Of the total foreign exchange spent by the G-5 central banks to defend the new par values, the United States contributed about 39 percent, Japan about 37 percent, and Germany, France, and Britain together about 24 percent. Calculated from data in *Federal Reserve Bank of New York Quarterly Review* 1985–86: 46–47.

provides a brief review with special attention to the exchange rate issue and the relevant domestic decision-making processes in the two countries.

3.1. The structure of governance and exchange rate policy making in Japan

In Japan, as in all parliamentary systems, the executive and legislative branches of government are fused (Lijphart 1984). In the terms used by Shugart and Carey (1992), the origin and survival of the executive and assembly are not constitutionally separated. As a result, there is no need to examine the separate branches of government so as to determine the nature of any interinstitutional bargaining game.

It is still possible, however, that bargaining would be necessary within the government. That is, if governments were formed by coalitions of parties, or by a highly heterogeneous single party, it might be necessary to model Japanese decision making as involving more than one "veto player." However, as discussed by McCubbins and Rosenbluth in Chapter 3 of this volume, one political party, the Liberal Democrats, controlled both houses of the Diet from 1955 to 1993, only losing its majority in the Upper House in 1989 and in the Lower House in 1993.[10] Therefore, the range of interesting questions concerning Japanese decision making is reduced to intra-LDP bargaining and to any potential bargaining between the party and its agents in the national bureaucracy.

Apart from the prime minister and the chief cabinet secretary, no other government official exercises even nominal authority that would appear necessary to bring coherence to the decision-making process. Nor is any single ministry within the bureaucracy in a position to dictate its policies or positions to any other ministry; the Ministry of Foreign Affairs (MFA) is said to have once dominated decision making on most major foreign policy issues, including those in defense and economic policy areas, but it has long since yielded large chunks of its responsibilities to other ministries and agencies.[11] Moreover, interministry turf wars have been a constant and conspicuous feature of the Tokyo bureaucracy, reducing the autonomy and effectiveness of both individual ministries and the national bureaucracy as a whole in their dealings with politicians and private interest groups.[12] Finally, the reversion point in these interministry disputes is drift along the lines of policies and priorities approved by the LDP.

---

[10] Since our story ends before 1989, there is no need to concern ourselves with the consequences of divided Japanese government in this paper.

[11] Interview with a senior MFA official, August 1988. See also Fukui (1979).

[12] Interview with a senior official in the Minister's Secretariat, MFA, September 1988. See also Richardson and Flanagan (1984: 350–52).

Political leadership, however, can be exercised and a degree of policy coherence achieved if and when the prime minister, the chief cabinet secretary, and the minister or ministers in charge of the policy at issue are united in and committed to pushing a well-defined policy line. They can then either persuade or coerce senior bureaucrats in the relevant ministries to fall into line to shift policy.

To cite an example from an area relevant to international macroeconomic policy coordination, the budget-making process in Tokyo is usually wide open and susceptible to all kinds of political, bureaucratic, and interest group pressures.[13] For much of the period under review, Ministry of Finance (MOF) and Bank of Japan (BOJ) bureaucrats, preoccupied with a serious budget deficit problem, strongly resisted the constant political pressure for adoption of expansionary fiscal policy emanating both from foreign governments and private groups and, more important, from scores of entrenched domestic special-interest groups and their representatives in the ruling party. Ultimately, however, pressures applied by the prime minister and MOF minister overcame the bureaucrats' resistance and led to their acquiescence in substantial public works spending.[14] (See McCubbins and Noble on budgeting in Chapters 4 and 5 of this volume.)

In comparison to the highly politicized budget process, decision making in the monetary policy area in general and exchange rate policy in particular traditionally has been far more effectively insulated from direct political and interest group pressures. To an important extent, this has been due to the government's monopoly on relevant information. As in most other governments around the world, there are only a handful of bureaucrats in Tokyo, divided between MOF and BOJ, who regularly follow and are knowledgeable about short-term foreign exchange and interest rate movements.

Moreover, and again as in most other governments, a combination of necessity and expediency allows those few experts to maintain a tight information blackout on their deliberations and decisions. Because a person or a firm with advance knowledge of an impending government action that might significantly affect interest or the foreign exchange rate could make a fortune at the expense of those without such knowledge, governments go a long way to withhold all potentially sensitive informa-

[13] Interview with a senior official in the Financial Bureau, MOF, September 1989. See also Campbell (1977).

[14] Funabashi (1988a: 128–29); interview with a senior official in the Financial Bureau, MOF, September 1989; interview with a middle-level official in the minister's secretariat, MOF, September 1989. The phenomenal appreciation of the yen in the period following the Plaza meeting caused deep and widespread concern among Japanese businesses about its recessionary impacts on the domestic economy, a concern that was inevitably and swiftly translated into concerted political pressure for large compensatory public works spending.

tion about prospective policy moves. The need for secrecy based on this consideration is accepted, if only grudgingly, by most bureaucrats in the Japanese government outside of MOF and BOJ, including those in MFA.[15] The information blackout is also often justified by the argument that, because the government has to take action in this area in response to external pressures, policy makers in MOF and BOJ have little time to consult and gain approval of either the Diet or affected private groups in advance.[16]

The upshot is the almost total exclusion of all but the principals from monetary and exchange rate policy decision making. Even MFA bureaucrats and the Cabinet Councillors' Office on External Affairs are kept in the dark.[17] The traditional rivalry between MOF and MFA may make the former even more secretive toward the latter than toward other ministries, such as MITI and the Economic Planning Agency (EPA). A former foreign minister remembers a fracas between an MOF minister and himself in the mid-1980s over the deliberate exclusion of the Japanese ambassador in Washington – an MFA official – from a high-level meeting of monetary policy makers from the two governments.[18,19]

In the management of exchange rates, the MOF contingent holds a formally superior decision making position vis-à-vis its BOJ counterpart. This is due largely to MOF's control of the Special International Financial Transaction Account (Tokubetsu kokusai kinyu torihiki kanjo).[20] The bulk of the funds in this account, derived mostly from the sale of govern-

---

[15] Interview with a former foreign minister and current member of the House of Representatives, September 1988.

[16] Interview with a senior official in the research and statistics department, BOJ, August 1988. Another important reason for the effective insulation of the decision-making process from political and societal pressures is the fact that Japan's major exporters of manufactured goods are at the same time major importers of raw materials and fuels. This dual role makes the impacts of a change in the yen's exchange rates with foreign currencies, especially the dollar, on their balance sheets uncertain and ambiguous. A higher yen might put them at a disadvantage in important foreign markets where they sell their goods, such as the United States, but provide an advantage in markets where they buy raw materials and fuels, such as Asia and the Middle East.

[17] Interviews with two senior MFA officials, September 1988. This outcome is consistent with the long-held position of MOF and the Ministry of International Trade and Industry (MITI) that MFA should concern itself only with "political" and national security issues and leave economic matters to the economic ministries. Interview with a former chief cabinet secretary and current member of the House of Representatives, September 1988.

[18] Interview with a former foreign minister and current member of the House of Representatives, September 1988.

[19] The decision at the May 1986 Tokyo summit to enlarge G-5 to G-7 (adding Italy and Canada) was made without the knowledge, let alone the direct involvement, of the MFA minister, a fact that led to a fierce verbal battle between the two ministers and their respective subordinates (Interview with a senior MFA official, September 1988).

[20] Interview with a senior official in the Financial Bureau, MOF, September 1989. See "Gaikoku kawase kanriho" [Foreign Exchange Control Law], Article 12, in Hoshino et al. (1988: 3349–3350).

ment bonds, is under MOF jurisdiction, with only a small fraction available to BOJ.[21] Routine decisions related to interventions in foreign exchange markets are normally made by middle-level bureaucrats in MOF's International Finance Bureau (IFB), while more difficult decisions go to MOF vice-minister and the counselor for overall coordination in the MOF minister's secretariat.[22] In this aspect of exchange rate policy making, the MOF–BOJ relationship parallels the Treasury–Federal Reserve relationship in Washington.[23] In practice, MOF and BOJ experts work closely together, and the relationship is usually smooth and amicable. For example, while a decision on whether, when, and how to intervene in foreign exchange markets is for MOF experts to make, it must be implemented by the BOJ staff. BOJ's policies are determined by the BOJ Policy Board, on which an MOF representative serves as a nonvoting member, although the evaluation of this group's actual role and influence varies greatly even among the experts themselves.[24]

Interagency disagreements do arise periodically, and these are referred to the MOF minister and the BOJ governor, who consult with each other and jointly make a final decision.[25] While MOF and BOJ bureaucrats see eye to eye on most issues, the MOF group tends to be more sensitive and responsive to pressures exerted by the political leadership, especially to demands for expansionary policy,[26] while BOJ bureaucrats typically view issues, including the balance-of-payments problem, more narrowly from the perspective of their effects on prices and inflation.[27]

Although experts in the two agencies frequently meet and work together in Tokyo, their roles in international negotiations occasionally lead

---

[21] Interview with a former senior MOF official, September 1989.

[22] Ibid.; interview with a senior official in the Financial Bureau, MOF, September 1989.

[23] Okabe (1987: 33). Formal authority to change the official discount rate, on the other hand, belongs to the BOJ governor with the advice of the BOJ Policy Board, although in practice it is exercised in consultation with MOF experts, especially the counselor for overall coordination and the director of the research and planning division in the minister's secretariat, as well as BOJ's own staff. The highest decision-making body within BOJ is the so-called *Marutaku* (roundtable) of seven senior officials, including the governor and deputy governor, where all major macroeconomic policy and related issues are reviewed, and decisions on issues within BOJ's jurisdiction are made. Below this level, the policy-making process revolves mainly around the BOJ governor's secretariat and the General Affairs and Banking departments. Decisions on the discount rate, however, are often made at the top without much direct staff-level involvement.

[24] A BOJ bureau director says it is an extremely influential decision-making body, citing the credentials of its seven members representing, respectively, industry, agriculture, city banks, local banks, the Economic Planning Agency, MOF, and BOJ. A former MOF deputy vice-minister, on the other hand, says it is a purely token presence (interviews, September 1989).

[25] Interview with a senior official in the Foreign Department, BOJ, September 1989.

[26] Interview with a former senior MOF official, September 1989; interview with a senior official in the Financial Bureau, MOF, September 1989.

[27] Interview with a senior official in the Foreign Department, BOJ, September 1989.

to conflict. BOJ experts wear two hats. As members of such central bankers' organizations as the Bank for International Settlements (BIS), BOJ experts are immersed more fully in the process of internationalization and tend to behave more like members of an "international money mafia" than do their MOF counterparts.[28] At the same time, in dealing with foreign pressures for adjustments to the discount rate, BOJ bureaucrats tend to be more conservative than their MOF counterparts because their primary mission under the conservative LDP rule is monetary and price stability.

For example, at the time when macroeconomic policy coordination among the major industrial nations was discussed at the Plaza Hotel meeting in September 1985, BOJ "nationalists" deliberately reversed the meaning of the term "flexible management of monetary policy" used in the Plaza Accord to lead Japanese banks to raise, rather than lower, interest rates.[29] They had hoped to blame the rise of the rate on "market forces,"[30] but the trick was caught by U.S. Federal Reserve Chairman Paul Volcker and the New York Federal Reserve Bank's E. Gerald Corrigan, both of whom accused the Japanese government of acting against the spirit of the accord.[31] Toward the end of October 1986, BOJ bureaucrats' opposition prevented another discount rate reduction, which Miyazawa had promised Treasury Secretary James Baker, despite BOJ governor Satoshi Sumita's personal effort to bring his subordinates around behind the MOF minister's commitments to Washington.[32]

These examples point to several important aspects of macroeconomic policy making in the Japanese government. While the process is exposed and sensitive to both domestic and international pressures, BOJ is relatively less susceptible to such pressures than MOF; the BOJ may be more nationalistic on such issues as the discount rate adjustments. Years of policy and political continuity reinforced these dynamics. So, it took an extraordinary degree of unity and determination on the part of the political leadership to force usually fractious monetary policy bureaucrats to support and implement internationally inspired coordination measures.

3.2. The structure of governance and exchange rate policy making in the United States

In contrast to parliamentary Japan, the United States has a presidential system of government with constitutional separation of the executive and

[28] Ibid.
[29] Interview with a senior MOF official, August 1988.
[30] Ibid.; Funabashi (1988a: 50).
[31] Okabe (1987: 25); Volcker and Gyohten (1992: 246).
[32] Funabashi (1988a: 79); interview with a senior official in the Research and Statistics Bureau, BOJ, August 1988.

legislative branches (Lijphart 1984). Powers are also shared, however, through a system of checks exercised by one branch upon the other. Any policy requiring legislation must pass through three separate veto gates, namely, the House of Representatives, the Senate, and the president. Moreover, the incumbents of these three legislative organs are chosen by different constituencies. Therefore, the a priori expectation is that they will be at odds with each other over most policy questions; the burden of proof is on those who would assert a convergence of preferences.

The constitutional separation of powers is overlaid with even more complexity during periods of "divided government," when one party controls the executive and the other party controls one or both of the legislative chambers. This was the case during the period in question here, the mid-1980s, when the Democrats controlled the House of Representatives, while Republicans held the presidency and, by a narrow margin, the Senate. Insofar as the two parties differ on questions of foreign trade and fiscal and monetary policy, our expectation of divergent policy preferences is all the stronger in this case. Even within the Republican Party, however, the different constituencies of President Reagan and the median Senate Republican affected their respective stances on the desirability of various policy options from trade protectionism to exchange rate adjustment.[33]

Evidence of these policy differences between the branches is presented later in this chapter. But the U.S. exchange rate policy system was not always so fragmented and permeated by societal demands, and the magnitude of the change that occurred during the 1980s is best appreciated against the background of its more centralized, historical pattern.

Under the Bretton Woods regime, from the end of World War II to 1971, the dollar's reserve status meant that the United States was much more tightly constrained from altering its exchange rate than were its trading partners. As the passive "nth country," the role of the United States was to maintain the regime, while other countries (Japan notable among them) adjusted their currency parities against the dollar in light of their economies' comparative export performance. In the United States, treating the exchange rate[34] as the residual outcome of policy choices – over other instruments or even by other countries – imposed no insuper-

---

[33] The constitutionally prescribed diffusion of veto power, combined with these differences in policy preferences, are sufficient for us to model the U.S. decision-making structure with three separate points in Figure 9.1. Of course, it is possible that the parties themselves were not cohesive, or that intrachamber differences were relevant for policy making. Since the outcome we are endeavoring to explain is, in part, the absence of a legislative agreement on protectionist legislation, however, any further fissures in the U.S. decision-making structure would only strengthen our story.

[34] More precisely, under the regime of fixed convertibility between the dollar and gold, the surplus or deficit on international transactions.

able costs, for the economy was relatively closed, and the U.S. GNP constituted the bulk of world production. Because few businesses relied on exporting, the exchange rate was largely unimportant to politically influential private sector actors. Moreover, because the international economic challenges confronting the U.S. government over this period centered on supporting the dollar and minimizing gold outflows, there was little incentive to develop the institutional processes needed to link exchange rate policy to a national economic strategy. As might be expected in this situation, the institutions that constituted the exchange rate policy process were relatively centralized and closed, with authority exercised by a handful of government officials in the executive branch; channels of communication with societal groups were attenuated or absent.

Over the past two decades, however, the U.S. economy has become more internationalized, with the result that satisfactory exchange rate management depends on a more subtle appreciation not only for international currency markets and the probable actions of other governments but also for the effects of the exchange rates on domestic firms and workers. If the context of exchange rate policy making was changing steadily from the late 1960s to the 1980s, however, the institutions, processes, and ideas guiding it in the United States hardly altered. This created problems at both tiers of the two-level game, in U.S. international monetary policy and in the political relationship between the U.S. government and businesses.

For instance, the consistency and quality of the American government's management of the exchange rate compares unfavorably with that of other countries. The symptoms of poor policy performance were clear during the regime of "managed floating rates" in the 1980s. During this period, the currencies of most other leading nations traced a relatively smooth, steady pattern – an outcome that served the private sector by minimizing transaction costs attendant on fluctuating rates (e.g., unpredictability of prices, the cost of insurance against unfavorable currency shifts) and that also helped to insulate domestic monetary policy from internationally transmitted instability. The dollar, on the other hand, fluctuated widely both over the business cycle and from one administration to the next.[35]

The politics of exchange rate policy were also in flux during the 1980s, with formerly uninvolved private sector interests pressing both the president and the Congress for action, and with both houses of the legislature

---

[35] The most dramatic example of this pattern is the period of "laissez-faire neglect" of the dollar's value during the first Reagan administration, followed by the active, indeed most would say adroit, American-initiated management of exchange rates via multilateral coordination during the second Reagan administration. Destler and Henning (1989) detail currency fluctuations during this period.

pressing the executive to allow wider participation in the policy process. During the early 1980s, the strong dollar was portrayed by President Reagan as a fitting symbol of America's newly rediscovered foreign policy hegemony. However, a strong dollar's economic effects were increasingly visible in the worsening plight not only of small, isolated firms, but in the overall trade deficit and the declining profitability of formerly successful exporting firms. The business press began devoting attention to news about the trade deficit and the diminishing competitiveness of U.S. exports.

Eventually a consensus began to emerge within the business community, a consensus that focused increasingly on the exchange rate as the culprit. The Business Roundtable, composed of the country's hundred or so largest firms, produced an analysis showing that American exporters had lowered their costs and prices in real terms, but that the rising dollar–yen exchange rate had reversed this advantage in third markets. As this interpretation was disseminated by the business press, it helped to politicize the business community, because it provided evidence that private sector efforts to close the trade gap had been undermined by currency movements that were beyond their power to influence.

As the business community mobilized, lobbying efforts were concentrated on the trade deficit. Focus on the trade deficit reinforced the salience of the problem, but it left open the question of what policy changes should be adopted to deal with it. This meant that the considerable influence of the business community joined what was fast becoming a virtual cacophony of policy proposals, ranging from incentives to encourage domestic savings and discourage consumption, to subsidies for training workers or buying new capital, to protectionist tariffs, and, in a distinctly secondary position, exchange rate adjustments. Highlighting the problem had the advantage that it allowed a unified presentation of the concerns of exporting firms with those of firms that compete against imports – something that could not have been accomplished if they had focused on policy solutions, where import-competing firms' preference for tariffs would have clashed with exporters' preference for free trade. Given the diversity of possible policy solutions and the number of separate executive agencies and congressional committees they implicated, however, the business leaders advocating a frontal attack on the trade deficit found no simple, straightforward way to press their grievance.

The greatest surprise to business leaders came in the consistent unresponsiveness of the executive-branch officials from whom they were used to receiving a sympathetic hearing; virtually every effort to influence the White House was rebuffed.[36] Eventually, business leaders, often with the

---

[36] Throughout the first Reagan administration, Donald Regan, the treasury secretary, and

support of unions and agricultural interest groups, turned to the Congress, taking their case to committees with mandates in the trade field. Congress was eager to respond to this broad-based expression of concern, and various bills were introduced calling for the immediate imposition of tariffs on imports from countries – especially Japan – that were running large and persistent trade surpluses with the United States. Until well into 1985, the first year of Reagan's second term, virtually all the domestic political pressure to correct the trade deficit was channeled through Congress, and resulted in an escalating chorus of protectionist threats.

With the White House firmly committed to a laissez-faire stance in the international monetary system, the business community's increasing concern with the strength of the dollar found no access to the executive branch. Moreover, unlike trade issues, the exchange rate is not an explicit part of the mandate of any congressional committee. Consequently, societal pressures to intervene in the exchange markets achieved only modest (and largely symbolic) satisfaction, less by way of explicit policy proposals than by way of "fire alarms" registering concern from congressional committees with oversight responsibilities that gave them a channel to the Treasury and the Federal Reserve.[37]

In this context, the opportunity for a relatively inclusive, clearly focused debate on the strength of the dollar or the appropriateness of the exchange rate was simply unachievable. Neither members of Congress nor aggrieved domestic producers had any experience in the exchange rate policy area; outside the bureaucracy, virtually all the participants were equipped with only ill-developed ideas about the exchange rate's impact on domestic and international economic goals. Given the fragmentation of policy authority and the White House's denial that a problem existed, they were uncertain about how to approach executive institutions to seek redress by adjusting the exchange rate as a feasible solution to the current-account deficit.[38] But the power of the commercial interests could not be denied. By the mid 1980s, U.S. exchange rate policy making – compared to the historical pattern, or compared to the Japanese policy process described above – had been unusually penetrated by domestic political pressures, and appeared to be ad hoc and disorganized. Indeed, the very unpredictability of the process, and especially of the prospective actions of the House and Senate, strengthened Treasury Secretary Baker's negotiating position in the weeks leading up to the Plaza meeting, for it connoted a

Beryl Sprinkel, the chair of the Council of Economic Advisors, were especially forceful and consistent advocates of the administration's ideological belief in free trade in goods and nonintervention in international currency markets.

[37] See McCubbins and Schwartz (1984).

[38] Interviews with senior economists at the Brookings Institution, Treasury Department, and Institute of International Economics, March 1989.

win set that tightly constrained a legislative coalition willing to use its veto power to reject any bargain it found unsatisfactory.

4. THE POLITICS OF THE PLAZA NEGOTIATIONS

4.1. The U.S. side

Several streams of influence in the American political process came together early in 1985, and the momentum of that confluence, partially channeled by Secretary Baker and his deputy, Richard Darman, carried the G-2 toward the Plaza agreement of September 22, 1985. From the U.S. perspective, the immediate anxiety arose from the steadily worsening current-account deficit, but concern about two medium-term issues – the prospect of a worldwide recession if a cut in the U.S. fiscal deficit were not compensated by demand growth in Japan and Germany, and the impact of high interest rates on the prospective costs of servicing the American debt – also required consultation.

Pressure from the American manufacturing sector propelled the issue to the forefront. Business leaders were less influential in dictating the government's international negotiating strategy because they could not agree on a unified lobbying effort on exchange rate policy for several reasons. These ranged from how the recession and then recovery masked the net impact of the exchange rate, to splits because distinct segments of the business community pressed separately for different ameliorative policies (e.g., tariffs to protect particular industries, more expansive domestic monetary policy, and direct capital controls).[39] What all business sectors shared was a cool reception at the White House. Eventually business leaders focused their efforts on Congress, hoping that the threat of trade legislation would force the administration to take some action against the trade deficit.

During the first Reagan administration, Congress held hearings on the trade deficit, and the dollar was often a secondary theme of the resulting committee reports. House Democrats took the lead in several wide-ranging hearings, but they focused on how the president's domestic economic policies undermined the nation's competitiveness, not on the exchange rate. Moreover, the influential business interests most responsible for pushing the trade deficit to the top of the congressional agenda were also sympathetic to the bulk of President Reagan's economic program, and they muted their opposition as the 1984 election approached. In a similar way, Reagan's personal popularity, combined with GOP control of

---

[39] Destler and Henning (1989, especially chapter 7). This section relies on the work of several researchers at the Institute of International Economics, including Cline (1989); Funabashi (1988a), Williamson (1986), and Williamson and Miller (1987).

the Senate, stymied concerted attacks in the Congress on the eve of the election.

Shortly after the beginning of Reagan's second term, however, domestic economic conditions and several foreign economic policy gaffes focused attention on the current account imbalance with Japan and, eventually, on the exchange rate. Although the recession had bottomed out, the U.S. position in the international economy showed no sign of improvement, with the dollar and the current-account deficit rising steadily. Political pressure on Congress increased sharply after the election, particularly from business interests demanding action on the budget deficit and the trade imbalance, but the administration continued to resist working with the Congress on deficit reduction.

By summer 1985, the congressional response to outcry over the trade deficit had moved from rhetoric to policy proposals along several lines. Initiatives came not only from the Democratic House but also the Republican Senate. While these bills included calls for a range of retaliatory trade controls and tariffs, they also took much more specific aim at the exchange rate than had previous legislative actions. For example, Senator John Danforth (R-MO) introduced a bill citing Japan for various predatory practices, and calling for the immediate imposition of new restrictions on imports from Japan. Other bills called for withholding U.S. participation in GATT until trade negotiations were explicitly linked with moves to right the exchange rate imbalance by coordinating monetary policies (Danforth and Lloyd Bentsen [D-TX]); for import surcharges on all products from countries running extraordinary surpluses with the United States (Bentsen, Richard Gephardt [D-MO] and Dan Rostenkowski [D-IL]); and, in a proposal jointly introduced in the House and Senate, for automatic foreign exchange intervention triggered by any large current account deficit (Bill Bradley [D-NJ], D. Patrick Moynihan [D-NY], and Max Baucus [D-MT] in the Senate along with Stanley Lundine [D-NY] and John LaFalce [D-NY] in the House).

The significance of these measures for the administration's emerging exchange rate policy was twofold: Virtually all linked trade problems (on which public dissatisfaction was intense and readily mobilized) to the exchange rate, and congressional support for them was genuinely bipartisan (signaling unaccustomed weakness in the administration's foreign economic policy coalition). Figure 9.1 registers the fact that trade-oriented initiatives were promoted more aggressively in the Democratic House, and that the Republican Senate appeared to be slightly less protectionist (and more sympathetic to the president's free-trade ideology); but it is important to note that clear signals came from both chambers that they were poised to support targeted retaliation against Japan. Secretary Baker referred to a "prairie fire" of opposition to the administration's laissez-faire policy, and this image captures the sense of irresistibly rising momentum behind these initiatives.[40]

If the trade deficit was the policy target, virtually every major player (with the notable exception of the president) acknowledged that the most straightforward approach to correcting it lay in righting the domestic budget deficit. But the White House and Congress had been at an impasse over the budget deficit since early in Reagan's first term, thus ruling out this policy instrument. Monetary policy was a second option; the dollar's value could in theory be lowered by expanding the money supply. But this option ran up against both the president's treasured image as an inflation fighter and the firm policy predilections of Federal Reserve Chairman Volcker. The imposition of protectionist tariffs constituted a third option. Tariffs would protect U.S. import-competing firms, and for the Congress they offered a means of responding directly, and visibly, to constituents' outrage at foreigners for taking American jobs and buying up American real estate. But the administration's free-trade ideology and the danger of retaliation by other countries against U.S. exporters led the White House to oppose this course. If the Plaza meeting had produced no agreement to reduce the trade deficit, however, a tariff bill would have almost certainly passed the Congress by a comfortable margin. It would have been politically difficult for the president to veto such a bill.

The Administration's distaste for any of these three alternatives might have led logically toward the exchange rate instrument in any event, but the incoming treasury secretary, James Baker, who had not been an enthusiastic supporter of the Regan-Sprinkel policy of nonintervention, had additional reasons for focusing on the exchange rate. As White House chief of staff from 1981 to 1985, Baker had been keenly aware of the intensity of the business community's concern about the trade deficit. And as experienced campaign operative, he recognized the value of finding a policy instrument that would ameliorate the problem without alienating either side of the tenuous coalition of exporters and import-competing firms. Baker perceived, moreover, that the trade deficit offered the opportunity to engage in an early and significant action that would, if successful, redound greatly to his personal credit – here the fact that foreign exchange intervention (unlike monetary policy, fiscal policy, or tariffs) was within the Treasury's mandate gave him a powerful additional reason to favor that instrument. Baker preferred the idea of a coordinated intervention to bring down the value of the dollar, but he calculated that the prospects would be good for successful unilateral action if this were necessary. Finally, on arriving at the Treasury, Baker found that cabinet secretaries with trade-policy mandates (Malcolm Baldrige at Commerce, U.S.

[40] *Business Week,* October 7, 1985.

Trade Representative William Brock, and John Block at Agriculture) were eager to support a more active exchange rate policy, as was Secretary of State George Shultz.

In short, Baker had support from business, agriculture, unions, members of both parties of Congress, and even from dissenters within the administration, to catapult the exchange rate issue to the top of the domestic political agenda and initiate negotiations over broader issues of policy coordination. Furthermore, international economic conditions – especially Japan's and Germany's understandable apprehension about growing protectionist sentiment in Congress, along with the temporary "honeymoon" ushered in by the departure of Regan and Sprinkel – contributed to the sense of opportunity for an adroit political entrepreneur.

4.2. The Japanese side

In the first half of 1985, the Japanese government was divided over how to respond to Washington's overture for cooperation on macroeconomic issues. Some cabinet members regarded it as just another manifestation of Washington's pressure tactics and opposed MOF's move toward cooperation.[41] Even within MOF, some senior officials, including International Finance Bureau (IFB) Director Toyoo Gyohten, opposed the proposed joint intervention in foreign exchange markets. They argued mainly on neoclassical theoretical grounds, but their negative reaction also reflected their skepticism about the Reagan administration's reported recanting of its long-standing commitment to the strong-dollar policy (Funabashi 1988a: 27). To the nationalist prime minister, Nakasone, however, the strong yen was an attractive symbol of Japan's rising international status and prestige, just as the strong dollar had been the proof of a powerful United States to Reagan (Funabashi 1988a: 123). Under the combined pressure from Washington and Japan's own top leadership, MOF and BOJ bureaucrats eventually overcame their own doubts and objections and fell into line.

In the meantime, preparations for the Plaza meeting proceeded under tight secrecy during the summer and early fall of 1985. Prime Minister Nakasone learned about the meeting only a few hours before it took place, while Chief Cabinet Secretary Takao Fujinami did so as the meeting was about to begin.[42] Japan's chief negotiator in the series of secret bilateral and multilateral experts' talks leading to the Plaza meeting was MOF

---

[41] Interview with a senior Ministry of Finance official, August 1988.
[42] Interview with an *Asahi Shinbun* economic affairs reporter, September 1988.

deputy vice-minister Tomomitsu Oba. He informed only four individuals in the entire Japanese government of what was going on: the prime minister, the MOF minister, and the IFB director-general and deputy director-general.[43] The four kept the news strictly to themselves.

When the Japanese negotiators met in New York to set the conference strategy immediately preceding the Plaza, the meeting was attended by no more than a dozen individuals, including MOF minister Noboru Takeshita, MOF deputy vice-minister Oba, and BOJ governor Sumita.[44] Tight secrecy was maintained also in discussions between monetary policy authorities of the United States and Japan (and subsequently between them and those of the other three G-5 member governments). Moreover, the agreement reached at the meeting was deliberately announced on a Sunday, when all major foreign exchange markets were closed.[45]

Before and after the Plaza meeting, to the delight of his subordinates in the bureaucracy, MOF minister Takeshita not only repeatedly told but apparently convinced most of his fellow LDP politicians that they would be wasting their time by meddling with the bureaucrats' work on monetary policy issues because such concerns were "way over their heads."[46] Some LDP politicians no doubt resented the tight secrecy and a few even called the MOF and BOJ bureaucrats "liars," but no significant pressure from the legislature emerged.[47] Takeshita was also worried about growing international pressure for increased public works spending by the Japanese government, which would jeopardize the Nakasone cabinet's long-standing policy to reduce the large budget deficits. Takeshita therefore pressed BOJ governor Sumita to take steps to bring down interest rates and Sumita complied, albeit not without considerable reluctance and resistance (Funabashi 1988a: 65).

By mid-1985, most MOF and BOJ experts were thus aboard the Nakasone cabinet's decision to participate in a concerted multilateral effort to drive up the value of the yen.[48] The MOF and BOJ experts, however, disagreed on whether the official discount rate should be lowered in order to dampen the expected recessionary impacts of the yen's appreciation on the domestic economy.[49] MOF preferred to cut the rate, noting that the substantial fall of prices for both imported and domestic

---

[43] Interview with a senior MOF official, August 1988.
[44] Ibid.; Okabe (1987: 13).
[45] Interview with a senior MOF official, August 1988.
[46] Ibid.
[47] Interview with a former chief cabinet secretary and current member of the House of Representatives, September 1988.
[48] Interview with a former senior MOF official, September 1989.
[49] Interview with a senior official in the Foreign Department, BOJ, September 1989.

wholesale goods made it possible to reduce the discount rate without triggering inflation. The majority of BOJ experts disagreed, perceiving the danger of inflation as much more likely. As already mentioned, BOJ deliberately encouraged city banks to maintain high interest rates for a month and a half following the Plaza meeting.

Kiichi Miyazawa, who replaced Takeshita as MOF minister in July 1986, was an even more articulate and aggressive advocate of cooperation with the United States in the management of both exchange rates and interest rates. His subordinates in MOF fell in line fairly quickly and began to support a series of discount-rate cuts, hoping to help stimulate domestic demand for imports and thus ward off pressure from the United States and other members of G-5 for larger public works spending in Japan. By the fall of 1986, Sumita and his BOJ subordinates also ceased to resist Miyazawa's initiatives, at least publicly. Below the surface, however, the conflict between Miyazawa and Sumita and between their respective subordinates, persisted.[50] The tension between Miyazawa and Sumita rose particularly in October 1986 when the finance minister promised Treasury Secretary Baker that the Japanese discount rate would be lowered by another half percentage point, only to find the BOJ governor and his agency defiantly opposed (Funabashi 1988a).

When prices of building materials began to surge early in 1987, the BOJ bureaucrats' inflationary fears were again aroused, and the bank formally pressed for an increase in the discount rate. Their recommendation, however, was rejected by a cabinet determined to stimulate domestic demand and dampen export pressure.[51] The discount rate was reduced in February 1987 to the historic low of 2.5 percent, following an agreement reached between Miyazawa and Baker a few weeks before, and this provoked another burst of opposition from BOJ (Funabashi 1988a: 81). The opposition was rebuffed one more time by the Nakasone government, which was determined to maintain the steady pace of growth of the Japanese economy, and in the process to earn international credit for helping the United States pare down its trade and budget deficits.

---

[50] Miyazawa's unconventionally individualistic way of conducting negotiations with his foreign counterparts deepened the BOJ leaders' discomfort and resentment. Known for his rare fluency in English, Miyazawa made his own appointments with Baker and other U.S. officials by telephone and visited with them alone to discuss not only exchange rates but also interest rates and other monetary policy issues (Okabe 1987: 44; interview with a senior official in the Financial Bureau, MOF, September 1989). Miyazawa's advocacy of an expansionary policy pleased the U.S. leaders but disturbed many MOF and, particularly, BOJ bureaucrats, even though the latter understood that an MOF minister was a politician who had little choice but to respond to the international and domestic political pressures (interview with a middle-level official in the minister's secretariat, MOF, September 1989; interview with a former senior MOF official, September 1989).

[51] Interview with a senior official in the Financial Bureau, MOF, September 1989.

4.3. The Plaza bargain

The trade imbalance itself motivated the countries to move toward the bargaining table. Like the profits of a monopolist, a growing trade surplus appears an unambiguous advantage in the short run, but like monopoly profits, an excessive trade surplus breeds resentment among customers and leads eventually to calls for political redress. By the mid-1980s, there was a growing sense in Japan that the falling value of the yen had produced an embarrassingly large trade surplus, most visibly with the United States, but there was no consensus on whether or what action the government should take to rectify the situation.[52] For reasons already spelled out, both countries rejected alternative policy responses because of domestic politics. For example, the most obvious unilateral action, the use of fiscal policy to stimulate Japanese domestic demand, was ruled out by the government's budget deficit and the perceived danger of inflation. Although each country would have preferred that the other bear the burden of adjustment, the acknowledged political impossibility of imposing unilateral sacrifice in either country made the idea of coordinated adjustment a more attractive option. If it was understood that the status quo was unsustainable, however, there was little indication of how to craft an adjustment mechanism.

The leaders of both countries understood the dangers of aggressive protectionist retaliation by the United States. The economic costs of such retaliation would have been visible in both countries: In Japan, exports would have fallen immediately and bilateral trade would have diminished steadily over the medium term; in the United States, decreased access to Japanese products would have hurt consumers and manufacturers alike. In the absence of any cooperative agreement, moreover, the United States very probably would have undertaken aggressive unilateral measures to lower the value of the dollar. Since the market value of the dollar was already declining before the Plaza meeting (Feldstein 1986), it is likely that such a strategy would have been at least partly successful. The danger was not so much that dollar devaluation could not have been accomplished, but that – without the confidence in the dollar signaled by coordinated intervention – the fall of the dollar could not be controlled and its "hard landing" would result in financial chaos.[53]

---

[52] Japanese leaders were strongly opposed to the idea of coordinated fiscal policy adjustments. Japanese negotiator Yamaguchi frequently reminded Oba that "Japanese strategy at the Plaza should be first to realign the currencies, and second, to reduce interest rates jointly, stressing the need to leave the 'main castle' [fiscal policy] free from attack'" (Funabashi 1988b: 40).

[53] Although all the major U.S. policy makers were not equally in favor of using exchange rate adjustment as the sole instrument to accommodate the trade imbalance, the Plaza Accord was clearly preferable to the status quo. For Baker himself, the cost of failure at the Plaza to

The political costs of a failed agreement were also visible. Having invested their political reputations in achieving good economic relations with the United States, LDP leaders like Nakasone, Takeshita, and Miyazawa would have suffered if the negotiation had fallen through. In the United States, protectionist retaliation would have garnered short-term political approval for its congressional sponsors, but its medium-term economic costs would soon have shown up in the political ledger. Widespread tariff protection would have embarrassed the White House, as it flew in the face of the president's free-trade ideology, but the administration's ability to keep its coalition in line depended on delivering a cooperative commitment from other countries that would serve in the same way to reduce the trade deficit.

Thus it appears that both the short-term political outcomes and the medium-term economic outcomes made it rational for Japanese decision makers to conclude an agreement with the United States. Moreover, the short-term political stakes in the United States gave the executive an incentive to negotiate with the Japanese in order to avoid being forced to go along with the Congress in imposing tariffs. The threat from Congress not only influenced the timing of the talks but also strengthened the U.S. negotiating position, by limiting the size of the win set; American negotiators could take a hard line (especially for a debtor country) – claiming credibly at the Plaza that their hands were tied, and that only a commitment to significant shared adjustment would be able to secure ratification, given the domestic political climate.

If the deficit and the immediate political threat from the U.S. Congress made it rational to negotiate, the outcome itself was by no means clear. Once the idea of coordinated adjustment was on the table, four policy instruments were available – theoretically if not politically – to begin restoring the Japan – United States current-account balance: (1) the exchange rate; (2) monetary policy; (3) fiscal policy; and (4) structural changes, that is, microeconomic adjustments intended to influence consumption, savings, and productivity.

The position initially espoused by American negotiators included the first three of these instruments; indeed, the original U.S. proposal was for a comprehensive package of measures including exchange rate realignment along with coordinated commitments by the G-3 nations to adjust

---

his reputation would have been high but probably not politically fatal. Volcker and other monetarists supported the Accord as a first step; their preference would have been for a more extensive agreement to force the administration and Congress to adjust domestic fiscal policy, and they worried that too easy and smoothly functioning an agreement to adjust only exchange rates might work just well enough that it would permit Congress and the administration to cease efforts to correct the budget deficit. (cf. *Business Week*, Oct. 7, 1985).

fiscal and monetary policy.[54] But the ratification of this package hinged on congressional action, and that could not be credibly assured, a fact that relieved the Japanese negotiators since fiscal policy adjustments would have been difficult for them to sell at home.[55]

Japan's domestic win set included exchange rate realignment and some increase in monetary policy flexibility, and thus the union of the American and Japanese win sets included some limited degree of coordinated monetary policy adjustment. Such measures were, however, largely excluded from discussion at the Plaza because of the Bundesbank's opposition. The two-level game metaphor illuminates the stumbling blocks that prevented a more extensive coordinated response. Although the preferences of some of the negotiators at the international table, such as Shultz, Baker, and Miyazawa, might have fostered a commitment to greater coordination of domestic policies, the need to ratify any agreement through the domestic political process narrowed the intersection of the two countries' win sets dramatically. Indeed, when we take into account Germany's vigorous opposition to monetary policy adjustment, the overlap among the G-3 win sets was essentially limited to exchange rate adjustment, and the discussion as well as the final communiqué kept to this focus (Volcker and Gyohten 1992: 245).

5. CONCLUSION

In sum, the most notable features of U.S. policy making during the early 1980s – the structural fragmentation of authority and the political refusal to employ the exchange rate as a policy instrument – contrast markedly with institutions and outcomes in Japan. The House, Senate, and president all sought identifiably different policy outcomes, which can be con-

---

[54] In the series of meetings between Baker and Takeshita (June 21), as well as Mulford and Oba (July 23 and August 21), and in the G-5D meetings just prior to the Plaza (September 15), the U.S. position consistently favored spreading the adjustment burden across all three instruments. In addition to currency realignment, the U.S. commitment at the Plaza included reducing the deficit by 1 percent of GNP for FY1986 and by a "significant amount" in later years.

[55] In April 1985, Shultz had even raised the question of structural adjustment, mentioning the need for agreement on fundamental measures to alter savings rates in the United States and Japan as the only sure means of achieving lasting correction of the current account imbalance. None of the Plaza negotiators, however, appears to have envisaged putting a proposal for changes this fundamental on the table. In Japan, policies to liberalize consumer credit and financial markets were underway in response to separate negotiations between the United States and Japan, and they were promulgated during this period and counted as part of the Plaza bargain. Baker repeatedly urged Takeshita to press forward with fiscal policy reforms that would diminish the tax incentives for savings, and tax reform was on the LDP agenda at the time, but Japanese negotiators refused to tie the timing or content of this reform to the Plaza agreement (Funabashi 1988a, b; Lincoln 1988).

ceived of as distinct points in a two-dimensional policy space measuring trade protectionism against change in the strength of the dollar.

Substantively, the House was the most protectionist, overrepresenting, as it does, northeastern industrial states with industries particularly hurt by the loss of international competitiveness caused by the overvaluation of the U.S. dollar. The Republican Senate was slightly less protectionist, but still much more willing to raise tariffs as a response to burgeoning trade and budgetary deficits than was President Reagan. The president, whose constituency was disproportionately made up of free-traders and opponents of government intervention in markets, preferred to avoid protectionist legislation, in favor of some sort of international deal to remove impediments to the "proper alignment" of exchange rates.

In Japan, on the other hand, the only veto player in the domestic policy game was the ruling party, the LDP. Moreover, the necessarily centralized and secretive nature of exchange rate policy meant that the party as a whole delegated policy making in this area to a very small coterie of top party leaders – backbenchers were hard pressed to intervene in policy making. The nature of the problem – exchange rates – as well as the delegation by backbenchers to party leaders of the responsibility for maintaining good relations with, and open markets in, the United States, combined to restrict decision-making authority to a select few. Thus, Japan profitably can be modeled as a unitary actor at the international level of the "two-level game," with the primary goal of forestalling unilateral protectionist legislation already looming in the U.S. Congress. In order to minimize its losses, Japan needed to make a deal with any one of the three U.S. veto players to stop the advance of protectionist legislation. But, since all three U.S. players rejected the status quo, the deal would need to be one that addressed the trade imbalance and avoided protectionism. Only the U.S. president, with his authority over the Treasury's foreign exchange activities, could credibly commit to such an agreement. We argue that the Plaza Accord represented just such a deal.

10

Conclusion

PETER F. COWHEY AND MATHEW D. MCCUBBINS

1. INTRODUCTION

The authors in this volume have demonstrated that a common framework can be used to understand the politics and policies of countries heretofore thought to be vastly different. We have argued that Japanese and American politics are neither exceptional nor incomparable. Beginning with a common understanding of the institutional bases of politics – based on the division of power and the electoral rules of each country – our authors have demonstrated the implications of these political structures for electoral behavior, party organization, spending policy, control of government bureaucracies, regulatory policy, and foreign policy. This final essay reviews the arguments of each of the previous essays, and then discusses how prospective changes in political institutions in both countries might alter their policy outputs in the future.

In Chapter 2, Cox and Rosenbluth used probit analysis to provide quantitative estimates of how much national partisan tides affect the reelection probabilities of politicians in Japan, the United States, and the United Kingdom. They found that the electoral fates of candidates in Japan are less tied to the fate of the party than is the case in the United States, with both countries falling well short of the tight correlation between candidate and party fortunes in Great Britain. The single-member-district system used in U.S. House elections creates incentives for members of Congress to establish personal vote coalitions. These incentives, to some extent, also serve to loosen the bonds of party discipline. Similarly, Cox and Rosenbluth argue that the incentives built into the SNTV electoral system used for Japan's Lower House are at the root of that country's low "electoral cohesiveness." Intraparty competition at the district level necessarily dilutes the meaning of the party label, and motivates party candidates to seek personal votes so as to improve their prospects for success.

McCubbins and Rosenbluth looked into just how this personal vote strategy works in Japan in Chapter 3. They showed that SNTV with multimember districts creates a vote-division problem for any party seeking a parliamentary majority. (Such perverse problems do not obtain in the single-member-district systems used in the United States.) In response to the need for "product differentiation" for same-district copartisans, the LDP does two things. First, it allows each candidate to make personalistic campaign appeals based on the provision of pork-barrel projects and through massive campaign spending. Second, the LDP oversees a division of credit claiming for public policy outputs by its candidates by maintaining a system of party committees with specialized policy jurisdictions and ensuring that there is as little overlap as possible in committee assignments among same-district copartisans.

Of course, a clearer understanding of electoral incentives, campaign strategies, and party organization would be nothing more than academic trivia if politicians were irrelevant to the policy-making process, as many observers of Japanese (and sometimes U.S.) politics assert. McCubbins and Noble argued that such a view is mistaken, that elected representatives do in fact control policy making in both countries. Budgetary policy making is one of the most important and ubiquitous processes of governments. Therefore, the authors looked to this policy to test the logical and empirical basis for claims of bureaucratic power. In Chapter 4, they argued that the assertions that politicians abdicate policy-making authority to unelected bureaucrats rest on a combination of assumptions that collectively do not obtain in either country.

In Chapter 5, McCubbins and Noble then tested several theories of budget making in Japan that purport to show that the budget reflects several key norms for resolving conflict among warring bureaucracies. Three norms discussed in the literature on budget making – fair shares, incrementalism, and nonretrenchment – were tested on a complete budgetary data set for Japan for most of the postwar period, and showed that none of these theories is borne out. Hence budgetary policy making is governed neither by bureaucratic whim nor by automatic "norms" of behavior.

Some analysts may wish to argue that budget processes are qualitatively different from policy in areas where governments are setting rules or defining international obligations. Part II of this book therefore examines regulatory and foreign policy. The first two chapters in Part II examined the differences between U.S. and Japanese regulatory policy. In both cases, the observation was that diffuse public goods aimed at consumers are much less likely to be provided in Japan than in the United States.

In Chapter 6, Noll and Rosenbluth showed that while both countries undertook reform of their telecommunications systems, the impetus for and results of those reforms were quite different. In the United States, the consumer was the big winner of deregulation and the breakup of AT&T. Prices of equipment and services tumbled in the face of the new competition. In Japan, however, the introduction of "competitors" to NTT was not done for the benefit of consumers, and did not really entail deregulation at all; pricing still requires ministerial approval, as does the introduction of any new service or of any new entrant into the market. The authors explained that the root of the differences lies, again, in the political institutions of the two countries. Japan's SNTV-induced, money-based politics places wealthy and highly organized groups such as industry in a strong position vis-à-vis consumers; this is not as important in the United States.

Cohen, McCubbins, and Rosenbluth found similar results in the area of nuclear power regulation. They argued (in Chapter 7) that the multiplicity of "veto players" (state and federal regulators, state and federal courts, several different federal agencies, and three independent legislative actors), brought about a brownout in nuclear power development in the United States. Each of these veto points provided potential access for opponents of each new project. In Japan, the sole policy arena was within the ruling LDP – as long as its members' opinions about the desirability of nuclear power did not waver, new projects would continue apace. Prominent opponents of nuclear projects such as environmentalists and non-proliferationists were not enfranchised by the LDP, as they were by the Democratic Party (in the House of Representatives) in the United States.

The final two contributions to the book demonstrated that the institutional differences between the United States and Japan are relevant for foreign policy as well. In Chapter 8, Cowhey showed that the electoral and governing institutions both determine the goals of foreign policy – by shaping what is politically optimal in terms of legislators' ultimate goal of reelection – and the means by which those foreign policy goals are pursued. Thus, expanded military commitments – indeed, even the discussion of foreign policy in general – were not good strategy in the context of Japan's SNTV, whereas U.S. presidential candidates had every incentive to discuss foreign policy. Furthermore, the "goal" of military policy in Japan was often to benefit the always-privileged industrial constituents of the LDP. Hence, while the security-minded military bureaucracy in the United States focused on the military use of civilian technologies, the focus was reversed in Japan. In both countries, political leaders significantly restructured the powerful military and foreign affairs bureaucracies to reconcile foreign policy objectives with domestic political imperatives. But the pattern of restructuring reflected differences between a government with divided powers and a parliamentary system under single-party dominance.

In Chapter 9, Fukui and Weatherford took the next step and showed how the different political institutions in Japan and the United States affected international bargaining between the two countries. They argued that the negotiated rise of the yen after 1985 occurred because the constellation of interests in the United States gave American negotiators very little room to compromise, while simultaneously issuing a credible threat of a dire reversionary outcome for Japan if adjustment did not take place. Thus, a nonlegislative deal with the U.S. president to inflate the value of the yen was the lesser of two evils in the face of a believable threat by the U.S. Congress to write protectionist legislation. As long as the LDP's most important constituents (big business) feared the reversionary outcome of American protectionism more than they dreaded the consequences of a stronger yen, the LDP would have to acquiesce to the latter.

2. INSTITUTIONAL CHANGE AND POLICY CHANGE

As of this writing, both Japan and the United States are undergoing important changes in their electoral systems, changes that promise to induce dramatic shifts in how and what policies are made in each country. Though prognostication is always dangerous, it seems appropriate to discuss these structural changes in the conclusion to this book. To so do, we will draw on the lessons learned from each of the chapters in this volume to suggest the likely effects of each country's electoral reform on each of the policy areas covered.

2.1. Political reform in Japan

In the summer of 1993, a series of bribery scandals at the highest levels of the LDP, in combination with the party's inability or unwillingness to pass an electoral reform package, led to a split in which enough LDP members defected from the party on a no-confidence vote to cause the government to fall. In the ensuing general election, those members ran as a new party, and again, the LDP was deprived of a parliamentary majority. After nearly a month of bargaining and bidding for coalition partners, a seven-party coalition – excluding only the LDP and the Japan Communist Party – joined together to form a government.

The declared core of the new coalition's platform was the enactment of the very sort of electoral reform over which the LDP stumbled. After the defection of several Socialists caused the defeat of the political reform bills in the Upper House, the coalition compromised with the LDP to allow the approval of a modified reform package. Soon after the passage of the political reform package, the coalition government fell, as Prime Minister Morihiro Hosokawa resigned, and the Socialists and *Sakigake* refused to join the government of his successor, Tsutomu Hata. Hata's minority government lasted only two months, and gave way to a coalition consisting of the Socialists, *Sakigake,* and the LDP. At this point (August 1994) a special commission has just submitted to the new Socialist prime minister, Tomiichi Murayama, its redistricting plan for the Lower House.

The new Lower House will consist of 500 seats, with 300 seats filled in single-member plurality elections, and the remaining 200 members elected from closed-party lists by proportional representation (PR) in eleven districts. Each voter will cast two ballots, one for the district seat and one for a party list. Unlike the otherwise similar German system, the allocation of the plurality seats will be completely separate from the allocation of the PR seats. That is, a party will win its proportion of the seats in the PR group plus (not "including") however many seats it can win in the single-member-district elections. Furthermore, each candidate will be allowed only one fund-raising organization to gather corporate donations of up to 500,000 yen apiece. According to the current plan, these donations will then be prohibited completely after five years. Finally, some measure of national campaign financing will be instituted.

The prevailing theme of the proposed reforms is to both centralize and programmatize party politics in Japan. Duverger's Law (Duverger 1954) argues that the number of competitive political parties (see Taagepera and Shugart 1989 on the "effective number of parties") should eventually be winnowed down toward two, as only two parties should be competitive in the 300 single-member districts.[1] This trend probably will not result in the elimination of third parties altogether, since the threshold of exclusion (Lijphart 1984; Taagepera and Shugart 1989) in the PR section will be so low.

More important, there will no longer be any intraparty competition in elections. Obviously, we would not expect any party to endorse more than one candidate in each plurality race. In addition, the closed-list rule for the PR section means that candidates can neither help themselves nor hurt their parties by seeking personal votes. Thus, the most "efficient" solution (see Cox 1987) for parties will be to campaign on the basis of party platform, in that doing so will provide a sufficient decision rule for voters. Finally, the concentration of corporate financing of campaigns at the party level further centralizes control within parties over electoral campaigning. No longer will it be as easy for maverick candidates to raise their own money in the event that the party is stingy with funds.

What does all of this imply for party organization and for policy? If it is true that the raison d'être of the PARC committee structure is to aid in

---

[1] Riker (1982) suggests that Duverger's Law applies at the district level, but not necessarily at the national level. Canada, Britain, and India are all examples of countries that have plurality elections but more than two national parties.

district-level vote division, then we should expect to see nothing short of its demise. Obviously, a PARC is not necessary for a party to make a policy decision or to run a campaign in elections based on party labels – just look at the example of British parties. Indeed, we should expect to see both the internal organization and the campaign behavior of Japanese parties more closely resembling those of their British counterparts than those of their own forebears.

As for policy, no specific predictions can be made until the party system actually shakes itself out. Duverger's Law predicted the number, not the platforms, of parties. However, with the emphasis in campaigns expected to shift away from personal votes and toward party programs, the enormous amount of budget money devoted to pork-barrel spending in the particularistic appeals necessary under SNTV undoubtedly will be scaled back. As the party component to the vote increases in importance relative to the personal component (Cox and McCubbins 1993; Cox and Rosenbluth Chapter 2 this volume), more emphasis will be put on the party's reputation as responsible governors, and the budgetary funding of personal claims to pork-gathering prowess will diminish.

Under SNTV, the funding and regulatory provision of public goods suffered even more than in most democracies due to the higher opportunity costs of foregoing particularism in favor of public goods. As Noll and Rosenbluth have demonstrated, the need to maintain an ever-increasing flow of campaign resources from big business caused the LDP to allow more firms to feed at the telecommunications trough, which remained protected by continued protection from market forces. Similarly, Cohen, McCubbins, and Rosenbluth argued that while U.S. institutions allowed a great deal of access for environmental concerns, these arenas for challenge simply did not exist in Japan. Or, if they did exist (e.g., the courts or the Diet itself) they were effectively controlled by the very majority party that had made the policy being challenged.

Under the proposed electoral law, however, we would expect both budgetary and regulatory policies to be much more public-goods oriented than ever before, as such policies will now work toward the enhancement of partisan reputations at a lower cost. In general terms, this might mean that the interests of the downtrodden Japanese consumer, which have long been held hostage by subsidized farmers and inefficient small business operators, might finally begin to form the basis of partisan appeals. In addition to the pricing structures of regulated industries, this might show up in the decline of trade barriers, in higher interest rates on savings, and in a more highly developed social safety net, along the lines of Japan's (Organisation for Economic Development and Cooperation) OECD counterparts.

Events over the last year support our theoretically based predictions concerning the future direction of Japanese policy. For example, one of the first reactions to the fall of the LDP concerned nuclear energy policy. The Hosokawa and Hata governments expressed a desire to cool down the nuclear energy program, specifically the construction of breeder reactors. The electric utilities responded by announcing they would cease investment in nuclear plants, because the investment risk (read "political risk") was now too high. Not surprisingly, the current LDP-led coalition has renewed the government's dedication to nuclear power.

Similarly, the Hosokawa and Hata cabinets both promised and embarked upon far-reaching economic deregulatory measures. From telecommunications to transportation to distribution, the coalition planned to strip away much of the "profit-padding" protection that had characterized the LDP's Japan. The last legislative act that Hata carried out was to introduce a comprehensive deregulation package to the Diet. Again not surprisingly, the return of the LDP to power in the current government makes deregulation less likely. No action has been taken on Hata's bill as of August. Finally, budgetary policy felt the effects of the LDP's departure as well. The budget bill, normally passed in March for the start of the following fiscal year on April 1, was delayed until July. It is too early to tell whether the net fiscal effect of the 1994 budget represented a sharp shift from previous trends due to change in governmental leadership, but there were several large shifts at lower levels of aggregation. It is the lesson of this book that all of these policy fluctuations can be attributed to changes in the preferences of the key political decision makers, stemming from the fall of the LDP. Similarly, we expect even more changes once the new Lower House electoral system has been used for the first time, creating a Diet made up of individuals and parties with fundamentally different sorts of electoral incentives, and, accordingly, different policy preferences.

2.2. Term limits in the United States

In the United States, the reformist trend has thus far focused on term limits for members of Congress. Several states have seen term limits approved in statewide referenda, and several others are in the process of following suit. The most immediate effect of these term limits, of course, will be that the organization of Congress itself will be called into question. The seniority norm for committee assignments, for example, may have to be revamped, or else it will work to the detriment of members (and perhaps voters) from those states that have instituted term limits (Polsby, Gallaher, and Rundquist 1969).

The ostensible goal of these term limits is to redirect the focus of congressional careers from biennial reelection campaigns in favor of the actual task of governing. Put another way, the goal is to overturn Mayhew's "electoral connection" altogether. The jury is still out on whether term limits will have their intended effect, whether they will simply work to the disadvantage of the affected members in a Congress that otherwise remains unchanged, or whether they will actually backfire.

The last of these three possibilities is a real concern for some who see the electoral system as actually working quite well as it is. These people would argue that elections are the very discipline that representatives need to induce them to act in their constituents' interests. The authors of this volume count themselves in this latter group. Indeed, if politicians are no longer able to make careers within the legislature, they may have to find ways to create political careers outside the legislature. This is reminiscent of the political machines of late-nineteenth-century American cities, where rotation of machine politicians through postings in legislative offices were just part of their career-long service to the machine. Recent work on the effects of term limits on political careers in Costa Rica bear out this concern (Carey 1993).

2.3. A final word

Beyond these broad generalizations, prognostication is a risky business. In sum, however, it is probably safe to predict that the structure, process, and policy outputs of Japanese politics will change. This is because all of these aspects of policy making are in some sense determined by the exigencies of electoral politics. New electoral rules will mean new mandates for reelection-seeking politicians when they organize their majority-seeking parties. Old solutions (including old policy logrolls) will no longer be optimal.

The new institutionalist approach to politics taken by the authors in this volume should be extended to the study of countries other than Japan and the United States. This approach has proved fruitful here, but its usefulness as a general approach remains largely untested. Broad comparisons of electoral rules and constitutional circumscriptions of legislative, executive, and judicial powers, and how these affect political organization, political behavior, and policy, are needed to test its usefulness.

Bibliography

Aberbach, Joel D. 1990. *Keeping a Watchful Eye: The Politics of Congressional Oversight.* Washington, D.C.: Brookings Institution.

Aberbach, Joel D., Robert D. Putnam, and Bert A. Rockman. 1981. *Bureaucrats and Politicians in Western Democracies.* Cambridge, Mass.: Harvard University Press.

Achen, Christopher H. 1982. *The Statistical Analysis of Quasi-Experiments.* Berkeley and Los Angeles: University of California Press.

Acheson, Dean. 1969. *Present at the Creation.* New York: Norton.

Administrative Case Litigation Law. 1963. (Law No. 139, May 16, 1962), EHS Law Bulletin Series, vol. 2.

Administrative Complaint Investigation Law. 1973. (Law No. 160, September 15, 1962), EHS Law Bulletin Series, vol. 1.

Aldrich, John H., John L. Sullivan, and Eugene Borgida. 1989. "Foreign Affairs and Issue Voting: Do Presidential Candidates 'Waltz Before a Blind Audience'?" *American Political Science Review* 83: 123–41.

Alford, John D., and David W. Brady. 1987. "Personal and Partisan Advantage in U.S. House Elections, 1946–1986." Unpublished manuscript.

Allison, Graham T. 1971. *Essence of Decision: Explaining the Cuban Missile Crisis.* Boston: Little, Brown.

Ando, Hiroshi. 1984. "Japan's Budget: Leadership and Control." *JEI Report* February 17, 1984.

Ando, Hiroshi, ed. 1987. *Sekinin to Genkai: Akaji Zaisei no Kiseki* [Responsibility and Limits: The Record of Deficit Finance]. Tokyo: Kinyu Zaisei Jijyo Kenkyukai. Two volumes.

Andrews, Edmund L. 1993. "Radio-Frequencies Bill Advances," *New York Times,* March 3.

Arrow, Kenneth. 1951. *Social Choice and Individual Values.* New York: Wiley.

Asahi Shimbun. 1982. "Denden Kaiho Dai Ichigo [The First Installment of NTT Deregulation]." *Asahi Shimbun,* February. 4.

  1983a. "Denden, Senbai wa Ashibumi [At a Standstill over NTT and Salt and Tobacco Monopoly]." *Asahi Shimbun,* May 15.

  1983b. "Sainen Suru Denden Masatsu [Trade Friction over Telecommunications Worsens]." *Asahi Shimbun,* May 18.

  1983c. "Denden Bunkatsu wa Tana'age [Putting Off the Break-up of NTT]." *Asahi Shimbun,* August 28.

  1983d. "Minkan Sannyu e Joken Seibi [Preparing for New Entry]." *Asahi Shimbun,* September 4.

1983e. "Gyokaku Hoan o Zenmen ni [Pushing Administrative Reform Bills]." *Asahi Shimbun*, September 7.

1983f. "Denden Kaikaku no Hoanka Ryosho [Drafting the NTT Bill]." *Asahi Shimbun*, September 14.

1983g. "Nichibei Kyotei no Koshin de Kochokai [Hearings on Extending the U.S.–Japan Agreement]." *Asahi Shimbun*, September 14.

1983h. "Denden Minei Ikogo no Gyomu [Business after NTT Privatization]." *Asahi Shimbun*, October 25.

1983i. "Sankoshi ga Jiyuka Teishin [A MITI Council Recommends Liberalization]." *Asahi Shimbun*, December 21.

1984a. "'Kyokasei wa Kaenu' ['We Won't Change the Permission System']." *Asahi Shimbun*, March 13.

1984b. "VAN Shuai Kettchaku Hakaru [Plans for an Agreement on VANs Within the Week]." *Asahi Shimbun*, March 21.

1984c. "VAN Kisei de Jimin wa Keikosen [No Meeting of the Minds on the VAN Issue in the LDP]." *Asahi Shimbun*, March 22.

1984d. "Jimin Chosei Nao Nanko [LDP Still Without a Solution]." *Asahi Shimbun*, March 23.

1984e. "Kettchaku Raishuu ni Mochikoshi [Putting Off a Decision Until Next Week]." *Asahi Shimbun*, March 24.

1984f. "Ozume no VAN Hoan Chosei [An Overarching Agreement on the VAN Bill]." *Asahi Shimbun*, March 25.

1984g. "VAN Hoan Aratana Mondaiten Fujo [More Problems Arise Over VANs Bill]." *Asahi Shimbun*, March 27.

1984h. "Aratana Choseian Fujo [A New Compromise Bill is Floated]." *Asahi Shimbun*, March 28.

1984i. "Choseian Dotai ni Kyogi [A Compromise Bill to be Discussed]." *Asahi Shimbun*, April 3.

1984j. "Denden Nihoan Kakugi de Kettei [The Cabinet Passes Two Telecommunications Bills]." *Asahi Shimbun*, April 6.

1988a. "Danmatsu Hanbai no Sezei Shido [Guidance on the Sale of Terminal Equipment]." *Asahi Shimbun*, June 25.

1988b. "Rikuruto Kanren no Hikokai Kabu [Recruit's Unlisted Shares]." *Asahi Shimbun*, June 30.

1988c. "Kokusai VAN Kikaku Mondai [The Problem of Standards for International VANs]." *Asahi Shimbun*, September 12.

1989a. "NTT Bunkatsu Ron Ichidan to Kappatsuka [The Argument for Breaking Up NTT Resurfaces]." *Asahi Shimbun*, January 3.

1989b. "Yuseisho no Bunkatsuron ni Teiko [Resisting MPT's Break-up Plan]." *Asahi Shimbun*, April 20.

AT&T Japan. 1992. "New Common Carrier Market Analysis." Tokyo: February 14.

Avant, Deborah. Forthcoming. *The Institutional Sources of Military Doctrine: The United States in Vietnam and Britain in the Boer War and Malaya.* Ithaca, N.Y.: Cornell University Press.

Bach, Stanley. 1986. "Representatives and Committees on the Floor: Amendments to Appropriations Bills in the House of Representatives, 1963–82." *Congress and the Presidency* 13: 40–58.

Baerwald, Hans H. 1974. *Japan's Parliament: An Introduction.* Cambridge University Press.

1986. *Party Politics in Japan.* Boston: Allen & Unwin.

Bank of Japan. 1991. *Comparative Economic and Financial Statistics: Japan and Other Major Countries.* Tokyo: Bank of Japan, Research and Statistics Department.

Barone, Michael. 1990. *Our Country: The Shaping of America from Roosevelt to Reagan.* New York: Free Press.

Beck, Nathaniel. 1983. "Time Varying Parameter Regression Models." *American Journal of Political Science* 27: 557–600.

Bobrow, Davis B. 1993. "Military Security Policy," in R. Kent Weaver, and Bert A. Rockman, eds., *Do Institutions Matter? Government Capabilities in the United States and Abroad.* Washington, D.C.: Brookings Institution, 412–444.

Bobrow, Davis B., and Steven R. Hill. 1991. "Non-Military Determinants of Military Budgets: The Japanese Case." *International Studies Quarterly* 35: 39–61.

Bradsher, Keith. 1993. "AT&T in a Deal in Japan: First Sale of Gear to Nippon Phone." *New York Times,* April 27.

Brady, David. 1973. *Congressional Voting in a Partisan Era: A Study of the McKinley Houses and a Comparison to the Modern House of Representatives.* Lawrence, Ks.: University of Kansas Press.

1988. *Critical Elections and Congressional Policymaking.* Stanford, Calif.: Stanford University Press.

Brady, David W., Joseph Cooper, and Patricia Hurley. 1979. "The Decline of Party in the U.S. House of Representatives, 1877–1968." *Legislative Studies Quarterly* 4: 381–407.

Breush, T. S., and A. R. Pagan. 1979. "A Simple Test for Heteroskedasticity and Random Coefficient Variation." *Econometrica* 47: 1287–1294.

Brock, Gerald W. 1980. *The Telecommunications Industry.* Cambridge, Mass.: Harvard University Press.

Brown, R. L., J. Durbin, and J. M. Evans. 1975. "Techniques for Testing the Constancy of Regression Relationships Over Time." *Journal of the Royal Statistical Society, Series B* 37: 149–192.

Bueno de Mesquita, Bruce, and David Lalman. 1990. "Domestic Opposition and Foreign War." *American Political Science Review* 84: 747–766.

Burness, H., W. Montgomery, and J. Quirk. 1980. "The Turnkey Era in Nuclear Power." *Land Economics* 56 (May 1980).

Burnham, Walter Dean. 1965. "The Changing Shape of the American Political Universe." *American Political Science Review* 59: 7–28.

1970. *Critical Elections and the Mainsprings of American Politics.* New York: Norton.

Butler, David, and Donald Stokes. 1969. *Political Change in Britain.* New York: St. Martin's.

Cain, Bruce, John Ferejohn, and Morris Fiorina. 1987. *The Personal Vote: Constituency Service and Electoral Independence.* Cambridge, Mass.: Harvard University Press.

Calder, Kent E. 1988a. "Japanese Foreign Economic Policy Formation: Explaining the Reactive State." *World Politics* 40: 517–541.

1988b. *Crisis and Compensation – Public Policy and Political Stability in Japan, 1949–1986.* Princeton, N.J.: Princeton University Press.

Calvert, Randall L., Mathew D. McCubbins, and Barry R. Weingast. 1989. "A Theory of Political Control and Agency Discretion." *American Journal of Political Science* 33: 588–611.

Bibliography

Calvert, Randall L., Mark J. Moran, and Barry R. Weingast. 1987. "Congressional Infuence Over Policymaking: The Case of the FTC," in Mathew D. McCubbins and Terry Sullivan, eds., *Congress: Structure and Policy.* Cambridge University Press.

Campbell, Angus, Philip E.Converse, Warren E. Miller, and Donald E. Stokes. 1960. *The American Voter.* New York: Wiley.

Campbell, John Creighton. 1975. "Japanese Budget *Baransu,*" in Ezra F. Vogel, ed., *Modern Japanese Organization and Decision-Making.* Berkeley and Los Angeles: University of California Press.

1976. "Compensation for Repatriates," in T. J. Pempel, ed., *Policymaking in Contemporary Japan.* Ithaca, N.Y.: Cornell University Press.

1977. *Contemporary Japanese Budget Politics.* Berkeley and Los Angeles: University of California Press.

1984. "Policy Conflict and Its Resolution Within the Governmental System," in Ellis S. Krauss et al., eds., *Conflict in Japan.* Honolulu: University of Hawaii Press.

Carey, John M. 1993. "Term Limits and Legislative Representation." Ph.D. dissertation, University of California, San Diego.

Cater, Douglass. 1964. *Power in Washington: A Critical Look at Today's Struggle to Govern in the Nation's Capital.* New York: Random House.

Catte, Piero, Giampaolo Galli, and Salvatore Rebecchini. 1992. "Exchange Markets Can Be Managed!" *International Economic Insights* 3: 17–21.

Chapman, J. W. M., R. Drifte, and I. T. M. Gow. 1982. *Japan's Quest for Comprehensive Security: Defence – Diplomacy – Dependence.* New York: St. Martin's.

Chinworth, Michael W. 1992. *Inside Japan's Defense – Technology, Economics & Strategy.* Washington, D. C.: Brassey's.

Claggett, William, William Flanigan, and Nancy Zingale. 1984. "Nationalization of the American Electorate." *American Political Science Review* 78: 77–91.

Cline, William. 1989. *United States External Adjustment and the World Economy.* Washington, D.C.: Institute for International Economics.

Cohen, Linda. 1978. "Essays on the Economics of Licensing Nuclear Power Plants." Ph.D. dissertation, California Institute of Technology.

1979. "Innovation and Atomic Energy: Nuclear Power Regulation, 1966– Present." *Law and Contemporary Problems* 43: 67–97.

Cohen, Linda R., and Roger G. Noll. 1991. *The Technology Pork Barrel.* Washington, D.C.: Brookings Institution.

Collie, Melissa. 1981. "Incumbency, Electoral Safety, and Turnover in the House of Representatives, 1957–1976." *American Political Science Review,* 75: 119–131.

Cooper, Richard. 1968. *The Economics of Interdependence.* New York: McGraw-Hill.

1985. "Economic Interdependence and Coordination of Economic Policies," in Ronald W. Jones and Peter B. Kenen, eds., *Handbook of International Economics,* vol. 2. Amsterdam: Elsevier, 1195–1234.

Cowhey, Peter F. 1993a. "Elect Locally, Order Globally," in John Gerard Ruggie ed., *Multilateralism Matters.* New York: Columbia University Press, 157–200.

1993b. "Domestic Politics and International Commitments: The Cases of Japan and the United States." *International Organization* 47: 299–326.

Cowhey, Peter F., and David Auerswald. 1993. "Ballot Box Diplomacy – The

War Powers Act and the Use of Force." Paper prepared for the 1993 annual meeting of the American Political Science Association, Washington, D.C.

Cox, Gary W. 1987. *The Efficient Secret: The Cabinet and the Development of Political Parties in Victorian England.* Cambridge University Press.

1990. "Centripetal and Centrifugal Incentives in Electoral Systems." *American Journal of Political Science* 34: 903–935.

1991. "SNTV and d'Hondt are 'Equivalent.'" *Electoral Studies* 10: 118–132.

Cox, Gary W., and Mathew D. McCubbins. 1986. "Electoral Politics and the Redistributive Game." *Journal of Politics* (May).

1991. "On the Decline of Party Voting in Congress." *Legislative Studies Quarterly* 16: 547–570.

1993. *Legislative Leviathan: Party Government in the House.* Berkeley and Los Angeles: University of California Press.

Cox, Gary, and Richard McKelvey. 1984. "Ham Sandwich Theorems for General Measures." *Social Choice and Welfare* 1: 75–83.

Cox, Gary, and Frances Rosenbluth. 1993. "The Electoral Fortunes of Legislative Factions in Japan." *American Political Science Review* 87: 577–589.

Crandall, Robert. 1992. *After the Break-Up.* Washington, D.C.: Brookings Institution.

Curran, Timothy J. 1982. "The Politics of Trade Liberalization in Contemporary Japan: The Case of the Tokyo Round of Multilateral Trade Negotiations, 1973–1979". Ph.D. dissertation, Columbia University.

Curtis, Gerald L. 1971. *Election Campaigning Japanese Style.* Tokyo: Kodansha.

1988. *The Japanese Way of Politics.* New York: Columbia University Press.

Davidson, Roger H. 1977. "Breaking up Those 'Cozy Triangles': An Impossible Dream?" in Susan Welch and John G. Peters, eds., *Legislative Reform and Public Policy.* New York: Praeger.

1981. "Subcommittee Government: New Channels for Policy Making." in Thomas E. Mann and Norman J. Ornstein, eds., *The New Congress.* Washington, D.C.: American Enterprise Institute.

Davidson, Roger H., and Walter J. Oleszek. 1977. *Congress Against Itself.* Bloomington: Indiana University Press.

Davis, Otto, M. A. H. Dempster, and Aaron Wildavsky. 1966. "A Theory of the Budget Process." *American Political Science Review* 60: 529–547.

1974. "Toward a Predictive Theory of Government Expenditures: U.S. Domestic Appropriations." *British Journal of Political Science* 4: 419–452.

Demski, Joel, and D. Sappington. 1987. "Delegated Expertise." *Journal of Accounting Research* 20: 117–148.

Destler, I. M., Leslie H. Gelb, and Anthony Lake. 1984. *Our Own Worst Enemy – The Unmaking of American Foreign Policy.* New York: Simon & Schuster.

Destler, I. M., and C. Randall Henning, 1989. *Dollar Politics: Exchange Rate Policymaking in the United States.* Washington, D.C.: Institute for International Economics.

Dickey, D., and W. A. Fuller. 1979. "Distribution of the Estimators for Time Series Regressions with a Unit Root." *Journal of the American Statistical Association.* 74: 427–431.

Donnelly, Michael. 1991. "Japan's Nuclear Quest." Paper delivered at the Conference on Japan's Foreign Policy, Grand Cayman.

Downs, Anthony. 1957. *An Economic Theory of Democracy.* New York: Harper & Row.

Dranove, David. 1987. "Rate-Setting by Diagnosis-Related Groups and Hospital Specialization." *RAND Journal of Economics* 18: 417–427.

Drifte, Reinhard. 1986. *Arms Production in Japan: The Military Applications of Civilian Technology.* Boulder, Colo.: Westview.

Duverger, Maurice. 1954. *Political Parties: Their Organization and Activity in the Modern State.* New York: Wiley.

Eads, George C., and Kozo Yamamura. 1987. "The Future of Industrial Policy," in Kozo Yamamura and Yasukichi Yasuba, eds., *The Political Economy of Japan, Volume 1: The Domestic Transformation.* Stanford, Calif.: Stanford University Press, 423–468.

Ebato, Tetsuo. 1986. "Okurasho: Seiko Kantei to Zaisei Hatan [The Ministry of Finance: Party High, Bureaucracy Low and Fiscal Bankruptcy]." *Seiron* (April): 173–184.

Eguchi, Yujiro. 1980. "Japanese Energy Policy." *International Affairs* 3: 263–279.

Eidenberg, Eugene, and Roy D. Morey. 1969. *An Act of Congress: The Legislative Process and the Making of Education Policy.* New York: Norton.

Encarnation, Dennis J., and Mark Mason. 1990. "Neither MITI nor America: The Political Economy of Capital Liberalization in Japan." *International Organization* 44: 25–54

Enelow, James M., and Melvin J. Hinich. 1984. *The Spatial Theory of Voting.* Cambridge University Press.

Enelow, James M., and Melvin J. Hinich, eds., 1990. *Advances in the Spatial Theory of Voting.* Cambridge University Press.

Epstein, Leon D. 1967. *Political Parties in Western Democracies.* New York: Praeger.

Erikson, Robert. 1972. "Malapportionment, Gerrymandering, and Party Fortunes in Congressional Elections." *American Political Science Review* 66: 1234–1245.

Esherick, Joseph W. 1987. *The Origins of the Boxer Uprising.* Berkeley and Los Angeles: University of California Press.

Evans, Peter B., Harold K. Jacobson, and Robert D. Putnam. 1993. *Double-Edged Diplomacy: International Bargaining and Domestic Politics.* Berkeley and Los Angeles: University of California Press.

Federal Communications Commission. 1989. *Telephone Rates Update.* Washington, D.C., February 3.

1991. *Statistics of Communications Common Carriers, 1990–91 Edition.* Washington: U.S. Government Printing Office.

1992a. *Preliminary Statistics of Communications Common Carriers.* Washington, D.C.: FCC.

1992b. *Trends in Telephone Service.* Washington, D.C., February and September.

Feldstein, Martin. 1986. "New Evidence on the Effects of Exchange Rate Intervention," NBER Working Paper no. 2052. Cambridge, Mass.: National Bureau of Economic Research.

Fenno, Richard F. Jr. 1966. *The Power of the Purse: Appropriations Politics in Congress.* Boston: Little, Brown.

1973. *Congressmen in Committees.* Boston: Little, Brown.

1978. *Home Style: House Members and Their Districts.* Boston: Little, Brown.

Ferejohn, John. 1974. *Pork Barrel Politics: Rivers and Harbors Legislation, 1947–1968.* Stanford, Calif.: Stanford University Press.

266

1986. "Logrolling in an Institutional Context: A Case Study of Food Stamp Legislation," in Gerald C. Wright, Leroy N. Rieselback, and Lawrence C. Dodd, eds., *Congress and Policy Change*. New York: Agathon.

Fiorina, Morris P. 1977. *Congress: Keystone of the Washington Establishment*. New Haven, Conn.: Yale University Press.

Fisher, Roger, and William Ury. 1981. *Getting to Yes*. Boston: Houghton Mifflin.

Flamm, Kenneth. 1988. *Creating the Computer*. Washington, D.C.: Brookings Institution.

Flanigan, William H. and Nancy H. Zingale. 1974. "The Measurement of Electoral Change." *Political Methodology* 1: 49–82.

Fort, Rodney, and William Hallagan. 1991. "Two Paths in the Woods: A Comparison of Public Policies toward Nuclear Power in the U.S. and Japan." Photocopy, Pullman, Wash.: Washington State University.

Fransman, Martin. 1992. "Japanese Failure in a High-Tech Industry?" *Telecommunications Policy* (April): 259–276.

Freeman, John Leiper. 1955. *The Political Process: Executive Bureau–Legislative Committee Relations*. New York: Random House.

1965. *The Political Process: Executive Bureau–Legislative Committee Relations*, rev. ed., New York: Random House.

Friedman, David. 1988. *Misunderstood Miracle: Industrial Development and Political Change in Japan*. Ithaca, N.Y.: Cornell University Press.

Friedman, David, and Richard J. Samuels. 1993. "How to Succeed Without Really Flying: Japan's Technology and Security Ideology and the Japanese Aircraft Industry," in Jeffrey A. Frankel and Miles Kahler, eds., *Regionalism and Rivalry: Japan and the United States in Pacific Asia*. University of Chicago Press.

Fujii, Mitsuru, and Michael R. Reich. 1988. "Rising Medical Costs and the Reform of Japan's Health Insurance System." *Health Policy* 9: 9–24.

Fukui, Haruhiro. 1970. *Party in Power*. Berkeley and Los Angeles: University of California Press.

1979. "The GATT Tokyo Round: The Bureaucratic Politics of Multilateral Diplomacy," in Michael Blaker, ed., *The Politics of Trade: U.S. and Japanese Policymaking for the GATT Negotiations*. Occasional Papers of the East Asian Institute, Columbia University, New York.

1984. "The Liberal Democratic Party Revisited: Continuity and Change in the Party's Structure and Performance." *Journal of Japanese Studies* 10 (Summer 1984): 384–435.

1987. "The Policy Research Council of Japan's Liberal Democratic Party: Policy Making Role and Practice." *Asian Thought and Society*. 12: 3–31.

1988. "Electoral Laws and the Japanese Party System," in Gail Lee Bernstein and Haruhiro Fukui, eds., *Japan and the World*. London: Macmillan, 119–143.

Fukui, Haruhiro and M. Stephen Weatherford. 1990. *Nichibeikan ni Okeru Keizai Boei Seisaku Men de no Kyocho* [Japanese–U.S. Cooperation in the Economic and Defense Policy Issues Areas]. Kaigai Sangyo Kenkyu Gen-4 [JIPRI Studies in Industrial Policy Issues Abroad, 1990, No. 4]. Tokyo: Japan Industrial Policy Research Institute.

Fukunaga, Fumio. 1986. "Sengo ni Okeru Chusenkyoku no Keisei Katei [The Process of Reintroducing the Medium-Sized District Electoral System in Postwar Japan]." *Kobe hogaku zasshi* 36: 403–457.

Fuller, W. A. 1976. *Introduction to Statistical Time Series*. New York: Wiley.

Funabashi, Yoichi. 1988a. *Tsuka Retsu Retsu* [Heat on currencies]. Tokyo: Asahi Shinbunsha.

——— 1988b. *Managing the Dollar: From the Plaza to the Louvre.* Washington, D.C.: Institute for International Economics.

Funada, Masayuki, and Kazumi Kurokawa, eds. 1991. *Tsushin Shin Jidai no Ho to Keizai* [The Law and Economics of the New Telecommunications Era]. Tokyo: Yuhikaku.

Gerth, H. H., and C. Wright Mills, eds. 1946. *From Max Weber: Essays in Sociology.* New York: Oxford University Press.

Gibbard, Allan. 1973. "Manipulation of Voting Schemes: A General Result." *Econometrica* 41: 587–601.

Gilligan, Thomas W., and Keith Krehbiel. 1990. "Organization of Informative Committees by a Rational Legislature." *American Journal of Political Science* 34: 531–564.

Goodwin, George. 1970. *The Little Legislatures.* Amherst, Mass.: University of Massachusetts Press.

Goss, Carol F. 1972. "Military Committee Membership and Defense-Related Benefits in the House of Representatives." *Western Political Quarterly* 25(2): 215–233.

Gowa, Joanne. 1988. "Public Goods and Political Institutions: Trade and Monetary Policy Processes in the United States," in G. John Ikenberry et al., eds., *The State and American Foreign Economic Policy.* Ithaca, N.Y.: Cornell University Press.

Green, Harold, and Alan Rosenthal. 1963. *Government of the Atom: The Integration of Powers.* New York: Atherton.

Grier, Kevin B. N.d. "Congressional Preference and Federal Reserve Policy." Photocopy.

Griffith, Ernest S. 1961. *Congress: Its Contemporary Role,* 3d ed. New York University Press.

Griffith, Ernest, and Francis Valeo. 1975. *Congress: Its Contemporary Role,* 5th ed. New York University Press.

Haley, John. 1978. "The Myth of the Reluctant Litigant." *Journal of Japanese Studies* 4 (2): 359–390.

Hamada, Koichi, and Hugh Patrick. 1988. "Japan and the International Monetary Regime," in Takashi Inoguchi and Daniel I. Okimoto, eds., *The Political Economy of Japan, Volume 2: The Changing International Context.* Stanford, Calif.: Stanford University Press, 108–137.

Hammond, Thomas, and Gary Miller. 1987. "The Core of the Constitution." *American Political Science Review* 81: 1155–1174.

Handbook of Japanese Financial/Industrial Combines. 1971. San Francisco: Pacific Basin Reports.

Harvey, Andrew. 1990. *The Econometric Analysis of Time Series,* 2d ed. Cambridge, Mass.: MIT Press.

Heclo, Hugh. 1977. *A Government of Strangers: Executive Politics in Washington.* Washington, D.C.: Brookings Institution.

Heclo, Hugh, and Lester Solomon, eds. 1981. *The Illusion of Presidential Government.* Boulder, Colo.: Westview.

Hellmann, Donald. 1969. *Japanese Domestic Politics and Foreign Policy.* Berkeley and Los Angeles: University of California Press.

Hinman, George, and Thomas Lowinger. 1987. "A Comparative Study of Japan and United States Nuclear Enterprise: Industry Structure and Construction Experience." *Energy Systems and Policy* 11: 205–229.

Hirose, Michisada. 1981. "Gyosei Kaikaku to Jiminto [Administrative Reform and the LDP]." *Sekai* (August): 245–257.

——— 1989. *Seiji to Kane* [Politics and Money]. Tokyo: Iwanami Shoten.

Hollerman, Leon. 1988. *Japan, Disincorporated: The Economic Liberalization Process.* Stanford, Calif.: Hoover Institution Press.

Holmström, Bengt. 1982. "Moral Hazard in Teams." *Bell Journal of Economics* 13: 324–340.

Hoshino, Eiichi, Koya Matsuo, and Hiroshi Shiono, eds. 1988. *Roppo Zensho: Showa 63 – Nenban* [Compendium of Laws: 1988 Edition]. Tokyo: Yuhikaku.

Hrebenar, Ronald J. 1986. *The Japanese Party System: From One-Party Rule to Coalition Government.* Boulder, Colo.: Westview.

Huber, Peter. 1987. *The Geodesic Network.* Washington, D.C.: U.S. Department of Justice.

InfoCom Research, Inc. 1992. *Information & Communications in Japan 1992.* Tokyo: InfoCom Research, Inc.

Inoguchi, Takashi. 1989. "Seisaku Kettei e no 'Ishiki Kozo' o Miru [Structure of Preferences in Policy Making]." *Ekonomisuto* 3: 84–91.

——— 1990. "The Political Economy of Conservative Resurgence Under Recession: Public Policies and Political Support in Japan, 1977–1983," in T. J. Pempel ed., *Uncommon Democracies: The One-Party Dominant Regimes.* Ithaca, N.Y.: Cornell University Press, 189–225.

——— 1992. "Four Japanese Scenarios for the Future," in Kathleen Newland, ed., *The International Relations of Japan.* London: Macmillan, 206–223.

Inoguchi, Takashi, and Tomoaki Iwai. 1987. *Zoku Giin no Kenkyu* [A Study of Zoku Diet Members]. Tokyo: Nihon Keizai Shimbunsha.

Inter-Parliamentary Union. 1963. *Parliaments: A Comparative Study on Structure and Functioning of Representative Institutions in Forty-One Countries.* New York: Praeger.

Ireland, Timothy. 1981. *Creating the Entangling Alliance – The Origins of the North Atlantic Treaty Organization.* Boulder, Colo.: Westview.

Ishida, Takeshi, and Ellis S. Krauss, eds. 1989. *Democracy in Japan.* University of Pittsburgh Press.

Ishihara, Shintaro. 1991. *The Japan That Can Say No: Why Japan Will Be First Among Equals.* New York: Simon & Schuster.

Ito, Daiichi. 1980. *Gendai Nihon Kanryosei no Bunseki* [An Analysis of the Contemporary Japanese Bureaucracy]. Tokyo: Tokyo Daigaku Shuppankai.

Iwai, Tomoaki. 1988. *Rippo Katei* [The Law-Making Process]. Tokyo: Tokyo Daigaku Shuppankai.

Izumi, Aizu. 1993. "Building Japan's Information Infrastructure." *Nihon keizai Shimbun*, April 16.

Jacobson, Gary. 1987. "The Marginals Never Vanished: Incumbency and Competition in Elections to the U.S. House of Representatives, 1952–1982." *American Journal of Political Science* 31: 126–141.

——— 1990. *The Electoral Origins of Divided Government: Competition in U.S. House Elections, 1946–1988.* Boulder: Westview Press.

——— 1992. *The Politics of Congressional Elections.* New York: Harper.

Japan Company Handbook. 1993. Tokyo: Toyo Keizai Shimposha.

Bibliography

Japan Electric Power Information Centre. 1986. *Nuclear Power in Japan.* Tokyo.

Japan Electricity Production Information Centre. 1988. *Electric Power Industry in Japan 1988.* Tokyo.

Japanese Legislation of Telecommunications, Volume 1: Telecommunications Business Law As Amended. 1991. Tokyo: Communications Study Group.

"Japan's $3 Billion Election," 1990. *Economist.* February 3: 31–32.

Jewitt, Ian. 1988. "Justifying the First-Order Approach to Principal–Agent Problems." *Econometrica* 56: 1177–1190.

Jichisho Senkyo Bu, ed. 1991. *Seiji Katsudo no Tebiki* [An Almanac of Political Activities]. Tokyo: Daiichi Hoki Shuppan.

Jiyu Minshuto Seimu Chosakai Meibo [LDP PARC Membership Roster]. Various years. Tokyo: Jiyu Minshuto Seimu Chosakai.

Johnson, Chalmers. 1975. "Japan: Who Governs? An Essay on Official Bureaucracy." *Journal of Japanese Studies* 2 (Autumn): 1–28.

      1982. *MITI and the Japanese Miracle: The Growth of Industrial Policy, 1925–1975.* Stanford, Calif.: Stanford University Press.

      1989. "MITI, MPT, and the Telecom Wars: How Japan Makes Policy for High Technology," in Chalmers Johnson et al., *Politics and Productivity.* Boston: Ballinger.

      1990. "The People Who Invented the Mechanical Nightingale." *Daedalus* 119 (Summer): 71–90.

      1992. "Japan in Search of a 'Normal' Role." *Policy Paper 3.* San Diego, Calif.: Institute on Global Conflict and Cooperation.

Jones, Charles. 1961. "Representation in Congress: The Case of the House Agriculture Committee." *American Political Science Review* 55: 358–367.

Joskow, Paul L. 1974. "Inflation and Environmental Concern: Structural Change in the Process of Public Utility Price Regulation." *Journal of Law and Economics* 17: 291–327.

Joskow, Paul L., and Roger G. Noll. 1993. "Deregulation and Regulatory Reform," in Martin Feldstein, ed. *Economic Policy in the 1980s.* University of Chicago Press.

Kakizawa, Koji. 1984. "The Diet and the Bureaucracy: The Budget as a Case Study," in Francis R. Valeo and Charles E. Morrison, eds., *The Japanese Diet and the U.S. Congress.* Boulder: Westview.

Kamishima, Jiro, ed. 1985. *Gendai Nihon no Seiji Kozo* [The Political Structure of Contemporary Japan]. Tokyo: Horitsu Bunkasha.

Kanodia, Chandra. 1987. "Stochastic Monitoring and Moral Hazard." *Journal of Accounting Research* 23: 175–193.

Katahara, Eiichi. 1990. "The Politics of Japanese Defence Policy Making, 1975–1989." Ph.D. dissertation, Griffith University.

Kato, Yoshitaro. 1992. *Nihon no Yosan Kaikaku* [Japanese Budgetary Reform]. Tokyo: Tokyo Daigaku Shuppanki.

Katz, Richard S. 1973. "The Attribution of Variance in Electoral Returns." *American Political Science Review* 67: 817–828.

Katzenstein, Peter J. 1978. *Between Power and Plenty: Foreign Economic Policies of Advanced Industrial States.* Madison: Wisconsin University Press.

      N.d. *Agents of Non-Violence: Police, Military, Normative Structures and Japanese Security.* Manuscript.

Keehn, E. B. 1990. "Managing Interests in the Japanese Bureaucracy: Informality and Discretion," *Asian Survey* 30 (November): 1021–1037.

Kernell, Samuel. 1986. *Going Public: New Strategies of Presidential Leadership.* Washington: CQ Press.

1991. "The Primacy of Politics in Economic Policy," in Samuel Kernell, ed., *Parallel Politics: Economic Policymaking in Japan and the United States.* Washington, D.C.: Brookings Institution, 325–378.

Kernell, Samuel, ed. 1991. *Parallel Politics: Economic Policymaking in Japan and the United States.* Washington, D.C.: Brookings Institution.

Kiewiet, D. Roderick, and Mathew D. McCubbins. 1991. *The Logic of Delegation: Congressional Parties and the Appropriations Process.* University of Chicago Press.

King, Gary. 1986. "How Not to Lie with Statistics: Avoiding Common Mistakes in Quantitative Political Science." *American Journal of Political Science* 30: 666–687.

King, Gary. 1989. "Constituency Service and Incumbency Advantage." Unpublished manuscript.

Kishimoto, Koichi. 1988. *Politics in Modern Japan: Development and Organization,* 3d ed. Tokyo: Japan Echo.

Kishiro, Yasuyuki. 1985. *Jiminto Zeisei Chosakai* [The LDP Research Commission on the Tax System]. Tokyo: Toyo Keizai.

Kitagawa, Zentaro, ed. 1987. *Kompyutaa Shisutemu to Torihiki Ho* [Computer Systems and Transactions Law]. Tokyo: Sanseido.

Koh, B. C. 1989. *Japan's Administrative Elite.* Berkeley and Los Angeles: University of California Press.

Koh, Harold Jongju. 1990. *The National Security Constitution.* New Haven, Conn.: Yale University Press.

Kohno, Masaru. 1992. "Rational Foundations for the Organization of the Liberal Democratic Party." *World Politics* 44: 369–397.

Kohno, Masaru, and Yoshitaka Nishizawa. 1990. "A Study of the Electoral Business Cycle in Japan: Elections and Government Spending on Public Construction." *Comparative Politics* 22: 151–166.

Krasner, Stephen. 1978a. *Defending the National Interest.* Princeton, N.J.: Princeton University Press.

1978b. "U.S. Commercial and Monetary Policy: Unraveling the Paradox of External Strength and Internal Weakness," in Peter Katzenstein, ed., *Between Power and Plenty: Foreign Economic Policies of Advanced Industrial States.* Madison: University of Wisconsin Press.

Krauss, Ellis S. 1984. "Conflict in the Diet: Toward Conflict Management in Parliamentary Politics," in Ellis Krauss, Thomas P. Rohlen, and Patricia G. Steinhoff, eds., *Conflict in Japan.* Honolulu: University of Hawaii Press, 243–293.

Krauss, Ellis, and Bradford Simcock. 1980. "Citizens' Movements: The Growth and Impact of Environmental Protest in Japan," in Kurt Steiner, Ellis Krauss, and Scott Flanagan, eds., *Political Opposition and Local Politics in Japan.* Princeton, N.J.: Princeton University Press.

Krugman, Paul. 1991. *The Geography of Trade.* Cambridge, Mass.: MIT Press.

Kumon, Shumpei. 1984. "Japan Meets Its Future: The Political Economics of Political Reform." *Journal of Japanese Studies* 10 (Winter): 143–165.

Kuni no Yosan. Various years.

Kuribayashi, Yoshimitsu. 1986. *Okurasho Shukeikyoku* [The Budget Bureau of the Ministry of Finance]. Tokyo: Kodansha.

Kurihara, S., T. Kubokawa, and S. R. Nakashima. 1982. "Japan's EIA Procedure for Nuclear Facilities." *EIA Review* 3: 289–295.

Lake, David A. 1992. "Powerful Pacifists: Democratic States and War." *American Political Science Review* 86: 24–37.

Leffler, Melvyn P. 1993. *A Preponderance of Power: National Security, the Truman Administration and the Cold War.* Stanford, Calif.: Stanford University Press.

Lehr, William, and Roger G. Noll. 1991. "ISDN and the Small User: Regulatory Policy Issues," in Martin C. J. Elton, ed., *Integrated Broadband Networks.* Amsterdam: North Holland.

Lesbirel, Hayden. 1990. "Implementing Nuclear Energy Policy in Japan." *Energy Policy* 4: 267–282.

Lijphart, Arend. 1977. *Democracy in Plural Societies: A Comparative Exploration.* New Haven: Yale University Press.

1984. *Democracies: Patterns of Majoritarian and Consensus Government in Twenty-One Countries.* New Haven, Conn.: Yale University Press.

Lijphart, Arend, Rafael Pintor, and Yasunori Sone. 1987. "The Limited Vote and the Single Nontransferable Vote: Lessons from the Japanese and Spanish Examples," in Bernard Grofman and Arend Lijphart, eds., *Electoral Laws and Their Political Consequences.* New York: Agathon.

Lincoln, Edward J. 1988. *Japan: Facing Economic Maturity.* Washington, D.C.: Brookings Institution.

1990. *Japan's Unequal Trade.* Washington, D.C.: Brookings Institution.

Linz, Juan J. 1990. "The Perils of Presidentialism." *Journal of Democracy* 1: 51–69.

Lowi, Theodore J. 1972. "Four Systems of Policy, Politics, and Choice." *Public Administration Review* (July–August): 298–310.

1979. *The End of Liberalism: The Second Republic of the United States.* New York: Norton.

Luce, R. Duncan, and Howard Raiffa. 1957. *Games and Decisions.* New York: Wiley.

Lupia, Arthur. 1991a. "Agenda Control Versus the Power of Information." Unpublished paper.

1991b. "Credibility and Learning From Liars." Unpublished paper.

Lupia, Arthur, and Mathew D. McCubbins. 1994. "Learning From Oversight: Police Patrols and Fire Alarms Reconsidered." *Journal of Law, Economics and Organization* 1: 96–125.

Mabuchi, Masaru. 1989. "Shiron 1970-Dai no Yosan Seiji: Itto Yui ni Okeru Yosan Hensei [A Preliminary Essay on Budget Politics in the 1970s: Budget Compilation Under a Predominant Party]." *Handai Hogaku* 39, no. 1 (August): 37–64.

MacKinnon, James. 1991. "Critical Values for Cointegration Tests," in R. F. Engle and C. W. J. Granger, eds., *Long-Run Economic Relationships: Readings in Cointegration.* Oxford University Press, 267–287.

MacKinnon, James, and Halbert White. 1985. "Some Heteroskedasticity Consistent Covariance Matrix Estimators with Improved Finite Sample Properties." *Journal of Econometrics* 29: 305–325.

Maddala, G.S. 1977. *Econometrics.* New York: McGraw-Hill.

Magee, Stephen P., William A. Brock, and Leslie Young. 1989. *Black Hole Tariffs and Endogenous Policy Theory: Political Economy in General Equilibrium.* Cambridge University Press.

Bibliography

Management and Coordination Agency. 1990. *Shigikai Soran* [General Directory of Advisory Councils]. Tokyo.

Manley, John F. 1970. *The Politics of Finance: The House Committee on Ways and Means.* Boston: Little, Brown.

Marshall, John, and Peter Navarro. 1991. "Costs of Nuclear Power Plant Construction: Theory and Evidence." *RAND Journal of Economics* 22: 148–154.

Masters, Nicholas A. 1961. "Committee Assignments in the House of Representatives." *American Political Science Review* 55: 345–57.

Matsubara, Nozumu, and Ikuo Kabashima. 1984. "Tanaka Ha Assho Jiminto Taihai no Kozu [The Logic of an Overwhelming Tanaka Faction Victory Amidst an LDP Defeat]." *Chuo Koron* (March): 74–85.

Mayer, Helmut, and Hiroo Taguchi. 1983. *Official Interventions in the Exchange Markets: Stabilizing or Destabilizing?* BIS Economic Papers, 6. Basle: Bank for International Settlements.

Mayer, Kenneth. 1992. *The Political Economy of Defense Contracting.* New Haven, Conn.: Yale University Press.

Mayhew, David R. 1974a. *Congress: The Electoral Connection.* New Haven, Conn.: Yale University Press.

1974b. "Congressional Elections: The Case of Vanishing Marginals." *Polity* 6: 295–317.

McConnell, Grant. 1966. *Private Power and American Democracy.* New York: Vintage.

McCubbins, Mathew D. 1991. "Government on Lay-Away: Federal Spending and Deficits Under Divided Party Control," in Gary W. Cox and Samuel Kernell, eds., *The Politics of Divided Government.* Boulder, Colo.: Westview, 113–153.

McCubbins, Mathew D., and Gregory W. Noble. 1993. "The LDP and the Determinants of the Japanese budget." Presented at the annual meeting of the Public Choice Society, March 1993, New Orleans, Louisiana.

McCubbins, Mathew D., Roger G. Noll, and Barry R. Weingast. 1987. "Administrative Procedures as Instruments of Political Control." *Journal of Law, Economics and Organization* 3: 243–277.

1989. "Structure and Process, Politics and Policy: Administrative Arrangements and the Political Control of Agencies." *Virginia Law Review* 75: 431–482.

McCubbins, Mathew D., and Thomas Schwartz. 1984. "Congressional Oversight Overlooked: Police Patrols Versus Fire Alarms." *American Journal of Political Science* 28: 165–179.

McKean, Margaret. 1981. *Environmental Protest and Citizen Politics in Japan.* Berkeley and Los Angeles: University of California Press.

McMillan, John. 1992. *Games, Strategies, and Managers.* New York: Oxford University Press.

Michels, Robert. 1915. *Political Parties.* New York: Collier.

Michisada, Hirose. 1981. "Gyosei Kaikaku to Jiminto [Administrative Reform and the LDP]." *Sekai* 429: 245–257.

Ministry of International Trade and Industry. N.d. "Electricity Rate Regulation in Japan." Photocopy, Tokyo.

Ministry of Posts and Telecommunications. 1986. "Denki Tsushin Ryokin Santei Yoryo [Outline of Telecommunications Pricing]." Tokyo: MPT, March 17.

1990a. "Measures to be Taken in Accordance with Article 2 of Supplatary Provisions of the Nippon Telegraph and Telephone Corporation Law." Tokyo: MPT, March 30.

1990b. *White Paper: 1990 Communications in Japan.* Tokyo: Minister's Secretariat.

1991. "Type One Telecommunications Market." Internal memo, July 6.

1992a. *Telecommunications Market of Japan: Open.* Tokyo: Telecommunications Association, January.

1992b. "An Outline of the Telecommunications Business." Internal memo, July.

Ministry of Posts and Telecommunications, Secretariat. 1992. "Denki Tsushin Shingikai Iin Meibo [List of Members of the Telecommunications Advisory Board]," October.

Ministry of Posts and Telecommunications, Telecommunications Bureau, ed. 1985. *Denki Tsushin Jigyoho, Kankei Shorei Kaisetsu* [The Telecommunications Business Law and An Annonated Compendium of Related Ministerial Orders]. Tokyo: Denki tsushin shinkokai.

Mirrlees, James. 1976. "The Optimal Structure of Incentives and Authority Within an Organization." *Bell Journal of Economics* 7: 105–131.

Mochizuki, Mike M. 1983–84. "Japan's Search for Strategy." *International Security* 8: 152–179.

Montgomery, W., and J. Quirk. 1978. "Cost Escalation in Nuclear Power." Environmental Quality Laboratory Memo No. 21, California Institute of Technology, Pasadena.

Morrow, J. D. 1991. "Electoral and Congressional Incentives and Arms Control." *Journal of Conflict Resolution* 35: 245–265.

Mowery, David C. 1988. "Joint Ventures in the U.S. Commercial Aircraft Industry," in David C. Mowery, ed., *International Collaborative Ventures in U.S. Manufacturing.* Cambridge, Mass.: Ballinger.

Munger, Frank J., and Richard F. Fenno, Jr. 1962. *National Politics and Federal Aid to Education.* Syracuse University Press.

Murakawa, Ichiro. 1985. *Nihon no Seisaku Kettei Katei* [Japan's Policy Making Process]. Tokyo: Gyosei.

1989. *Jiminto no Seisaku Kettei Shisutemu* [The LDP Policy Making System]. Tokyo: Kyoikusha.

Muramatsu, Michio, and Ellis S. Krauss. 1987. "The Conservative Policy Line and the Development of Patterned Pluralism," in Kozo Yamamura, and Yasukichi Yasuba, eds., *The Political Economy of Japan: Volume 1: The Domestic Transformation.* Stanford, Calif.: Stanford University Press, 516–554.

Muramatsu, Michio, and Masaru Mabuchi. 1991. "Introducing a New Tax in Japan," in Samuel Kernell, ed., *Parallel Politics: Economic Policymaking in Japan and the United States.* Washington: Brookings Institution, 184–207.

Murphy, James T. 1974. "Political Parties and the Porkbarrel: Party Conflict and Cooperation in House Public Works Committee Decision-Making." *American Political Science Review* 68: 169–186.

Nakane, Chie. 1971. *Tate Shakai no Ningen Kankei* [Interpersonal Relations in a Hierarchical Society]. Tokyo: Kodansha.

Natchez, Peter, and Irving Bupp. 1973. "Policy and Priority in the Budgetary Process." *American Political Science Review* 67: 951–963.

National Association of Regulatory Utility Commissioners. Various Years. *Bell Operating Companies Exchange Service Telephone Rates.* Columbus, Ohio: NARUC.

Navarro, Peter. 1988. "Comparative Energy Policy: The Economics of Nuclear Power in Japan and the United States." *Energy Journal* 9: 1–15.

1989. "Creating and Destroying Comparative Advantage: The Role of Regulation in International Trade." *Journal of Comparative Economics* 13: 205–226.

Nemoto, Koichi. 1992. "Denki Tsushin Jigyo to Tsushin Meekaa no Kankei to Tenkai [The Relationship Between the Telecommunications Industry and Equipment Makers, and its Development]." *Tohoku daigaku keizai gakkai* 53, no. 3 (January).

Nihon Ginko Chosa Tokei Kyoku. 1985. *Nihon Keizai o Chusin to Suru Kokusai Hikaku Tokei.* Tokyo: Bank of Japan.

Nihon keizai shimbunsha, ed. 1983. *Jiminto Seichokai* [The LDP PARC]. Tokyo: Nihon Keizai Shimbunsha.

1989. *Gekishin: dokyumento NTT [Earthquake: A Documentary of NTT].* Tokyo: Nihon Keizai Shimbunsha.

1992. "Zosho, 'NTT Kabuka Taisaku o Kento' [The Finance Minister: 'We Are Studying Ways to Boost NTT Stock']." *Nihon Keizai Shimbun,* May 12.

Nincic, Miroslav. 1990. "U.S. Soviet Policy and The Electoral Connection." *World Politics* 42: 370–396.

Nippon Telegraph and Telephone Corporation. N.d. "History of Rates for Direct Dialed Calls."

1992a. *NTT Procurement Activities, 1992.* Tokyo: NTT.

1992b. *Summary of Changes for Telecommunications Services.* Tokyo: NTT, January.

Nishii, Taisuke, and Ken Fujimori. 1989. "Nakasone Zenshusho wa Nani o Shita Noka [What Did Former Prime Minister Nakasone Do?]" *Asahi jaanaru,* March 3: 14–17.

Nishii, Taisuke, and Teruo Nishimae. 1989a. "NTT ni Sukuu: Seizaikai no Riken Kozo [Building a Nest in NTT: The Structure of Power in the Political and Business Worlds]." *Asahi jaanaru,* January 6: 102–105.

1989b. "'Shinto Taiho' De Honmaru ni Semaru Kensatsu no Mesu [Circling in on the Heart of the Scandal with 'Shinto's Arrest']." *Asahi jaanaru,* March 17.

Nishioka, Takeo, and Susumu Narahashi. 1981. "Gyoaku wa Kitokuken to no Taiketsu Da [Administrative Reform is a Battle with Vested Interests]." *Bungei shunju,* August: 178–186.

Niskanen, William. 1971. *Bureaucracy and Representative Government.* Chicago: Aldine-Atherton.

Noam, Eli M. 1983a. "Federal and State Roles in Telecommunications: The Effects of Deregulation." *Vanderbilt Law Review* 36: 949–983.

Noam, Eli M., ed. 1983b. *Telecommunications Today and Tomorrow.* New York: Harcourt, Brace, Jovanovich.

Noble, Gregory W. 1989. "The Japanese Industrial Policy Debate," in Stephan Haggard, and Chung-in Moon, eds., *Pacific Dynamics: The International Politics of Industrial Change.* Boulder, Colo.: Westview, 53–95.

1992. "Flying Apart? Japanese–American Negotiations over the FSX Fighter Plane." Policy Paper in International Affairs no. 42. Berkeley, Calif.: Institute of International Studies.

Noguchi, Yukio. 1979. "Decision Rules in the Japanese Budgetary Process," *Japanese Economic Studies* 7, No. 4 (Summer): 51–75

1980a. "A Dynamic Model of Incremental Budgeting." *Hitotsubashi Journal of Economics* 20, no. 2 (February): 11–25.

1980b. *Zaisei Kiki no Kozo* [The Structure of Fiscal Crisis]. Tokyo: Toyo Keizai Shinposha.

1982. "The Government–Business Relationship in Japan: The Changing Role of Fiscal Resources," in Kozo Yamamura, ed., *Policy and Trade Issues of the Japanese Economy: American and Japanese Perspectives.* Seattle: University of Washington Press.

1991. "Budget Policy Making in Japan," in Samuel Kernell, ed., *Parallel Politics: Economic Policymaking in Japan and the United States.* Washington, D.C.: Brookings Institution.

Noll, Roger G. 1979. "Regulation and Computer Services," in Michael L. Dertouzos, and Joel Moses, eds., *The Computer Age.* Cambridge, Mass.: MIT Press.

1985. " 'Let Them Make Toll Calls': A State Regulator's Lament." *American Economic Review* 75: 52–56.

1989. "Telecommunications Regulation in the 1990s," in Paula Newberg, ed., *New Directions in Telecommunications Policy.* Durham, N.C.: Duke University Press.

Noll, Roger G., and Bruce M. Owen. 1988. "The Anticompetitive Uses of Regulation: *U.S. v. AT&T,*" in John E. Kwoka, Jr. and Lawrence J. White, eds., *The Antitrust Revolution.* New York: Scott, Foresman.

1989. "*U.S. v. AT&T:* An Interim Assessment," in Stephen Bradley, and Jerry Hausman, eds., *Future Competition in Telecommunications.* Boston: Harvard Business School Press.

Noll, Roger G., and Haruo Shimada. 1991. "Comparative Structural Policies," in Samuel Kernell, ed., *Parallel Politics: Economic Policymaking in Japan and the United States.* Washington, D.C.: Brookings Institution, 211–229.

Noll, Roger G., and Susan R. Smart. 1991. "Pricing of Telephone Services," in Barry G. Cole, ed., *After The Breakup.* New York: Columbia University Press.

North, Douglass C. 1990. *Institutions, Institutional Change, and Economic Performance.* Cambridge University Press.

Odell, John S. 1982. *International Monetary Policy: Markets, Power and Ideas as Sources of Change.* Princeton, N. J.: Princeton University Press.

Ogul, Morris. 1976. *Congress Oversees the Bureaucracy.* University of Pittsburgh Press.

Ohkawa, Masazo. 1985. "The Role of Political Parties and Executive Bureaucrats in Governmental Budget-Making – the Case of Japan," in Karl W. Roskamp et al., eds., *Staat und Politische Okonomie Heute.* Stuttgart: G. Fischer.

Ohmae, Masaomi. 1979. "Nase Dendenkosha wa Nerawaretaka [Why Was NTT Targeted?]" *Chuo koron* 94: 251–265.

Okabe, Naoaki. 1987. *Oshu: En Doru no Seiji Rikigaku* [Retaliation: The Political Dynamics of the Yen–Dollar Exchange Rate]. Tokyo: Nihon Keizai Shinbunsha.

Okimoto, Daniel I. 1989. *Between MITI and the Market: Japanese Industrial Policy for High Technology.* Stanford, Calif.: Stanford University Press.

Olson, Mancur. 1965. *The Logic of Collective Action: Public Goods and the Theory of Groups.* Cambridge, Mass.: Harvard University Press.

Ordeshook, Peter C. 1986. *Game Theory and Political Theory.* Cambridge University Press.

Pacific Telesis. 1992. *Pacific Bell White Pages: San Diego* and *Pacific Bell White Pages: Palo Alto.*

Packard, George R., III. 1966. *Protest in Tokyo.* Princeton, N.J.: Princeton University Press.

Paglin, Max, ed. 1989. *A Legislative History of the Communications Act of 1934.* New York: Oxford University Press.

Park, Yung Chul. 1986. *Bureaucrats and Ministers: Contemporary Japanese Government.* Berkeley and Los Angeles: University of California Press.

Peltzman, Sam. 1989. "The Economic Theory of Regulation after a Decade of Deregulation." *Brookings Papers on Economic Activity: Microeconomics,* 1–41.

Pempel, T.J. 1982. *Policy and Politics in Japan: Creative Conservatism.* Phillidelphia: Temple University Press.

——— 1986. "Uneasy Toward Autonomy: Parliaments and Parliamentarians in Japan," in Ezra N. Suleiman, ed., *Parliaments and Parliamentarians in Democratic Politics.* New York: Holmes Meier, 106–153.

——— 1986. "Uneasy Toward Autonomy: Parliaments and Parliamentarians in Japan," in Ezra N. Suleiman, ed., *Parliaments and Parliamentarians in Democratic Politics.* New York: Holmes Meier, 106–153.

——— 1987a. "The Tar Baby Target: 'Reform' of the Japanese Bureaucracy," in Robert E. Ward and Yoshikazu Sakamoto, eds., *Democratizing Japan: The Allied Occupation.* Honolulu: University of Hawaii Press, 157–187.

——— 1987b. "The Unbundling of 'Japan, Inc.': The Changing Dynamics of Japanese Policy Formation," in Kenneth B. Pyle, ed., *The Trade Crisis: How Will Japan Respond?* Seattle, Wash.: Society for Japanese Studies, 117–152.

Plott, Charles. 1967. "A Notion of Equilibrium and Its Possibility Under Majority Rule." *American Economic Review* 57: 787–806.

Polsby, Nelson, Miriam Gallaher, and Barry Rundquist. 1969. "The Growth of the Seniority System in the House of Representatives." *American Political Science Review* 63: 787–807.

Popkin, Samuel L. 1991. *The Reasoning Voter: Communications and Persuasion in Presidential Campaigns.* University of Chicago Press.

Prestowitz, Clyde V., Jr. 1988. *Trading Places: How We Allowed Japan to Take the Lead.* New York: Basic.

Putnam, Robert. 1988. "Diplomacy and Domestic Politics: The Logic of Two-Level Games." *International Organization* 42: 427–60.

Pyle, Kenneth B. 1988. "Japan, the World, and the Twenty-first Century," in Takashi Inoguchi, and Daniel Okimoto, eds., *The Political Economy of Japan,* vol. 2. Stanford, Calif.: Stanford University Press, 446–486.

——— 1993. "Japan and the Future of Collective Security," in Danny Unger, and Paul Blackburn, eds., *Japan's Emerging Global Role.* Boulder, Colo.: Lynne Rienner, 99–117.

Ramirez, Anthony. 1993. "Cellular Telephone Industry Counts 11 Million Customers." *New York Times,* March 3.

Ramseyer, J. Mark. 1983. "Japanese Antitrust Enforcement After the Oil Embargo." *American Journal of Comparative Law* 31: 395–430.

——— 1985. "The Costs of the Consensual Myth: Anti-trust Enforcement and Institutional Barriers to Litigation in Japan." *Yale Law Journal* 94: 604–645.

——— 1988. "Reluctant Litigant Revisited: Rationality and Disputes in Japan." *Journal of Japanese Studies* 14, no. 1: 111–123.

Ramseyer, J. Mark., and Frances Rosenbluth. 1993. *Japan's Political Marketplace.* Cambridge, Mass.: Harvard University Press.

Reich, Michael R. 1990. "Why the Japanese Don't Export More Pharmaceuticals: Health Policy as Industrial Policy." *California Management Review* 32, no. 2 (Winter): 124–150.

Reichard, Gary W. 1986. "The Domestic Politics of National Security," in Norman Graebner, ed., *The National Security: Its Theory and Practice 1945–1960*. New York: Oxford University Press, 243–274.

Richardson, Bradley M., and Scott C. Flanagan. 1984. *Politics in Japan*. Boston: Little, Brown.

Riker, William. 1980. "Implications From the Disequilibrium of Majority Rule for the Study of Institutions." *American Political Science Review* 74: 432–446.

  1982. "The Two-Party System and Duverger's Law: An Essay on the History of Political Science." *American Journal of Political Science* 76: 753–766.

Ripley, Randall B., and Grace A. Franklin. 1984. *Congress, the Bureaucracy, and Public Policy*, 3d ed. Homewood, Ill.: Dorsey.

Rochon, Thomas R. 1981. "Electoral Systems and the Basis of the Vote: The Case of Japan," in John Creighton Campbell, ed., *Parties, Candidates, and Voters in Japan: Six Quantitative Studies*. Ann Arbor: Michigan Papers in Japanese Studies.

Roeder, Phillip G. 1993. *Red Sunset: The Failure of Soviet Politics*. Princeton, N.J.: Princeton University Press.

Rohde, David W. 1991. *Parties and Leaders in the Postreform House*. University of Chicago Press.

Romer, Thomas, and Howard Rosenthal. 1978. "Political Resource Allocation, Controlled Agendas and the Status Quo." *Public Choice* 33: 27–43.

Rosenbluth, Frances McCall. 1989. *Financial Politics in Contemporary Japan*. Ithaca, N.Y.: Cornell University Press.

  1993. "Financial Deregulation and Interest Intermediation," in Gary D. Allinson, and Yasunori Sone, eds., *Political Dynamics in Contemporary Japan*. Ithaca, N.Y.: Cornell University Press, 107–129.

Rosston, Gregory. 1993. "The Economics of Spectrum Allocation: The Case of Mobile Radio." Ph.D. dissertation, Stanford University.

Ruggie, John Gerard. 1992. "Multilateralism: The Anatomy of an Institution." *International Organization* 46: 561–598.

Sakakibara, Eisuke. 1991. "The Japanese Politico-Economic System and the Public Sector," in Samuel Kernell, ed., *Parallel Politics: Economic Policymaking in Japan and the United States*. Washington, D.C.: Brookings Institution, 50–79.

Salomon Brothers, Inc. 1992. *Global Telecommunications Review*. New York.

Samuels, Richard J. 1987. *The Business of The Japanese State: Energy Markets in Comparative and Historical Perspective*. Ithaca, N.Y.: Cornell University Press.

  1991. "Reinventing Security: Japan Since Meiji." *Daedalus* 120: 47–68.

  1994. *Rich Nation, Strong Army*. Ithaca, N.Y.: Cornell University Press.

Samuels, Richard J., and Benjamin C. Whipple. 1989. "Defense Production and Industrial Promotion: The Case of Japanese Aircraft," in Chalmers Johnson, Laura D'Andrea Tyson, and John Zysman, eds., *Politics and Productivity: The Real Story of Why Japan Works*. New York: Harper, 275–319.

Sandholtz, Wayne, et al., eds. 1992. *The Highest Stakes – The Economic Foundations of the Next Security System*. New York: Oxford University Press.

Sasaki, Takeshi. 1991. "Postwar Japanese Politics at a Turning Point,"*Japan Foundation Newsletter* 18: 1–7.

Sato, Seizaburo, and Tetsuhisa Matsuzaki. 1986. *Jiminto Seiken* [The LDP Regime]. Tokyo: Chuo Koronsha.

278

Bibliography

Schaller, Michael. 1985. *The American Occupation of Japan.* Ithaca, N.Y.: Cornell University Press.

Schattschneider, Elmer Eric. 1935. *Politics, Pressures, and the Tariff: A Study of Free Private Enterprise in Pressure Politics, as Shown in the 1929–1930 Revision of the Tariff.* Englewood Cliffs, N.J.: Prentice-Hall.

Schelling, Thomas. 1960. *The Strategy of Conflict.* Cambridge, Mass.: Harvard University Press.

Schoenbaum, Thomas J., and Joseph H. Ainley. 1988. *The Regulation of Nuclear Power in Three Countries: the United States, France, and Japan.* Athens: University of Georgia School of Law.

Schoppa, Leonard J. 1991. "*Zoku* Power and LDP Power: A Case Study of the *Zoku* Role in Education Policy." *Journal of Japanese Studies* 17: 79–106.

Schwartz, Thomas. 1986. *The Logic of Collective Choice.* New York: Columbia University Press.

Sen, Amartya. 1970. *Collective Choice and Social Welfare.* New York: North–Holland.

Shapiro, Martin. 1988. *Who Guards the Guardians: Judicial Control of Administration.* Athens: University of Georgia Press.

Shepsle, Kenneth. 1978. *The Giant Jigsaw Puzzle.* University of Chicago Press.

——— 1979. "Institutional Arrangements and Equilibrium in Multidimensional Voting Models." *American Journal of Political Science* 23: 27–59.

——— 1988. "The Changing Textbook Congress." In John Chubb and Paul Peterson, eds., *Can the Government Govern?* Washington, D.C.: The Brookings Institution.

Shepsle, Kenneth A., and Barry R. Weingast. 1984. "Legislative Politics and Budget Outcomes," in Gregory B. Mills and John L. Palmer, eds., *Federal Budget Policy in the 1980s.* Washington: Urban Institute.

——— 1987a. "The Institutional Foundations of Committee Power." *American Political Science Review* 81: 85–104.

——— 1987b. "Reflections on Committee Power." *American Political Science Review* 81: 935–945.

Shirk, Susan L. 1993. *The Political Logic of Economic Reform in China.* Berkeley and Los Angeles: University of California Press.

Shugart, Matthew S., and John M. Carey. 1992. *Presidents and Assemblies: Constitutional Design and Electoral Dynamics.* Cambridge University Press.

Simms, Christopher A. 1988. "Bayesian Skepticism on Unit Root Econometrics." *Journal of Economic Dynamics and Control* 12: 463–474.

Sinclair, Barbara. 1983. *Majority Leadership in the U.S. House.* Baltimore: Johns Hopkins University Press.

Smith, Steven S., and Christopher J. Deering. 1984. *Committees in Congress.* Washington, D.C.: Congressional Quarterly Press.

Soma, Masao. 1986. *Nihon Senkyo Seidoshi* [A History of Japanese Elections]. Fukuoka: Kyushu Daigaku Shuppankai.

Sone, Yasunori, and Masao Kanazashi. 1989. *Bijiuaru Zeminaru: Nihon no Seiji* [Visual Seminar: Japanese Politics]. Tokyo: Nihon Keizai Shimbunsha.

Spence, A. Michael. 1974. *Market Signalling: Informational Transfer in Hiring and Related Screening Processes.* Cambridge, Mass.: Harvard University Press.

Stewart, Michael. 1984. *The Age of Interdependence.* Cambridge, Mass.: MIT Press.

Stockwin, J. A. A. 1987. "Japan: The Leader–Follower Relationship in Parties," in Alan Ware, ed., *Political Parties: Electoral and Structural Response.* Oxford: Basil Blackwell, 96–116.

1989. "Political Parties and Political Opposition," in Takeshi Ishida, and Ellis S. Krauss, eds., *Democracy in Japan.* University of Pittsburgh Press, 89–112.

Stokes, Donald. 1965. "A Variance Components Model of Political Effects," in John M. Claunch, ed., *Mathematical Applications in Political Science.* Dallas, Tex.: Arnold Foundation.

1967. "Parties and the Nationalization of Electoral Forces," in William Nisbet Chambers, and Walter Dean Burnham, eds., *American Party Systems: Stages of Political Development.* New York: Oxford University Press.

1973. "Comment: On the Measurement of Electoral Dynamics." *American Political Science Review* 67: 829–831.

Strahan, Randall. 1990. *New Ways and Means: Reform and Change in a Congressional Committee.* Chapel Hill: The University of North Carolina Press.

Strange, Susan. 1988. *States and Markets.* New York: Blackwell.

Strom, Kaare. 1990. *Minority Government and Majority Rule.* Cambridge University Press.

Suleiman, Ezra N. 1977. "The Myth of Technical Expertise." *Comparative Politics* 10 (October): 137–158.

Sundquist, James L. 1981. *The Decline and Resurgence of Congress.* Washington, D.C.: Brookings Institution.

Suttmeier, Richard. 1981. "The Japanese Nuclear Power Option: Technological Promise and Social Limitations," in Ronald Morse, ed., *The Politics of Japan's Energy Strategy.* Berkeley, Calif.: Institute of East Asian Studies.

Taagepera, Rein, and Matthew Soberg Shugart. 1989. *Seats and Votes: The Effects and Determinants of Electoral Systems.* New Haven, Conn.: Yale University Press.

Tajima, Hiroshi. 1991. *Giin no Tame no Horitsu Sai Jiki* [An Almanac of Laws for Diet Members]. Tokyo: Gyosei.

Takano, Yoshiro. 1992. "Nippon Telegraph and Telephone Privatization Study." World Bank Discussion Papers 179. Washington, D.C.: World Bank.

Tanaka, Akihiko. 1990. "International Security and Japan's Contribution in the 1990s." *Japan Review of International Affairs.* 4: 187–208.

Tanakadate, Shokitsu. 1986. "A Summary of the Limitations on Administrative Adjudication under the Japanese Constitution." *Law in Japan* 18: 108–117.

Taylor, Dean. 1982. "Official Intervention in the Foreign Exchange Market, or Bet Against the Central Bank." *Journal of Political Economy* 90: 356–68.

Tejima, Takashi. 1976. *Gyoseikokka no Hori* [The Legal Theory of an Administrative State]. Tokyo: Gakuyo Shobo.

Temin, Peter, and Louis Galambos. 1987. *The Fall of the Bell System: A Study in Prices and Politics.* Cambridge University Press.

Trenkler, H. 1976. "Costs of Construction Time Extension in Nuclear Power Plants." Photocopy. Vereinigungen Deutscher Elektrizitatswerke, Frankfurt.

Tsuji, Kiyoaki. 1964. "The Bureaucracy Preserved and Strengthened." *Journal of Social and Political Ideas in Japan* 2: 3.

1969. *Nihon Kanryosei no Kenkyu* [Research on the Japanese Bureaucratic System], rev. ed. Tokyo: Tokyo Daigaku Shuppankai.

Tufte, Edward. 1975. *The Political Control of the Economy.* Princeton, N.J.: Princeton University Press.

Bibliography

U.S. Department of Commerce, Bureau of the Census. 1991. *Statistical Abstract of the United States*. Washington.

U.S. Department of Energy, Energy Information Administration. 1980. *Nuclear Power Regulation*. Energy Policy Study No. 10. Washington.

Upham, Frank. 1987. *Law and Social Change in Postwar Japan*. Cambridge, Mass.: Harvard University Press.

Van Evera, Stephen. 1985. "Why Cooperation Failed in 1914." *World Politics* 38: 80–117.

van Wolferen, Karel. 1989. *The Enigma of Japanese Power: People and Politics in a Stateless Nation*. New York: Knopf.

Vogel, Steven. 1992. "The Power Behind 'Spin-Ons': The Military Implications Of Japan's Commercial Technology," in Wayne Sandholtz, et al., eds., *The Highest Stakes – The Economic Foundations of the Next Security System*. New York: Oxford University Press.

Volcker, Paul A., and Toyoo Gyohten. 1992. *Changing Fortunes: The World's Money and the Threat to American Leadership*. New York: Times Books.

Walton, Richard, and Robert McKerzie. 1965. *A Behavioral Theory of Labor*. New York: McGraw-Hill.

Waltz, Kenneth N. 1979. *Theory of International Politics*. Reading, Mass.: Addison-Wesley.

Watanabe, Yoshiaki. 1985. "Shuno Jinji Koso to Shindenden no Yukue [What Top Management Personnel Struggles Mean for the Future of NTT]." *Ekonomisuto*, April 20.

Wattenberg, Martin P. 1986. *The Decline of American Political Parties, 1952–1984*. Cambridge, Mass.: Harvard University Press.

Weingast, Barry. 1980. "Congress, Regulation, and the Decline of Nuclear Power." *Public Policy* 28: 231–255.

Weingast, Barry R., and Mark Moran. 1983. "Bureaucratic Discretion or Congressional Control? Regulatory Policymaking by the Federal Trade Commission." *Journal of Political Economy* 91: 775–800.

Westefield, Luis P. 1974. "Majority Party Leadership and the Committee System in the House of Representatives." *American Political Science Review* 68: 1593–1604.

White, Halbert. 1980. "A Heteroskedasticity-Consistent Covariance Matrix and a Direct Test for Heteroskedasticity." *Econometrica* 48: 817–838.

Wildavsky, Aaron. 1964. *The Politics of the Budgetary Process*. Boston: Little, Brown.

Williamson, John. 1986. *Equilibrium Exchange Rates*. Washington, D.C.: Institute for International Economics.

Williamson, John, and Marcus H. Miller. 1987. *Targets and Indicators: A Blueprint for the International Coordination of Economic Policy*. Washington, D.C.: Institute for International Economics.

Williamson, Oliver E. 1975. *Markets and Hierarchies: Analysis and Antitrust Implications*. New York: Free Press.

World Almanac and Book of Facts. 1992. New York: Pharos.

Yamamoto, Shichihei. 1989. *Habatsu* [Factions]. Tokyo: Bungei Shunju.

Yamamoto, Yujiro. 1983. "Denden Min'eika wa Naze Kinkyu Kadaika [Why NTT's Privatization is of Pressing Concern]." *Chuo koron* (June): 160–166.

Yayama, Taro. 19982. "Denden Fuamirii ga Kyofusuru 'Shinto Kakumei' [The

'Shinto Revolution' That the NTT Family Fears"]. *Bungei Shunju* (August): 122–135.

Young, Michael K. 1985. "Judicial Review of Administrative Guidance: Governmentally Encouraged Dispute Resolution in Japan." *Columbia Law Review* 84: 923–983.

Zaisei Seisaku Kenkyukai, ed. 1985. *Kore Kara no Zaisei to Kokusai Hakko* [Public Finance and Issuance of National Bonds From Here On], rev. ed. Tokyo: Okura Zaimu Kyokai.

   1991. *Kore Kara no Zaisei to Kokusai Hakko* [Public Finance and Issuance of National Bonds From Here On]. Tokyo: Okura Zaimu Kyokai.

Zaisei Tokei, various years.

Zhao, Suisheng. 1989. "The Politics of Institutional Design: The Choice Between Presidential and Cabinet Government in Nationalist China, 1925–1937." Ph.D. dissertation, University of California, San Diego.

Author Index

Author Index

Author Index

Subject Index